SELLING THE NIGHT

Andy Crysell spent the 1990s as a music and subculture journalist, interviewing a who's who of pioneers for iconic publications like NME, The Face, Muzik, i-D, Dazed & Confused, Mixmag, Spin and DJ magazine.

In more recent years, he has founded and grown successful agencies across London, Singapore, Amsterdam, Los Angeles, New York City, Sydney and Stockholm, shaping global cultural strategies for clients like Nike, adidas, Apple, Netflix, Spotify, Ballantine's, Heineken and IKEA. He divides his time between London and Brooklyn, and still spends as much of it close to big speakers and under stroboscopic lights as life permits.

First published by Velocity Press 2025
velocitypress.uk

Printed and bound in Poland by Totem.com.pl Printing House

Cover design: Hayden Russell

Typesetting: Paul Baillie-Lane

Editor: Paris Ferguson

Print ISBN: 9781913231828
Ebook ISBN: 9781913231835

GPSR
Publisher: Velocity Press, London, United Kingdom
EU Authorised Representative: Easy Access System Europe - Mustamäe tee 50, 10621 Tallinn, Estonia, gpsr.requests@easproject.com

SELLING THE NIGHT

When club culture meets brands, advertising and the creative industries

ANDY CRYSELL

Dedicated to Susan and Patrick.
With me at the start of writing this.
With me in spirit at the end.

CONTENTS

PROLOGUE

KFC at UMF

"Y'all hungry for some beats?"

April 2019. Wedged between the warm waters and glass skyline of downtown Miami's Bayfront Park, the Ultra Music Festival has never been known for subtlety, but this is shaping up to be something else. Described by Billboard as a 'premier global dance destination', the consistently brash UMF – its name taken from Depeche Mode's Ultra album – is about to go WTF. Adam Beyer, Carl Cox, Marshmello, Maceo Plex and Armin van Buuren are among the vast array of talent spread across the three days of UMF, which, having launched in 1999, has both expanded hugely in scale in Miami and spawned franchises from Croatia to Colombia. Right now, though, the audience is advised to give it up for a DJ who's come all the way from Kentucky. A DJ called Colonel Sanders. He of the fried chicken empire.

Enter stage someone in a Colonel Sanders get-up – white suit, black string tie, signature goatee – topped off with a massive Deadmau5-style helmet. From there, five minutes (yes, he played a five-minute set) of pumping up the crowd with strangely off-key EDM, the screens awash in giant Colonels with love-heart eyes. With the disassociated mood characteristic of these events, the crowd doesn't dance, but they don't boo either. They mostly just stick it out, capturing the whole spectacle on video.

If the reaction at UMF was *meh,* by the time the clips hit YouTube, it had evolved into something more robust. 'What level of capitalism is this?' asked a comment that garnered 1,000 likes. 'This episode of Black Mirror sucks,' said another. One person simply wrote, 'This made me sad'. Word from the KFC camp was more upbeat. A tweet from the Colonel blurted: "One thing a lot of people don't know about me is that I have been a huge fan of electronic music for the last few days, and I can't wait to show off the DJ skills I've developed in that time." Another tweet from the Colonel: "Being on this stage was a wild ride. I couldn't ask for a better crowd of folks at @ultra today!"

By the time news of this wild ride collided with the specialist music media, incredulity was hitting a peak. 'A line finally may have been crossed at this year's Ultra,' snarled Pitchfork. 'The stunt's bald crassness is, in many ways, a logical extension of an industry dogged by accusations of ghost production, buying social-media followers and other signs of general spiritual decay. It's possible to wonder why it took so long for things to reach this point.' The view from the 909 Originals website was similarly damning: 'It's been said that in this era of Trump, Brexit et al, that politics is beyond satire. In the realm of electronic dance music (or should that be event-driven marketing?), aka EDM, it's probably fair to say that we are now, similarly, beyond parody.'

Details about how this turn of events came to be, what the strategy behind it even was, or how much exactly does it cost to grab 300 seconds of stage time for someone pretending to be a fast-food tycoon who died 35 years ago was, unsurprisingly, not the type of thing anyone was rushing to disclose. But those on the marketing communications side were broadly on the same page as those in dance music. Industry outlet, The Drum, remarked: 'Many saw the inclusion of a brand on the main stage as an interruption or disrespectful to the artists at the festival.' Speaking to Campaign, Kate Umfreville from experiential marketing agency, The Producers, observed: "All too often, brands decide to be the publisher and curator of cultural content. They don't have permission or authenticity to do it. Yes, create a vehicle for DJs to perform – stage, arena, hotel, motel, Ferris wheel, boat, tank, you name it. It's been done and it works. But be the canvas, be the facilitator."

Courtesy of a giant and unskippable on-stage advertisement, we have started *Selling The Night* at what, by most people's reckoning, is the bottom of the barrel. The you-couldn't-make-it-up moment when America's already hyper-commercialised EDM industry jumped the shark (or perhaps the chicken). It's a good place to start – for effect, at least – but it doesn't mean this story will permanently remain in disapproval mode. There's much ground to cover, charting how dance music interfaces with a wider world of commerce and creativity – the opportunities this creates, and the threats raised. It's not all as silly or dispiriting as KFC-goes-EDM. Concerns will be aired and shortcomings pointed to, but also brilliant projects and noteworthy collaborations. Smart ways in which dance music has been platformed and celebrated, and in which wider culture has been influenced.

As such, expect to hear as much in this book about ad campaigns, sponsorship deals and how ideas permeate from club culture to other fields, as legendary DJ sets or detailed unpacking of genres. In this pursuit – and alongside drawing from a wealth of editorial and research materials – I go after a range of perspectives. I interview people club culture-side, agency-side, brand-side, as well as academics, archivists, activists, policymakers, photographers, writers, designers and more. Among this mixed crowd, some take pride in the interaction club culture has with the outside world, while others are suspicious, if not downright hostile (indeed, the notion of a dance music industrial complex, packaging raw creative energies for mass consumption, is real for some). Dance music's backstory also offers insight, early signals of brand partnerships and ideas from nightlife that have impacted on other fields. Looking in the other direction, many are eager to share thoughts on the future – mostly optimistic, centred on practical outcomes and rooted in the principle of 'knowledge as power'.

Across its chronology, what's fascinating is how dance music and club culture (terms I use fairly interchangeably) navigate their relationship with their surroundings – who's pulling the strings, and how the circumstances evolve. The strong argument throughout: regardless of adversities, don't bet against its capacity for rapid reinvention and adaptation. From Fiorucci at 1970s discos to modern-day venture capitalism landing in club culture, there is, for sure, a lot going on here. But how to make sense of the moving parts and multiple inputs?

Two directions of travel

Dance music is part of wider culture – it doesn't have much say in this – and, depending on your stance, can also be considered part of the broader creative industries. This book explores how the raw creativity of club culture, born in the margins, has reshaped industries and influenced cultural movements globally. It examines the complexities of this relationship – both the symbiotic and the parasitic – and asks: what happens when brands and institutions enter this space, and how can we preserve its democratising power? There's nothing particularly straight or linear about any of it, but, to my mind, it is a story with two main directions of travel:

1. **Brands moving into club culture:** A relatively concentrated story, but one loaded with big challenges for those grappling with notions such as authenticity and value exchange as they design collaborations between brands and dance music. We'll look at both past and present examples of friction and harmony in the relationship between club culture, brands and advertising. We'll also hear about the challenges in proving the effectiveness of these collaborations, the perils of short-term thinking and brands' increasingly layered efforts to position themselves as supporters, not just sponsors.

2. **People and ideas that emerge from club culture:** A more expansive and sprawling story, rather dizzying in scope when considering what to include and how wide to set the aperture. Media, advertising, design, gaming, fashion, hotels, alcohol, beauty and tourism certainly all figure in where club culture has left a mark. But so do questions about how equitable club culture's opportunities are, especially in a time when operating without a safety net of privilege is more challenging than ever.

Resistance and dissent

All aboard? Not quite. Before we guzzle too much of the corporate Kool-Aid, there are plenty I speak to, representing different communities and perspectives, who do not recognise the value in letting brands take space in dance music whatsoever. Some also view ideas taken from club culture more as theft and appropriation than something to be celebrated. One of the people I reached out to, an acclaimed voice on New York City disco, got back by email with: 'My take is that brands should be kept well away from the dancefloor, or at least dancefloors that value community and egalitarianism. Corporations are anti-democratic and the ruination of the world. I'd rather they paid proper taxes on their profits rather than piggy-backing on grassroots culture to whitewash their embedment in neoliberalism and often reactionary governments, Israel being the most notable.'

The premise that brands, the creative industries and dance music are cosy bedfellows, and that it's just about improving, *optimising*, the relationship between them is not how some see it at all. They picture a future in which clubs are self-supporting and self-sustaining, keeping those external forces at bay. Another person I reached out to, someone with a detailed perspective on music, club culture and design from the 1980s and 1990s, responded to my request to chat with: 'ANYTHING to do with brands and advertising is the LAST thing I am interested in.

Ditto, in our current moment, what passes for creative 'industries'. But best of luck all the same.' I took the last part with a pinch of salt.

Other themes of dissent encountered include the harm caused by the influx of investment money into club culture – followed by the profit extracted and the growing divide between the haves and the have-nots this is creating. There is also, unsurprisingly, growing scrutiny of how dance music has responded to the wider calls for accountability and action against systemic inequality and social injustice, particularly in the wake of the Black Lives Matter movement. Parallel to this, and often intertwined, is the threat posed by the gentrification of cities, which now jeopardises the very existence of club culture.

Next to commoditisation and commercialisation, another theme of disquiet is the so-called over-intellectualisation of nightlife – an irony noted when writing a book about dance music – even its 'academisation'. A 2024 piece in Quietus opens with: 'Clubs are closing, a new generation is less keen on going out and bashing their bonces with garries – yet raving is discussed more than ever, with endless books and academic articles discussing the dancefloor as a utopia.' The music journalist Chal Ravens opines in the piece: 'I can't remember a time when people talked about dancing as much as they are right now, despite apparently not doing it as much. In the last few years I've bought three books specifically about dancing – more than in 10 years of writing about dance music – and noticed rave-themed reading groups popping up to analyse them. At the ICA in London, for instance, participants have been discussing 'what it means to rave in the contemporary moment' via close readings of writers and choreographers.'

Much of what we see in dance music – the frictions and concerns – echo broader debates playing out across society. And, just as elsewhere, voices are growing louder and more confident. The role of brands in club culture, and its co-option by the creative industries, therefore, does not get a free pass.

Who's writing this?

I'm going into this with what could be viewed as a foot in both camps (though for me it's much less binary than that). I have a love of, and fascination with, dance music and its surrounding culture that goes back quite a soberingly extensive number of decades. Alongside this, I've worked in marketing communications for the past 20 years. It probably comes as little shock that many in that field share this passion for dance music, quite a few probably crediting it as important in whatever success they've had – whether through inspiring ideas or valuable connections made.

It was certainly important for me. In fact, I owe huge amounts to it. I didn't go to university. Courtesy of a Jobcentre ad, I started work at 16 as a foot messenger in a late '80s, pre-gentrified Soho, London, scooping up experiences from the characters, occasional chaos and regular conviviality of the place, listening to hip-hop on my Walkman and delivering photos to ad agencies. I was also scooping up glimpses of what life looked like in those ad agencies. It was a particularly flourishing period for that industry in London. It all appeared very exciting, but the catch was I was going in the tradesman's door. Not the front door, the one into well-appointed lobbies where, invariably, a wall of screens blasted out the agency's latest work. I felt close to all of that creativity but also a million miles away from it. Job offers in advertising were not forthcoming (absurdly, ways in for those without a university education have drastically diminished in the time between then and now – so much for progress).

In the midst of my Soho runner days came 1988 and acid house. How it exploded into being is a story that has been told so many times now as to have lost a little of its kick, but it genuinely changed everything for me. Though I'd always loved music, as with the inner sanctums of those ad agencies, it all felt out of reach. I couldn't see a way in. Acid house upturned that. While many of the records were made far away in Chicago and Detroit, those DJing, promoting the parties and cooking up so many of the other cultural activities that orbited the night out, if you didn't know them yourself, there was a good chance someone else you knew did.

Suddenly a thrilling sense of being closer, *much closer*, to the centre of the action took hold. And as intense and mind-blowing as the music and the club or warehouse party were, many of us were switched on by the adjacent ideas and DIY entrepreneurialism that came along in tow. The empowering and democratising reverberations had you thinking that, just maybe, you could start a fanzine or a T-shirt line, set up a club night or some other kind of enterprise that fed off, and contributed to, the energy of that moment. I wouldn't have heard about the 'creative industries' concept by then, but if I had, and that all of this experimenting in underground culture was a part of a bigger cause, I'm pretty sure I would have been immediately sold.

As it was, I ran some small parties, sold tickets to, and helped others organise, bigger parties. I had a record deal (didn't get beyond some test pressings). I never started a fanzine but I wrote for other people's fanzines, and this was the bit that stuck. I spent the next decade making a career (I use that term loosely) as a music and subculture journalist, never quite getting over the shock of being sent records for free, or flown places to interview fascinating/visionary/famous/absurd people, and experience all kinds of subcultural inspiration firsthand.

I spent time with Carl Craig, Derrick May, Wu-Tang Clan, Jay-Z, Nas, Björk, Massive Attack, Aphex Twin, Jeff Mills, Daft Punk, Frankie Knuckles, Public Enemy, Dr Dre, Masters At Work, Snoop Dogg, Mary J Blige, Missy Elliott, De La Soul, Fabio & Grooverider and countless others. I got to chart the deepest recesses of the underground, alongside the explosive commercialisation that marked the 1990s – superclubs, Ibiza, dance music festivals and so forth. Despite the swelling coffers of dance music, I barely made a living during that time – certainly not one that had me thinking about savings or pensions. But in many ways, the lessons learnt and portals opened more than paid the bills.

Later, after a brief stop-off in the boom-crash beginning days of dot-coms, by a mixture of design and happenstance I made a swing into marketing communications and agencies. Since then, and truly using so much of what I found in acid house – confidence, how to join dots, the value of subculture, turning hustle into a kind of business savvy – I've launched, grown and subsequently sold a couple of companies that had offices in all places from London and New York City to Sydney and Singapore. The first focused on creative outputs and so-called branded content. The second on cultural insights and strategy. At both, we worked with big, demanding brands in categories like media, tech, apparel and alcohol, all essentially seeking to connect with culture for commercial gain.

While the commissions at these agencies covered a range of themes, music was ever present in the mix. Early on, I worked with Sony PlayStation on initiatives that placed them within the DIY culture of grime. Also way back when, on strategies for (blast from the file sharing past) Napster, unpacking music and youth culture for Channel 4, and advising an array of music magazines and specialist radio stations on preparing for a digital future (mixed results there, frankly). More recently, with Ballantine's on their True Music platform, learning what clubbers, DJs and promoters need from brands, and helping shape their principles for playing a role in a safer, fairer industry. In between: Apple, Spotify, Nike, Bacardi, Peroni – these are just a handful of the other brands who called us in to explore the direction music subculture was headed in, strategising what their own point of view or position may be.

Like many in marketing communications whom I've spoken to for this book, I've sometimes felt conflicted by making a living from coalescing culture and commerce. The briefs usually presented an honourable goal of how a brand could support a scene, movement or community. But positive intentions were prone to getting jumped on by factors such as brand guidelines, budget cuts, 'return on investment' wrangling and the fear of stepping outside the safer confines of traditional marketing.

Often it was evident that while the team working on the project had their hearts in the right place, higher-ups in the organisation saw it as just another line on a spreadsheet, no more important than pay-per-click campaigns or popup ads.

I grew up too obsessed with adverts, media and game-changing companies like Nike and Apple – alongside more underground things – to draw a hard dividing line between brands and subculture. My fairly rudimentary view has always been that if brands want to engage in these spaces, they should provide tools, resources, platforms and exposure that others need – offering utility, not trying to be the life and soul of the party. But they don't always see it that way – which, no doubt, is exactly how you end up with DJs dressed as Colonel Sanders.

When I started this book, I kept an open mind but suspected I wouldn't come away with a tidy answer on how brands and dance music should coexist (spoiler: I didn't). It reminds me of the unresolved debates from the early days of acid house in the UK. Was it a countercultural escape – a rebellion against Margaret Thatcher's nascent neoliberalism? Or was it a symptom of Thatcherism itself? Entrepreneurialism, oversized mobile phones and a milieu where anyone could rise above their station by grafting – perhaps unwittingly acid house was all of this writ large.

Maybe it was both things at once. That, I believe, was the fuzzy conclusion reached back then, and nearly 40 years on, not much seems to have changed. For some, dance music is a community and support network – it's political. For others, it's escapism and consumerism – a space ripe for brand involvement. For most, there's no succumbing to easy binaries. It is both – which is awkward, messy, prone to friction but ultimately reflects how many of us live, with feet (like mine) in multiple camps, lurching between underground and mainstream, culture and commerce, resistance and participation.

Considerations

Some observations from writing this book – specifically, aspects I grappled with or that impacted the course of the story. I began with more streamlined ideas of what was in and out of scope. But the conversations I had with the many people who generously gave their time introduced new subjects. As a result, I found myself confronting topics I hadn't initially considered. For instance, the role of funding in club culture (beyond standard brand partnerships) became a more prominent theme than anticipated, and the role of education in dance music and club culture well and truly forced its way into the story.

Some chapters have us firmly on a chronological path. Others are more thematic in form. I'd love you to read all of this book – no kidding – but I think each chapter can be considered a stand-alone read, too. Some of these chapters stay in lane. Others, let's just say, are a little more discursive. For instance, themes like minoritised and marginalised communities in dance music are not – and to my mind, should not – be ring-fenced to a single chapter. These debates are fundamental across the full timeline of club culture, present in every facet of it, regardless of how commercial or otherwise nightlife finds itself. Similarly, the impact of gentrification and urban change are never far from the page.

At times, it has felt like an exercise (albeit a mighty fun one) in boiling the ocean. Club culture, after all, has near endless touch points with other aspects of culture and creativity. I'd describe this book as comprehensive, then, but not definitive – by which I mean that while many threads could have been explored (some known to me, many not), I've chosen to look closer at some intersections – such as which fields have been influenced over the decades, and how these influences have compounded into present-day club culture – over others.

I also wrestled with how much to cover hip-hop – and its adjacent genres – in this story. It appears in places, but ultimately, I think it has a narrative that deserves its own space. In ways both positive and less so, it has a different relationship with brands and advertising, and its own dealings with wider culture. Sometimes the focus in this book drifts closer to festivals than clubs, but it's all now part of the broader dance music culture. In fact, there's a term for this: the 'festivalisation' of dance music. While much of what I cover has global relevance, I acknowledge that my focus in terms of research and interviews was on big clubbing cities and destinations in the Global North. There are undoubtedly other perspectives and stories from different regions that deserve more thorough exploration.

Creativity from the night

They say nothing good happens after midnight, but in the case of creativity, that's just not so. The night fosters a different kind of creativity: something urgent, spontaneous, carved out of necessity and often from those living marginalised lives. It's a creativity that you can't summon up in an agency or studio environment, via an officially sanctioned arts body or a shiny innovation lab. It grows in the dark but, for decades, has filtered through to influence everything from media, advertising, design and visual culture, to gaming, fashion, hospitality, alcohol, beauty, tourism and far beyond. Myriad stunning ideas emerge from it. Very bright and resourceful people, too.

The UK's Night Time Industries Association (NTIA), much as they have skin in the game, puts it nicely in their 2022 report titled Dance Music's Impact On Communities And Culture: 'Nightclubs may seem like blackboxed utopias, but participants take the inspiration, positive attitudes, relationships and interpersonal skills forged within repurposed basements and warehouses back out into the wider world. People emerge from clubs inspired, happier, more tolerant and more community-spirited.'

But who gets to leverage this out-the-box talent and creativity, for reasons communal or commercial? Amid considerable societal change, how can we preserve the egalitarian role that this creativity plays? Much here is in flux and deep in debate. The creativity itself, however, remains loud, booming and beyond question. If you're as fascinated as I am by transformative power born of the night – and its capacity to change lives – you should find catalytic ideas and inspiration in these pages. And no more chicken colonels, promise.

1. A STATE OF PERPETUAL SURPRISE

Early signals before dance music as we know it, with brands seeking a presence in jazz and among Black communities

The first moves towards 'culture marketing', and how ideas journey from subculture to mainstream

Pepsi in Harlem

That it's in New York City where we first encounter a brand stepping into dance music shouldn't come as much surprise. It makes perfect sense that it should be here, in the frenetic swirl of subcultural change and accompanying commercialisation that is the hallmark of the place. But the decade we're in is less expected. We will get to the NYC of the 1970s, to the dressed-down underground and uptown decadence, but for now, we're further back. It's the 1940s and we're in Harlem.

Here, above Central Park, in a neighbourhood synonymous with activism and social change, the Lindy Hop emerged – an energetic mishmash of jazz swing dances. Named after aviator Charles Lindbergh's 1927 Atlantic crossing, the Lindy Hop was an early street dance and a cornerstone of the African American community. Its epicentre was the Savoy Ballroom on Lenox Avenue (now Malcolm X Boulevard), dubbed the 'home of happy feet'. It's remembered as one of the country's first racially integrated public places. Through the 1920s and 1930s, up to 5,000 people packed the Savoy nightly, dancing to house bands like Al Cooper's Savoy Sultans and Chick Webb, with guests like Dizzy Gillespie and Ella Fitzgerald. The energy was unmatched on its famous 'track' dancefloor – named for its unique elongated shape.

As is often the case in clubs, there was a special spot on the dancefloor where you'd encounter the wildest enthusiasm. At the Savoy, this was 'cat's corner', near the bandstand and informally reserved for the best dancers. In Steppin' On The Blues, Jacqui Malone describes it as a space where 'an invisible rope surrounded a dancing area that met the requirements of ritual, recreation and performance'.

By the 1940s, a so-called third generation of Savoy Lindy Hoppers emerged in the neighbourhood. Before they were old enough to dance in the ballroom, many could be found further along Lenox Avenue, at number 121 – home of the Pepsi-Cola Junior Club. Created for teens aged 15–19, it was described in an April 1945 edition of the New York Age, a prominent African American newspaper, as a 'gift to the community'. Run by the club members themselves under the motto 'good citizenship through self-government', the club featured a soft drink counter (stocked, we assume, with plenty of the fizzy stuff), ping pong tables, a jukebox and, most importantly, a dancefloor. Just a short walk from the Apollo Theatre, the club became where the new generation of Lindy Hoppers danced their hearts out – at least until the 10pm closing time.

And what brought Pepsi-Cola to Harlem? The junior club was launched during the tenure of business president Walter Staunton Mack Jr, who was known for investing heavily in art exhibits and civic engagement. Yet, as jazz historian Harri Heinilä of the University Of Helsinki notes, the motives weren't purely altruistic: 'Despite a noble idea of creating good citizens by providing Harlem youngsters a place where they can learn principles of self-government and socialize with each other, practically, the reason for the club was economic. In the 1940s, there was a rivalry between the Coca-Cola and Pepsi-Cola companies. The latter had an idea of marketing Pepsi-Cola to African Americans by getting them involved in the company's activities, starting in 1940 when the company hired three African Americans for its sales team. The Harlem Junior Club was likely part of this strategy to win African Americans over to the Pepsi-Cola company.'

Some of the dancers – notably the couple George and Sugar Sullivan – would rise to national fame in the 1950s. You can find clips of them on YouTube from around then, their moves bringing everything from breakdancing to Chicago footwork to mind. Pepsi, however, gave up on their club in 1947, claiming a lack of support from the community (though just as likely due to a strategic pivot or cost-cutting measures, believes Heinilä). They offered the place rent-free for 18 months to anyone who wanted to take the space over and came forward with good plans and intentions.

It's unclear what offers were received, but in the following decades the site would become a rehearsal room and a Woolworth department store. In the 1970s, music found its way back inside, and it transformed into the Harlem World Disco. Disco by name, but more hip-hop by reputation: before eventually closing in 1985, 121 Malcolm X Boulevard would claim a further place in music history as the setting for shows by Grand Wizard Theodore & The Fantastic Five, Cold Crush Brothers, Treacherous Three and Busy Bee.

Jazz's relationship with brands and marketing took other forms as well in the first half of the 20th century. From the 1930s onwards, cigarette manufacturers became heavily involved in early radio programming, much of it centred on jazz. Among the first were the Lucky Strike

Radio Hour, Camel Pleasure Hour and the Philip Morris Playhouse. Jazz duly began to grow in the North American popular consciousness, and the cigarette brands got to associate with music that was beginning to represent notions of freedom and rebellion.

Coming later than Pepsi-Cola's Harlem endeavours, though with rather more credibility and a through-line to the present day, Hennessy also made moves into Black culture around the mid-20th century. American GIs were first exposed to the warm and spicy flavours of the French cognac, now part of the vast LVMH luxury group, when stationed in Europe in the 1940s. The presence of jazz in European cities, particularly Paris, adds to the cultural relevance. By the 1950s, Hennessy was making the most of these connections, becoming among the first brands to recognise the existence of a successful Black professional class in the US, running adverts in magazines like Jet and Ebony, and signifying its place among emergent African American confidence through striking up endorsements from Miles Davis, Marvin Gaye and Josephine Baker.

In 1968, Hennessy appointed African American Olympic champion Herb Douglas as vice president for marketing, breaking barriers and setting an example for diversity and inclusion in the corporate world. Speaking to Dazed.com in 2023, Julie Nollet, then chief marketing officer at Hennessy, explained: "As time progressed, Hennessy's involvement in the cultural fabric of the Afro-American community continued to deepen. It became more than just a beverage; it was embraced as a symbol of celebration, triumph and unity." The brand has reportedly been name-checked in over 4,000 rap tracks, and links into hip-hop, grime, reggae and beyond have been maintained.

These were among the opening interactions in the significant and multidimensional relationship between music subculture and brands that was to come. Though it's unlikely that they would have brandished terms such as 'cultural relevance' and 'authenticity' inside whatever constituted the marketing department of 1940s Pepsi-Cola or 1950s

Hennessy, this is essentially what they were seeking with their support of junior dance clubs and jazz music. It wasn't just about showing up in the neighbourhood; it was about showing up in the culture. They figured that, rather than buy billboard space, they would provide resources and utility. Countless brands have followed this path since, though not always with success. By the mid-1980s, Pepsi's own music initiatives looked questionable, epitomised by the Guess The Fat Boys' Weight competition, where the winner received 898 cans of Pepsi and $898 to match the then-notable rap trio's combined weight in pounds.

Rudimentary as their strategies would have been back then, brands like Pepsi and Hennessy were undoubtedly starting to grapple with the questions of legitimacy and purpose that bother boardrooms today. What meaningful role could they occupy? What 'permissions' did they have to participate in cultural spaces? And once they had established themselves, they faced another challenge: determining the success metrics. How do they measure if the needle has moved, and what exactly is the sentiment or perception they want to move anyway?

Brands, culture, influence

Before we go any deeper on to the dancefloor, it's worth level-setting on a few fundamentals of marketing communications. From relatively humble beginnings – when early ad men in the US were regarded as little more than smooth-talking wide-boys (and they were always boys) – it's an industry that has undergone a profound 75-year transformation. It has been lavishly romanticised along that path in the cultural psyche. Conjuring visions of Mad Men and Madison Avenue, it's become loaded with the machismo of the pitch, limitless nights out on expenses and much flitting around the world. The rise of mega-brands like McDonald's, Nike, Apple, Pepsi and Levi's has been put down as much to how they've communicated as the products they've offered. In its day, the TV spot became as conversation-worthy as the programmes it bookended. The lure of life as 'the creative' or 'the strategist', with its fashionable – and more recently hipster-ish – trappings, has proven strong for many. While it doesn't quite command the salaries of finance or tech, there's good money to be earned nonetheless – and a strong sense of cultural cachet to go with it.

But it's also an industry facing challenges, perhaps fearing that the glory years – particularly the expense accounts and global flitting – are fading into the past. Budgets are squeezed, clients are taking services in-house and generative AI looms as a tempting option for doing the work at twice the speed and zero the cost of humans. Concerns over representation appropriately feature, alongside handwringing about where the swagger and bravery have gone. Adding to the angst are the mega-scale management consulting groups – think Accenture – determinedly refusing to stay in their lane, snapping up creative, insights and design agencies with gusto. Probably not unlike many other industries – though marketing communications has a greater knack than most for getting dramatic about it all – it doesn't feel much like 'situation normal' right now.

All that said, it remains a vast and eminently global industry. A 2019 report by equity research firm Redburn and professional services group PwC valued it at $1.7 trillion worldwide. Such is its vastness that it spans everything from advertising to PR, SEO to sponsorship, events to influencers. With an appetite for change that is equal parts thrilling, desperate and disorienting, this is an industry that questions itself relentlessly – conjuring up new disciplines while discarding old ones. For all the self-flagellation, it is remarkably adept at adaptation – such as when TikTok rockets to prominence and an entirely new set of ways of working need to be rapidly devised. Because of all this, it can be an energising world to work in – but also harsh and sometimes absurdly demanding.

One simple (some would say simplistic) way to make sense of how marketing communications work – and what is expected of it – is to slice it into two: performance marketing and brand marketing. The former focuses on driving measurable actions and achieving specific goals, such as sales, leads or website traffic. It's all about programmatic advertising – automated, data-driven ad buying – and near-immediate results. Performance marketing has grown significantly in the digital age and, depending on your perspective, has either brought greater accountability and trust in return on investment or sucked most of the soul out of the industry.

On the other hand, brand marketing concerns itself less with driving immediate actions and more with growing fame over time: creating lasting relationships and cementing unassailable positions in the firmament of modern consumer life. Its long-term nature means it lacks the measurability of performance marketing, often leaning more towards art than science. This makes success harder to quantify, with definitions of it conveniently – or inconveniently – malleable. Brand marketing is also the stuff of glamour and glory in the advertising game – the kind that embeds advertising into popular culture and, at least once upon a time, made people remark that the ads were better than the TV shows. Over more than a century, it has built an expansive web of businesses, from fabled names like J Walter Thompson, Ogilvy & Mather and Saatchi & Saatchi to relative upstarts like Uncommon Creative Studio, 72andSunny and Mojo Supermarket.

Within brand marketing, there's a mindset that pays particular attention to the idea of embedding brands in culture. It's not new, but it's certainly been getting louder. Pinning down exactly what it is can be tricky, but most agree it's about placing brands among the things that matter to people – instead of getting in the way with adverts. It involves embracing the messiness of culture, not trying to force a perfect framework. It's often proclaimed to be about *engaging* with culture, rather than interrupting it. In some cases, it can even mean leading culture (Nike and Apple are often cited as examples here), but more frequently, it's about contributing – though what that contribution looks like is often up for debate. Many people, myself included, have earned a decent living helping brands navigate that debate.

But… culture? That word carries a lot of complexity and confusion. For some, when you talk about culture, it's a conversation about the arts. For others, it revolves around themes like purpose and representation. In different circles, it is about youth culture, or something tied to early adopters and opinion formers. In a broader sense, culture is everything. It's vast and expansive. It can refer to the most underground corner of music or the most mainstream aspects of family life. It's religion and generational change. It's walking the dog and making a sandwich. It can move at a crazy pace or creep along with glacial stealth. It can be utterly frivolous or painfully important. It's everywhere – and, in another sense, nowhere.

Sure thing, but run that lot past the average time-poor chief marketing officer – who has a CEO with little tolerance for long-winded reflections – and you won't get very far. While no proponent of marketing himself (he was a Marxist), cultural theorist and activist Dr Stuart Hall's work offers useful direction. Born in Kingston, Jamaica, and arriving in Britain in 1951, Hall later became the director of Birmingham University's Centre For Contemporary Cultural Studies. There, a new interdisciplinary approach to cultural studies emerged, informed by the 'classless society' principles from the US in the 1950s, amid the rise of mass communication. Central to Hall's perspective was rejecting the top-down view of culture, where the upper classes define it. Instead, he argued that culture comes at us from all angles: the subcultures of youth, the power of popular media, gendered and ethnic identities and decolonial perspectives. Hall's cultural studies embraced this complexity, acknowledging a variety of influences shaping culture.

Hall articulated culture as something expansive and unrefined: as experience lived, experience interpreted, experience defined. Culture, he believed, is shared meaning given to people, objects and events. Shared meaning that others can interpret, and that produces a sense of identity. The draw for brands and those who market them to become part of this shared meaning is obvious. It speaks of deeper connections, emotional resonance, relevance and authenticity. To note: at the time of writing, I'm not sure how many times 'authenticity' will be referenced in this book, but I'm assuming many. As DJ, producer and activist Honey Dijon put it: "The word authentic gets tossed around in dance music like French fries."

Dr Stuart Hall, who passed away in 2014, would likely be aghast at how some of his thinking has been co-opted into marketing communications. Pop-up, collabs, endorsements and branded content, one assumes, were not high among his priorities. Since his time, other writers have tackled culture's role in branding. In 2010, Douglas Holt and Douglas Cameron's Cultural Strategy: Using Innovative Ideologies To Build Breakthrough Brands took a more practitioner-focused approach. They argue for moving beyond traditional marketing industry tactics, instead integrating deeply rooted cultural meanings and pinpointing shifts in orthodoxy as a way to compelling brand narratives. This is particularly appealing in crowded categories like alcohol, where product innovation is scarce. The idea: sell the same beer but create a distinct cultural position around it – breaking away from industry norms and conventions.

The anthropologist and author Grant McCracken also weighed in on the topic with his 2009 book Chief Culture Officer. In it, he proposes that while major corporations tend to have their finances, operations and technology sorted, they're often caught off guard by the rapid changes in contemporary culture. McCracken suggests that adding a chief culture officer to the C-suite – taking a seat next to the chief financial, marketing, technology and operating officers – would help remedy a company's fuzzy relationship with cultural trends, addressing this proactively and strategically.

One of the key distinctions McCracken calls out in Chief Culture Officer is between fast and slow cultural shifts. By 'fast' he's referring to rapidly evolving spaces like music, sport, food and fashion. Shifts here are explicit, observable and on the surface. Often when people think about trends, what's happening here comes to mind. Meanwhile, slow culture operates beneath the surface, encompassing deeper values and rituals that shape shared meaning over time. Slow culture is what ultimately drives and sustains fast cultural trends; it determines what will stick, what will continue to gain momentum and what will fade away. Examples of slow culture include evolving societal attitudes towards family, spirituality and mindfulness – shifts that take time but influence everything from fashion choices to corporate policies.

Adding to the focus on culture – and always hungry for a new angle – the marketing communications industry has also fixated on principles of fandom in recent times. Once, being a fan of something was treated with suspicion, considered 'just a phase', something to 'grow out of'. But increasingly, it's recognised as a mighty cultural force, celebrated by the media and coveted by brands. Whereas once, being a fan might have marked you out as obsessive or nerdy, now it shows you are passionate, creative and engaged. It's a way to make sense of and form identity in our chaotic, challenging world. It has a lot to do with shared meaning, too.

There has been a significant shift in the power balance here. Fan culture used to be primarily controlled by the 'fan object' (aka the star), who decided when interactions would happen and when information would be shared. Now, fans are far less passive. Fan communities and ecosystems are just as much about the interactions between the fans themselves as with the fan object. Modern fans can be creators, collaborators, advocates and even investors. In a time when marketers are questioning the value of traditional demographic segmentation (such as males aged 18–24 or mothers aged 35–44), being present within people's passions and designing with those shared interests in mind presents a new, compelling opportunity to engage.

It's not hard at all to see where dance music and club culture fit in here. Dance music thrives on active participation, with fans as collaborators.

By tapping into this fandom and the nocturnal energy that comes with it, brands hope to connect with – gasp – credibility. Not just as advertisers, but as part of the culture. It promises an organic but powerful approach to building relationships with fans who are already deeply invested.

On paper, this makes so much sense. Go towards people and their passions. And, please, do talk about *people* – not 'consumers' or 'customers' (as hard as it is for many in marketing to accept, people are not walking around in customer mode all day). There are tribes and fandoms to collaborate with right now (the fast-culture stuff) and you can design with empathy for the future (the slow-culture stuff). But making this work in practice is another story. The biggest challenge often lies in measuring the return on investment. Long-term campaigns, partnerships and sponsorships across multiple online and offline channels are difficult to track. By comparison, spending that money on TV ads offers clearer measurability (though not necessarily better results).

The other question brands often grapple with is a more existential one: do we belong here? This ties back to relevance and authenticity. Does a brand truly have a place in a subculture, and can it add anything of value? Surely the need for bang for the buck will eventually piledrive cultural sensibilities? And what does authenticity even mean anymore? Some argue that the term has been so overused and hollowed out that it is now empty. As far back as 2011, a New York Times article told us: 'That 'authentic' has become a fad word is not surprising to scholars like Naomi S Baron, a linguistics professor at American University in Washington and the author of Always On: Language In An Online And Mobile World. She said it's common for some words to be used so often that they actually become devoid of meaning.'

There's even a growing school of thought in the marketing world that we're now in a post-authentic era, where no one cares about brands claiming to have a meaningful role in anything. Depending on your viewpoint, this makes for either a fascinatingly fluid shift to leverage or just another messy set of complications to keep you awake at night.

So far, we're addressing why brands engage *in* subculture. But there are also the ideas that emerge *from* it. This refers to the principles of influence; how trends and behaviours spread. These days, you'd be forgiven for thinking this is solely the doing of the often derided 'influencer' – those who use their social clout to promote products across fashion, beauty, fitness, travel and technology. However, the discourse around influence and how it circulates and grows in significance goes back long before worldwide social titans like MrBeast, Huda Kattan and Bretman Rock rose to fame.

Dick Hebdige's Subculture: The Meaning Of Style (1979) ran the rule over how subcultural symbols become commodified and integrated into the mainstream. Hebdige (who, by no coincidence at all, studied under Dr Stuart Hall at the Centre For Contemporary Cultural Studies) focused on UK youth tribes like teddy boys, mods, rockers, skinheads and punks, analysing their initial resistance to mainstream infiltration, before entrepreneurially-minded outsiders found a way in. He traced the journey of these styles from subversive acts of defiance to commercialised products, highlighting how cultural forms, though often born from opposition, eventually integrate into the broader cultural economy.

This theme of subcultures being hijacked and commodified was further explored in Naomi Klein's No Logo (1999). Hitting the shelves just as the notion of globalisation came to prominence in the West, Klein discussed the concept of 'cool hunting', where companies seek out cutting-edge subcultural trends and use them to market products to a larger, often more mainstream audience. Looking at the brand Tommy Hilfiger, then having a moment in hip-hop and R&B, and finding favour with Snoop Dogg, Mary J Blige, Usher, Aaliyah and their followers, she wrote: 'Like so much of cool hunting, Hilfiger's marketing journey feeds off the alienation at the heart of America's race relations: selling white youth on their fetishization of Black style, and Black youth on their fetishization of white wealth.'

In the same year came Malcolm Gladwell's The Tipping Point: How Little Things Can Make A Big Difference. In it, the Canadian journalist and public speaker tries to make sense of the small, hidden forces that explain why some ideas, trends and products burst from the fringes and find major-scale appeal – and why others don't. He introduces the individuals – 'connectors', 'mavens' and 'salesmen' – and networks that act as catalysts. Also, what makes some things 'stickier' and therefore more memorable and alluring than others (he uses the unexpected resurgence of Hush Puppies shoes in 1990s New York as a case study), providing a framework for understanding how influence works in a world where trends can emerge from anywhere.

A decade later, Jonah Berger's Contagious: Why Things Catch On (2013) added a new layer to the conversation, focusing on the social and emotional dynamics that make things go viral. Berger's model for virality included factors like emotion, storytelling and social currency – how people prefer to share things that make them feel special or look good in front of others. He argued that the most contagious ideas are often those that evoke strong human responses or are embedded in compelling narratives.

Of course, the most contagious ideas these days are the ones that light up on TikTok and Instagram. While many longstanding principles of influence still apply, social media has blown others to smithereens. Ideas now spread further and faster. Influence has been decentralised. We contend with algorithms and echo chambers. What exactly is a trend versus a microtrend versus an aesthetic versus a vibe? That's a debate that plays out at a frantic pace. Though not as frantic as the trends/microtrends/aesthetics/vibes themselves roll through. Brands are left facing the dilemma of what to chase and what to skip. Should they tell their own story or get closer to the story of others? To make a play on Charli XCX's 'brat summer', as so many did in 2024? To become a Duolingo-like meme, or stay in lane? Either way, the days of simply slotting 30-second commercials between TV hits are behind us. And some in marketing are adapting more gracefully than others.

In practice

Some get to write and theorise about these look-away-and-they've-changed-again themes. Others have to get on and do something with them. Indeed, through the rest of this book, we'll hear from many marketing practitioners – particularly those whose work overlaps with dance music. Some are in the employ of huge global brands or network agencies; others in more niche and boutique affairs. Some major on the strategy; others on the execution of campaigns and activations. Between occasional unease over whether commercial and creative imperatives can ever truly be squared, they mostly seem to love what they do. They also all have a story to share about underground music culture. Not just of the fun of the night out, but the lasting impact. Of attitudes they've carried forward from those experiences, contributing to how they make sense of the world, relationships and the right ways of working.

For instance, Leila Fataar. I check in with her first, less for the close-up view of dance music and more to tap into the fact that she has 30 years of experience making sense of where brands and culture come together. But she's got tales from the dancefloor, too. Originally from South Africa, her goals in her formative years in Cape Town included taking style cues from Tank Girl and immersing herself in the first waves of a post-apartheid rave scene that came into town. When she moved to London in 1995, she found her tribe among the city's buoyant drum 'n' bass movement. "Jungle, drum 'n' bass, hardcore rave culture – this was my community. It's where I started to meet friends that I still know today. But more than that, it was a training ground for the way I work. It changed everything. It shaped me in how I think about brands and business."

After a stint in PR and marketing for the hairdressers Toni & Guy, Leila leapt into the unknown, launching her own agency, Spin, in 2002. It started with a focus on PR services and a skew to fashion clients. But, as the internet took off and the opportunity to work differently grew, she started to think in broader communications terms. "I found a new niche," she says. "Integrating the online, and then the social, with the offline. Also integrating youth culture, fashion and music. Guerilla marketing, flash events, pop-up stores, unexpected collaborations – all of these things were starting to take shape."

Leila has also seen the evolution of how brands think about culture from the client side. She next took the role of global director for PR and social at adidas Originals in Germany. A bold relaunch of the Stan Smith shoe was a highlight. In her time there, in 2013, Business Insider dubbed the sportswear giant as among the '20 brands that have mastered Instagram'. Things turned even more culture-specific when she moved back to London in 2015, becoming head of culture and entertainment at the alcohol group, Diageo – home to a huge portfolio that includes Smirnoff, Johnnie Walker, Baileys, Guinness, Gordon's Gin and Captain Morgan. At the time of the appointment, Ed Pilkington, marketing and innovation director at Diageo Europe, told the Campaign trade title: "As marketers, we are very lucky at Diageo to have an incredible range of brands to work with that play an authentic part in culture. Leila will be leading a team to ensure we are capitalising on this, shaping how our brands show up and ensuring that we are and remain culturally relevant." Leila comments today: "I didn't know anything about alcohol – I was from a fashion and music background. But that's what they wanted, someone who could come in to disrupt the category, make them do something different. Someone who really didn't understand the rules."

Projects at Diageo saw Leila getting more involved with music. Among them were Smirnoff's Equalising Music programme, which aimed to double the number of female-identifying music headliners at festivals through thought leadership initiatives and partnerships with non-profit organisations; and the Smirnoff Sound Collective, with objectives of promoting greater visibility in dance music for the under-represented through mentoring and guidance. For Guinness, the work included collaborations with Boiler Room at the Notting Hill

Carnival, featuring appearances from heavy dub system operators like Aba Shanti-I.

Exciting stuff, but the lure of independence eventually had Leila stepping away from corporate security and starting a new business. In 2017, she opened as Platform13. It terms itself an 'independent global partner that creates and maintains cultural relevance for some of the world's best-known brands'. Among a long list of Platform13 clients, there is Birkenstock, Beats By Dre, Under Armour, Pinterest, Guinness, Vans, Bumble, adidas, The LEGO Group and Moet & Hennessy. "I wanted to come up with a new way of working," Leila says. "I felt I knew what the gaps were in how brands were operating in and thinking about culture."

Cultural relevance is a term, an ambition, that surfaces consistently in conversations about brands making links with dance music. Leila, who, when we speak, is nearing completion of a book on the topic of cultural relevance for brands, thinks there are still some fundamental misunderstandings in what is being got at here. "Too many people talk about culture marketing as if it's a channel, an output, compared to TV or social media," she says, talking to me shortly after wrapping up a big project that, as tends to be the way with these things, has left her half elated, half exhausted – "Yesterday was a shut-the-curtains day." For her, the conversation around brands and culture needs to start at a place before anything executional is considered. "It's not an output; it's an input. It's a perspective that then shapes business strategy. I connect all of this with business growth, not only marketing outputs."

So how does she define cultural relevance for brands? "It's a brand that impacts people enough that they'll buy it, consume it. But also that they'll work for it. They'll advocate for it; they'll defend it. That's a culturally relevant brand. This, for me, is the holy grail because it's not just about people buying your brand. It's about adding so much value to the world, to the culture that you're trying to be part of, that people believe in you on levels beyond simply purchasing and consuming."

She says one of the challenges here is working with clients to even agree on what culture means. As we've described, it's a big and messy subject, and you need people to accept it for what it is, rather than try to slot it into a sausage machine. She eschews the marketing world's predilection for frameworks and prescriptive models, preferring a more 'get your hands dirty' approach. For similar reasons, she also thinks too many marketers have got just a bit too good (or perhaps robotic) at their jobs – meaning they've lost the ability to think like an everyday person.

"It might sound strange to say, but it can be a problem," she laughs. "It's part of the rigidity that brands often suffer from. They have a lot of processes; a lot of 'the computer says no'. I work with them to get to an understanding that culture is lots of things and things you can't just feed into a black box and expect results to get spat out the other end. For instance, for me, culture is my background. I'm South African, mixed race. My family's Muslim. Then there are the things that influence me, like fashion, music, sport and art. Then you have business culture, company culture. You've got to be ready to think about how all of these things intersect. But it's not a thing to be scared of – all of these intersections are quite beautiful really."

Where she concedes there is a need for something more systematic is around measurement – showing the success that comes with being culturally relevant. It's another recurring theme in this book. Brands, unsurprisingly, do like their metrics, and they can call upon quite the range of them: awareness metrics, engagement metrics, conversion metrics, brand perception metrics, market share metrics, influence and advocacy metrics, return on investment metrics. Whether any of these are really fit for purpose in ascertaining the benefits of cultural relevance is up for debate.

"I think there's still a job to be done here; something that feels more standardised," she explains. "This kind of work can come across as more of a 'nice to have' because people don't understand the impact it has on business growth. It's hard to measure more emotional stuff like this.

Hard to measure things that are more to do with community. But 'hard' shouldn't stop us – we need to solve this."

Another barrier to brands engaging meaningfully and sustainably in culture that frequently gets raised is short-termism. Specifically, the short-termism which comes from factors such as quarterly profit and performance reporting cycles. Also from many senior figures in client-side marketing roles moving between jobs at a faster-than-ever rate. If you only expect to be at a brand for two years, you may not be inclined to invest in a cultural initiative that will take far longer than that to show results. "That's why you need to create a cultural positioning in the business that sits outside of just the marketing department," she believes. "So that any CMO *(chief marketing officer)* can come in and begin to develop their own translation of it, rather than start from scratch."

In some respects, music has more to compete against now in the type of cultural opportunities that brands will consider and what they'll weigh it up against. Sport, for instance, would once have been considered quite a different kind of investment. Leila explains that's no longer the case. Football, basketball and so forth are cross-pollinating with art, fashion and, indeed, music, showing a convergence is underway. Nevertheless, she affirms that music still offers fertile scope within this mix and that careful project design is key to getting it right. Which includes listening to those you intend to engage with. Obvious, you'd think, but not necessarily a strong trait among brands.

"It's so important to have people who truly represent those communities involved from the very beginning, during the ideation phase, not just at the execution stage," Leila continues. "You can't understand the nuances of what's needed without those voices at the table from the start. Too often, I see big, traditional agencies rushing in with ideas without considering if anyone on their team really understands the culture or the community. That's where they miss the mark. As I say, stop being such a good marketer and become a better human!"

Regardless of the challenges, Leila is not short on optimism. She and others are finding space to educate brand teams on what they mean by cultural relevance. Also, as the years tick by, there's a generational change in the boardroom to consider.

"As a new wave comes through, stepping into leadership roles and the C-suite, I'm hopeful it will bring a better understanding. It's part of having a better awareness of the responsibility brands now have in the world. There's a growing recognition that relevance can't just be bought by money. Since everything that happened in 2020 *(specifically the pandemic and the Black Lives Matter movement)*, people have started to look behind the curtain, understanding more about brands, businesses and their values. I really think this has come to a head now with Palestine and other issues. It's like everyone is finally critically thinking about everything they see and know. That's the hope, and for my sins, I'll keep hoping for it.

"It's an interesting time for culture. Music, sport and even fashion are real connectors of people around the world," Leila concludes, reflecting on all that's changed since she stepped off her flight from Cape Town three decades ago. "That's the opportunity. Despite geopolitics and other forces that can divide us, these are the spaces where we can come together. That's what dance culture, rave culture and club culture did for me personally – and I know it did that for lots of others. It wasn't about where you were from or how much money you had. It wasn't like that. Those in business still have a lot of learning to do here. They need to really grasp how important this stuff is for people – and therefore how important it should be for their brands."

2. DISCO WAS A SWEET THING

Denim, vodka, art, dancing – reflections from NYC's disco days

You won't find partnerships in the modern sense. Instead, early dalliances between brands and dance music. And one (unwelcomely) materialising long after

We're a community

On a Hell's Kitchen dancefloor in July 2024, the closest thing remaining to New York City disco's origin story is rolling out again. From the Musica venue's expansive DJ booth, François K (real name Kevorkian) – 70 years old, with a fantastical history that encompasses playing at The Loft, the Garage, Better Days and Studio 54, and an abundance of edits, remixes and productions – eases down the music and addresses the remarkably diverse crowd. "We're doing this together. We're a community. We're a group of loving, absolutely dedicated people who think of this as such an important part of our lives that we can't possibly let go of it."

He's reflecting on 28 years of Body & Soul, the storied night he hosts with Danny Krivit and Joe Claussell. But really, he could be reflecting on closer to 50 years of the most immense club culture narrative of all. The Sanctuary, The Loft, The Gallery, Paradise Garage, Fun House, Area, Danceteria, Mudd Club, The Saint, The Tunnel, Sound Factory, Twilo, Body & Soul. These are just a few of the clubs that mark this kaleidoscopic journey through after-dark creativity and the quest for both escape and belonging. At every stage, the notion that 'we're a community' can be pointed to. Community with many facets to it, but often carrying a particular relevance to those living marginalised lives through racial discrimination, sexual orientation, gender identity and socioeconomic challenges. This is complex and emotive stuff, deep-set in how to survive and, at times, even thrive in the city.

With all of this in mind, some argue that brands have no place in spaces so oriented to community, with their codes of support, pride, expression and protection. Brands aren't human – they don't, and can't, care about humans. They are constructs designed to generate revenue. Naomi Klein's seminal critique of corporate branding in 1999, No Logo, put it this way: 'The astronomical growth of brands and logos is not a triumph of marketing; it's the market triumphing over us.' Some from the disco era firmly agreed – and their present-day advocates have taken up the cause on their behalf.

The Loft, the party that started in early 1970 at 654 Broadway, has, in many senses, played on forever in the minds of the devoted – both the relative few who've attended and the numerous who wish they had. The incongruity between brand objectives and the club as a community probably feel most striking in the case of this anti-commercial, pro-audiophile space. Writing on his website in 2022, Tim Lawrence, the academic, music historian and author of weighty disco explorations Love Saves The Day and Life And Death On The New York Dance Floor, robustly presented the argument for why brands have no place in the world of The Loft. Or in close company with its founder, David

Mancuso. The touch paper for this was a press release from Louis Vuitton, claiming that the Fall In Love men's collection that year – work that design luminary Virgil Abloh started on before his passing in 2021 – was inspired by Mancuso's familial, egalitarian vision for The Loft.

Hypebeast reported on the collection as follows: 'Built upon Virgil Abloh's belief that the function of a DJ is akin to that of a designer, Louis Vuitton has unveiled its Pre-Spring 2023 Fall In Love collection. The upcoming range explores how DJs and designers sample established genres to create sounds and looks that resonate with the outlooks of new generations.' This makes for slick PR copy, but while The Loft was known for inclusivity and immersive sonic experiences, what it wasn't known for was high fashion or exclusivity. Across 7,500 words – including slight detours to note that another luxury brand, Moncler, currently occupies the building that was home to The Loft from 1975 to 1985 – Tim pulls apart any sense that there's something to be admired in the style nod being made here.

'News of the collection reached me when Tina Magennis – a dedicated regular at The Loft ever since David held his first Love Saves The Day party on Valentine's Day 1970 – sent me a link to a Mixmag article published on 26 July,' he writes. 'The matter-of-fact report left me feeling uneasy, as did other journalistic accounts of the launch of the collection. There was no suggestion that Louis Vuitton's alignment with David could be anything other than cool and positive, bringing a form of 'deserved attention' to The Loft, with gratitude due to a fashion corporation that was forward-thinking enough to support the cause. I wondered: what about The Loft being the absolute inverse of everything Louis Vuitton stands for?'

Tim continued: 'Can we access the essence of what it is to be human, entering into a form of collective joy and maybe experiencing a form of cosmic transcendence by putting on a pair of shoes, a shirt, matching trousers and a jacket? Is this what goes down in the changing rooms of Louis Vuitton's stores?' By October 2022, a Resident Advisor article reported that the Mancuso estate had given no form of approval for the collection. "We know David would have refused this association if he was still alive," said an estate representative. "We do not approve of the way they have used David and The Loft's name, reputation and pioneering life's work to market their collection and brand. We know David would have refused this association if he was still alive."

But would everyone from then, from that fabled era of NYC nightlife, have refused this association? That seems unlikely. It was a broad church and, even if a credible connection wasn't there with Mancuso – who Tim Lawrence remembers as having a distinctly relaxed attitude to fashion, typically wearing a T-shirt, collarless overshirt, regular slacks and construction boots – it's safe to say others would see relevance in affiliations of this kind. More polished ideals of style were, of course, integral to many aspects of the disco era.

Nicky Siano certainly recalls fashion designers, and therefore the notion of the fashion brand, on the dancefloor. "New York was in a lot of chaos *(it was the era when the city nearly declared bankruptcy)*, the Vietnam war, the *(Stonewall)* riots – all of these things were coming to a head, and people needed change. Disco was part of that, and fashion designers were part of that," he says on a video call from his place in Sheepshead Bay, Brooklyn. Nicky is just back in full view, with his dog sleeping in the background and a cat jumping across surfaces. A second ago, he was only visible from the torso down, a sinewy ball of energy as he dances to illustrate how brands sponsoring clubs need to "get more strategically rhythmic".

Born in 1955 and raised in an Italian American family in Coney Island, Brooklyn, his story is as good as Disco Year Zero. He loved high-quality sound from as early as he can remember. By the time he was 12 – played through the best home stereo system he could get together with the money raised from a part-time job – he was embracing the sonic minutiae of everything from symphonic recordings to singer-songwriter Laura Nyro. "This was something I took with me into

DJing. Hearing things that other people didn't notice," he explains. "I would take songs and create little paths. I would play with the tone, so that it would be more exciting, and people would go nuts. And then they'd know exactly where we'd do it every week, and they'd be screaming like four or five pieces before it was actually gonna happen."

He's talking about nights at The Gallery, the club he started with his brother, Joe, in February 1973 on 10th Street in Chelsea – it eventually moved to a new spot on Mercer and Houston in 1974. He was just 17 at the time (his brother was 10 years older). Incredibly, his first DJing residency came when he was 16, at The Round Table, situated in the ballroom of an old hotel. But his disco story doesn't even start there.

"I started going down the West Village, and I began hearing dance music through the doors that were opening and closing at the bars. Bars I couldn't get into. I was 13 when I started going down there; 14 when the riots happened. This was 1969 – David (Mancuso) didn't even open yet when I was hearing these songs. I just became focused on dancing. I'd ask people coming out of the clubs, 'What was that song?' And I'd write down the name. Then, the real journey was finding the record. It took me about a month to work out there was only one place selling these 45s – Colony Records *(which survived until 2012)* on Broadway and 49th. It was the best kept secret. It was DJs-only."

The power of music and dancing started to manifest for Nicky when a boring night in Coney Island led him to The Loft. His brother was hosting a party. It was dull, recalls Nicky, so he pulled out his box of Colony-sourced 45s and started playing. A woman who was dating his brother came up to him and asked: "'You like this music? I'm going to take you somewhere.' And she took us to The Loft. And it was the first year, 1970. And it was just after the summer, so I started going to The Loft in September of 1970. That influenced me more than anything."

The Gallery took the intimacy of The Loft and made things bigger, louder and more hedonistic in form. A bit more commercial in outlook, too. Clubbing as it would become was therefore moving into view. Francis Grasso, spinning at The Sanctuary, was first to start mixing records (with others like Michael Cappello and David Rodriguez warranting a nod), but with Mancuso eschewing the beat-matching style, it was Nicky who really furthered the art of blending tracks together to create dancefloor euphoria. It wasn't just tracks, either. Dropping in jet plane sound effects over staples such as MFSB's Love Is The Message was part of the drama.

"The whole thing about The Gallery is it was designed to blow your mind while you are on the dancefloor. It was designed to maximise the dancing experience. And we had LSD to help us – not alcohol. I mean, the music made me want to *really live.* It was making love to my ears. And picking the right records to make the room go nuts – I enjoyed the shit out of that."

Writing about a night at The Gallery in the New York Sunday Daily News in 1975, Sheila Weller enthused: 'The wildness is exquisitely wholesome. Furious dancing. Gentle laughter. Crepe paper and tinsel. Body energy shakes the room… The floor is a drum to the dancers – many of them gay, most of them black – whose upsprung fists and tambourines lob the balloons and streamers above what seem to be collectively chosen intervals.'

Beyond partying, what role did these places play in fostering creative possibilities? Nicky subscribes to the view that clubs in that period provided opportunities for the otherwise marginalised. You needed to mix in the right circles, but you sure as hell didn't need an education or a privileged background. There was a support network, of sorts, that enabled people to rise. A certain pair of friends called Larry Levan and Francis Warren Nicholls Jr (soon to be better known as Frankie Knuckles) caught an early break by helping out at The Gallery. Next to taking cues from Nicky's DJing techniques, duties included hanging up decorations and mixing acid into the house punch.

Set against the epic backdrop of 1970s NYC, with high style and street style beginning to sashay around each other, that fashion was the first of the creative industries to integrate with club culture is hardly surprising. A domino effect followed: fashion influenced graphic design, which shaped media, then advertising, interiors and beyond. Nic Allum, a cultural anthropologist currently based in Los Angeles but having lived in most corners of the world, offers a perspective on this. In the past, she's worked for the Mo' Wax, Acid Jazz and Ninja Tune labels; for promoters the Mean Fiddler Group; as a cultural strategy advisor to will.i.am and his equity partners; for umpteen brands through her Cultureland consultancy; as a guest lecturer on cultural branding at Northwestern University; *and* as creative director of Do The WeRQ – an organisation seeking change in LGBTQ+ representation in the marketing industry. She's also explored – and thought deeply about – music subculture's influence on the world around it.

Nic draws a connection between disco and fashion that goes back as far as 1973 and the Battle Of Versailles. This high-profile fund-raising event was an orchestrated face-off between French and American fashion designers, with Yves Saint Laurent and Pierre Cardin among those starring for the former and Stephen Burrows and Halston for the latter. Trade title WWD (known back then as Women's Wear Daily) reported on it as: 'A triumph of sportswear ease over couture fussiness. More than an uber-glam party, the show sparked the internationalization of fashion, elevated the prestige of American labels, transformed runway shows and opened more opportunities for Black models.'

Indeed, 10 of the 36 models brought across by the American contingent were Black. Among them was Bethann Hardison, who later became an activist and co-founder of the Black Girls Coalition in 1988, supporting African American models. "But as well as everything else, it was totally disco," Nic says. "In terms of how it was presented, how it was highly choreographed, it felt very much like disco. It's an early part of that long, long tail of influence that disco has had. It made people think about fashion, both luxury and street, in a different way. And that impact has stayed a part of fashion through to today."

Back with Nicky Siano. He witnessed these cultural connections being made firsthand. "Disco influenced all kinds of things. 100%, undoubtedly, and across so many areas. But it started with fashion," he nods. "I mean, The Gallery, it was a fashion industry hang-out. The number of designers who came through the doors was unbelievable, and it must have influenced them all. Thinking about clothes and style in a way they wouldn't have before, and for a new audience. Calvin Klein, Willi Smith, Stephen Burrows *(the latter two he struck up friendships with)*. Everybody who was in fashion came down. It was intense and it was influential."

Willi Smith, who was to become arguably the highest-profile Black fashion designer of the 1980s, is credited in many circles as having laid the foundations for the catwalk's collision with streetwear. Stephen Burrows was the first Black American designer to achieve international acclaim, with his trademark colour-blocking and truly disco-primed use of fabrics taking substantial influence from the dancefloor. He said at the time: "Dancing is always in my clothes… you can do anything and feel free in the garment."

If designers like Burrows heralded a disco aesthetic that was emergent and cosmopolitan, sequined and bold, a contrasting style code thrived at places like The Loft and Paradise Garage. In these settings, it was dressed down, home-customised and ready for sweat. Writing for NME in 1983, Paolo Hewitt caught the born-of-necessity style in an interview with Michael de Benedictus, a Larry Levan acolyte and co-founder of the Peech Boys outfit. "And the fashions!" the keyboardist exclaimed when asked about the Garage get-up that year. "They all look so incredibly different, but they can't go to Jumping Jack Flash *(East Village boutique known for glitter-heavy fashion)* to get that look, so they go to their closet and they see something, rip it apart and sew this part to that part and suddenly there's a look there."

You could argue it was the cursory start of a dress-down versus dress-up style divide that has permeated nightlife ever since. Nicky feels he saw both taking shape at The Gallery. "Capped-sleeved T-shirts. That was Larry's idea," he says, referring to his sometimes lover Larry Levan and the shorter-sleeved tees, created with maximum scope for movement in mind. These would feature in so many pictures of dancers at Paradise Garage. "I had never seen a capped-sleeved T-shirt until Larry started working for me. And one night he rolled in with one. It was not turned up – it was cut that way. He was like, 'This is my latest design – I'll make you one.' And I started wearing it. And then eventually the stores went crazy with his idea, and those T-shirts started selling everywhere."

Since those early days at The Gallery, Nicky has had as many highs and lows as he'd wedge into one of his sets – including a lot of years lost to heroin. He played at Studio 54. He was DJing when Bianca Jagger was famously photographed riding a horse through the club on her birthday. 54 co-founder Steve Rubell was obsessed with the lights at The Gallery, taking ideas from that club uptown with him. But Nicky was sacked after a few months at 54 due to his drug habit. Some wilderness years followed. Then, he co-wrote a book with author Suzanne Lipsett, No Time To Wait, offering guidance on managing and living with HIV. More recently, there has been a glorious return to the decks, with a lot of (well-earned) love shown by younger audiences and opportunities to play at festivals and clubs worldwide.

Thinking back on his days at The Gallery and what differs from the 21st century version of NYC, he says: "It would be easier for a 17-year-old me today in some ways. Social media means you can reach out that much more. But there's no way me and my brother could've got a club in Manhattan today. The relationship I had with the dancers back then – that's hard to duplicate now. And those friendships from then, they've lasted a lifetime."

While the likes of Burrows and Smith were the first to show up in the clubs – drawing influence from and ultimately contributing to the style codes they encountered on nights out – it was an Italian brand that started to leverage these cultural currents in at least nominally strategic terms. That brand was Fiorucci. It was bright, fast, unabashed and it took the city by a neon-lit storm.

"Fiorucci!" Nicky beams as he remembers the Italian fashion brand arriving in NYC. "They opened their store right around the corner from Bloomingdale's. We'd go there every week to see what they had. Their jeans, they fitted me like a glove. I loved Fiorucci stuff and they made such a big impact in the clubs from the first second we came across them. Oh, Fiorucci!"

Fiorucci at the disco

In 1999, the contemporary British artist Mark Leckey released a video called Fiorucci Made Me Hardcore. Starting with northern soul footage from the Wigan Casino and building through to 1990s rave, this rather wonderful and highly mesmeric piece of work splices together footage from across the decades of underground UK dance culture. Jamie xx subsequently samples it on his 2014 track, All Under One Roof Raving – also a homage to particularly British, and hardcore, flavours of dance music. Leckey was quickly dubbed the 'artist for the YouTube generation' and later won the 2008 Turner Prize with his exhibition Industrial Light And Magic.

Revisiting Fiorucci Made Me Hardcore in 2015, The Guardian wrote: 'It portrayed subjects – working-class, mostly white, mostly male teenagers – rarely accorded dignity and grace in the wider culture. At the same time, in an art world that could often seem wry, or ironic, or knowing, Fiorucci was different: disarmingly sincere.' Of its title, Leckey noted his view that "something as trite and throwaway and exploitative as a jeans manufacturer *(Fiorucci)* can be taken by a group of people and made into something totemic, and powerful, and life-affirming."

Trite or not, this is one of those through-line moments that make exploring subculture so fascinating. Though sometimes less by the brand's intent than through cultural adoption, Fiorucci has tracked alongside music and related style tribes over time. It became a staple of the UK football casual wardrobe for a period. Mark Leckey was himself an Everton-supporting football casual.

Down in London, the Boy's Own club collective was also straddling football and music culture. Speaking to Eddy Rhead for the Oi Polloi fashion store's blog, the DJ Terry Farley from Boy's Own recalls: "From the mid-70s you would get coaches and coaches come down to the King's Road. Coach-loads would come in from Leicester, the Midlands, South Wales and the like, and people would just walk up and down. Clothes shops were more important than record shops in a social way. You'd go in, pick up flyers, hang around, chat to other people and the people working in the shops always knew exactly where the best places to go were. You'd start at World's End, down the King's Road, up Sloane Street to Knightsbridge where a Lacoste shop had opened in about '77, then back down to the Fiorucci shop, which was a big deal back then."

Fiorucci gained further kudos among UK football fans through its shirt sponsorship of Internazionale (Inter) in the company's hometown of Milan – a place with Mecca-like qualities for football casuals. Actually, this was a different Fiorucci – Cesare Fiorucci, a dairy and meat producer best known for its salami – but that didn't seem to matter too much.

The through-line keeps on going back across time. As Nicky Siano has enthusiastically recalled, it takes us to the vivid night culture of New York City in the 1970s. Fiorucci wasn't the only label showing up amid that vividness. We've already encountered Calvin Klein, Willi Smith and Stephen Burrows. And as Sister Sledge would reference in He's The Greatest Dancer there was 'Halston, Gucci, Fiorucci'. But Fiorucci went the furthest in bringing 'brand' to the dancefloor – and then bringing the club to their store. It sponsored parties at Studio 54, including the 1977 launch night. That party included a performance by the Alvin Ailey dance company, with costumes by Antonio Lopez, who also designed clothes and styled windows for Fiorucci. While this particular sponsorship initiative was doubtless less formal in nature than the type that would happen today – fewer contracts, less checking on 'alignment' with brand values and audience fit, no attempt to measure the return on investment – it can reasonably be highlighted as the first instance of a brand engaging in, and seeking leverage from, the type of club culture that still lives on today.

Interviewed for the Free Spirit documentary about his life, founder Elio Fiorucci recalls: "For me, disco was a sweet thing, like a return to Romanticism. A lady comes to me. She did the PR for these two gentlemen *(Ian Schrager and Steve Rubell)*, and she tells me that they have got the most famous disco in Long Island City *(Enchanted Garden, Schrager and Rubell's pre-Studio 54 club in Queens)*, but they want to move to Manhattan and they have found a TV studio, and they want to convert it into a disco and it will become the most famous club."

It's unsurprising that dance music first saw brand patronage in the more extravagant and privileged setting of Studio 54, owned by Schrager, Rubell and the often-overlooked other co-founder, Carmen D'Alessio. The club, complete with its moon and cocaine spoon sign, attracted a roll call of celebrities, ranging from drag star Divine to Donald Trump. This was in contrast to spaces popular with marginalised club kids, like The Loft and Paradise Garage, or the grittier downtown spots like the Mudd Club. Fiorucci – the man and the brand – liked freedom and counterculture. But Elio also liked fame, high profile and life on the right side of the velvet cord. Studio 54, situated at what originally opened as the Gallo Opera House in 1927 and later became the CBS broadcast studio, offered plenty of that.

Fiorucci-endorsed nights at Studio 54 largely played out the same as regular nights at Studio 54, though perhaps with more focus on the guest appearances. The flyer for one, in May 1983, marked the 15th anniversary of Fiorucci. It listed electro pioneer Man Parrish and

Madonna & Dancers. By that stage, Madonna had already played live at the multi-storey and less exclusive Danceteria club, where Mark Kamin resided as DJ in the main room, and scenes in Desperately Seeking Susan were shot. It didn't stop with sponsorship. Fiorucci's striking colours and innovative cuts were splashed liberally across the club's clientele, too. Disco-friendly sexiness and high-waist jeans. The Fiorucci angels design (modelled after Raphael's cherubs) and never-ending variations on the brand logo. Jumpsuits, nods to gender fluidity and a mishmash of high and low fashion influences. The marketing fit, even without the benefit of modern metrics to pore over, was good.

The fit was also evident in the Fiorucci store, which opened on 125 East 59th Street (currently, underwhelmingly, home to a branch of Muji) in 1976. The location: at the bottom end of the Upper East Side, far from the scuzzy chaos and creativity of the Lower East Side. 'A dollop of downtown atop a bland soup of midtown blahs', as the Flaming Pablum blog put it. It was called a concept store, and the concept was decidedly club-like. To the point that it would eventually be dubbed the 'Studio 54 of the daytime'. The music, naturally, was throbbing – mainly string-laden four-to-the-floor disco to start with, more Ze Records-style no-wave as the years went by. Strobe lights flickered and people danced as they shopped.

Ettore Sottsass and Andrea Branzi designed the store. Sottsass would go on to found the Memphis Group, the Milan design collective whose clashing colours and heavy use of plastic became an equally loved and reviled influence on the look of 1980s furniture and furnishings, earning the description 'a shotgun wedding between Bauhaus and Fisher-Price'. All of this was evidenced in the very neon, intentionally throwaway visual codes of the Fiorucci store, which would embrace a new thematic direction every three months.

The slew of famous people who frequented the store was similarly as expansive as those who went to Studio 54. The mood, if not quite so debauched (more free espressos than cocaine), was equally high energy and flamboyant. Photographer, stylist and artist Maripol was the store manager. She was the director of the celebrated Downtown 81 film, which Fiorucci partly funded. Maripol also styled Madonna. Madonna's brother, Christopher, worked at Fiorucci, as did i-D magazine founder Terry Jones. Keith Haring painted murals there. Andy Warhol was given desk space in the store to run Interview magazine. In his diary in 1983, Warhol wrote: 'Went to Fiorucci and it's so much fun there. It's everything I've always wanted, all plastic.'

Interviewed for a New York Times piece about the store, Kim Hastreiter, the founder of the downtown chronicling Paper Magazine, which was sold at Fiorucci, said: "It was really for people who were out at night dancing. That's what Fiorucci was for. It wasn't really for what you'd wear to the office." In the same piece, artist Kenny Scharf – who, prior to collaborating with Absolut, had his first solo exhibition in the Fiorucci store – remarked: "There was never any place like it before, and never any place like it after. It was like a daytime disco. Any time of day, you'd go there and there'd be the music and the visuals and the people. Basically, someone would call you on the phone and say, 'Hey, you want to go to Fiorucci and dance in the window?' And it would get on the news, while we were up there, just dancing."

One such occasion was in 1979 when NBC's Real People reality series turned up to film the fashion kids dancing in the window. Also, the regular New Yorkers looking perplexed from the *other* side of the window. "Would *you* buy clothes from these people?" asks the presenter in a tone that strongly suggests she wouldn't. In the clip, Fiorucci salesman and performance artist Joey Arias, and musician and fellow performance artist Klaus Nomi, lead the fray. There's robotic dancing in the window (another small claim to cultural fame would be Fiorucci bringing break-dancing to that part of Manhattan; not, it's fair to say, a very break-dance-y part of town). One woman exclaims: "I think the more tacky the better. Tacko is where it's at." Another, musing on what draws New Yorkers to the store, adds: "They want to be appropriate to the situation. And the situation is mad." One of the bemused onlookers, big sideburns and bigger tie, can only muster up: "It's something I don't know. Ha ha ha. I'm not used to seeing this."

Beyond its novelty to the average New Yorker, the Fiorucci store and the city's club culture had a mutually influential relationship. It spanned a range of aesthetic touchpoints, from fashion to design and spatial layout. Bringing the night's energy into the day, the store positioned itself as much about community and entertainment as transactional retail. At its peak, it reportedly attracted 100,000 visitors on a Saturday. As Elio noted in Free Spirit: "In a short time, it became a meeting point for all Americans. People came here just to spend time, have fun, look at the pictures and listen to music."

Elio Fiorucci, who passed away in 2015 at 80, seemed destined for the disco life. Though his beginnings were ordinary, working in his father's shoe shop from the age of 14, he was travelling to London by the time the 1960s arrived, drawing inspiration from the vibrant scenes of Carnaby Street and Kensington Market. With it, a way to dress that felt freer, less constrained by rules. "You need to be very brave to break religious precepts," he reflected, recalling the traditional values presiding over his childhood in Milan and the surrounding countryside. "Stopping the unnecessary fears to begin life."

He took the energy, freedom and prototype fearlessness he experienced in London back to Milan, opening a store in 1967 that featured the work of London designers like Ossie Clark and Zandra Rhodes. His travels around the world brought back various ideas and products – from beaded jewellery to thongs – gathered in places like India and Brazil. In 1974, he created Italy's first concept store, a vast space that housed everything from denim and record departments to houseware, a restaurant, a travel agency and a particularly grand fountain. London called him back, too, with his first overseas store opening on the King's Road in 1975, where job seekers were put through auditions and casting sessions.

As the Fiorucci brand gained momentum through the late 1970s and early 1980s, including turning its attention to the US, it employed a team of young trend-spotters who circled the globe in search of fresh ideas – many of which were found in the burgeoning network of clubs springing up in major cities. The brand collaborated with Disney on Mickey Mouse-emblazoned clothes, released brightly hued sticker books with Panini and produced an endless stream of brilliantly designed posters and advertisements.

Fiorucci also organised parties in Ibiza at Pacha. It was on the Balearic island that Elio first conceived what would become the brand's most lucrative innovation: Lycra-infused stretch jeans. Elio was captivated by the sight of hippie women wearing (and washing) their Levi's denim in the sea. He set out to create jeans that similarly clung to bodies on dry land. The brand's skintight jeans – despite Elio's talk of inclusivity, he refused to design for women above a UK size 10 – came in colours as bold as the store's interior. They quickly became a staple of NYC nightlife, sparking a designer denim revolution that spread out from disco through wider culture, influencing brands like Gloria Vanderbilt and Calvin Klein.

Denim brings us back to Studio 54, a club that never shied away from consumerism or commercial opportunity. Gloria Vanderbilt, the blue jeans success story, held catwalk shows there. Ian Schrager and Steve Rubell also saw a space for Studio 54 to have its own jeans brand, bringing in designer Norma Kamali. She was famous for the red swimsuit Farah Fawcett wore in an iconic (and 12 million-selling) pin-up poster from the period that later appeared in Tony Manero's room in Saturday Night Fever (in another ad campaign, Fawcett posed on a skateboard in Fiorucci's stretch denim). While there's little evidence that Studio 54 jeans sold well, they remain memorable for the magazine ads. Featuring otherwise nude men and women stepping into the jeans, the strapline poked fun at the venue's exclusivity: 'Now everybody can get into Studio 54.'

Studio 54 jumped into partnerships and commercial ventures with the utmost gusto. In contrast, those NYC clubs that get talked about in considerably more hushed tones, notably The Loft and Paradise Garage, took longer to overlap with the world of brand communications and did so indirectly. Their impact came more from their aesthetic and energy. They fashioned a blueprint for global club culture to run with from the late 1980s onward. The rise of the DJ (something not embraced at Studio 54, where the DJs were held in low esteem by the management). The allure of the underground. The dressed-down, urban streetwear cues of baggy pants and ripped T-shirts. The liberation and inclusivity these nights fostered. Brands did not feature in those clubs, but eventually they sure would want a piece of their attitude and authenticity. Refined, translated and almost always polished up too pristinely, nonetheless, these codes of rebellion were essential ingredients in how many brands would seek to present themselves to discerning young consumers. "The best clubs from then," says Nicky Siano, "brands would die for just a fraction of the connection those places had with people."

For reasons of taste and decadence, history hasn't looked too kindly on Studio 54. It is viewed as more symbolic of excess (see Jagger and horse), of disco culture's overlap with America's inglorious and status-seeking elite, than great music, or the gritty vitality of elsewhere in NYC. Its resident DJs (the mainstay was the relatively overlooked Richie Kaczor, who's credited with popularising Gloria Gaynor's I Will Survive, and who passed in 1993 with complications from AIDs) rarely warrant coverage compared to appraisals of the selectors and their playlists from other night spots. In Bill Brewster and Frank Broughton's book, Last Night A DJ Saved My Life, Danny Tenaglia comments: "Studio 54 was like going to see a movie, you know? It wasn't about the music. When you went there, it was gimmicky." The brash, beyond-reproach attitude of the place is what mostly gets remembered. It was an attitude that led to the Studio 54 dream crashing down to earth amid IRS raids, tax evasion charges and, ultimately, Rubell and Schrager serving time.

The animosity some directed at Studio 54 was succinctly captured in the origin story of Chic's most famous hit, Le Freak. It's 'Freak out!' refrain started as 'Fuck off!' – aimed at the knock-backs that Chic's Nile Rodgers received from the club's notoriously hard-to-please doorman, Marc Benecke. "I thought that by now Marc Benecke knew me because I had been there many, many times with my girlfriend and with a guy who used to manage Fiorucci. But Marc totally disregarded us," Rodgers says in Anthony Haden-Guest's The Last Party account of Studio 54. He consequently headed back through the snow to his apartment, bought coke, grass and champagne, and started playing with Chic co-founder Bernard Edwards. "We resorted to using music therapeutically… We were just yelling obscenities… 'Fuck Studio 54… Fuck them!'" Rodgers now counts Benecke as a friend, and Le Freak, with cleaned-up lyrics, shifted over seven million copies.

But in Nicky Siano's mind, this critical narrative does obscure some good early intentions at Schrager, Rubell and D'Alessio's palace of excess. It was, he believes, a club that started with "purer motives" and a passion for music very much the North Star – for Steve Rubell in particular. "I'm not sure they wanted it to go the way it did. I think what fucks you up most is the fact that you set your goals, and then you attain everything immediately, and where do you go from there?"

Absolut advertising

It's certainly the purer, earlier days of Studio 54 that the Swedish vodka brand Absolut has opted to carry forward memories of and inspiration from. Next to Fiorucci, it's the company that most often gets referenced in the embryonic days of what would transform into an industry of after-dark brand activations, cultural marketing and strategic sponsorship opportunities. Absolut has been remarkably consistent in their presence ever since. That many brands dip in and out of club culture, switching direction at the whim of new marketing regimes or under duress from oscillating budgets or uncertainties over the benefits derived, is remarked on by many that I speak to. Staying power is recognised as a virtue, the way to build credibility and permission. But also something that faces many barriers. Absolut, however, is the clearest counter to such fickleness.

The vodka company's story before prominence in club culture is long and complicated. It started life as Absolut Rent Brännvin in 1917. It wasn't until far later, in 1979 – and in the wake of decreasing home country sales – that the brand went global. By then, the pharmacy-style bottle that Absolut is famous for had been conceived (a nod back to the 16th and 17th centuries, when vodka was sold as medicine). Carillon Importers distributed and marketed the brand in America. French-born CEO Michel Roux led that company. Sensing a city in flux – tense and on edge but intoxicatingly aspirational – he saw a vital role for NYC club culture in Absolut's future growth. He was convinced it would connect the brand to a sense of liberation sought in these new times and by new audiences hungry for style and conspicuity. Studio 54, in particular, offered precisely the setting he was looking for.

Roux was determined to get his vodka in front of the right kind of people. In his book, My Absolut Life, one story demonstrates his initial tactics, recounting the role of Swedish socialite and proto-influencer Christina 'Titti' Watchmeister. She reportedly would ride around Manhattan on a custom-made Hermes bicycle, its basket stuffed with bottles of vodka. "I agreed to pay her a small stipend in exchange for whatever work she did promoting Absolut – which usually meant getting her friends to drink it at the city's hot clubs. A part-time model and party girl, she was a regular fixture at Studio 54."

Running parallel with Roux's enthusiasm for getting Absolut into clubs was the opportunity he saw among the gay community. Against the grain of most in big business, he recognised their taste-making potential, including setting the agenda for the more adventurous straight fraternity. At today's Absolut, Maxime Henain is the global head of culture, collaborations and partnerships. Safe to say, that's not a job title that would have existed in the business in the 1970s. It's a much more recent addition to the many strands of marketing communications within the organisation – emblematic of how culture is seen as a significant lever to pull. Maxime comments: "Michel Roux really saw the LGBTQ+ crowd as a future trendsetting one and what was happening at night in New York was so vital and influential back then. It was very fluid, very much of a mix. At least in the beginning – because it did change – he saw it strongly in Studio 54. There was this cocktail blend of different people from different walks of life – and then all of the surprises that can happen from that. It was a community that was important for us. We've been pushing the agenda that everyone's invited to the party, no matter who they are, ever since."

It's a theme picked up via another of Roux's masterstrokes: appointing the advertising agency TBWA. Starting in Europe but finding much of its fame on Madison Avenue, the story goes that they outgunned 93 other agencies to pick up the Absolut account. It was a partnership that would run for over 30 years, built on striking principles of centring the work around the distinctive shape of the bottle and two-word headlines; beginning with Absolut followed by a word that reflected the theme of the ad: Absolut Perfection, Absolut Manhattan, Absolut Festival and so on.

'Absolut Heaven was the first ad to run,' continues Roux in his book. 'It made a big splash, even if it did appear in the New York Times as a full page directly across from the obituaries. The macabre placement wasn't planned – though a lot of people certainly thought it was funny.' Later in My Absolut Life, he continues: 'These first ads, so simple but fun, set up the notion that Absolut would be all about surprises. We'd be constantly pushing the envelope, unveiling new ideas, month after month, all year long.'

Getting their adverts in the right places, in a way that complemented the brand's uptick in visibility in clubs, saw Absolut start advertising in LGBTQ+ magazines – in The Advocate in 1981, followed by After Dark and New York Native. They weren't the first to do so – Miller Lite and Jägermeister reportedly started placing ads in regional queer newspapers in the late 1970s – but they were first to with a more specific leaning to nightlife and celebrating creativity. Maxime talks of the allyship they've shown with the queer community since then. It has evolved, he explains, from the days of Regan and the AIDs crisis to showing their support for equal rights issues and same-sex marriage equality. But none of this should come as a surprise, he also remarks, when you consider that Sweden is a country where a gender-neutral personal pronoun was first proposed in a newspaper in 1966.

Viewed retrospectively, this all starts to look like the most brilliantly laid out of strategic plans. In reality, less so. KPIs (key performance indicators) are integral to justifying Absolut's participation in cultural fields such as music and art today (and we'll hear more from Maxime about this in later chapters). In the after-dark NYC of all that time ago, happy accidents were more pivotal in how partnerships and opportunities came into being.

"Oh yes, and a lot of word of mouth," Maxime explains. "Someone connects you with someone else, and then they connect you with someone else. The way Michel Roux operated in that world was very casual. He just found his way to people like *(Keith)* Haring and *(Andy)* Warhol. And because it was casual and word of mouth, it reinforced the appeal of the brand because it was a new player with a bottle that looked like a kind of pharmacy shape. And then you'd get strange conversations going around like that Warhol was wearing Absolut as a perfume in clubs, dabbing it behind his ears. There was an air of mystery around this Swedish brand. Not everyone even knew where Sweden was! But there was something about this brand and something about that world. Different people were mixing together, and that has served us ever since."

Some pretty iconic names just got dropped into the conversation there. The bottle, the advertising and the presence in clubs coalesced to form a further dimension of Absolut's place in NYC. Contemporary art and graffiti were exploding out of the galleries, onto the streets and into the clubs. New attitudes to creativity combining with the gritty realities of economic hardship and social change meant there was a lot to reflect through art. Roux was taking notice – and getting to know Andy Warhol in the process.

The connection begins with Absolut taking out advertising space in Interview, the magazine that Warhol founded with journalist John Wilcock, previously part of the launch team of The Village Voice. In fact, Roux suggests the pages they were buying were keeping the title afloat. After a bias toward cinema to start with, Interview found its groove through a more expansive blend of downtown cool and uptown gossip, low and high culture, with Diana Ross, Madonna, Grace Jones, Truman Capote, Divine, Jean-Michel Basquiat and John Travolta among the cover stars (often presented with very Warholian silkscreen effects). Next to using the bottles as decor, NYC clubbers started plastering the walls of their loft spaces and walk-ups with Absolut adverts. The ones in Interview, with their outsized format and high-quality paper stock, were the best of all.

Quite where Roux and Warhol first met is shrouded in apocryphal stories, but at Studio 54 is as close to consensus as we seem to get. Their subsequent meetings led to the artist's noted collaboration with Absolut – two paintings for which they paid $65,000, heralding the start of the brand's now extensive art collection. One of the paintings was used as an advert. It was the first of what would eventually be more than 500 ads to feature artist renditions of the bottle's outline. 'Spectacular, iconic, exciting – a black bottle on a golden background with letters in shades of blue, purple and pink' is how Roux describes it in his book.

Christo Kaftandjiev is a Sofia University professor specialising in advertising and marketing communications. He's also written various books, one of which is Absolut Semiotics. Semiotics is an academic discipline with roots among foundational thinkers such as French theorist

Roland Barthes and some commercial uptake within the broader field of cultural strategy. It can be summarised as the study of signs and symbols, how they are used to communicate meaning and, in turn, how meaning is constructed and understood. "Thanks to his painting, some people still incorrectly believe that Andy Warhol actually designed the iconic bottle," Christo laughs. "Brands reflect the psychological values of the cultures that create them and, in some respects, Swedish culture had common characteristics with the liberal NYC lifestyles of that era... These artists were geniuses. They defined the development of postmodern painting for decades to come. With their help, Absolut became an integral part of pop culture at the time."

Warhol's work with Absolut was a logical extension of his fascination with the commodification of culture, though apparently not an instant hit with TBWA. 'What are you advertising? Is this a vodka ad or an ad for Andy Warhol?' Roux claims they asked him. He also says that Warhol wanted to do more work for Absolut, but he declined ('It's like you said, everyone gets their 15 minutes') and instead asked to be introduced to other artists.

He connected with Basquiat, but that didn't work out ('I don't need to be in business with an addict'). Then came successful collaborations – even if, by all accounts, it sounds like Roux didn't find either collaborator easy to work with – with two downtown luminaries: Keith Haring and Kenny Scharf. The sci-fi themes and absurdism routinely featured in Scharf's art and installations were translated in his Absolut project as trippy desert scenes with ringed planets overhead. Awash with dancing figures, radiant babies and barking dogs, Haring's hugely enduring, often street-oriented style of art showed up as bold yellows and reds against Absolut's blue, his animated people lifting the bottle skywards. It positions Absolut as more than a product. Instead, part of a vibrant social movement and a cultural conversation. "The human body, from the point of view of semiotics, is a sign system," continues Christo. "With the help of the human body, communicators express different meanings. For example, that of freedom. The Absolut Haring ad definitely expresses freedom and positive pathos." Freedom or otherwise, Roux needed a little winning over. He thought Haring's bottle looked reminiscent of a condom.

Creativity, modernity and social engagement – this work had it all for Absolut. These two artists would figuratively, sometimes literally, take the art, the bottle and the brand with them into clubs like Mudd Club, Paradise Garage, Area and Club 57, embedding Absolut deeper and deeper into the culture. The latter of those clubs, which ran from 1978 to 1983 in the East Village and considered itself an optimistically-minded escape from the famously mean streets outside, had particularly strong links with this pair – and, therefore, with Absolut. Haring designed countless flyers for the club and appeared at art and poetry events. Scharf staged the first art show there, a celebration of the space age, no doubt with one of resident DJ Dany Johnson's eclectic playlists as accompaniment. "There was an intermingling of the nightclub and the night world with the art world, the young kids – and that was not what was going on in the established art world," Scharf told the Artspace website in 2017. "The aesthetic at the time was conceptual and minimal, and we were the opposite. We were just celebrating excess, I guess."

While Mancuso would no doubt not have let Absolut through the door, looking at NYC club culture more broadly, it's a brand that has been there almost since the beginning. It staked a claim in times less crowded and before debates around the brand/culture value exchange had even been dreamt of. There were fewer rules and, really, what was down to marketing strategy versus just for fun or by chance is nearly impossible to ascertain.

That time spent now manifests as foundations in art, clubs, music and the LGBTQ+ community which are so sturdy that Absolut has been able to build on them assuredly ever since. Just in the context of NYC, the brand keeps leveraging what it's forged in ways big and small.

Absolut Truth, for instance, was a 2018 campaign uncovering opinions about what makes the city tick and which of the many shuttered clubs – Mars, Palladium and Area all get mentions – should be resurrected. Running since 2022, Out & Open on Absolut.com combines photography and oral history to discuss the role played and the importance of preserving the city's LGBTQ+ bars. There are layers upon layers to this. A 2013 exhibition and accompanying book about Area, the vast space at 187 Hudson that from 1983 to 1987 constantly reimagined itself with wildly ambitious theme nights, and where Absolut featured as a small but prominent element within a much broader aesthetic tableau, sees the brand showing up as the sponsor.

It would be inaccurate to claim that Absolut's heady ascent in that period (by 1986, it had broken the one million case barrier and was the best-selling imported vodka in the US) was solely down to its exploits in art, clubs and after-dark creativity. Simultaneously – and somewhat incongruously – it sponsored everything from ski events to sailboat races. But those urban adventures are the ones that the company has stuck with. They are what makes for a master class in authenticity, the topic that dominates so much of the modern marketer's headspace.

Absolut, like any brand, is not unblemished. They've faced criticism for greenwashing and, in the wake of the invasion of Ukraine, for continuing to sell products in Russia. In the queer community, questions sometimes arise about the harm alcohol has caused – from violence to illness – and whether they really should be considered a meaningful advocate. Yet these critiques around allyship are marginal compared to the support and engagement the brand continues to receive. Absolut has never departed from club culture and shows no sign of planning to. While every 20-something dancing to the over 800 artists at Belgium's Tomorrowland event – sponsored by the brand – may know little of this backstory, the deep roots in nightlife create a unique kind of permission for the vodka that comes in the apothecary bottle. It presents a thread to follow, Maxime Henain confirms: "Even if you cannot always pinpoint exactly what, or put it into clear words, the things they did back then always help direct what we do today."

Who needs revenge?

In 1990, Frankie Knuckles famously described house music as disco's revenge. It's a wonderfully evocative line – one founded around the narrative of the commercial plummet suffered by the music at the start of the 1980s and the bias that was tangled up in that decline. Routinely considered the beginning of the descent was the July 1979 Disco Demolition Night at the Chicago White Sox's Comiskey Park (across prior years, the same ground was host to Disco Night events, organised by the Step By Step disco dance TV show, sponsored by Coca-Cola; also White Sox game days that featured Salute To Disco interludes). For an entrance fee of 99 cents, fans got to bring along, and then blow up, their (not so favourite) disco records. Steve Dahl, the Chicago shock jock who orchestrated it, claims it was all a bit of fun – a twist on the Salute To Disco spots. It's patently easy to see, however, why others saw this gathering of young white males, destroying the work of the marginalised and minoritised, as something more racist and homophobic.

Anthropologist Nic Allum remarks: "Steve Dahl was like, 'I can't fit into a white suit. I can't afford a white suit.' He corralled these angry, straight white men in this home of angry, straight white men, the baseball park. And in Chicago, the birthplace of house music, of all places. He was like a pre-social Andrew Tate."

"It felt to us like Nazi book-burning," Nile Rodgers from Chic told the Independent in 2004. "This is America, the home of jazz and rock, and people were now afraid even to say the word 'disco'." Around the same time, major labels like Warner Bros were shuttering their disco departments, radio was deprioritising the sound and the American nation was swinging right towards the neoliberalism of Ronald Regan.

Things did not look good, with the cultural tide turning against disco. All meaning that pointing to the Chicago house sound as disco's revenge has some truth to it. But as is widely accepted, a rich lineage of music and culture wasn't wholly levelled on an evening in the windy city in July 1979 or in the 'disco sucks' discourse of that time. The years between peak disco and proto-house in fact produced some superlative records (to merely scratch the surface: Serious Intention's You Don't Know, Klein & MBO's MBO Theme, Strafe's Set It Off). It produced its own tally of epochal clubs, too; in many instances bringing with them a back-to-basics reset, as a 1983 NME piece about the Fun House club at 526 West 26th Street, Manhattan, recounts. "Have you been to Studio 54, Xenon? Those places are for people that are there for social reasons. This place plays hard disco for people that are into dancing," said an 18-year-old Puerto Rican called Idales, who's interviewed in the piece. The Fun House was where DJ and Madonna collaborator Jellybean Benitez found fame, a place that appealed to working-class kids from New York's outer boroughs. "This is real," Idales continued. "For real people."

Disco's reach extended to real people – or, at least, beyond the inner city to those closer to the mainstream – in other ways, too. Beyond music and clubs, disco had cultural facets that couldn't be stuffed back into the genie's bottle. To borrow a current term, an 'aesthetic' was moving outwards. Fashion, design and hospitality were the most obvious touchpoints, but disco's influence stretched far beyond a societal penchant for platform heels and sequins. The aerobics craze of the 1980s – Jane Fonda's Workout videos owe a considerable debt to disco – and new beliefs in body consciousness and positivity draw inspiration from nightclubbing. Modular furniture, conversation pits and low-slung seating reflected disco's communal ethos. Shifts in attitudes toward recreational drugs, sex and relationships echoed its hedonistic spirit. Visual media and lighting design embraced hypnotic elements like neon, strobes and mirrored surfaces. Even the mainstreaming of high style glamour, transitioning from nightclub to department store, bore disco's signature.

Nic Allum adds: "Disco never went away. The sound didn't, but in the context of what we're talking about here – the feel of it, the mood and attitude, and how that then manifested in products and media. It has had the longest tail. You had the impact of club lighting, club design, mirrorballs and lit-up floors. All of that, even in subtle ways, started influencing home interiors. The clothes – metallics and silvers, diamantes and rhinestones. Beauty – metallics again; reflective and big and striking. Designed for the night, even if worn in the day."

"People who understand know that disco didn't die," continues Nicky Siano. "It changed how things looked, how people felt and what they wanted to spend their money on. The music and the vibe stayed with us, whatever it says in the history books." What's recorded, or as likely not, in the history books is important here. Everyone I speak to agrees that disco isn't afforded the same credit for its creative and social impact as movements like punk or psychedelia, and much of that comes down to who its pioneers were: predominantly queer, Black and Latinx communities. Not the white men who dominated those other movements or who tend to write the history books.

Of course, you can debate for hours the 'cause and effect' component here – what disco created versus what disco was following. But it was right in this mix of influence. Much as with acid house and Thatcherism in the UK at the other end of the 1980s, there was a cultural duality, too. Aspects of disco's aesthetic both in opposition and support of the burgeoning Reagan-era values. Liberation, diversity and community versus excess and consumerism. That duality surfaces in other ways. Alice Echols, professor of history at the University Of Southern California, looked at it in terms of how women were represented within disco in her 2009 book, Hot Stuff: Disco And The Remaking Of American Culture. Objectification, sexualisation, exploitation – yes, all of the above. But then something else, as she explained in a radio interview: "You can't really make sense of how the culture moved from the white-gloved Diana Ross to Lil' Kim in a fairly short period of time, without exploring disco and disco's role in opening up and validating female sexuality."

Another I spoke to about the topic was Dr Lulu Le Vay. She's a journalist, author, academic, DJ (going by the name Lulu Levan) and lecturer – the latter at BIMM Music Institute, University Of Westminster, University Of West London, Roehampton University and the Institute Of Contemporary Music Performance. Lulu plays disco tracks, studies disco's legacy and integrates disco's history into her teaching. For her, part of the cultural impact was about the strength in numbers it gave people. "There was a mutual understanding of what it meant to be a minority between Black females and the gay community," she says. "Jocelyn Brown talked about this. She said it was about love and rebellion in equal measures. This then has wider reverberations. It helped lots of people to consider the presence they could start to have in the world."

Nic Allum thinks along similar lines: "There were aspects of misogyny. There always are! But there was also a growing freedom of expression for women, for which disco can take credit. And particularly for Black women. Prior to disco, the female soul singer would stand there in a pretty dress, looking kind of gospel. That was the acceptable face of Black women in media and entertainment. Black female disco artists brought in something which we'd then also see in film, TV and adverts. More movement and expression. Less standing still and being static. The confidence that you can be alone, not one of a lineup or obscured in a group. Something much looser and more fluid. That affected people in ways outside of just music."

Dance music culture in this period was congruent with deeper conversations about identity and self-expression that would eventually snowball. It would still be a rocky road ahead, but disco can lay claim to acting as a launch pad for the fight for broader representation –

a fight that would, through the 1980s, begin to permeate society via sitcoms, adverts and films. While not exactly blockbuster hits, movies like Personal Best and Desert Hearts – regarded as milestones in lesbian cinema – gained attention beyond niche audiences. Also in the early 1980s, Making Love was a formative example of a Hollywood movie that addressed same-sex attraction with greater sincerity. Likewise, Victor/Victoria, starring Julie Andrews and James Garner, tackled themes of gender ambiguity and fluid sexualities.

Billy Crystal's portrayal of Jodie Dallas in the sitcom Soap – though picking up criticism for its stereotyping – nonetheless did help normalise the presence of a gay character in mainstream TV. Later to be made for television, Armistead Maupin's Tales Of The City book series presented an unvarnished take on the LGBTQ+ community in San Francisco and one that resonated with straight society. And The Golden Girls, of course – the colossal sitcom success that won support for its positive LGBTQ+ representation and sensitive handling of the AIDs crisis.

In advertising, brands like Subaru, United Colors Of Benetton and IKEA began featuring gay couples, often embedding subtle cues that resonated with LGBTQ+ audiences while flying under the radar for straight viewers. These campaigns were sometimes labelled 'gay vague'. Subaru's taglines, for instance, included 'We're completely comfortable with our orientation' and 'It's not a choice, it's just how we're built'. In pop music, meanwhile, particularly the strains coming from the UK, queer culture and identities were pushing the boundaries of what was considered acceptable in mainstream media. Culture Club, Frankie Goes To Hollywood, Erasure, Soft Cell, Bronski Beat, Pet Shop Boys – it was quite the shift from the decade before.

None of this progress diminishes the dreadful impact of the AIDS crisis, nor the homophobia that accompanied it. But while the queer community endured the cruel label of the 'gay plague', often threatening to push them into the shadows, the cultural shifts of the 1980s – seen in film, TV and advertising – still marked a significant step forward in

LGBTQ+ visibility. In the face of adversity – including the right-wing politics of 1980s America – each of these moments helped elevate the story of queer representation in popular culture.

"You started to see things in the media, in entertainment, that weren't just gay-coded like they might have been before," agrees Nic Allum. "They were more overt and open." Alice Echols goes on to talk about how "widespread, and lasting, the interventions and changes that disco made were... The way it broadened the contours of blackness, femininity and male homosexuality."

But not everything we see today has depth to it, cautions Lulu Le Vay, believing it's wise sometimes to question the authenticity of the change that has happened. "One example for me when I think of that disco ideal, I see it in the Soho House Group, but lots of other places as well. A capitalising on a Black queer aesthetic. It's like this identikit thing across all the Soho Houses – a gay Black man front-of-house. It's a type of queer-cool-pinkwashing. It doesn't mean that all of the homophobia, racism and inequality aren't still underneath that surface."

Several people I speak with talk about disco as part of a prototype culture wars. Early salvos leading to the painfully divided times we find ourselves in. "I guess the difference between Mancuso and The Loft, Paradise Garage, places like that, and Studio 54 flows through to today," says Nic Allum. "It's kind of the culture wars. Greater acceptance and representation on one side; neoliberalism and the likes of Trump – literally Trump, he went to 54 – on the other. A fight for different types of freedom."

Lulu Le Vay continues on a related theme, cautioning that it's disco's place in nurturing community, rather than its influence on design, lifestyle and the creative industries, that most needs platforming. "That disco legacy is everywhere, such a huge influence on popular culture and one that's been so heavily commercialised. But what's sad in all of that is the meaning of the dancefloor has been lost. This simple, pure notion of it as a safe environment for minorities when, in the outside world, there was so much trauma for them. With Trump back and this nasty current mood, that need for safe environments, for an escape from trauma, is the most important thing that should stay alive from disco – not just the look or the design aesthetic."

It's an unfeigned purpose for dance music that rings out through time. It takes us back to François Kevorkian's words at the top, from a hot night in Hell's Kitchen at Body & Soul. Loving people. Absolutely dedicated people. Doing this together. A community. Amen to that.

3. IT GROWS IN THE DARK

There are two directions of travel in *Selling The Night*. Brands moving into club culture, and ideas and influences moving out of club culture

Here, it's the latter. Pop-ups, design, boutique hotels, tourism, gaming, art, fashion, exhibitions and beyond

In the Area

New chapter, same city. We're back in NYC, in 1983 at 157 Hudson Street in Tribeca. This is the home of Area, another fabled club from the city's voluminous annals. Situated in a vast warehouse space, it was leased for just $3,000 a month by, as a Vogue article explained, 'a few enterprising art-school kids with a letter of recommendation from Interview magazine'. Soon after opening, Area set the town alight, exciting and bewildering to an equal measure. This place was something different, something else.

DJs included stalwarts of the Manhattan night, Johnny Dynell and Justin Strauss, along with noteworthy guests such as Jean-Michel Basquiat. Musically speaking, Area operated between disco and, as

Frankie Knuckles termed house music, disco's revenge. By the time of the last night in March 1987 and, captured on a boisterous mixtape that does the rounds on Mixcloud, there's everything from the pulsating freestyle of Company B and electro-pop of Information Society to the emergent Chicago sounds of Chip E and Robert Owens getting an airing.

But really, it wasn't the music that made Area remarkable. The source of that came from this being a club with an *art department.* That wasn't the way it usually worked. It promoted itself using what Jesse Kornbluth, writing in New York Magazine in 1985, called 'oblique advertising'. That wasn't normal, either. Speaking to DJ History, Strauss described Area as: "An art project with a Richard Long sound system." Still not normal. All of this made the club remarkable for its appetite for drama and – that most brand-approved of words – experience.

Experiences plural, in fact. Ever-changing ones. They were showing the way for what, a decade or so on, would pick up the tag of experiential marketing, with brands nowadays creating immersive, temporary events strongly reminiscent of the kind that Area pioneered. The constantly changing themes that the club specialised in prefigured the pop-up retail concept, too. It would be remiss to suggest that every modern-day marketer was tapping indirectly into Area's legacy, aware of every backstory detail. But its influence has certainly made its way into their working practices.

At the nub of this influence was a complete redesign of the 13,000-square-foot space every six weeks, becoming an entirely new universe of fun and adventure. Presented through abruptly titled themes like Natural History, Fellini, Confinement, Obsession, Hollywood, Acid Flash, Suburbia and Gardens, these tended to involve naked performers, elaborate works of art and spicy antics. 'Area is the number one cause of marital breakup in New York,' nightlife columnist Michael Musto announced in The Village Voice. One night featured a urinal-lined entryway. The one called Disco had a cordoned-off, empty VIP area into which no one could tread. The night named Gnarly boasted a strobe-lit electric chair and a skateboarding ramp. There were actors on hand to breathe life into the themes on every occasion. Hungry for more experience? Live enemas would feature from time to time.

The New York Times reported from an Absolut-funded one-off return for Area in 2013 (no sign of enemas on this occasion, though surfaces were sprinkled in dust, à la fake cocaine). Marking the launch of a self-titled book celebrating the club's brief but significant reign, they spy a certain octogenarian fashion force at the party – one quick to raise the topic of 'experience', too. 'Calvin Klein showed up, standing before a wall of Ronald Reagan posters created for a Hollywood party in 1984. "It was a different experience every time," Mr. Klein said of the club. "You never knew what to expect. It was such a creative moment."'

Those art school kids that Vogue referred to: Area was the brainchild of four childhood friends from California; brothers Eric Goode and Christopher Goode, Shawn Hausman and Darius Azari. Highest profile of the foursome, Eric went on to launch hotels, make videos for Nine Inch Nails and, in quite the plot twist, direct the Netflix smash Tiger King. He's also a prominent conservationist, pioneering the Turtle Conservancy to protect threatened turtles and tortoises. Which runs rather at odds with the live animals that featured in the entertainment at Area – monitor lizards and owls, included.

The Area founders were inspired by much that permeated subculture back on the West Coast. The 'happenings' of performance artist Allan Kaprow in the late 1950s and 1960s, 'fourth wall'-splintering creative collisions of audience and performers. Also, the LSD-fuelled escapades of Ken Kesey's Merry Pranksters. Transferring that kind of freaked-out creative energy to the meaner streets of NYC made perfect sense to them. "The culture of New York was different," Eric Goode told The Daily Beast. "It was lawless. We could do pretty much anything we wanted with reckless abandon."

Kornbluth's 1985 New York Magazine piece explained that the Area name showed 'they wanted something ambiguous, free-floating, cryptic, something that didn't suggest a club. They did, however, want to play off the one important fact about the place: that it would change. The space was just raw material, a staging ground, a generic environment – an area.'

Serge Becker headed the club's art department, dubbed a "cultural engineer" by hotelier André Balazs, and someone who's since gone on to launch a slew of bars and restaurants across Manhattan and beyond. With another member of the Goode family, Jennifer (sister to the brothers), also working in the art department, their brief was to design the nights and the communications to go with each of them. For the opening night, guests were mailed a velvet ring box. Inside, a blue capsule with instructions not to swallow the pill but to drop it into hot water instead, whereupon it would dissolve, and an invitation would appear. Another was a mousetrap that smashed open an amyl nitrate-like capsule.

King Britt, the DJ, record producer and – through the Blacktronika college course – educator, is among the many who took inspiration from the club. One of his first endeavours in his native Philadelphia was a club called Vagabond alongside a DJ called Blake and his future Ovum Records partner, Josh Wink. "Area was it, man. It was such an influence on me. Whenever you went, you thought you were in a new club. It was kind of like a movie set," he says. "We had the DJs, but we also had an interior designer and a painter. Area was totally the motivation for that. There's something about creating your own world. Not just with music but with how you use space."

'Worlds' are referenced is another take on Area's influence – and specifically on marketing communication – from Jochen Eisenbrand, chief curator at the Vitra Design Museum: "When I look at their parties and their invitations, to me it's a precursor to these so-called 'worlds' that brands are trying to create: brand worlds. It starts with the moment you get the invitation and this is similar to brands aiming for a consistent and cohesive experience that runs all the way through their events or campaigns. It feels like the start of the pop-up experience."

Located in Weil am Rhein, Germany, the Vitra Design Museum is privately owned by the iconic Swiss furniture company of the same name. It hosts an array of beautifully assembled exhibitions (one was Nike: Form Follows Motion, examining the brand's place in design innovation and social change). In 2018, Night Fever, Designing Club Culture 1960–Today opened (it would later move to the V&A Dundee). Its brief: examining how nightclubs have acted as spaces for experimentation in interior design, new media and alternative lifestyles. From speaking to designers, club owners and promoters, the exhibition team started to amass materials for Night Fever. "All of it demonstrated interconnections between the world of clubs and the world of design and architecture," Jochen says. But most materials were 'flat' – drawings, record covers, film, posters. They then worked with industrial designers to create 'volume' through music and light installations, and the exhibition came to life. Area was one of the venues that Night Fever paid particular attention to – and where demonstrating the volume of the experience was most important.

"Can you imagine how many people in a city like New York and who went to Area would later form branding agencies, that type of thing," continues Jochen, who's every bit as calm and studious as you'd anticipate a chief curator at a very stylish museum to be. "It seems so obvious to me that it will have influenced people in those fields. Fashion as well. We're doing an exhibition on fashion and we're seeing invitations written on porcelain plates and catwalks designed like dining tables. All of this sounds very Area to me."

In 1984, Leo Burnett agency creative director and writer Jay Conrad Levinson coined the term 'guerrilla marketing' in a book of the same name. In it, he explored surprising and unconventional interactions between brand and consumer. He covered pre-digital forms of word-of-mouth. Early references to what would come to be known as FOMO, too. Outlined subtypes of guerrilla marketing included ambient, grass-roots, stealth and street marketing (viral wasn't yet a thing).

The expression guerrilla marketing has drifted out of favour, but the thinking behind it – and the parallels with Area, with its thematic take-overs and oblique advertising – is very much coded into the modern experiential marketing operating system. We've seen flash mobbing and all manner of unconventional events. Urban art and the aforementioned pop-ups. We've had the online and the offline blending in ever more curious ways. And we've seen collabs – lots and lots of collabs.

It's hard to know where to start when trying to reel off a list of pop-ups and experiential hi-jinks engineered by brands in recent times. The Taco Bell Hotel & Resort was in the fashionable desert town Palm Springs – a four-day takeover with 70 themed rooms and plenty of merch. With the first opening in Pennsylvania and Dallas, Netflix House is the streamers' leap into 'experiential entertainment venues', a chance for deep interaction with the stories and characters of shows like Bridgerton, Money Heist, Stranger Things and Squid Game. IKEA has hosted sleepovers in its stores. Airbnb has done sleepovers, too, except in places like Paris' Louvre. Dubbed the 'ultimate brand strengthening exercise', Diesel opened a pop-up store in NYC's Chinatown with products based on 'authentically fake' bootleg designs. For the credible knock-off effect, the signage featured deliberate misspellings: 'DEISEL – For Successfull Living'. In areas adjacent to brands, creative studio Bombas & Parr, with their blending of food, art and experiential design, and the immersive screenings of Secret Cinema, warrant a mention. Club culture, a platform for subversive creative experimentation, can claim to have lit the fires for these unconventional marketing initiatives.

The Area effect goes further into retail than simply the pop-up format, too. With online shopping offering customers all the convenience they need, brick-and-mortar retail has been searching for a new role. In many categories, this means ramping up the emphasis on experience over the transactional. Speaking on an expert panel at Milan Design Week, Gary Bott, the UK managing director of innovative Korean eyewear brand Gentle Monster, explained: "It's about shifting the focus from selling. Instead, stores should focus on the audience and creating an outstanding experience for them. Hyperphysicality means creating something that is 'hyper real' in an unexpected context, something almost fantastical that speaks to all senses." Immersive storytelling, limited-editions, subcultures, communities and shared identity are watchwords for concept retail futurists today, which all sounds highly akin to Area 40 years ago.

"Really, it was like a theatre set," Jochen from Vitra continues. "They hired actors to play along with each theme, and then all the clubbers would play along. That's incredible. I'm sure it was a strange and fascinating mix: all of the artists of that time were in attendance, but also Reaganomics *(a term used to describe the economic policies promoted by President Ronald Reagan)* was starting. A lot of money was moving in and these people wanted to be entertained in new and different ways."

When Area was at its prime, there had been talk of taking its concept further. With offers on the table to branch out into restaurants and even department stores, it had the makings of a bigger, more extensive brand in tune with 1980s American demands to be entertained in the different ways that Jochen refers to. But alas, it was not to be. New York moved on, and Area drifted out of fashion. Again drawing parallels with all things pop-up and ephemeral, it's a turn of events that seemingly was met with a nonchalant shrug from the Area founders. "People always measure the success of a thing by its longevity," said Eric Goode, "but the entire point of Area was its impermanence."

These themes of pop-up impermanence in clubbing and their intersection with brands live on long after Area. Prada's three-day Double Club at Art Basel Miami Beach in 2022, for instance. The creation of German artist Carsten Höller (among his other work, a 2010 show at the Hamburger Bahnhof that offered visitors a night exposed on a circular platform, above '12 castrated reindeer, 24 canaries, eight mice and two flies' – yours for €1,000), it was described as an artwork that doubled as a nightclub. "It really works," Höller enthused to Wallpaper. "If you have been a little bit in the outside space and then go into the inside space, it's like cutting your brain in two in some ways. You feel like a Rumble Fish."

A Rumble Fish theme sounds *exactly* the kind of thing that the Area crew would've got behind. Less likely, though, a thing Jochen from Vitra would have experienced in his formative years. "It was just ordinary gigs and indie bands where I grew up," he laughs. "There was no credible club scene. I only discovered the beauty of techno through this exhibition." Understandably, then, he went into the Night Fever project without much knowledge of club culture. But he came out of it excited by the uninhibited ideas it produces and just how much they mean to people.

"I was struck by the degree of identification that clubs offer people," he remarks. "Just how important and memorable the experiences created inside them can be. Brands are absolutely desperate to match that: to create memorable experiences that create loyal customers. You can also think about the kind of gender-blending that starts in the safe spaces clubs provide and later appears in fashion and then ultimately on the streets. It's now so much more normal and accepted. Depending on where you live, often people don't have to be so afraid anymore. And these once-radical expressions are now celebrated and normalised, finding their way into media and brand advertising. Clubs are the root of that communication evolution."

Of all the clubs featured at Night Fever, one senses Area left the strongest impression on Jochen. Another he points to in establishing the modern brand experiential blueprint is New York's Electric Circus. The earliest of the clubs showcased in the exhibition, it started in 1967, heralding a kind of the multimedia sensoriality that marketers view as crucial to emotional connections. Situated in an old ballroom on St Marks Place in the East Village, there was theatre, dance, music, light projections and even a merry-go-round. Artists who played there included The Velvet Underground, The Grateful Dead, Ike & Tina Turner and the more avant-garde Terry Riley and Morton Subotnick. Electric Circus' days were over in 1970, when a bomb went off on the dancefloor. Not as in a track, but as in an actual bomb, injuring 15 people. At first, it was claimed that the Black Panther Party was responsible, but they denied this. The venue made a brief return, of sorts, to club culture in the 1980s, when it became the home for an Alcoholics Anonymous dry disco.

Jochen had two co-collaborators on the Night Fever project. One was Katarina Serulus from Design Museum Brussels, who'd previously researched Belgian clubs, notably the heavily mirrored and Studio 54-influenced new beat temple, Boccaccio in Ghent. The other, Cat Rossi, a design historian and professor of architecture at the Canterbury School Of Architecture And Design. She had been exploring the design of the 1960s Italian clubs for a while, which provided the initial spark for Night Fever.

Space Electronic, the Italian club which came under the microscope at Night Fever, is another that inspired how space – retail, entertainment, work, hospitality – would start to look and behave in the future. Opening in Florence in 1969, it is (present tense: incredibly, it still exists today, if in a more mainstream form) one of several breathtaking clubland architectural endeavours in Italy from that period. Opening in 1966, Piper in Turin was another, known for modular furnishings, booming audio capabilities and coloured strobe lights.

Space Electronic was as experimental as could be. It was the work of the Gruppo 9999, one of a number of revolutionary architecture collectives in the country, and proponents of radical new ways of living. With Carlo Caldini from the collective taking the lead, compared to the entertainment spectacles of NYC, this space was informed by somewhat more studied principles around ecological, technological and societal change. It had furniture made from washing machine drums, raised platforms for dancing on, large-scale installations, live interventions, nods to theatre and even greater references to Andy Warhol. The music majored on the big and dramatic: prog rock, psychedelic jams and proto-synthpop (itself leading to Italo disco). Brilliantly, next to being a club primed for a generation of Italians looking for fun and surprising experiences by night, it doubled as an architecture school by day.

"The thing that drew me to the club was a photograph of it in 1971, where they had planted vegetables on the dancefloor," says Cat. "And then on the basement level, another dancefloor, they flooded that and turned it into a lake. You had to walk across the stepping stones to get into this space upstairs. What an amazing undertaking. It still grips me 10 years after first learning about it."

Cat explains that Gruppo 9999, like other collectives (such as Superstudio and Archizoom), were part of a movement called 'radical design' – one that set out to reject the norms of architecture and its relationship with the commercial world and the dominant modernism of the time. Much of what they focused on was determinedly temporary (and pop-up) in form – performances, films, installations, exhibitions, multimedia experiences. But it was the disco setting that anchored it all.

"Absolutely, it was key. They sought out the nightclub as the optimal spatial typology for their multidisciplinary experimentation. One key reason was that, at the time, the idea of nightclubs as defined spaces hadn't really been formed. There weren't set rules, and they certainly hadn't been commercialised. They were associated with the underground – often quite literally – which gave them an important sense of freedom. This freedom manifested in all sorts of ways. The architects were particularly drawn to nightclubs as spaces that encouraged participation and flexibility, where furniture could be moved and programming spanned poetry, live theatre, art performances and more. The concept of discos or nightclubs was fundamental to that."

Cat – who's quick to point out she's not an "expert raver" – says that, as these have been forgotten histories for so long, those studying them are still making sense of the influence venues like Space Electronic have had. "I'd say it's been hugely important and, weirdly perhaps, is becoming increasingly influential through more people's exposure to the story. But more work is needed to trace the impact. What's fascinating to me, though, is that what we're seeing here is the origins of clubs as actually very multidisciplinary spaces – different to the narrower definitions of clubs that we became used to in the 1990s and 2000s, but perhaps more like how we'll consider clubs in the future."

Next to the mark left on what was to become experiential marketing, venues like Space Electronic also show signs of the kind of responsive architecture – adapting to climate, light and user behaviour – that now garners coverage. Moreover, these venues reflect the community-led design practices that are increasingly common in placemaking. There was an unreservedness and ingenuity for how space could be used that the commercial and brand worlds are only just catching on to.

Aside from Area, Space Electronic and Electric Circus, other club spaces explored at Night Fever included Munich's Yellow Submarine (1971), New York's Studio 54 (1977) and Paradise Garage (1977), Manchester's Haçienda (1982), Glasgow's Sub Club (1987), London's Kinky Gerlinky (1989), Beirut's B018 (1998), Berlin's Berghain (2004) and Detroit's Mothership (2015) – though the latter is less a club, more a P-funk-inspired Afro-futurist, mobile DJ booth. Be it clubs steeped in space age outlandishness, opulent trappings or concrete and industrialism, these hubs of dance music that go on to influence so much around them, from retail to hospitality, brand experiences to third spaces, are always a product of a "transitioning moment in a city; gaps appearing in the fabric," Jochen from Vitra concludes.

"So often it's about being part of the changing city," he adds. "Around a similar time to Area you had the Haçienda in Manchester – another city that was in transition as the industry moved out. But whereas Area was about covering up the space, about inventing worlds and escapism, the Haçienda was about embracing that industrial aesthetic. Coffee shops and stores today – they have followed that through. Just the bare, exposed walls and this attitude of keeping it rough and as it is."

Those bloody columns

"For better or for worse, the Haçienda was the starting point of the regeneration of Manchester." We are hearing from designer Ben Kelly. Speaking from his cottage-cum-studio in bucolic East Sussex, he's animated, no-nonsense and reflecting on the legendary venue he imagined into life. It's an imagining that turned into his life, too. Forty years on, it is still with him in so many ways.

The club was partly modelled on New Order's manager Rob Gretton's hankering for a New York-type venue (he was inspired by hanging out with Arthur Baker at Danceteria and Fun House) in Manchester. Draining Factory Records and New Order's cash reserves close to zero, after a rocky start with poorly attended events (unfathomably, crass comedian Bernard Manning starred on the opening evening), it would find its groove at much the time that house music found its groove in the UK. The place has been closed for nearly 30 years, but in many ways, its own groove continues to this day.

Haçienda's peak period, circa 1986 to 1993, was the stuff of nightlife utopia: democratic, spontaneous, fast-evolving and madly exciting. Epochal nights such as Nude and Hot, presided over by DJs like Mike Pickering, Greg Wilson and Graeme Park, ensued. The mid-1990s brought tougher times before, in 1997, the Haçienda met a messy and ignominious end amid rising debts and marred by the city's significant gangland problems.

Despite those sad final days, nothing is dislodging the Haçienda from high-grade status in global after-dark folklore. All this time after its closure, Ben says the Haçienda cult remains as potent as ever. He receives weekly emails with some kind of request related to the old place. People ask him to sign materials and artefacts. "Bricks, signage, that type of thing. That's the level of obsessiveness out there. It's a passion. It's meaningful to people."

He says that the Haçienda, and that obsessiveness, has been with him most of his life – in ways good and bad. The baggage created has frustrated him like silly at times. But it's also defined a red thread to incredible, unforeseen opportunities. As for how it all started, like much that happens in and around clubs, there was happenstance in the turn of events. One thing leading to another and then to another. Great design work as the output – but little of it brought about by great design. "Good God, no," he snorts. "It was one giant and highly chaotic guessing game."

Born in 1949, Ben grew up in the Yorkshire Dales. He studied interior design at Lancaster College Of Art, then drifted down to London. There he gravitated to the emergent punk scene. He got to know Malcolm McLaren and Vivienne Westwood, designing aspects of their Seditionaries store using industrial materials. He then got the gig to develop the Covent Garden boutique Howie through his then-girlfriend. The same heavy-duty finish was on display again, early indications of the style he would bring to the Manchester club.

The boutique work led to him getting friendly with Peter Saville, the designer responsible for the broader look and feel of Factory Records – the posters and sleeves and other items that, famously, all came coded with the label's cataloguing system (FAC 61 was a lawsuit filed against Factory by wayward producer Martin Hannett; FAC 501 was Factory boss Tony Wilson's coffin). With a friendly rivalry between the pair lasting until this day, Ben and Peter Saville first collaborated on designing the cover for the self-titled 1980 debut album by Orchestral Manoeuvres In The Dark (OMD). A lot of the inspiration for the cover, notes Ben, came from the perforated doors he'd fashioned for Howie.

Then, the big turn of events. Factory Records and New Order purchased the dilapidated old yacht showroom that, on opening in 1982, would become the Haçienda (FAC 51). Initially, Mancunian motormouth Tony Wilson had assumed this would be a design job for Saville. Not so. When Saville decided that devising the visual language of an entire club was too much for him, he reckoned it was instead an undertaking for Ben... even though his level of experience in doing anything like this was only one notch higher.

"The wonderful naivety of it all," Ben laughs. "We didn't have much, but we had our independence. My clients were Factory Records and New Order, and that's what they stood for. This independent spirit that gave us creative freedom." So much of the Haçienda design was a product of necessity and functionalism. Materials that would stand up to stomping feet. Cat eyes and traffic bollards. Big arches and bold blocks of colour. Most prominently of all, zigzagging black-and-yellow stripes around the venue's columns to avoid collisions.

Those stripes have truly been with Ben ever since. As is often the case with designers, musicians, film directors and so forth who strike it big with something so early in their career, the Haçienda, its legacy and those stripes are things he's wrestled with over the years. "The Haçienda closed but it never went away," he continues. "It never fails to amaze me the level of interest it generates. I started to call it the monkey on my back. It annoyed me for quite a period of time, but then I realised I should think of it as a gift, think of it in a positive way. You see, eventually the penny dropped with me that, had the opportunity not come along to design the Haçienda, I would have had a very different life. It changed me back then and there have been moments over the years where it has changed me again."

One of those moments is a relationship that began uncomfortably and with distinct traces of cross-generational suspicion. It brings us back to Virgil Abloh. In chapter two, we heard how his nod to The Loft, with his Louis Vuitton Fall In Love collection, was met with a rebuff. The street fashion superstar's enthusiasm for the Haçienda only just avoided a similar fate to start with. Ben recalls how their relationship began: "I got this email from Matches Fashion talking about a guy called Virgil Abloh, who I'd never heard of. I didn't know if it was a waste of my time or not. So I printed off the email to show my wife, and then my son, who was 15, overheard us. He said, 'If it's Virgil Abloh, you have to, have to, *have to* do it.'"

Virgil Abloh's passion for music was undoubted. Dance music included. He DJed at Detroit's Movement festival and Ibiza's DC10. He struck up friendships with Honey Dijon and The Blessed Madonna. Moreover, before pivoting into fashion and interning at Fendi alongside Kayne West, he'd earned a master's degree in architecture from the Illinois Institute Of Technology. The striped columns of the Haçienda had caught his eye, sparking his own ideas for brand and for design (Abloh wasn't alone in fashion circles in his admiration for the Haçienda stripes – Raf Simons and Yohji Yamamoto have also cited them as an influence).

When he relaunched his Pyrex Vision label as Off-White in 2013, he created an 'anti-hierarchical' merger of luxury and streetwear that turned fashion upside down. And there were those bold stripes, featuring heavily on his garments and the brand messaging. 'Imagine hundreds of thousands of Off-White fans seeing diagonal lines all of the time and automatically thinking of Abloh's label,' a piece in Complex commented in 2016. 'That's extremely powerful, because it makes the brand seem larger than it actually is.'

At the time of the email, in 2016, Abloh's Off-White was launching with Matches Fashion, and they liked to mark every new designer who came on board by hosting a party. Abloh was contacting Ben to see if he'd like to collaborate on something for it. Ben had closed his main practice in the late 2010s, now focusing mainly on smaller projects. This, though, was the start of something big and out of the ordinary.

"Eventually an arrangement was made for me to have a phone conversation with this Virgil character in Chicago," Ben continues. "And we spoke and he just kept referring to columns. What the hell is he talking about, I wondered. Columns? And then it clicked. He meant the columns in the Haçienda. At first I was pissed off. I felt he'd ripped me off. He took the stripes from those bloody columns and built his Off-White business from it. He put those stripes on his clothes and made a fortune." It was an inauspicious start, but then Ben switched to thinking about this turn of events, this serendipitous interaction with just about the hottest streetwear design on the planet, as something intriguing; perhaps even something to feel honoured by.

"I thought, hold up, he's a DJ and what do they do? They sample things. That's all he's done – he's sampled me. So here he was kind of sampling three-dimensionally, which I found an interesting concept. And then we kept on talking, and the more we did, the more I discovered he was the nicest person and a fascinating one, too. I went along to this night he DJed at in the East End of London. All of these young people were there on their phones. I wondered what they were all doing. Someone told me they were influencers, so a whole new world opened up to me there and then!"

It was the beginning of a series of collaborations with Virgil which Ben is clearly so very proud of. He designed a mobile DJ rig – featuring striped columns in the design, naturally – for him to use as part of runway fashion shows. Called Off-Set, it eventually made its way to Art Basel. The columns he designed for an Off-White fashion week party headed to the Open Eye gallery in Liverpool – then to Somerset House. Mark Wadhwa, property developer and owner of London venues like Vinyl Factory and 180 The Strand, and his wife, designer and creative director Alex Eagle, decided they wanted some columns, too, for their Store X project. In this case, it was about 'the totemic properties of columns, from power and classicism to romanticism and decay', no less. Columns and stripes, humble ones and high falutin ones – they were breaking out everywhere.

"Virgil came along to various events and it went on and on from there," Ben recalls. "It all feels quite unbelievable really. Virgil rose to the dizzy heights of being Louis Vuitton's creative director of menswear and this gave him scope to do different things, bigger things. And it opened up a bigger world for me, too."

Another Kelly/Abloh collaboration was 2017's Ruin, a huge installation depicting abandoned nightclubs and fragments of disco culture (smashed mirrorballs, broken dancefloors), which was launched at London's Store Studios and then reconfigured in a Paris club, among other places. By then, Ben had taken to describing Abloh as the "roaming Haçienda ambassador" – the one who could communicate the power of its raw, unfettered design aesthetic to a new generation. It was a wonderful example of the deep and sometimes unexpected bonds that can be made through music, and all that surrounds it. Sadly, that was to come to an end with Abloh's passing, aged just 41 in 2021, from a rare form of cancer. "He was a lovely guy. He inspired me, and it was an incredible turn of events for me, really," says Ben, clearly upset to have lost such an immense partner in creative adventures.

As fantastic as those adventures with the Off-White genius were, the impact and influence of the Haçienda by no means stopped there. "The language, the materiality and the vibe of the Haçienda has seeped into various public spaces," Ben says. He was back on the dancefloor with Good Night: Energy Flash in 2019, an exhibition-meets-club backed by Hyundai Card in Seoul and investigating new dimensions in dance culture. Kelly designed the DJ booth, with Peggy Gou among those who graced it. And yes, it featured black-and-yellow stripes.

He's excited by how far outside nightclub parameters he's been able to stretch his design form. In 2023, he collaborated on the Aviva Studios complex, built on the old Granada Television Studios site in Manchester. "It's full of references to the Haçienda, the Dry Bar *(also owned by Factory, and designed by Ben Kelly)*, to the OMD sleeve I did with Peter, including perforated bright orange and blue metal. It's all in there." Unsurprisingly, the Haçienda look has been adopted on many fronts in Manchester. Just recently, posters mysteriously popped up around town, protesting against gentrification. Black and yellow posters, complete with a remix of Tony Wilson's "This is Manchester, we do things differently" line – now saying, 'This is Manchester, we do things exactly the same as any other city that has sold its soul to the higher bidder…'

Back in 1995, and down in London, he was tasked to reimagine the basement floor at the Science Museum, primarily a space for visiting parties of school children. "The guy who was the design director there, he said, 'Ben, wouldn't it be fantastic if you could do a Haçienda for kids.' And I just thought, 'Jesus, this is genius. How have I got here?'" Touches of the Haçienda have shown up in Kelly's architectural design work for advertising agencies, libraries, galleries, student accommodation and private properties. An even more stark example of how club design can touch on different environments came in 1999 when he designed new superstores in Sheffield and Swansea for Halfords. Yes, Halfords. The influence of the Haçienda on both of these warehouse structures is clear and striking.

In 2008, he started working with the fitness chain Gymbox. "This guy was looking to open a new gym brand and he was talking to a designer, who said, 'We should make them look just like the Haçienda.' Thankfully, the guy starting the gyms took the trouble to track down the person who *actually* designed the Haçienda. Me. We spoke, and I ended up designing 10 Gymbox spaces." Situated in unusual settings, from underground carparks to bank vaults to old Post Office premises, they came loaded with many familiar Ben Kelly stylings. "They changed the look of gyms in the UK. We made them look like nightclubs."

We get talking about Pret a Manger and the checker plate steel panels they use. It's something they lifted from his work, he insists. "I get pissed off about these things and then I stop with that. It's the way of the world and I prefer to feel flattered," he explains with trademark bluntness. "You know, if I earned a penny for all the black-and-yellow stripes in the world now. This idea from the Haçienda has become a global currency. The ethos, the visual language, whatever you want to call it, has filtered into the wider public domain. There's no doubt about that, but it becomes a watered-down version. Commercialised. I see it everywhere but rarely done properly."

This dilution that Ben Kelly describes – where the Haçienda's ideas are commodified into a watered-down version – echoes the cultural compression Kyle Chayka critiques in his 2024 book, Filterworld: How Algorithms Flattened Culture. Chayka explores how algorithmic recommendations shape our experiences, including the spaces we inhabit and share with others. Kelly's Haçienda aesthetic – its repurposed materials, industrial edge and functionalist skew – has permeated countless environments, from gyms and cafes to co-working spaces and boutique hotels. As Chayka observes, these are spaces where time is temporarily spent and cultural cachet flaunted. Physical environments duly become products. Kelly's vision, once groundbreaking, has been absorbed into this algorithmic palette, replicated endlessly but rarely with its original intention or depth intact.

Writing for The Guardian in 1999, lifestyle journalist Alix Sharkey pinpointed early (and pre-algorithmic) signs of this permeation of the club design aesthetic elsewhere. It took the form of retail spaces becoming increasingly akin to club environments. 'The really big changes are happening in the high street now, where stores such as Hennes *(aka H&M)* and TopShop bear an increasing resemblance to big nightclubs. They play the same music, use similar fittings, men's and women's clothing are no longer segregated in terms of presentation, there are communal changing rooms. There is no sharp definition of gender in the environment. Instead, you have coloured spotlights, pounding house music, multi-levels that correspond to dancefloor, bar area, chill-out room etc, and banks of video screens. Thanks to the demands of marketing, the look and feel of nightlife is increasingly ingrained in our built environment, from department stores to travel agencies, from coffee bars to health clubs.'

Once easily miffed by this cultural buying, borrowing and stealing, Ben Kelly now takes it in his stride. He wraps up our conversation with:

"Really, that the design of an underground club in Manchester could play a part in all of this change. Something created by people who didn't have a clue what they were doing. That's just bizarre. Am I proud of it? As much as I like to play it down, too right I am."

Check-in & dance

From the vivid stories of Area, the Haçienda and other landmark dance music venues, we have drawn lines between club design and gyms, museums, pop-up stores, immersive brand experiences and more. Step back into the world of Studio 54, track the story of its founders, and we can draw another clear and bold one. This time, following the trail (or velvet rope) takes us to the incarnation of the boutique hotel concept.

Journalist Deanna Ting's fascinating and highly detailed (we're talking 60,000 words) Complete Oral History Of Boutique Hotels for travel industry website Skift relays how this burgeoning section of the hospitality landscape has evolved in the last 40 years. Loosely defined as smaller in size and more independent in nature (if not necessarily in corporate ownership) than regular hotels, boutique establishments go big on curation, embracing local culture and, often, music that resonates more powerfully than the 'lift' variety of other chains. The global 'mass affluent' consumer, with their appetite for new settings and premium experiences, are sold on them. Industry data valued the global boutique hotel market at $9.8 billion in 2023, projected to hit $18 billion by 2033.

Rewind to the early 1980s and Studio 54's Ian Schrager and Steve Rubell are all over the germinal phase of this travel and tourism success story. They saw something in club culture that they thought would resonate in other contexts. A new way to benefit commercially from bringing people together amid a carefully assembled blend of luxury and subculturally sourced cool. The trigger for them to enter this new market? It seems there's nothing like a stint behind bars to focus the mind. Spending 1980 in jail for tax evasion associated with their 54 club was, Schrager has said, the spur to explore new business ideas. In tandem, they observed that someone else was getting into the NYC hotel game. One Donald Trump. As Schrager recalls: "We decided, 'We can do better than him.'"

Ting's account explains that two early stage iterations of the boutique hotel phenomenon were effectively running in parallel. A West Coast variant conceived by Bill Kimpton at his Kimpton Hotel in San Francisco, where the emphasis was on the food, the restaurant and a calming ambience. And then on the East Coast, Schrager and Rubell's Morgans, opening on Madison Avenue in 1984. 'Schrager and Rubell were intent on elevating the allure and magic they had perfected in their nightclubs and bringing them directly into their hotel lobbies and bars. This is where boutique hotels as we know them today got their start,' Ting explains.

It's reported that Rubell, who died of AIDs-related causes in 1989, was the first to use the term boutique hotel as a way to distinguish from the department store feel of the bigger, more established hotel chains. Schrager, meanwhile, is credited with the phrase 'lobby living', asserting that he would make hotels the nightclubs of the 1990s. Hotels as a destination for hip locals, not just affluent out-of-towners. He worked with the French industrial designer and architect Philippe Starck on many of his fêted and distinctly clubby hotel projects, from the Paramount in midtown Manhattan (with its famous Whiskey Bar, designed in a 'semi-industrial' manner with Polaroids on the walls) to the Delano in Miami (the location for high profile parties for Madonna and Winter Music Conference gatherings).

Speaking in the Skift article, Bill Walshe, CEO of the luxury-oriented Viceroy Hotel Group, explained: "I think Ian was somebody who not only had the commitment to the individual components of design meeting hospitality, but he also had the background in entertainment and nightlife to elevate boutique from being something which was design-led to something which was a very interactive and an emotional experience for the guest, where the hotels became the backdrop for a lifestyle that a lot of people aspired to. Not only in terms of the design aesthetic of the hotels, but of the vibe."

Niki Leondakis, formerly president and COO of Kimpton Hotels & Restaurants, said: "Ian's hotels, you would walk into them and arrive at a scene. It was sort of a velvet ropes type of experience and you were with all the beautiful people and, with his experience and fame from Studio 54, I think that drove a lot of the tone of his boutique hotels." KC Kavanagh, former senior vice president of global communications for Starwood Hotels & Resorts, added: "It was just a total mind shift that a hotel could look like this, like a cool nightclub. I remember visiting New York and staying at one of Schrager's hotels and it was like seeing the Wizard Of Oz in colour."

Jochen Eisenbrand from the Vitra Design Museum got to speak to Ian Schrager about the role clubs played in shaping ideas and exploring practices that could migrate into the hotel business. "He told me that clubs were the perfect test bed and that so many ideas transitioned over. It was all about the right mix. The right mix of music and people. All the way through to getting the interior design right. Even getting the smell right."

Schrager picked up on this theme in a 2014 interview on Radio WNYC (with Alec Baldwin, no less). People generally associate him with the glitz and fame of the entertainment/hospitality business (with an emphasis on the business), but here, he relates his nightclub adventures to something closer to the principles of DIY creative culture. "Nightclubs used to be like a garage business. Like making music in a garage or inventing a technology company in a garage. Now, you need millions of dollars to get started. But then, you didn't have to know anything; you didn't have to have a lot of money. It was like, you roll up the carpet, you put on a record player and you have a nightclub."

Schrager, who also talks about growing up in Brooklyn dreaming of making it big in Manhattan – and that now he lives in Manhattan and everyone wants to make it big in Brooklyn – continued: "We did a club we liked and from that we wanted to do a hotel we liked. Something that manifested the culture; our culture, not our parents' culture. No rules. Start from scratch."

He goes on to compare the nightclub business, the hotel business and another area of commercial interest for him, the real estate business. "If you strip it down, your primary goal in the nightclub business is to look after people and make sure they have fun. Elevate the experience. Same goal in the hotel business. Same goal in the condominium business."

Schrager is your archetypal hard-nosed Brooklynite. Not one to wax poetic about aesthetic principles or the trajectory of modern culture. But when he talks about 'elevate the experience' – that's the rub, the language of brands today. He found in the night the wisdom that others now search for through MBAs. The term 'experience economy' (the millennial-oriented trend for favouring experiences over possessions) has moved into common parlance. Industry experts, gurus and hot-take influencers espouse ideas like 'designing feelings into all aspects of a brand'. Jeff Bezos from Amazon puts it like this: "Your brand is what people say about you when you're not in the room." The world has had a lot to say – good and bad – about Schrager's clubs and hotels.

In his radio interview with Alec Baldwin, Schrager enthuses that he still programmes club nights in his hotels – such as for his Edition chain – when he sees a role for them and the opportunity for a "positive impact". He explains: "And still with sweaty, serious dancing at the heart of it." Hotels and clubs have crossed paths on many other occasions since the birth of the boutique concept. In the early 2000s, back in the boom years of the so-called electroclash sound (think DJ Larry Tee, Fischerspooner, angular hair and much lipstick), the Grand Hotels group, from Shoreditch to Tribeca, was hosting fashionable nights that gave another boost to the notion of the hotel as more than just a place to get some shuteye. Or at least in the view of some. Mr Saturday Night club DJ Justin Carter complained to Resident Advisor: "Tribeca Grand, what a dumb idea. I even DJed there, but those rooms were never meant to have music played in them. It was the epitome of a luxury brand tapping into an existing scene to try and make itself cooler."

Paris' Hôtel Costes is another prime example. This was a hotel that talked about having a 'musical direction', then delivered on that through compilation albums, tie-ins with labels and launching a recording studio. The New York Times covered the Costes story in 2005: 'Who is a hotel's most important employee? The general manager, concierge, chef or even the chief housekeeper might come to mind. But at many newer properties, especially boutique hotels aiming for a younger crowd, the answer could be completely different: the DJ. Once it would have been unheard of to see a DJ anywhere except in a dance club, a radio studio or behind a folding table at a wedding or bar mitzvah. In the last several years, though, DJs have been popping up all over the place – music shops, department stores, bars and now, with apparent success, in hotels.'

King Britt shares a DJ perspective: "You would walk into somewhere like the Delano, and you were hearing how specifically they were programming the music through the day, like a DJ set. Then that would follow through to other hotels. You'd go to the W and there's Andrew Jervis *(now chief curator at Bandcamp),* also programming a very specific sound. So this became another extension of dance music and of DJ culture. The opportunity to bring a different focus on sound to hotels was something new for us once-unimportant DJs to think about."

In late 2024, the Miami branch of The Standard completed a cultural loop of sorts, hosting an Art Basel exhibition called Disco + Design, celebrating disco-era aesthetics in modern music, art, fashion and interior design. From rooftop sessions at the W Hotel during the Amsterdam Dance Event, to DJ Harvey's nights at Pikes Hotel and legendary types such as DJ Pippi entertaining the beautiful people at the Balearic branch of The Standard, clubs and hotels have stayed firm accomplices of the night ever since those early moves by Schrager and Rubell. A wrap-up of underground and premium, embraced by some, met with chagrin by others.

Departure desk

British entrepreneur Freddie Laker's taste in music is not widely documented, but it can reasonably be assumed that club tracks did not figure highly. Nonetheless, unwittingly, he can lay claim to a support role in shaping UK dance music culture. In 1966, he founded Laker Airlines, a very early mover in the shift towards budget flights offered since then by operators, loved and disliked in equal measure, like Ryanair, Southwest Airlines, easyJet and AirAsia. After much legal wrangling with the government and disgruntled competitors like British Airways and Pan Am, Laker's flagship Skytrain service finally took to the air in September 1977, with flights from London Gatwick to New York JFK coming in at a then extraordinary £59 one-way.

For a generation of DJs, promoters and clubbers this was a thrilling turn of events. It still wasn't cheap for the average young person, but with a bit of graft and much saving, it was within reach. Suddenly, these Meccas of dance music they'd heard tales of, clubs like Paradise Garage and Fun House, record stores like Greenwich Village's Vinylmania, weren't so out of reach or restricted to the imagination. Eager to experience this relatable but different culture firsthand, young Brits would head to NYC, stay in the cheapest hotels or YMCAs they could find and spend every remaining dollar on clubs, records and clothes. They brought back stories and ideas, too. Ideas that, for some, would shape careers.

There are many narratives of DJs and club organisers from that era who took a Skytrain to NYC, lots of them coming back with bundles of 12-inches that otherwise weren't likely to grace the shores of the UK for some time. Norman Jay is one of them. Speaking to DJ History, he enthused: "Freddie Laker! God bless him, because without him I'd probably have taken another 10 years to get out there. But with £99 return you could go every couple of months if you saved up." In an interview for Billboard, Pete Tong said: "A profound influence was when I managed to go to New York when I was, like, 19, on a charter jet. There was an airline called the Freddie Laker Airways, and you could get a flight to New York for $99. I went a few times and got into a few clubs. It was just totally alien to anything I'd experienced in the UK… It was all the formative stuff that is the foundation of what we take for granted today."

It was also a foundation, of sorts, for dance music tourism. What started as a trickle of diehards heading to club culture epicentres eventually became a deluge of party-seeking travellers, hungry for nights out by the beach or in cities other than their own. While it's difficult to pinpoint specific figures for dance music, consumer intelligence platform Future Market Insights valued music tourism more broadly at USD $7.17 billion in 2024 and on course to reach $15 billion by 2034. Though how much of that is spent on dancefloors, as opposed to pop concerts or rock nostalgia tours, remains unclear, the scale to which dance music tourism has grown over the last two decades is undeniable. We've already discussed how club culture has left its mark on hotel trends, but here, it's the very reason for travelling in the first place.

Next to UK club kids hot-footing it to NYC, another early example of dance music tourism (albeit more short-haul) was the summer season on Fire Island, located off the southern shore of Long Island, New York. A popular getaway (The Pines and Cherry Grove hamlets, in particular) for NYC's gay community, the island holds a special place in dance music history thanks to The Sandpiper. This restaurant-cum-club shook to the sound of disco throughout the 1970s. Producer Tom Moulton (later to work with Grace Jones, First Choice and MFSB) created the first tape of 'overlapping songs' for the venue in the early 1970s. He'd spend up to 80 hours laying down reel-to-reels of the hottest tracks, supplying these to The Sandpiper every few months. All of this led to him, in 1975, creating the first continuous mix album from Gloria Gaynor's Never Can Say Goodbye. He was duly anointed the father of the disco mix and the inventor of the 12-inch.

A decade or so after those formative trips to Manhattan by Pete Tong and his contemporaries, a more global dance music landscape began to emerge. There was Goa in India, long a stop-off on the hippy trail, with parties from the early 1970s onwards that blended local folk rhythms with psychedelic rock, occasional outbreaks of synth music and an emphasis on lights and visual effects. Come the late 1980s, DJs like Goa Gil, Laurent and Fred Disko were playing embryonic forms of a fast trance sound that, by the early to mid-1990s, would entice a new generation of tie-dyed, backpacking party people to the western coast of India.

And then, Ibiza. Where to start with Ibiza? "I still have an image in my mind of the British kids arriving," Amnesia club DJ and Balearic beat founding father Alfredo, who passed away in 2024, told me when I interviewed him in the mid-1990s. The former journalist, who'd left his homeland of Argentina when the right-wing military took over in the 1970s, continued: "I've got this picture of them going absolutely crazy; trying to dance inside the speakers, even."

That story of Paul Oakenfold, Danny Rampling, Nicky Holloway and Johnny Walker's jaunt-that-spawned-a-scene has been told so many times not to need telling again here. But it is worth noting that the White Island was playing host to kinds of subcultural tourism before clubs were the central facet. In Hippie Hippie Shake, Oz magazine editor Richard Neville's memoirs of the 1960s, there's talk of wild full-moon parties on the island, with folk singer Donovan and feminist writer Germaine Greer among the notable attendees; of people 'floating free' on a 'jewel of decadent splendour'. Those floating included a growing contingent of hippies and bohemians, including Americans dodging the Vietnam War. Earlier still, when the right-wing dictator General Francisco Franco came to power in 1936, Ibiza clung tight to its liberal soul. Consequently, Spain's queer community gravitated to the tolerant island through the 1950s.

The role of club culture in Ibiza's tourism success story has, on numerous occasions, had a mixed reception from those less itinerant to the place. The island's authorities insisting all venues add roofs in the late 1980s still raises laments for the good old days among more seasoned visitors – no more dancing under the stars. Ibizan laws remain strict around noise. In 2018, legislation was introduced to stop music exceeding 65 decibels. Some of the earliest of the campaigns in Spain against 'over-tourism', advocating for more sustainable approaches and less pandering to holidaymakers and affluent second-home owners, took place here. And yet, club culture as a business seems to grow and grow in Ibiza regardless. The 2024 IMS Business Report assessed club ticketing revenue in Ibiza at €141 million in 2023, up 14% from 2022 and 76% from 2019. It also noted that the average ticket price has climbed from €44 in 2022 to €51 in 2023.

In terms of escalating outlays, that ticket price hike is nothing. Somewhere in all of this growth, Ibiza has increasingly pivoted upmarket. It's always had its bougie side and its elite side. Part of its folklore emanates from the idea that, out there on the dancefloor, you could be next to some hippies from Germany, various south London football casuals, a group of jetset kids from all over and minor royalty from Luxembourg. But it's become less the great leveller and more the premiumised experience. Now, it's bottle service and eye-wateringly expensive VIP areas. It is articles in Spain's El País newspaper, too, complaining about the noise of Lamborghinis roaring along the dusty lanes.

King Britt believes that the premiumisation of Ibiza also had a massive impact on brands wanting to show up there: "Ibiza, that really is what changed the game as far as brands and dance music. It's a destination, it's exotic. These brands could come in, and it was like the perfect storm for brands and marketing."

Also in El País, a 2022 piece made a hopeful claim that a multidimensionalism of life, even if unlikely to be present on the same dancefloor, still blesses the island: 'First it was the hippies, then the clubbers. In recent years, the mega-rich have joined. None of the previous groups has been totally displaced; none has wanted to leave Ibiza. Rather, they have spread out across the island, living side by side, creating small social archipelagos. The groups shape the different faces and masks of Ibiza, an island that embraces and expels, sometimes at the same time.'

According to a 2019 report by the University Of The Balearic Islands, clubs made up 35% of the island's gross domestic product and workforce. However, the rising cost of living in Ibiza means that workforce is increasingly found living in cars and vans. A BBC article in 2024 quoted one such worker on the island: "Things aren't going to change; in fact they're only going to get worse. This is an island for rich people." It's not just hitting those who work in clubs and bars, either. You'll find teachers, firefighters and police officers sleeping in vehicles in this place of high-net-worth escapism.

Though it may be particularly proficient in luxury clubbing, this isn't solely the preserve of Ibiza. In a 2023 feature bombastically headlined Elite Music Tourism Is the Latest 1 Percent Flex, Vanity Fair examined an ultra-exclusive entertainment world operated by event organisers and livestreamers like Cercle. It's one where Disclosure play at Croatia's Plitvice Lakes National Park, and Nina Kraviz on the first floor of the Eiffel Tower in Paris, for a select few. Reporting from one of Cercle's parties, the Vanity Fair piece declares: 'The sun is setting on Croix-de-Coeur, a mountaintop restaurant nestled 7,000 feet above sea level in the Alps Of Verbier, Switzerland. On the patio are two internationally renowned DJs, Derek Barbolla and Philippe Tuchmann *(they're in fact the founders of Cercle)*, mixing Fred Again and Peggy Gou for a crowd of no more than 30. Inside, a recently retired German CEO reveals his professional status, declaring, Aperol Spritz in hand, that he and his model girlfriend are currently "focused on enjoying life". He looks no older than 35.'

Elsewhere, the piece quotes Carly Van Sickle, the senior director of global brand marketing at upscale W Hotels: "The future of luxury music travel is poised for distinctive growth. In a post-pandemic world, prospective travellers are looking to embark to destinations that transcend the ordinary itinerary."

Stepping back, at least a little, from the pinnacles of premium, Ibiza once held a near monopoly on summer season clubbing of all flavours and budget points. However, a proliferation of new destinations has of course emerged, with places like Tulum, Croatia, Ayia Napa, Rimini, Las Vegas, Mykonos and Thailand each attracting their own club tribes. Demonstrating that clubland never stays stationary, Time Out insisted in 2024 that Manila and Rio de Janeiro were the go-to spots. Sometimes 'the spot' is a moving one. The frankly alarming idea of EDM cruises has become a reality in recent years. At the time of writing, Groove Cruises is advertising its January 2025 Miami to Labadee trip aboard the Allure Of The Seas with Eric Prydz. A 2023 research survey conducted in the US by Carnegie Mellon University-funded organisation Civic Science suggests they're on to something: Gen Z was recorded as the most likely generation to show interest in going on a cruise, a higher proportion than any other age demographic.

Back in the less sunny climes of the UK, Finlay Johnson, chief operating officer at the Association For Electronic Music (more from him in later chapters), recalls observing a club tourism occurrence that threw him. It was one he felt symbolic of nightlife splitting in two. "One time I was at Fabric, a large group of French kids came in," he remembers. "They had taken a coach over and were planning to leave at 4am. I was thinking, 'This really is club tourism.' And I was in two minds. They'd bought tickets, they'd invested in club culture. But it was also very much 'take-a-photo-and-go' and not necessarily about a community they will ever revisit. Maybe we end up with a splintering – destination venues and then those that exist outside of the bucket list thing.

Club tourists certainly head to the UK, but it's hard to see that much has happened to promote the country's night culture globally since the British Tourist Authority vaguely announced plans to do so far back in 1997. It would be about 'recognising the dance music industry as a way of attracting younger tourists,' they assured us. In contrast: Berlin – the closest contender to Ibiza as a hugely appealing dance music epicentre (if one more likely checked out for a sleepless weekend as 14 nights) – has undoubtedly worked hard to promote itself as such.

The start of this city's acceleration through the ranks of clubbing destinations was Love Parade. Kicking off in 1989 with strong political intentions, Dr Motte and Danielle de Picciotto's electronic dance music festival grew into the mother of all techno parties, with crowds of 1.6 million at its peak. Though it had moved to Duisburg by then, the event ended in tragedy in 2010, with 21 people killed and more than 600 injured, when a crush occurred at the entrance to a tunnel.

Tresor, Berghain and KitKatClub are just a few of the clubs that have taken on a legendary status in the city since then. Berlin has benefited from a distinctive techno sound. A dark aesthetic, too. A sense of a more forbidden and libidinous nocturnal pulse than you'll find in the Balearics. With much gusto, it also celebrates its no-curfew laws and the fact that clubs never need to shut. 'Go partying till the sun comes up – and goes down again! Unlike other German cities, Berlin has no official closing time,' trumpets the city's visitBerlin website.

In 2009, journalist Tobias Rapp published the book Lost And Sound: Berlin, Techno And The Easyjetset. It popularised the term 'techno tourist'. It told the story of a decade of budget airlines and a changing demographic in the city's underground venues. Interviewed for Resident Advisor, he recalls the moment in 2004 when the change was apparent to him: "I was standing in the line of a club waiting to get in. I realised, 'Wow, all of these people around me speak different languages.' Nobody was speaking German. People from all over the world are standing in line to get in, and I'm the only German here."

Liz Hunter was among those who visited around this time. She, however, hung around, becoming editor of Deutsche Telekom's Electronic Beats, a magazine and website that flew the flag for Berlin's burgeoning creative movement. "It was an amazing time in the city," she recalls fondly. "So much to get excited about that it's hardly surprising you had all of these kids getting on their easyJet flights, not even booking a hotel, and then flying back and going straight to work on a Tuesday.

"Without sounding too lofty, there was this real baseline respect that came from having had to fight so hard for this opportunity *(she's referring to the end of the Berlin Wall and the reunification of Germany)*. I think visitors to this underground culture, at least the early ones, really recognised that. I think it made going out clubbing a bit more profound. And then, of course, the mayor and others realised there was lots and lots of fucking money to be made out of it all."

Dr Luis Manuel Garcia-Mispireta is an associate professor of ethnomusicology and popular music studies at the University Of Birmingham. He researches electronic dance music scenes, examining their impact on sexuality, tourism and the creative industries. Many of his perspectives are derived from ethnographic fieldwork in Berlin. He shares a similar view on why Berlin recognised the soft power in techno's hard beats and steely sounds. "It was very much linked to money. It was techno tourism. Suddenly, it's a sector where you can look at the numbers. You can see the money coming in that is directly tied to clubbing. And it was in that moment that Berliner politicians were like, 'Yeah, techno has *always* been culturally really important, and actually a distinctive thing of ours.'"

As much as dance music has influenced fashion and cosmetics, advertising and design, its mark on travel and tourism is among its most substantial. There is much to be positive about here. Introducing people to new artistry and different communities, bringing together those who may otherwise never have met, extending horizons and forging connections. This all sounds very much part of the club culture blueprint that most sign up for. However, for reasons already described, it has brought downsides, too. Of course, the negative consequences of tourism aren't all the fault of dance music, but it's contributing. Moreover, we haven't touched on likely the most significant issue of all: tourism's detrimental role in the health of the planet.

Someone who has all of this on his mind on a daily basis is London-based Sam Blenkinsopp. He's the CEO and co-founder of Trippin, a digital platform and events business that seeks to 'connect travel, culture and creativity' for a primarily young audience. Trippin's mission statement says: 'We collaborate with our community to uncover stories that are found at the intersection of social and cultural boundaries. Combining guides and experiences with audio, film and written word to create an ecosystem that empowers people to travel with more purpose, this means making us, as travellers, more conscious of our impact on the environment, its people and its culture. Together we can make travel more sustainable for generations to come.'

Sam got to this positioning for Trippin when working in a culture marketing role at adidas. He was travelling a lot but wasn't coming across the type of content, editorial, or perspectives that resonated with him or provided insight and inspiration on the world he sought. "You'd have things like Tripadvisor, but I wasn't sure the demographic of the person writing their review was aligned with mine, or if their point of view was relevant to me," he explains. "And then with the more curated media approach, I felt like frequently it was catering for different types of traveller, maybe your family, or your backpacker, or your luxury traveller, or your student traveller. And then sometimes it feels like really voyeuristic perspectives – I think travel media has had a challenge historically of always being people from the Global North, maybe from New York or LA or London, probably white and middle-class, reporting back on other cultures from a very particular outsider perspective."

What started in 2005 as a private group on Facebook, with friends invited to share lists, recommendations and Google maps, grew in a couple of months from 20 members to 2,500. "That's when we realised it was more than a Facebook group, but this really special community, founded on this positive exchange of ideas and inspiration." Since then, working with co-founders Kesang Ball and Yasmin Shahmir, Sam's developed Trippin into a fully-fledged platform and much larger community, offering travel advice and resources, long-form content and partnerships with myriad international creators and collectives. Partnerships with brands, too, now the primary means of monetisation at Trippin. They've launched an agency division called All Corners to add to how they can work with brands. Its services include strategy and insight, storytelling and creative production, and experiences and events. But unlike a regular marketing communications agency, all are anchored to the expertise in, and passion for, more progressive ways to travel and explore.

Music features strongly, too. When we speak, Sam is prepping for an initiative at Public Records – the club venue, bar, restaurant, record shop, workshop space and outdoor garden all wrapped into one, in Gowanus, Brooklyn. Called Assemble, the events series is in partnership with the dating app Hinge, which touts itself as being about fostering meaningful connections rather than casual encounters. It sees them working with local collectives and programming activities across the day and evening that extend from workshops and learning sessions on childhood nostalgia, screenwriting and decolonised approaches to wellness to DJ sets later on.

"Love Parade, Café Del Mar, Amnesia, Tresor, Berghain – there's a lot of history out there now," Sam starts, when asked how he thinks dance music tourism is changing. "Once people just took a vacation, now it feels more like a cultural pilgrimage, you could say. But people are wanting to move beyond these popularist clubbing destinations. There's a stronger desire to gain access to culture that's more local and authentic."

One example he gives of how people are moving away from the more established institutions is Open Ground, which opened in Wuppertal, in the North Rhine-Westphalia region of Germany, in late 2023. A six-hour car ride from the action of Berlin, a buzz has developed at pace around this 1200-capacity space, situated in a converted bunker, with members of the Hard Wax record store and distributors playing a role in its design.

"Word gets around about their sound system, their programming and the sense of spiritual connection you get there," says Sam, who started in the worlds of culture and media at age 17, setting in motion a blog called Second To None, documenting streetwear, music and graffiti. "Then artists say it's the best space they've ever played in. All of that moves forward very quickly, and suddenly you start noticing people from across these key cities like London, Paris, Berlin and New York, all wanting to go to this place called Wuppertal, to go and experience this."

Another example he gives is Lisbon's Musicbox venue and nights there focused on the Angolan diaspora. It evidences the growing appetite to experience electronic music that emanates from beyond the typical Western epicentres and from Africa in particular. "You get this twist of the kaduro *(intense, fast-paced dance music born of a time of civil unrest)* from Angola in with the *(equally frenetic)* batida sound from Portugal. There are bigger artists and nights you can go to in Lisbon, but people increasingly want to experience something in its purest form and among the community that created it."

Sam acknowledges this creates a double-edged sword. It helps people to connect and to learn from new experiences. But it also runs the very real risk of eroding culture and heritage, disrupting economies and social structures. "Which is why it's so important to inspire and educate people to travel in a way that is more conscious of the local community," he continues. "In ways that support and uplift their economy, customs, rituals – and make it more sustainable for generations to come."

As he sees it, there's a responsibility both on the side of the clubs and the travellers. "With the clubs, it's: 'Okay, we're appealing to the international audience, but how are we ensuring that we're supporting, enriching and engaging the local community? Is this through programming and through who we are hiring? Are we giving apprenticeships or internships and opening up opportunities? Are we supporting local stores and businesses? Are we creating a good ecosystem? Are we supporting other venues and building a healthy scene?' Closer to home, but I think Fabric is an example of how some clubs have got lost in tackling this. They're doing okay at reinventing themselves now, but for about a decade, they were only really appealing to tourists. No one local would've been seen dead in there, because they weren't reflecting anything local.

"And with the traveller," he continues, "there's a responsibility to learn more, to research more. We need to think about how we spend our money as a form of support or protest, to vote in favour of or to boycott something. Do that, and we can uphold scenes and drive funds in the right direction. We can visit a space as an outsider, someone travelling there, but be respectful of it. We should also go as far as to question if it's even a space we should be going into. Ultimately, we need to be more conscious of our impact."

Another way Trippin factors music into world exploration orientates around 'travelling without moving' – or, at least, not moving far. They've staged events called Undercurrents at London's Corsica Studios, merging music and film to shine a light on subcultures from locations as widely spread as Tanzania, Brazil, Mexico and China. They've hosted parties in Glastonbury's Shangri-La field, where clubs, collectives and artists work to a different theme each year, with sets from Angelita, Batu, Bianca Oblivion, Blenk and Bushby.

"There can be something beautiful in bringing cultures to people, instead of people going elsewhere to experience that culture," Sam beams. "And I think a club and a dancefloor is an exciting space to experiment with how people engage with different ways of seeing the world. It's through the medium of music, but ultimately, you're exploring the identities and cultures of different people. So, in terms of how we do it, it's either about artists and DJs who we bring in from different parts of the world, or it's those who credibly represent a certain diaspora. Either way, we're transporting people to different corners of the world while staying on the dancefloor."

Prevalent media debate around travel and tourism rarely strikes a positive chord. Carbon emissions, cultural disruption, upending local economies – it's a narrative markedly less picturesque than many of the destinations we choose to head to. But with his mind set on seeking solutions, Sam signs off with a reminder of the reasons why travel matters so much to so many people and how there are deeply felt benefits we shouldn't lose sight of.

"The toxicity of social media, things like work-from-home, disconnectedness, loneliness – people feel isolated and driven apart. We've got to help people make more meaningful connections, and nightlife is one of those ways," he concludes determinedly. "Bringing clubbing together with travel amplifies this further. It becomes a spiritual connection – with the space you are in, your fellow dancers and the music you're listening to. It's not just about looking out there and understanding what's happening around you. It enables you to look inside and learn more about yourself."

Designing the night

In 1991, a book called Design After Dark: The Story Of Dancefloor Style by journalist Cynthia Rose was released. It shone a light on a new wave of young British designers, inspired by all corners of club culture, from acid house to acid jazz, from Soul II Soul's championing of Black entrepreneurialism to opportunities created by former pirate station Kiss FM going legal. Among those whose stories were told: Ian 'Swifty' Swift, the artist and graphic designer who made his mark with the Straight No Chaser magazine and Mo' Wax label. Also, a young Trevor Jackson, the omni-talented designer, moviemaker, producer and DJ behind Output Records, commissions for BMW and Comme des Garçons, and whose work has been shown at the ICA and Guggenheim.

Design After Dark blew my teenage mind. It captured the sense that you, too, could go out there and do things. That dance music wasn't just something to consume. That, in some way or another, and not limited to design, you could contribute as well. As the book's preface explained: 'During the latter half of the 1980s, London witnessed the making of remarkable social history. From illicit radio stations to improvised nightclubs, young Londoners helped to construct a completely alternative leisure landscape. Its aim was celebration, its glue was music and the changes it engineered and explored now affect the music industry, the advertising business and many related areas of design. Socially, this world united Britons of many ages who differed widely in background, race and taste. And the inspiration they took from each other was broadcast across the globe.'

Also among those showcased was a duo named the Thunderjockeys (aka Graham Elliot and John England). They started off doing projects in clubs. Then they were doing sleeves for Todd Terry. Then they get taken under the wing of global advertising agency BMP DDB Needham. Rose writes: 'They dip into every technology going. They will do a band's sleeve and also direct its promo; design a TV station's logo as well as its onscreen graphics.' Further in, she continues: 'In 1989, the Thunderjockeys decided to go into advertising. "Infiltrate might be a better word," says Elliot. "What happened was that, through agencies, we were giving people all these ideas. But we got a little bit tired of handing 'em over, waving goodbye and never hearing a peep again. We thought, why aren't we in there, doing those ideas..." Much of their work is inspired by keeping an eye on cultures around the world. Graham Elliot: "You've got to look outside of yourself to find out what you're about. That was the lesson behind the whole acid house thing."'

Before and since then, near-endless design codes and aesthetics have presided over different phases of dance music culture. Sonically, it's been a broad church and the visualisation of it – bleak, spangly, gritty, futurist, sexy, political, obtuse, literal and so on – has proven likewise. In the case of disco, for instance – or at least when it became commoditised and commercial – there was flesh on show. Lots of it and, uncomfortably, it was generally female flesh and the context was objectification. It wasn't just found on the tacky compilations, with names like Extasy, Hot Disco Takes and Do It!, that took the music to the masses. Salsoul Records, home to releases by Skyy, Double Exposure, Loleatta Holloway and First Choice, followed a similarly risqué visual path. Elsewhere in the disco years, there was a space-age thing (touched on in chapter two with Kenny Scharf's Absolut work), homoeroticism, exotica and airbrush effects.

Techno, when it did break from the anonymity of the plain 12-inch sleeve, brought different design stimuli with it. Wolfgang Voight has produced under names like Gas, Mint and Mike Ink. He also co-founded Cologne's minimal techno stalwart label Kompakt, for whom he has designed many covers. Interviewed for the book Rave And Its Influence On Art And Culture, he said: "I have visual visions and musical visions. Some of them go together – like minimal repetitions, ideas of looping. Some of my images, like my music, are about loops and repetitions and the variation of these loops and repetitions. And the other aspect is about work with external material, samples, in visuals as well as music, in order to create something different out of it."

Similar design thinking flowed through in the work of Pfadfinderei, the Berlin collective who forged their style working on flyers and record sleeves for Ellen Allien's BPitch Control imprint. Later, they brought their ideas to audio-video installations and then to brands like Lacoste, Red Bull, Netflix and Volvo. Codec Völker from the collective – which has now parted ways – explained to Format in 2018 the importance of the city's warehouse rave environments and accompanying art aesthetic in formulating a style: "We learnt a lot about emotion and spatial installations without having a direct client, just by having that experience."

Collectives abound in the realm where electronic music meets design. Another of particular repute was Tomato, which formed in London in 1991 and, if vague in form, continues to this day. Contributing artists, designers and musicians included Simon Taylor, Dirk van Dooren, Graham Wood, Michael Horsham, Dylan Kendle, Jason Kedgley, John Warwicker, Steve Baker, and Karl Hyde and Rick Smith of Underworld. Located in D'Arblay Street, Soho, next door to the Black Market Records store, they wanted to shred up design agency rules as much as they could. This included working with clients strictly on their terms, ditching hierarchical structures and the rule of any singular creative director. Their work for Underworld on covers (such as for Dubnobasswithmyheadman) and stage designs is likely most familiar to those into electronic music. But brands like Chanel, Channel 4, Microsoft, Samsung, Nokia, Nike, Renault and even the Royal Mail have also commissioned them in extremely multidisciplinary ways.

Speaking to Richard Turley in It's Nice That, Graham Wood from Tomato described the influence of having Underworld on the firm: "When Rick and/or Karl would arrive with a new cassette of work it would be a brilliant moment. Always energising, propelling work to happen, and causing us to think about how emotion could be embodied through image. I think that making emotional images from music can sometimes be quite hard; if I try to equate it, it is as if only 10% of the full emotion one invests in that kind of imagery ever really becomes manifested, whereas it seems to me to be the opposite with making music. What I'm trying to say is that it was intense, hard work. And lots of it. Never stopping producing, never stopping learning."

Dylan Kendle adds more about how music and its intersection with technology informed the outputs of the Tomato studio: "Not only did the collective count several musicians as members, and therefore music as an output, it also served the music industry as creatives, designers and video directors. Practically, I think it borrowed from the sample culture that defined much of the music of the era; in that it used the computer as a sampler and filter to create something new and 'other'. Its point of difference perhaps was that the inputs or sources were more often its own, rather than archive, stock or commissioned, and consequently the visual output was more unique."

For designers working in the music space in more recent times, cover art has, of course, lost much of its cultural capital. But there are other ways. Ukrainian animator and illustrator Elena Gumeniuk spent her youth creating art inspired by London grime, far from the scene of the action. From listening to the music of Dizzee Rascal, Wiley and co, she imagined the far-off urban environments of the UK capital. When she made it to London, she found work making illustrations for the music videos of AJ Tracey, Dread D and Jammz, using that as a springboard to work with Fred Perry, Apple Music and the creative agency Mother.

Vicky Grout's high status as a grime photographer, primarily shooting on analogue, opened doors for work with Nike, Havana Club and the New York Times. Such is the trend for recycling and recontextualising that some believe the influence of 1990s rave aesthetics is in the 2012 London Olympics logo. Speaking to Eye On Design, commercial director of branding consultancy Bugler Smith, Paul Gosling, looked back on that much debated visual emblem: "If you look at the 2012 Olympics identity and its font design *(by Wolff Olins)*, for me that's just '90s rave culture. Rave aesthetics clearly set a trend for hyper density, overlays, and that movement towards bold designs and patterns. I remember nostalgically thinking about things like having multicoloured dots on your face at Global Gathering, and that's all back in now. Even the bucket hats."

The designer and artist as a multidisciplinary being is hardly new. But in a time of the creator economy and portfolio careers, it has a growing effect on the ideas that emerge from club culture. Kesshia 'KESH' Kumari, from the suburbs of London, symbolises this. She didn't start specialising in one art form and then move on to others. She started doing music, visual art, design and fashion all at once. "All were in the flow at the same time," she has said. In that seamless flow, along with her trademark black-and-white eye graphic, there's been DJing, designing bottles for Hennessy, collaborating with American Apparel, installations in W Hotels and creating looks for Jammer, Dizzee Rascal and Kanye West. The London club culture she grew up with converged with creative and commercial opportunities from the full 360-degree range.

We could go on. But trying to cover every design perspective that has carved out a space in dance music would be a whole other book. However, Ian Anderson from The Designers Republic is one person who can make a particular claim for work in 1990s club culture that went on to influence much outside of that scene. Anyone who's owned a Warp Records or R&S release will be familiar with his collisions of colour and typography, shapes, symbols and Japanese-oriented elements. Anyone who saw the communications from Leeds club night turned dance music empire Gatecrasher as well. More recently, there have been releases for the likes of Róisín Murphy. But the pathways have traversed far out of dance music, too – to gaming, fashion, TV, even fizzy drinks.

Speaking on a video call from his longstanding base in Sheffield, he's musing on the journey that design has taken him on across 40 years. Bits of it make sense to him. Other bits he talks about like he's still struggling to figure them out. "I couldn't really tell you how it all happened. But I guess it *did* happen," he laughs. "So much of it was by chance. We weren't trained as graphic designers, not formally. And we didn't know how, in those pre-laptop days, to work with photography. But we did know how to draw shapes with Rotring pens, and that suited this new crop of bands, the likes of Plaid and Autechre, who didn't want to be on the cover. It was a bit like, well, if that's the case, you better talk to The Designers Republic."

Working with Warp put Ian and his fledgling The Designers Republic business on the map, his designs resplendent on the covers at the moment that imprint grabbed the zeitgeist. But his connections with the steel city and its music started earlier. Indeed, for someone who's not from the place ("I grew up in the south, but the music coming out of Sheffield sounded better than the stuff coming out of London. I wanted to be in a proper city, a socialist city."), he's certainly made himself at one with it. He headed to Sheffield in 1979 and, having already been in a punk band, wanted to be in a post-punk band. He was a bassist, but not a very good one, he admits, so he called time on that. The prototype band he had been in transformed into the influential industrial funk outfit Chakk, which included Mark Brydon (later in Moloko with Róisín Murphy) among its number. Chakk would then fund the launch of FON Studios – a place that saw wave after wave of Sheffield's underground, from Cabaret Voltaire to Forgemasters to Sweet Exorcist, come through its doors.

Ian was DJing a bit, also designing flyers. He was asked to manage a new Sheffield band, Person To Person, formed by ex-members of early '80s pop sensations ABC. The band signed to Epic Records, and because he'd designed those flyers, he started doing their covers. He's described that first cover as being motivated by "a headful of Russian constructivism, Festival Of Britain design, Ealing comedies, Star Trek and early Face magazines." It was a mix of inputs and influences that he would refine in subsequent design work – and now under The Designers Republic banner, joined by Nick Phillips, a former sculptor and the organ player in indie band World Of Twist. Early commissions came from Age Of Chance and his Chakk mates; also for early British house missives from Krush and The Funky Worm.

"In Star Trek, the Klingons had their own font," Ian muses, explaining his influences further. "In an early black and white Dr Who, they saw some markings on the wall, which apparently they could translate as meaning Dalek City. And weirdly, that got me into Japanese visuals – and typography that I couldn't read. So this was all a big fascination for me – how far can you abstract typography, once you start drawing your own letter forms and things?" Further into our conversation, he also talks about a childhood spent drawing imaginary flags and football kits – that's somewhere in the busy mix, too.

Soon enough, and very much inspired by what they saw at FON, Steve Beckett, Rob Mitchell and record producer Robert Gordon launched Warp Records. Within a few years, it was on course to become one of the most successful and pioneering electronic music labels ever. The Designers Republic, which opted for the revolutionary vibes of Bastille Day to launch on, became synonymous with so much of the visuality of the label and of artists like Autechre, LFO, The Black Dog and Aphex Twin. The sound and look expanded in appeal further with the electronica gateway compilation series, Artificial Intelligence, replete with uncanny valley glitch artistry from TDR. Thanks to all of the intertwining threads, the friendships, the experiments and the collaborative adventures, Ian says this all went much deeper than a standard contractual, buyer/supplier relationship. "It never felt like we were just the hired design agency with Warp. The connections, the thinking we shared – it all went further than that."

The work on those Warp releases put Ian's studio firmly on the map. It was distinctive and playful stuff. It was as exciting as the music and, looking back, it summarised the age as much as the tracks did, with him fostering what he describes as a 'visual lingua franca' for electronic music. He's maintained relationships with many of the key Warp artists to this day, noting how he's got his head around different working styles and expectations.

"With Autechre, for instance, there's a lot of discussion that's based on concepts. Conversations about art and the minute details of things. Rob *(Brown)* will be asking me questions about the thickness of a line I'm using. We've worked together for so long now and come so far. I think I've trained them into thinking of design as being about what they want people to perceive an album to be about, as opposed to just what they want on the cover."

He calls out Aphex Twin's Syro as one of his favourite Warp projects. It comes adorned with a long list of all the costs incurred making the record – from radio advertising in France and putting up posters in Italy to the various outgoings incurred in music production. "Ha, getting Warp to give us the breakdown of all of the costs associated with the record, and me telling them they're going to be on the cover, and them saying, 'Yeah, yeah, that's really cool.' And then we actually did it, and they were like, 'Oh, you really *are* doing that?' That freedom we had, it left space for us to be able to occupy and use as we wished. Club culture gave us so much freedom to do what we wanted. In general, these artists didn't want to be on the cover. That wasn't their thing, and that meant we could use that cover space in so many different ways.

"Still," he adds. "It's never going to happen, but I've been trying desperately hard for years to get Autechre to pose for a cover as Simon & Garfunkel. Either that or wear Kiss makeup."

We get talking about what's stayed the same and what's different since then; and how some have brought a face to so-called faceless music. Come David Guetta and albums like Nothing But The Beat and One More Love, and we have effectively turned full circle. There he is, big and loud on the cover. More reminiscent – depending on how the wind and/or his stylist takes him – of a MOR rock star or a kooky new wave kid than anything embedded deep in a dance underground. If he hasn't dressed as Kiss yet, one suspects he could be persuaded. "Faces on covers – not for me," Ian grimaces. And it was The Designers Republic's emphasis on symbolism over faces that enabled so much of his thinking – all of those visual obsessions he'd been storing since childhood – to move beyond record covers and find relevance in other fields.

Much as when speaking with Ben Kelly, there are moments when Ian expresses frustration that he's not always been the one to benefit from his ideas. The sense that others have been handsomely paid for the groundwork he put in, communicating his methods to broader audiences. He's seen it everywhere from TV idents to T-shirts. But also much like Kelly, he eventually turns himself around to accepting that it's how things work.

"There was a time when I was younger and more bothered about this sort of thing, when it was a real issue for me. You had bigger agencies just taking our work and copying it. They were getting the returns for our ideas. I was talking with the guy who started YO! Sushi about a new chain he was opening. And he said he'd wanted to get to work with me because they'd basically copied my style for YO! Sushi. He was talking about this with some pride, and I was thinking, hmm… And someone else told me that a design agency had dumped a load of my Gatecrasher album covers on the table at an RAC rebrand pitch and said they would do it like that." Then the more sanguine Ian kicks in. "I suppose you either do stuff that people like and then get copied or if you're not being copied, it's because no one likes or notices your work. So you have to deal with it in your head after a while."

But it hasn't just been a story of theft or his design aesthetic touching on the broader creative industries without permission. Comme des Garçons came calling when designer Junya Watanabe became so enamoured with The Designer Republic's cover for The Business Of Basslines release by German acid techno duo Hardfloor – or HRDFLR as their name appeared in this case – that he wanted something similar for his latest collection. There's been merchandising work for Issey Miyake (a back and forth with Japanese commerce and communications is a recurring theme). Campaign work for utility provider Powergen, imagining electricity as packaged goods. Imaginative formats for bespoke billboards for Fosters Ice sit in the extensive portfolio, too.

Even if YO! Sushi did the dirty on them, sushi came calling in the end. Ian got to design Moshi Moshi Sushi on the top floor of London's Canary Wharf tower. Coca-Cola, meanwhile, requested that he dream up bottles informed by 'love and optimism' and then convert them into advertising work that appeared across Europe, North and South America, Australia, and South East Asia. Whatever the media, whatever the business category, so much of the conceptual freneticism and unorthodoxy of those early electronic dance covers surfaces in this work.

'The music and club culture stuff has led to so much," he acknowledges. "With someone like Coke, obviously they were thinking about it in a different way than just record labels. They interpreted that work as us being experts in youth communication. I think a lot of this goes back to how we thought about design in the first place. The premise for us was that if you're designing a record cover, it should never look like a record cover. It was a good attitude to start with – a really simple equation. Then if you're working for a gallery, don't make it look like something for a gallery. Same with gaming and so on."

Game on

Gaming ranks in a special place at The Designers Republic in how they've stretched beyond club culture, using those after-dark beginnings as a launch pad to wider means of expression. Namely, their work on WipEout, WipEout 2097 and Wip3out. A futuristic, anti-gravity racing franchise, these titles did much to change the rules of gaming – the look, the feel, the music soundtracking them and the intended target audience for them. Synced with the European launch of Sony Computer Entertainment's PlayStation One, the game's debut iteration landed in 1995. It wasn't the first time electronic music and gaming had crossed paths. Japan's Yellow Magic Orchestra had been sampling arcade games years earlier. And, released in 1989 for the Amiga and Atari ST, Xenon 2: Megablast came with a soundtrack by Bomb The Bass. But WipEout, as that capitalised E gives away, took things to a whole different and more club-informed level.

Nick Burcombe, lead designer at the Liverpool game studio Psygnosis, apparently started cooking up the idea for WipEout while playing Mario Kart with Age Of Love's self-titled trance track playing in the background. "I was trying to explain this to Jimmy *(Bowers, fellow Psygnosis developer),* at the time in the pub, of how excited I was to have this music crescendoing with the victory," he told gaming industry trade website MCV in 2016. Psygnosis being asked to produce a gameplay sequence for the 1995 film Hackers, which featured a slew of dance tracks from the likes of Carl Cox, Kruder & Dorfmeister, Leftfield and Moby, also fed into the planning.

"The target audience they decided on wasn't bedroom gamers anymore," Tim Wright, also from Psygnosis, told Mixmag in a 2024 feature looking back on the 'world's first rave-inspired video game'. Tim was the in-house music producer at Psygnosis. He was schooled in the ways of dance music, so he could contribute tracks alongside the established artists, by being taken on visits to Liverpool clubs Cream and Voodoo. "They wanted people coming back from the nightclubs or on the Sunday morning after the club. To be something that would be in the living room and be a shared experience, rather than a solo thing."

Accompanying racing spacecraft at blistering speeds, navigating sharp turns, jumps, loops and rockets, Leftfield, The Chemical Brothers and Orbital throbbed along in the first version of WipEout. Previous games from Psygnosis had come with cover art by prog rock era mainstay Roger Dean (think wizards and so forth). Drafting in The Designers Republic, with all of their electronic music credibility in tow, was a master stroke. The brief given: 'Change the way computer games look forever.'

The upshot was an agitated explosion of typography, shapes and colours – it was the TDR trademark style whacked all of the way up. It didn't stop with the cover art. Ian and team also had a hand in promotions and advertising that brought a healthy infusion of controversy to the release. The advert showed a young couple, seemingly both dead and with blood gushing from their noses. The copy implied this was the result of extreme G-force, but the parallels with a drug overdose were clear to see. The young woman in the advert was a yet-to-be-famous Sara Cox, later of Radio 1 and ladette repute. Throw in Red Bull as sponsors of a WipEout tour, and you had the 1990s encapsulated.

"We were streets ahead of other people at the time," says Ian, reflecting on The Designer Republic's achievements in a rare moment of bravado. "We had our own vision and were on our own mission. By the time people thought they were catching up with us, we were moving on again, and that's what we were doing with WipEout." The second edition, WipEout 2097, nudged up even closer to clubland. There was a CD release of the game's soundtrack (brief aside: I wrote the – in hindsight, rather over-excited – sleevenotes to this), with contributions from Future Sound Of London, Fluke, Photek, Daft Punk and Chemical Brothers. The game promoted the album, and the album promoted the game. It was marketing perfection. WipEout remains a reference point for designers today. Its enduring legacy and wholesale revamp of gaming design norms are celebrated in the book WipEout Futurism: The Graphic Archives, published nearly three decades after the title's release.

Even if "rave culture helped gaming become cool," as Burcombe told Mixmag, not all attempts to combine them have been so successful. DJ Hero – from the makers of the considerably more popular Guitar Hero – never really found a way to nail the armchair DJ experience, even if Grandmaster Flash, DJ Shadow, Daft Punk, Jazzy Jeff were among the playable characters you could assume the form of. But beyond the games themselves, the integration has taken on different dimensions. In the 1990s, Sony PlayStation hosted chill-out lounges at Ministry Of Sound and sponsored Charlie Dark's multidisciplinary Blacktronica sessions, described by painter Chris Ofili as "part house party, part revolutionary meeting and part social gathering." Dark would later go on to bring club-tinged energy to street running culture with his much-praised Run Dem Crew initiative.

Chris Cunningham, director of Aphex Twin's most freaky videos, such as Come To Daddy and Windowlicker, was drafted in to create TV spots for PlayStation – notably 2003's Mental Wealth, starring a digitally-altered teenage female human/alien hybrid, who uttered an eerie monologue that seemingly had little to do with gaming. All of the tricks of surrealism and body horror that he'd acquired making videos for camera-shy electronic music artists were being regurgitated across mainstream media and for the benefit of a global corporation.

More recently, the convergence between dance music and gaming has also been platform-oriented. Twitch, the livestreaming service that started with roots firmly planted in the latter community, has been building bridges with the former – and thus between the two. Their DJ Program launched in 2024 on August 8. Spotting an opportunity, and as a nod to the Roland TR-808 drum machine, they promptly named this 8.08 Day, drafting in the likes of Jazzy Jeff, Anastasia Rose, Grandmaster Flash and Steve Aoki to share the news. Where previously DJ sets on Twitch often resulted in copyright-related takedowns, muted streams and even bans, now DJs could register and source from a catalogue of cleared tracks, with rights holders receiving a share of the revenue generated by those streams.

Contributing to the company blog, Twitch CEO Dan Clancy enthused: "DJs have a special place on Twitch. Since early 2020, the number of DJs streaming on our service has more than quadrupled, and tens of thousands have been able to build and monetise communities of music fans here. Simply put, the Twitch community loves DJs, and we believe we are the best service in the world to help these creators reach their full potential." What started as dance music soundtracking gaming has moved to more integrated and structural crossovers. And with it, the boundaries between subcultures continue to blur and dissolve. Ideas from the night move further into the day.

Clubs to catwalks

Games, hotels, museums, pop-ups, sushi restaurants, TV idents, advertising, car part superstores – as we've seen, a plurality of sectors across the creative and cultural industries have felt dance music and club culture's influence. The permutations are near endless. The possibilities are enticing. It presents a compelling argument for those who represent the creativity of the night to tub thump for, too. Electronic Beats, Economic Treats, the 2024 report from the UK's Night Time Industries Association, states: 'Electronic music's influence stretches far beyond the confines of the music itself, permeating into fashion, media, film, and technology… The widespread appeal of electronic music is greatly attributed to its dynamic connection with various forms of entertainment. This genre's interconnectedness with broader cultural movements and social change underscores its significant influence.'

Sometimes this interconnectedness is about talent being recognised and steered through from music culture to more commercial settings. When it goes well, the work of this talent in these settings reflects a broader cultural validation, explicit or otherwise, of underground creativity. In other cases, it's more a matter of brands directly commodifying subcultural trends for profit, creating things that appeal to those immersed in – or aspiring to – dance music. Therefore, with less interest in lifting up people in the process. There are different directions of influence and control in this, of what integrity means and determining who ultimately benefits. It's a negotiation of power, with both credibility and revenue at stake. At its core, the question remains: who shapes the narrative, and who profits from these creative shifts?

One of the most apparent examples of this interplay between underground influence and mainstream commodification lies in fashion and beauty. Dance music is an inherently physical thing. As testified through a thousand song titles, choruses, heady chants and sample refrains, it's about how you move, how you feel and, often, how you look. It takes no great leap of imagination, then, to recognise that what's been scooped out of clubland by the multi-billion dollar beauty and fashion businesses ranks among the most significant transfer of ideas. This is route one material – certainly compared to, say, those Halfords superstores or RAC rebrands referenced earlier.

As we've already seen with the likes of Fiorucci, fashion has maintained a connection with dance music since the days of disco. Elsewhere pre-rave, the new romantics look took over suburban UK and the b-boy look took over the world. Another notable example from club days past was London's 'hard times' style – essentially a push against the theatrical excess of the new romantics, leaning toward beaten-up clothes and 1950s touches. What started off-the-cuff, soon enough was processed and packaged.

In a 1982 piece for The Face called A Tale Of Hard Times, journalist, author and all-round 1980s scenester Robert Elms hailed the new look: 'Ubiquitous Levi's worn into holes, sweatshirts serving their purpose and losing their sleeves, leather dominating everything; sandblasted for effect if you're rich and Italian, genuinely old and ragged if you're not. Leather caps, leather jerkins, big boots or no socks and espadrilles. Trousers are getting tighter, T-shirts ripped and torn.' Reflecting on the look – initially a precursor to modern-day thrift style, then entering mass-production by mainstream fashion stores – Elms more recently said: "I think genuinely the biggest reaction to the hard times cover being published is that within about a month there were jeans with rips and holes cut in them on sale in high street shops – and there have been ever since!"

Shifting from clothes to cosmetics, and for a more present-day perspective, a 2022 headline on the beauty, fashion and wellness industries website Glossy enthusiastically proclaimed: 'Rave culture has turned beauty into a giant dance party.' The story goes on to detail how 'rave-style aesthetics' were influencing cosmetics and makeup. Among those quoted, Doniella Davy. Her big break came as a makeup artist on Euphoria, then securing funding from the innovative entertainment company behind that show, A24, to launch the cult brand Half Magic Beauty. One of the products they offer is the Angel Rave lip kit. "I wanted to inspire joy and creativity from the outer packaging, the inner packaging, the colours," Davy said of her dancefloor-inspired creations in another interview, for Glamour.

If Davy's Half Magic Beauty represents the independent (albeit a well-financed one) taking inspiration from night culture, with MAC Cosmetics it's performed at scale. In 2019, they launched a Raver Girl palette. Eye shadows in the set included Happydaze, Mirrorball, Flash-beams, Sly Girl, Wild Card, Fabness, Rave-Cave and 120 BPM. Also in the range is an opalescent highlighter named Glow Stick. The Glossy piece explains: 'Pop culture, DJs with style influence and a light party mood have all helped drive the trend, and flashy looks are making their way from the dancefloor into real life.' While cosmetics and beauty effects have transitioned from disco to daylight for decades, this is it happening with much greater commercial intent.

Another trend in beauty and self-expression taking cues from the clubs has been stickers as makeup. Among the purveyors are new-era beauty businesses like Simihaze, PaintLab and Face-Lace. The founder of the latter, Phyllis Cohen, talked to Glossy about how they'd found a following in clubs: "People take lots of pictures wearing them in clubs, going in and out of the UV light because it's a dense material, and it's neon under ultraviolet light. You can see it across the room in a club." From there, they started to gain wider popularity, not least when singer, songwriter and actress Olivia Rodrigo picked up on the trend. Her 2021 Sour album, which racked up a mighty 385 million streams in its first week on Spotify, had cover art with Rodrigo with her tongue out and face covered in colourful stickers.

Palestinian twins, influencers and DJ duo Simi and Haze Khadra head up Simihaze. You'll find them playing on NTS Radio from Los Angeles, with everything from Dexter Wansel to Soulwax in the mix. Their Rave Pack and Dance Pack eye stickers get promoted via 'rave-themed influencer parties' and partnerships with Peggy Gou. The Glossy story notes that other female DJ/influencers, such as New York City's Brittany Sky and Vashti, collaborate with beauty brands. 'Makeup experts agree the rave aesthetic is making its way from parties to everyday life,' the piece concludes.

When not about makeup and face stickers, it can of course, much as with disco, still be about the clothes we wear. Like beauty, the relationship between dance music and fashion has swayed and sashayed across the decades, from catwalk to street and back again – from premium labels to tracksuits, couture to DIY. It's a relationship that gathered newfound energy as people looked for opportunities for self-expression after the pandemic. Givenchy creator director Matthew M Williams staged a show that had all the hallmarks of a warehouse rave and even called on heavy techno legend Robert Hood to soundtrack it. Fashion trade website WWD duly sought the perspective of Professor Carolyn Mair, author of The Psychology Of Fashion, to explain proceedings: "Fashion reflects the zeitgeist. Uninterrupted music and dancing with a lot of other people over a period of time enables us to lose ourselves in the moment. It takes us away from our thoughts outside the rave."

Matching Robert Hood in proving the overlap of fashion and dance music doesn't need to be the sole preserve of a younger generation of DJ/influencers, another techno veteran to weigh in is Richie Hawtin – though in fairness, with ventures like his own brands of sake and DJ mixer, he's never stuck to the techno script. He collaborated with Prada on live events. But collaboration in this case didn't mean just bowling up to play some tunes. Hawtin instead worked closely with the label's co-creative director, Raf Simons (described as a longtime fan of the Canadian's Plastikman incarnation), on a meticulously curated events series called Prada Extends. Labelled as a Berghain for fashionistas, each session – in cities such as Miami, Tokyo and London – consisted of a pairing of four DJs and four visual artists.

Speaking to The Face, Hawtin responded with characteristic earnestness when asked to consider the intersection of fashion and electronic music. "I think it has been there for as long as there's been both of those art forms. Sometimes it works well, sometimes it's not real or authentic and it crumbles. I think that's what people from electronic music are afraid of, especially the more original techno underground scene, who may argue that fashion and music shouldn't come together. But think about David Bowie. Think about his ideals and personality, and how his music became something more when he fused fashion and his musicality together.

"Think about Kraftwerk," Hawtin continued. "If you strip away the image of the robots, the music is still incredible. But it's what you take from the image of Kraftwerk and how it gives the music even more of a futuristic edge. I was brought up on Kraftwerk, Tangerine Dream and Mute Records, who had a real visual sense. Also, going into record stores and choosing records because the cover looks cool. It doesn't always mean it is going to be cool, but when it looks as good as it sounds, or vice versa, it's just so much more powerful. I've always remembered that in all my musical endeavours."

Elsewhere, with support from Comme des Garçons, Honey Dijon has her Honey Fucking Dijon label. The fashion backstory with Dijon includes hitting the runway for Off-White. With her own label, she speaks of a determination to platform Black queer culture and the roots of Chicago house music in the designs and the communications that come with them. Boiler Room's clothes range now features in the US luxury store Nordstrom. Their spring/summer 2024 collection goes big on utilitarianism – plenty of pockets and functional fabrics. Their T-shirts come emblazoned with arch lines such as: 'This is bedroom DJ level. No pacing, no artistic coherence, no message.' Having previously worked with Céline, Supreme and Stüssy, Benji B became musical and sound director for Louis Vuitton menswear in 2021. Along with Tyler, The Creator, he designed all things sonic for Virgil Abloh's final show, which was eventually staged several months after the designer's passing.

When exploring the more recent connections between dance music and fashion, it's little surprise that many roads lead us to the Korean DJ, producer, singer, songwriter, festival organiser, influencer and entrepreneur Peggy Gou. It was in her blueprint from the start: her first job was as an editorial assistant for Harper's Bazaar Korea. She's played at Off-White shows. Abloh reciprocated by endorsing her Kirin label, funded by Italian luxury fashion enterprise New Guards Group (they had deep pockets, having sold to Farfetch for US$675m). The current collection from Kirin (that means giraffe in Korean) ranges from satin wrap dresses ('decorated with neon contrast piping as a nod to the dance scene') at £400 to black T-shirts with 'Personal DJ' across the chest.

Vogue quizzed Gou about the relationship between designing clothes and being a DJ. "Somebody did ask me if I've approached this in the same way that I approach music, and the answer is, yes, in a way, it is. For me, music is about taste. If I like it, I like it, and if I don't, I don't. That is very hard to rationalise because, if you like something, you just like it... because it's your taste. I'm somebody who always wants more and always wants better. When I'm DJing, I'll go back to the hotel afterwards and think about what I've just done and know that I can do better than that the next time around."

Whenever the critics come at Gou, questioning her craft and credibility, clearly she works harder to achieve. She's the archetypal DJ as brand, and fashion is her ideal partner in climbing loftier heights. What started as ideas and concepts birthed on the dancefloor finding favour with designers and fashion houses, has mutated into something that also brings the DJs out of the night, alongside the ideas and concepts. Prada and Givenchy are brands, but so are these DJs. Not quite their equal, but certainly capable of taking fashion into new environs. The DJ as brand leverages social media at full tilt, presenting luxury to an audience unreachable through more conventional channels. They design their visual identity as much as their musical identity (plenty would scoff more so). They collaborate, they collaborate and they collaborate some more. They craft their narrative, and they sure-as-fuck network. The low-key, out-of-sight DJ they are not.

Roughly about now, many – particularly older clubbers raised on more purist ideals of the selector as someone to be heard but not seen – will be responding with high degrees of dismay. They have a point, and one assumes dance music will continue to be a broad church. But this course of travel, from specialist to crossover entrepreneurship, isn't unique to the modern-day DJ. Footballers, basketballers, models, artists, actors – all are making records, launching tequila businesses, opening restaurants, establishing online courses, mixing up signature cocktails, hosting fitness programs and generally refusing to stay in their lane. Ruminations over the good old days seem unlikely to dent Peggy Gou and co's commercial (ad)ventures.

Looking, not dancing

Another thing those older clubbers would never have foreseen – though may be more willing to spend their money on – also at odds with staying in the predicted lane, is dance music's entry to more hallowed cultural institutions. It's one of the more intriguing transfers, one that would have seemed unlikely in decades past: dance music, from disco to rave, techno to jungle, moving into galleries, museums and exhibition spaces, environments considered more highbrow and rarified.

In big cities worldwide, seemingly not a month goes by without the launch of some kind of curated celebration of dance music. And with it, clubbing and dancing have become a different kind of culture and entertainment. Something to observe, to lose yourself in cerebrally rather than viscerally. There have been examples further back (in 2013, London's V&A hosted Club To Catwalk: London Fashion In The 1980s; a year later in Sheffield, E-Vapor-8 concentrated on the relationship between contemporary art and rave music), but among the first grander scale transportations of night into day was 2019's Sweet Harmony at London's Saatchi Gallery – 10 rooms embracing all points from Castlemorton to Ayia Napa. Also in 2019, Electro, From Kraftwerk To Daft Punk at Philharmonie De Paris came with its own soundtrack by Laurent Garnier; Jean-Michel Jarre, meanwhile, leant out his synths and Daft Punk's Thomas Bangalter and Guy-Manuel de Homem-Christ advised.

Since then, these spectacles have come at us in forms as dizzyingly diverse as club culture itself. They have been broad and designed with mass appeal in mind in the case of something like Amsterdam's Our House. Dubbed the world's first electronic dance music museum, it (past tense, as it closed in 2024) ran the rule over 30 plus years of house music, with a feel that was part interactive learning opportunity, part noisy playground. Others have opted for a more specific angle. Contrary to its name, 2019's No Photos On The Dance Floor! in Berlin was a photo exhibition of the city's techno history, with work from Wolfgang Tillmans, Romuald Karmarkars, Sven Marquardt and Camille Blake. Naturally, it came with a book and a compilation album, with contributions from Alec Empire, Monolake and Ellen Allien.

In Milton Keynes in 2021, the city's main gallery proudly presented Sanctuary: The Unlikely Home Of British Rave – dedicated to the warehouse space that hosted countless raves in the 1990s. Writer and curator Emma Hope Allwood commented: "It wasn't until I became a journalist and came across the flyer for Dreamscape 1 that I learned of The Sanctuary. For me, this project is about doing justice to the youth culture history of MK – a place which is too often unfairly maligned as a cultural void."

The Vinyl Factory: Reverb at London's 180 Studios skewed to audio-visual installations and sonic experiences, with Theaster Gates, Caterina Barbieri, Virgil Abloh, Jeremy Deller, William Kentridge, Jenn and Gabriel Moses contributing; and a space called the Hi-Fi Listening Room Dream No.1, wherein New York artist Devon Turnbull provided a meditative space to listen to 'an evolving programme of unheard music, including exclusive test pressings and studio outtakes.'

The London Museum – also the setting for exhibitions such as Grime Stories and Dub London – has struck up a particularly close relationship with the club Fabric. In 2022, they announced it would become the 'world's first nightclub-in-residence at a museum'. Along with donating a sign created to mark the club's 20th anniversary, Fabric co-founder Cameron Leslie said: "It's great to see the club recognised for the community we have built and the vital role we play in London – as both a cultural space and tireless champions of electronic music as an art-form."

Making connections with community of another kind, move/003 opened at London's Dazed Studio in 2024 with a manifesto to showcase the often obscured role of Black and LGBTQ+ communities in rave culture. Built around the theme of a night out, it offered artistic reinterpretations of 'moments' at the rave. Conversations recorded with DJs and musicians at move/003, such as with Nia Archives, Loraine James and Roska, later appeared on Spotify's GLOW hub – described as an 'equity program for LGBTQIA+ creators'. Kobi Prempeh, founder and curator of fynn studio, who devised move/003 in partnership with DJ/producer SHERELLE, said: "Black and LGBTQ+ creatives haven't just had an impact that defines the dance music scene. Black and LGBTQ+ creatives *are* the dance music scene. When you and I talk about dance music – music that people dance to – it's been born from the people of Black and queer communities. And that story has been whitewashed, misappropriated and diluted time and time again."

Rave culture in the context of art galleries, museums and exhibitions is evidently here to stay, with nostalgia – for your own past or indeed someone else's – holding strong currency (not all of these events have used the rearview mirror, though the appeal of looking back, digging into dance music's multi-textured past, is obvious). Not unlike when dance music and after-dark creativity result in new interpretations of hotels or seep into the advertising aesthetic, this represents an institutionalisation and commodification of what was once a rebellious, underground movement. From abandoned warehouses into a polished, retrospective narrative.

Here, rave culture is recontextualised – its ephemerality, subversion and sense of communal freedom become artefacts for analysis and discourse. The gallery space offers legitimacy (whether requested or not) but detaches the culture from its original spirit of resistance, spontaneity and escape. It's a form of cultural gentrification (note to self: but then so is this book). Can dance music operate in both dimensions at once? Or, in these times of blended experience and hybrid artistry, perhaps it's not a distinction particularly worth making.

Reviewing Carl Craig's Party/Afterparty at the Geffen Contemporary at the Dia Beacon Museum, New York Times critic Jason Farago begged to differ. "Art is the luxury asset that moves in when the party's over," he said of the exhibition, which, at nearly five years in the making, looked to pay homage to the Black creators of dance music through a flurry of loops, lights, pulsating subwoofers and evolving soundscapes. When Party/Afterparty – with accompanying shows where Craig was joined by such luminaries as Moodymann, Kenny Larkin, DJ Holographic, Felix Da Housecat and King Britt – switched to the Museum Of Contemporary Art in Los Angeles, writer Michelle Lhooq picked up on the theme in her Rave New World Substack. In an entry titled The Museumification Of Techno, she ruminates on how 'raving's anarchic freedom, sweaty licentiousness and un-surveilled freedom are antithetical to the codifying authority of the museum.'

Jochen from the Vitra Design Museum remarks that Night Fever received far more media interest than any other exhibition he's been involved with. On the club culture side, meanwhile, there were some reservations to overcome. "We encountered scepticism from some of the people in the music scene. They weren't sure they wanted to become museum-ised," he smiles. "I remember meeting with the team at Tresor and they were like, 'What, you are a museum…'"

Fellow Night Fever director Cat Rossi also considers what it means to marshal the activities of the night into more brightly lit settings. "I think from an architecture, design and art history perspective, that lots of these practices were devalued, or not even known about, because they happened in the nightclub sphere. It means it's important to give it a platform. Something like the Vitra Design Museum can show people these incredible designers that hardly anyone has heard of, highlighting the importance of these kinds of spaces for developing careers and creating opportunities.

"Perhaps that's different than trying to put the latest things from club culture in a museum," she continues. "First of all, that would be kind of impossible. Secondly, those types of fleeting, underground undertakings are not things I find out about, and it's important people like me *(she's referring to her non-"expert raver" status here)* don't find out about them. If they last, at least in specialised circles, if they come to the surface more, that is when we think about what should be preserved, I feel."

On the day I'm writing this, I learn that London's Design Museum has an exhibition on the Blitz club ('the music, fashion and design stories that shaped Blitz – the club, the people, and the movement that transformed 1980s London style') slated for 2025. Also, that A Guy Called Gerald is getting a blue plaque (presumably to be placed where his Manchester home studio was) for penning the 'UK's first acid track', Voodoo Ray. He takes to Instagram to share the news, thanking those who supported him on the journey and sharing a photo of him proudly clutching the plaque. Social media debates inevitably breaks out over whether it was *really* the UK's first-ever acid track. Still, if preservation works for Gerald, perhaps it should work for all of us.

All that's been covered here – and so much that could have been covered here (truly, this is a chapter that mightn't have ended) – we can safely say it grows in the dark. Wherever it ends up, that's where it starts: in a place of independence and unstudied energy. Whether it's makeup stickers, museum exhibitions or new global clubbing destinations, the early signals of these ideas belong not to gatekeepers or the self-appointed, but to everyone who steps on a dancefloor. There are many reasons why ideas that yield here do not come from other sources and settings – from those more officially mediated, managed and funded. Perhaps at the core, it's because of a unique combination of reality (human connection, social purpose, making the most of not much) and a surreality (hypnotic beats, escapism, altered states) at play that could never have come from more contrived and controlled places. Where else but in clubs would you find this unpredictable collision, after all?

Clubs make for subcultural Petri dishes – each different from the other in what has gone in, but all capable of springing surprising ideas onto the world. Though it's unrealistic to think we can control what happens to the ideas that do surface, where they travel and how they are commercialised, what we can think more about is what goes into the dish in the first place: the mix of people, representation and fostering open platforms for expression. With that comes opportunities and licence – the avoidance of ideas spawned from monoculture. Because monoculture breeds monotony, and club culture should never be about that. In the next chapter, we hear mixed views on how equitable the nature of club culture-derived opportunities are these days. We listen to a lot of people very set on improving the situation, too.

4. ALL RISE TOGETHER

It's commonly believed clubs once created incredible opportunities for people

Is this still the case? Operating without a safety net of privilege isn't easy – but people are getting organised

Creativity from belonging

It's not just ideas, designs and product innovations that are pulled through from the night into the light, assuming relevance for those who aren't in tune with every twist and turn of the underground. It is people, too – included among them, those who might otherwise struggle to find outlets for their creativity or pathways into the creative industries. Clubs have served as test grounds for their ideas. Places to forge networks and, just as vitally, the necessary confidence in what they can create and contribute. These (often literally) underground spaces have provided a nurturing environment for progression, either in the sense of developing bigger, bolder ideas in dance music or extending into adjacent creative fields.

You won't find hard data or reliable stats for how many people have used a start in club culture in this way. There are too many junctions and bends in the road for maths to take account of. Too many variables for a clean read. Some will put the dent they've made in fields like fashion, advertising, design, media and, of course, music almost entirely down to the start they got in the night – to the connections made, the sense of self shaped and the visions germinated. For others, perhaps the role was more supporting. Yes, they'd have got there anyway, but the impact of the night was still a factor. At least a rite of passage, and often more.

While there are no stats to support this, there are plenty of stories to bring it to life. I'm told them by many I speak to in writing this book. They come wrapped in vivid memories of occasions, venues and scenes that unlocked doors into the industry or psychological ones into their minds. Such sentiments come from many marketers and music industry people whom we'll hear from through this book, and these are stories they really love to tell.

Tom Dodd is a London-based brand partnerships agent at William Morris Endeavor (WME) – a global talent agency (among many other things these days) that, incredibly, has existed since 1898 and represented such silver screen luminaries as Charlie Chaplin, Al Jolson, the Marx Brothers and Mae West. He affectionately recalls the sense of belonging felt through contributing to the small-but-wholehearted club scene of his native Carlisle, near the Scottish border in northwestern England. For him, the kind of work he'd go on to do with Red Bull Music Academy, Aphex Twin, Fat City, Night Slugs and more all stems from the insight and energy garnered in those under-the-radar spaces.

"Community is the buzzword of every creative agency right now," he starts. "They want to support communities and find little mini-fandoms and different worlds to tap into. What community gives you in creativity is really important. You're in Carlisle or wherever. It feels isolated, but at least you can go and meet people who are into music, and you can all chat and do things together. We create this little community, and that gives us a collective confidence to maybe then move to a bigger place, like London, and do more things and meet more people."

Of course, some dip in and out of these scenes. But for a noteworthy minority, the urge to actively participate rather than spectate comes close to overwhelming. For Tom, it all started with a love for hip-hop and, as time went by, the energised and party-primed big beat genre. "I was 17 and wanted to be a promoter," he smiles. "My dad gave me an old fax machine, and I worked out who the agents were, and I was sending out these faxes, trying to book people. Eventually I was successful. I booked Bentley Rhythm Ace *(big beat stalwarts known for playing live from behind a car windscreen, complete with working wiper blades).* I wasn't actually old enough to get into the club. My brother would let me in the fire exit. But I loved it and I made money from it. I was like, 'Right, I want to do this again.'"

His studies took him to London, where he organised Friends & Family club nights for Manchester's Fat City and Grand Central collectives. "The DJs would fly in from America. I'd pick them up at Heathrow, do the London party, drive them to Manchester, do the Manchester party, drive them back to Heathrow, and they'd fly out." He got more into the marketing aspects of the industry through a job at the sneakers-oriented creative consultancy Unorthodox Styles (first known for Crooked Tongues, a pioneering collectable trainer platform that launched in 2000). Stints working abroad followed before becoming head of music at Shoreditch's Cargo venue, and then as a live agent in and around the grime scene, working with the likes of Night Slugs label artists such as Bok Bok and Girl Unit. From there, as we'll hear later, he moved to roles at Red Bull, followed by WME.

"As weird as it sounds, things in life started to make sense to me in nightclubs," Tom reflects with a smile. "I saw I could make things happen, and I'm just one of endless people who've done it *(running club nights, managing DJs and artists)* for themselves. I didn't learn these things at school. I learnt them in club culture. I saw I could set up a business that puts on DJs and make some money from this thing I was in love with."

Ollie Oshodi is a brand and culture consultant who acknowledges that her own love of clubbing has driven so much of her career in the marketing communications field. She's worked at entertainment-focused creative agency Frukt; as UK managing director of Fader magazine and its well-regarded Cornerstone agency; and as a freelance consultant for the Warm Street agency and Resident Advisor. She concurs that these underground spaces can have you developing at a hyper-fast pace, thinking widescreen, too: "It teaches you things, and quickly. There's all of that entrepreneurialism of putting on the nights, posting content and learning about business, and you need to learn it all fast! I think there's also something about nightlife culture that allows you to, I suppose, dream. To let out your inner child. It opens up new avenues of creative thinking that you can take into other parts of life, whether art or fashion or whatever."

Speaking of Warm Street, I chat to the agency's co-founder Theo Gentilli. Similar to Tom from WME, he found kinship and common ground in a scene, if not quite a niche as Carlisle's, certainly one with a warmer, smaller town feel than London's. "I wanted to be part of the music scene, not just as a fan of it. It was more than just *attending* clubs. I had an insane passion for it and I loved meeting people in that world, especially in Bristol, where I was fortunate to be based at the time. It was a close-knit and respectful scene. Different promoters had their own dates, and we all communicated regularly and tried not to tread on each other's toes. Like, if another promoter had already booked an artist, there was always a conversation before any decisions were made about also booking that artist."

There are principles here that he's tried to carry through to Warm Street. Part of a new wave of culture marketing specialists, the agency counts Lush, Netflix, Nike and Ray-Ban among its clients, developing collaborative ideas in and around music scenes – and trying to do so in ways that tangibly support those scenes.

"There was a real sense of camaraderie despite the competition," Theo continues, further reflecting on learnings from his early days in club culture. "We all supported each other, and that made the experience feel exciting and special. It wasn't just about running events – it was about being part of a community. I think this vibe still exists in Britain today, regardless of the pressures, which is quite rare and exciting."

Few I speak to are ashamed to admit that making some money was part of the package they anticipated from switching from consumer and fan to an active contributor in club culture. It's a skewed sample, for sure (comprised mainly of brand and marketing-oriented people; maybe the responses would be different from those who transitioned to academia or activism, say) but seeking entrepreneurial routes, or at the very least sustainable careers, is paramount. It's not merely about profit but it is about leveraging their passions into something that can support them in the long term. The desire is to build something that's creative but viable, not fanciful.

"The creative industries, when they're working right, should allow you to have a go, shouldn't they?" continues Tom Dodd. "Same with art or music or fashion or whatever. Whereas getting into finance, you have to go through a finance company in the city, and you need to get a degree first, the creative industries shouldn't be like that. It should feel closer to being a footballer – the feeling that anyone can do it and make something from it if they want to."

That said, while they cherish club culture's role in their journeys, plenty I speak to raise questions over how valid this sense that 'anyone can do it' remains today. Also, how effective club culture is as a springboard, in fashioning opportunities in the broader creative industries for those from marginalised backgrounds. Further, they wonder if its role will diminish even more in the future. Dr Luis Manuel Garcia-Mispireta, the associate professor in ethnomusicology and popular music studies who we heard from in the last chapter and who has a particular view on how dance music works within Berlin's creative industries, paints a picture here.

"You can have careers in the industry that spark off of being a raver and your immersion in this culture from early on. You can leverage your accumulated knowledge to become something like a good venue manager or tour organiser. And I think more broadly, especially in a city like Berlin, what's evident is a creative cluster effect. A kind of symbiotic thing where someone might work for a tech company or do something in the creative industries like design or copywriting, but they're also raving their tits off and using some of their income to support a music career that eventually takes off. They're surfing back and forth between music, tech and the creative industries.

"So, does club culture create opportunities? The short answer is yes. But the longer answer adds, 'But for how many of us, and to what extent?' You can make a comparison to asking the question of what sports like basketball and football mean for Black and Brown folks, especially coming out of impoverished neighbourhoods. That a few of them do spectacularly well is not exactly the full story. We could say the same about those from low-income backgrounds in general. I would strongly advise against us getting too carried away with this optimistic thinking."

Working-class zero

Sipping coffee outside a Shoreditch cafe, Tom Armstrong is here to tell me about Common People, the community he co-founded with fellow strategist Jed Hallam. Its purpose is addressing a striking absurdity in the UK creative industries. Paraphrasing Common People's Substack page, significant soft power has been fostered for the country through advertising, music, fashion and design excellence that has taken cues from working-class people and culture. Yet, the possibility of people from these backgrounds actually getting to work in the creative industries has been shrinking at pace. When asked about the power and potential of club culture for democratising opportunities, Tom offers a response that is not dissimilar to Dr Luis Manuel's.

"I would say yes and no," he responds. "Yes, because there are undoubtedly examples, me being one of them, of people who have gone from the club world into the creative industries. Because I think the club world opens your eyes, broadens your horizons and inspires you. And without club culture, there aren't many opportunities for inspiration in your everyday life as a young, working-class person. School maybe is not as engaging as it could be. Or your home life might not be as culturally rich as others.

"So club culture is a way for you to go out and be like, 'Wow, there's another way to live. There's all this opportunity.' You see that club culture is being built from the ground up as a grassroots thing, often by working-class communities. It's a DIY culture and that in itself is inspiring. If I know these people from down the road, and they put this night on, and they're making money, I think I can do that. And that DJ, they're getting paid. And the people who are making the music, they're getting paid. So I'm going to get involved in this, or I'm going to make a magazine. Or I'm going to make some T-shirts and make a mark that way."

Here comes the no: "I think if you spoke to somebody that grew up around acid house, they would probably really believe in that DIY thing because it seems to have been a period *(late '80s to early '90s)* that accelerated all of that. But that doesn't remove the fact that these barriers exist to entry to the wider creative industries. That, with all the will in the world, and regardless of how much passion you have, that's not always enough to overcome the things that stand in your way or how to make proper long-term money."

Tom grew up in east London, holding firm with time-honoured coming-of-age influences of music, fashion and football. He noticed the way people were dressing. "I saw that certain lads would have this patch on their arm. I didn't know what Stone Island was, but I knew it marked you out somehow." He recalls chanting along to jungle track MCs in the primary school playground. He remembers sitting on a coach on a school trip, driving along Lea Bridge Road and past The Dungeons, the club that cultivated a particularly east London take on rave, with DJs like Rob Acteson, Linden C and Rhythm Doctor. "I recall thinking, 'That's what I want to do. I want to be in there. I want to be with those people.'"

Not that he could necessarily spot a link between all of this and actually getting to work in the creative industries, however. He bounced around a bit, working in a clothes store but also getting a little too close to a life of crime and seeing mates serving time. Then he got further, deeper, into music. He started DJing – proto-house, '80s boogie and beyond – and joining the dots between his world and the queer scene through parties such as Horse Meat Disco and NYC Downlow in Glastonbury's Block9. He started picking up freelance writing opportunities for Resident Advisor, Sabotage Times and others, eventually launching The Move, a quarterly music and culture title stocked in Rough Trade, MoMA and the ICA. From all this, he's now carving out a career as a creative strategist with a focus on the fashion sector.

"Club culture was the vehicle that took me out of a pretty shit and negative time, and into something positive, optimistic. Getting into clubbing just opened me up to a whole new world. I remember meeting this person, my friend Sophie. I remember saying to her, 'You're the poshest person I've ever met.' She's not even that posh – just like lots of people in London, living in places like Clapham or wherever. But I'd never been in surroundings where I could meet people like that."

What started as a WhatsApp group has turned into Common People joining the dots between those from agencies, government and education – often in the form of facilitating talks and presentations. "We wanted to find a way for people to connect because we saw that, if you hadn't come from certain backgrounds or gone to certain schools, you could feel isolated in these industries, like you weren't part of the conversation. You experience everything from unconscious bias to outright prejudice."

A 2020 Creative Industries Policy And Evidence Centre report noted that only 16% of people in full-time creative roles are from a working-class background. Incredibly, that's less than in academia, law and finance. So much for the open-mindedness and supposed inclusivity of the creative spheres. Other reports about the creative industries have painted a similarly troubling picture. Data from the Office Of National Statistics reveals that 16.4% of creative workers born between 1953 and 1962 had a working-class background, but that had fallen to just 7.9% for those born four decades later. There's some debate over whether this drop is partly because fewer people identify as being from working-class backgrounds in Britain these days, but regardless, it's a bleak statistic. As Common People put it: 'Due to a combination of social bias, government cuts and unequal access to education, the creative industries are becoming a playground for a privileged few.'

Other research reports and attendant commentary explain more about the rules in this particular playground. 2024 research from social enterprise Creative Access collaborating with PR firm FleishmanHillard exposed how wildly different perspectives can be from those within the creative industries, depending on their background. In their survey, 44% of upper- and upper-middle-class respondents believed social mobility in the UK is easier than ever, but only 16% of working-class respondents shared this view.

It calls out the lack of working-class representation at more senior levels within companies, in particular. Also unsurprising, how much all of this is exacerbated further by intersectional factors, such as race, gender, sexuality and ability/disability. For instance, Black (75%), mixed or multiple ethnic groups (78%) and Asian (64%) respondents are more inclined to observe class disparities in industry access compared to white respondents (61%). Unpaid internships and their favouring of those from wealthy backgrounds remain an issue. As does nepotism – to the degree that 'nepo babies' has entered the argot, and long lists of those who've benefited and subsequently shot to fame litter the web. The Creative Independent ('a resource of emotional and practical guidance for creative people') shared that 35% of industry professionals consider one of their most significant challenges in pursuing a rewarding career to be nepotism and unfair gatekeeper culture.

From educational inequalities to barriers to entry, low self-confidence to limited social and cultural capital, the obstacles to overcome – and which Common People seek to highlight – are manifold. Perhaps most acute among them in the context of club culture is trying to operate without a safety net. Tom expands on this: "As the cost of living grows, especially in cities like London, your safety net shrinks and shrinks. Creativity, thinking creatively, wanting to be creative – there is no time for taking risks on things like that. You think that's something for other people. And really, you could even say it's not even just about people from economically disadvantaged situations these days. It's more that if you're not from a particularly *advantaged* situation, there's just not very many levers you can pull that will help you out anymore."

Against this backdrop, he's understandably wary of an argument that there's a solid through-line from underground dance music to making yourself a career in the more conventional creative industries. Also, to avoid thinking that – as with boxers and footballers – just because some do it, all will do it. In addition, he notes that much of clubland is ruled by those who come from privilege anyway.

"They know how to set up the infrastructures of a business; how to play the game, raise the money. I've heard stories about how people like Judge Jules *(London DJ and promoter from a comfortable background, armed with a law degree)* in the days of warehouse parties and acid house would be pushed to the front when there was an issue involving the police or authorities. He was seen as the legitimate face, and just him being there, with the way he spoke, gave him a power which would not have been afforded to working-class people. That's a great example of the difference it makes."

Ollie Oshodi picks up on the theme that there are limits in how much clubs can act as a levelling force: "There are ups and downs. When you look at some of the sounds and genres that have broken through, things like grime, you can clearly see the DIY energy and the sense that you don't need others. The means of distribution *(less reliance on major labels)* being so much easier and so forth. But when you look more widely, you cannot argue with the statistics – fewer and fewer working-class people are making it into the creative industries. You have to come from a certain amount of economic privilege to have a place among these creative exploits."

As Tom Armstrong sees it, this representation deficit has knock-on detrimental effects on the quality of the creativity itself. "Certainly in this country, club culture has been a test bed for ideas from the streets and from working-class communities that wouldn't have found acceptance through other means or traditional media. You have to be a participant in culture to understand what authenticity and integrity are. I don't think you can just read about it in a book or a marketing paper. You must have lived it, and this is the problem with the creative industries being so dominated by near-identical people. In particular, most in decision-making positions haven't lived it, so they don't recognise it. It just passes them by, and as a result they sign off on poor creative work that doesn't click with ordinary people."

Beyond class

Social class is, of course, only one angle in considering issues of representation in club culture. As we've already touched on, intersectionality (a term now afloat in mainstream consciousness) and the impact of different aspects of identity – such as class, race, gender, sexuality and ability or disability – figure as strongly here as in any walk of life. Clubs, particularly in underground spaces, have historically offered marginalised communities not just a place for self-expression and freedom but also, in some instances, a route to more mainstream success and acceptance. Granted, sometimes only their ideas and innovations make it through, with the originators taken advantage of. But – from artists, filmmakers and designers to singers and producers – in better moments, it can be the creators who benefit, too.

However, the commercialisation of club culture runs a high risk of eroding these opportunities. As wealthier patrons and sponsors become involved, marginalised communities typically have been sidelined, more ghettoised. A growing sense of exclusivity in club culture limits prospects and despite this world's reputation for openness, stereotypes and tokenism are present. Tom Armstrong summarises what's at risk here: "Authenticity, integrity – you hear these words more than ever, but also more than ever, we're not creating the environment for them. How can you achieve these things if everything is monocultural?"

In 2021, I worked on an insight and thought leadership project, Resetting The Dancefloor, for Ballantine's whisky. With a brief to explore fan and industry perspectives on a safer, fairer future for music, its role was to support the brand's True Music initiative (more on that in chapter six) and its pledge to be a 'trusted and leading voice for diversity and inclusion within music culture'. Specifically, the brand was pledging to guarantee lineups and content would represent diverse communities (benchmarking against the demographics of the city where the activation takes place). To ensure artists and DJs are paid and treated fairly (creating a central database of global talent fees to track any disparity in payments). Also, to give fans safe and inclusive experiences (including briefing all venue security on the 'safe dancefloor policy' and real-time monitoring of online content to tackle negative comments and trolling).

I can't speak to how adequately realised these measures have been in practice or the checks and balances involved. However, the thought leadership work itself – despite the tendency for brand objectives to often influence findings in such projects – felt approached in the right spirit by Ballantine's, with a desire not to candy-coat.

I got to write the introduction to the report, shared via the True Music website and partnerships with Mixmag, i-D and others: 'The extent of diversity and inclusivity issues on the dancefloor have caught some people by surprise. Obscured by the positive aspects of music culture, problems have gone unchecked for too long. Dancefloors have always stood for freedom, right? The place where everyone is equal. So what could be so wrong? In truth, there have always been inequalities, but the explosive growth of the industry in more recent times has also accelerated the challenges. From the monocultural 'tech bro' mindset to the treatment of female DJs on social media. The recent rise of the scene's #metoo movement, with a slew of sexual assault claims coming to light. A marked drift away from the people of colour and queer origin stories of much that we listen to on the dancefloor. Dubious door policies and artist (non-)payment practices. Lineups that fail to take account of local music communities. Rising concerns over after-dark safety and accessibility. All of these factors and more mean there is much to work at if dancefloors are to live up to their billing as unbiased, non-judgemental spaces.'

Further into the report, our survey results supported this intro. One in three had experienced discrimination at a music event. Significantly, even if respondents hadn't suffered discrimination themselves, there's a high probability they would have seen others affected by it. An overwhelming 84% had witnessed discrimination on the dancefloor. As the report said, 'Make no mistake, there are issues, and we cannot let the dancefloor's freedom narrative obscure them.'

We got to those Resetting The Dancefloor statistics by surveying 2,300 clubgoers in five countries (Spain, South Africa, Brazil, the US and the UK) and interviewing a number of industry experts and insiders. Also starkly apparent was that intersectionality – that term again –

figured highly in the discrimination. Of those with intersectional identities, 60% reported having been discriminated against at events, with gender and race the most commonly cited aspects of a person's identity that were the basis of this discrimination.

As Georgia Taglietti – a senior voice at the Association For Electronic Music and Laurent Garnier's manager – told us: "The term intersectionality is the most important one. It's the word that lots of people, regardless of the narrative that they are part of, relate to. You can't put these topics into individual bubbles and just leave them there. That's not only inaccurate – that's a wrongdoing."

Honey Dijon, the Chicago-born, Berlin-based DJ, producer, activist and, in partnership with Comme des Garçons, mastermind of the Honey Fucking Dijon fashion line, was also one of those interviewed. She told us about intersectional dimensions of discrimination based on very real personal experience: "I have so much intersectionality to deal with. I deal with being queer. I deal with being a woman. I deal with being a Black woman. I deal with being a Black trans woman. I deal with being an artist who doesn't fit into the mainstream. That's a lot, but then no one is just a single thing.

"I think that narrative *(of dancefloors as places of freedom and diversity)* has been coerced for capitalist means," Honey continued. "Dancefloors are not as diverse as they once were. I think it's a very idealistic way to view things now. This music came from queer spaces and straight people went to those spaces to hear that music. But that's not how it works today."

Steven Braines is another who we checked in with. He's the co-founder of He.She.They, a house and techno record label, fashion label and inclusive party whose website 'about' page starts with the question: 'Can you remember when dance music culture was all about breaking down barriers, rather than building them?' When asked about clubs today, he laughed: "They're meant to be these amazingly diverse spaces, but it's more diverse in supermarkets than in most clubs. And when dancefloors turn corporate, it becomes straight white men booking other straight white men."

Honey continues on the theme that we need to look at all links in the chain: "People in tastemaker positions – those organising festivals, or booking agents, or club owners, or people that impact the lives of artists – they are not diverse. It's pretty much run by cis, heteronormative white men. There are very few women in these positions. Very, very few women of colour. And I'm just about the only artist who is trans and Black and female and headlining."

Straight white men booking other straight white men to play is a pattern that has not gone unmissed by Rachel Brosman, founder of New York City's Support Women DJs. It's an organisation with stated goals of 'getting women DJs booked on stages throughout NYC, which will in turn allow them more opportunities with other event promoters, at more venues, in more cities, and with record labels.'

A case in point of someone motivated both by their love of club culture but also by the things they can see wrong with it, she's based in Brooklyn these days, but grew up in Wisconsin. There she was listening to the likes of Daft Punk, Skrillex and Deadmau5 at school. This might as well have been a million miles away from the nearest club or rave, but that changed when she got to New York City and took a path from more mainstream club nights in Manhattan to distinctly cooler ones in her Bushwick neighbourhood.

There was much to love. Echoing the kind of baptism description many have gone with, she says: "I dived headfirst into that rave scene. It was like, 'This is my place; these are my people; this is my scene.'" But she also spotted a glaring misbalance to be rectified. "I was annoyed with the lack of women I was seeing on stages, whether it was the bigger stages or the smaller stages. And seeing a headliner who's not a guy was incredibly rare. It's still very unequal, and I had an experience last year where I met a group of guys who had their own collective and were putting on events. They were the first people I'd ever met on the organising side. And I was like, 'Um, these are just some average mid-20s dudes. I'm definitely *at least* as smart and determined as them.'"

Something demonstrated by the fact that with zero experience in the dance music industry (she was working in e-commerce for a toy company at the time), Rachel started running nights to further her Support Women DJs cause. "I didn't know any DJs personally, but I put a request out on my *(Instagram)* story, asking my friends for recommendations for their favourite female DJs in New York, and I got a good amount of responses. From there, I DM'd those DJs asking if they would be interested in playing. Then, I asked them for referrals for more women DJs. And pretty much every single one of them has been so supportive. Within a week I had a contact list of at least 100 DJs, and they all loved the idea. I was amazed by how receptive everyone was, particularly as I was transparent that I'd never organised a club night before."

Putting together a lineup that she felt would gel, her first event was a sell-out at Bushwick's Sultan Room. At the time of writing, that was around six months ago. Since then, there have been follow-up parties and a growing ambition for what Support Women DJs can become. "So there are a lot of ideas, but in particular, I'd like it to become a media brand for advocacy. Promoting releases from women DJs, pointing out which festivals do not include women in their lineups, and things like that. A platform that creates awareness."

She talks about the podcast series she's working on, narrating the stories of women and non-binary pioneers in dance music that have got lost over the years. Staging a festival is another goal, along with opening a club venue and a studio space. "A studio for women to record in, because I've learnt that to get real recognition and growth within this world, DJs have to start producing their own music. Otherwise it's hard to get the traction to bigger headline spots. For that to happen, we need to ensure that women feel included in studios. And I've had women tell me that though creating music is meant to be a collaborative process, they've been in a studio with some guys and felt silenced, not really a part of the group. I would love to create, I guess you could call it, a safe space for women to come together and collaborate, to make music to propel their careers to the next level."

There's a lot to change, Rachel acknowledges. It's structural stuff, not just about who's making and playing the tracks. "The clubs are almost always owned by men, which is why their DJs are mainly male. The music industry and the record labels – that's male-dominated as well. We need more diversity within all of these areas. And we need to do something about this frat culture that has become ingrained in clubs in the US in the last five years. This bro culture that's latched on to electronic music, meaning we now have a battle between the more alternative groups that think in terms of freedom to express and to dance, and those that want to get girls and get clout from DJing. So being in it for the right reasons versus the wrong reasons."

With so much ambition to realise, Rachel would welcome commercial sponsors and partners. She hopes they would see the value in backing initiatives that push for change rather than rolling out more banners at the places where bro culture is loudest and, therefore, tacitly supporting it. "Yeah, supporting the things that educate and that come from community. It means a world of difference between people like me being able to do these things and not being able to." She also believes that brands should request the clubs and festivals they support get to 50/50 female-to-male bills and provide greater pay transparency. It's no secret that many lineups consist of one or two artists receiving impressive payments and the remainder expected to 'play for exposure', with this overtly impacting those from more marginalised backgrounds.

Many others are lining up alongside Rachel Brosman to champion female and non-binary representation. Fèmmme Fraîche, best known for nights at London's Dalston Superstore, labels itself a 'debaucherous, frolickingly-fun, forward-thinking club night and community support platform, whose aim is to merge cutting-edge house, techno and art to queer wmxn fèmmmes, butch, trans, NB & EVRy1 in between.' Then there's Femme House. Running workshops across the US, an online academy and a yearly boot camp, they create 'opportunities for women, gender-expansive, BIPOC, and LGBTQIA+ creatives in the technical and behind-the-scenes areas of music.'

Sisters In Sound is a grassroots collective running showcases and workshops in New York, Miami, Washington DC, Puerto Escondido, Puerto Vallarta and at festivals to 'champion women and other under-represented DJs and producers, providing the tools and support for them to flourish, engage with local communities and connect with their sisters around the world.' Dubbed in media coverage as 'Fearless Females Of The Nightlife Industry', from its Brooklyn base, Collective Bae started as a series of events representing women and BIPOC creators. Since then, it's spawned an event production company, booking agency, label, mentorship platform and a consultancy wing.

2022's Progressing Gender Representation In UK Dance Music report by the Jaguar Foundation – headed by Jaguar (Bingham), the DJ and Radio 1 presenter on a mission to 'make electronic music a more equal place for the next generation of creatives and emerging artists' – dug deep into the issue. Themes explored included obstacles to career progression, how marginalised groups are sometimes 'othered' by being given their own rooms or stages to play on, the male gaze and stereotyping around looks and age.

"I think society would quite like us to have our babies and then fade away into the background," DJ, label manager and club impresario Madam X commented in the report. "It's really unfair. There's a double standard and I don't understand it. I think if you still want to DJ, why not? We need to normalise having a career and babies. We need more Anna Lunoes of the world. More Jamz Supernovas and Annie Macs paving the way and removing the fear."

Another who's quoted in the report is Manchester's DJ Paulette (and more from her shortly): "The glass ceiling is there for white women, the ceiling for Black women is underneath it, and it's made of a lot tougher substance. So getting even through to where there's a glass ceiling is twice as difficult."

Among the recommendations in the Jaguar Foundation report was the need to demystify dance music – 'Making it more accessible for anyone and everyone interested. Focusing on initiatives targeted at marginalised groups, especially into more 'malestream' institutions, leading to a more diverse workforce across gender, race and socioeconomic backgrounds. This helps artist representation to be more closely aligned with people who understand them innately, because they share a common identity.'

In the debate around diversity and representation, Theo Gentilli from Warm Street sees issues with the current skew to big ticket, big venue events and the so-called 'festivalisation' of club culture. He believes this shift impacts the community dynamics essential for fostering creative connections in dance music. "If you speak to 10 people in the smoking area at *(Ikea-space-turned-industrial-scale-club)* Drumsheds, I imagine probably one of them would work in the creative industries, and the rest might work in banking, finance, real estate, etc," he says. "That's wonderful in bringing lots of people into the world and, of course, making money. But if you go to the smoking area at Corsica Studios, I imagine probably 60% of those you speak to work in some form of the creative industries. That allows people to build connections, to move forward together."

Without the deep pockets of dance music ventures backed by institutional investors, he's also concerned about reduced opportunities for the type of communities and collectives, which have been the breeding ground for new talent for so long, to continue playing such a significant role. "A friend of mine, Ludo *(DJ Saint Ludo)*, she came up through collectives and community-based things like Rinse FM, Keep Hush and Foundation FM. She speaks to up-and-coming producers today, people sending her tracks, and they struggle to find the equivalent communities and collectives – new ones that resonate with them. It feels like we've lost so much of those things in recent times – we need to get that balance back."

Megasize clubs taking over, 'play for exposure' expectations for all but the biggest names, collectives and communities losing their clout – these developments all bring into question where the next wave of DJs will emerge from. Parallel to this, Theo identifies potential issues with what we expect producers and DJs to have in their professional toolkit these days. Of course, for some, being content creators and influencers, working with brands, and launching their own products is all part of the fun (and financials). But then, not all creative people want to assume that type of multi-hyphenate identity.

"When you think about what makes a successful artist. Either you have amazing music-making abilities, or you're good at thinking like a brand. Of course, there's always been an element of that in music, but never more than now. You're asking people to be real hybrids these days, and what's sad is that we'll lose a whole class of brilliantly creative people who don't want to do that or try things like getting their social following going but don't succeed. You shouldn't always look to the past for solutions, but there are things from back then that we've lost sight of."

Better days?

Anyone I speak to for this book who's over the age of around 40 tells a pretty rosy story when asked about club culture's role in creating and democratising opportunities. Location and personal experiences certainly play a part, but the prevailing message is that, once upon a time, anything felt possible. Clubs were incubators for those on the fringes – people who didn't fit in but had ideas they cared about and thought others might, too. Being involved for the right reasons versus the wrong ones, as Rachel from Support Women DJs articulated it, just didn't seem a major point for discussion.

It's a sentiment I'm on board with. I have no doubt I owe plenty to acid house – how it sparked my imagination and the path it set me on. I can't speak for club culture everywhere, but in the UK, what has always stood out is that, as much as it's the music we love, it's also the alternative world in which to exist. The sense of belonging this provides – and through it, the confidence to see how far ideas can be taken. If this magical knack for unlocking potential perhaps all sounds fanciful and far-fetched on paper, there are no shortage of true stories to hear that chime with this view, and it didn't start with acid house, either.

With rare groove another contender, acid house's clearest UK precursor in terms of a club culture that generated wider creative and entrepreneurial ripples was the so-called new romantic movement (aka the romantic rebels, new dandies or futurists). Surfacing primarily in London at the end of the 1970s, its building blocks were the sounds of David Bowie and Roxy Music, punk's attitude for intense change and a fashion bent that careered from frilly shirts to dressing as Thunderbirds or space Cossacks. It was somehow both down-to-earth and highly elitist. It generated ideas at an incredible pace; ideas that would spread from basement clubs to impact on fashion, retail, music videos, advertising, beauty trends, media and more on a national scale. Dylan Jones' deeper-than-deep dive into London at the turn of the 1970s and 1980s, Sweet Dreams: The Story Of The New Romantics, tells copious tales of those who found their way through club culture. Those beating a path from the Blitz club to jobs at 'yoof'-oriented, early stage Channel 4, or from nights at Le Beat Route to shooting adverts for Levi's.

Writer and broadcaster Robert Elms, who used his start as a new romantics chronicler and Spandau Ballet ally to launch a 40-year media career, describes in Jones' book first seeing his club culture friends finding fame in the style magazines.

"It somehow felt correct, felt like this was our due. I think we had what I describe as the arrogance of ignorance. We had no idea you couldn't do what we did. Britain at the end of the seventies was broken, grey, grim; it's got strikes. Well, you can have two responses to that: you can either get really grumpy or you can put on your best clothes and dance, and that's what we did. There is no doubt that we were fiddling while Rome burned. On the one hand, we were all terribly left-wing, and yet on the other, we were all baby Thatchers. There was an entrepreneurial edge, an individualistic edge, but I would say that in the early days, at least, it wasn't about making money. The first warehouse party that *(later to be Wag club founder)* Chris Sullivan and I did at Mayhem Studios, we didn't even charge people to come in. We had no conception that you could make money out of doing this.

"It was only later on that it started to be about people making money," Elms continues in Sweet Dreams. "For me, it was about being perceived in that small world. I didn't realise that you could reach out to a bigger world until quite a lot later, but I absolutely thought, when it started happening and all my friends started to get famous and be on Top Of The Pops or designing this and doing that, that it was fair and just. Media became important once we started to go beyond our own group. At first, you're doing everything to impress Andy Polaris *(from funk group Animal Nightlife)*, because he's a great dancer on the dancefloor and always dresses well, and you want him to be impressed by you. Then you're doing it to impress *(founder of Smash Hits and The Face)* Nick Logan, and then you suddenly realise actually you're now on Newsnight. It sort of went like that. I never, ever remember thinking, 'This is weird, as all my friends are famous.'"

That same sense of possibility, the 'arrogance of ignorance', swept through the 1980s, seeking other scenes and stirrings in youth culture to connect with. In the acid house sound, a willing recipient was found. The new romantics had the hair and the clothes, but rave had the scale, the inclusiveness and the first influences of a technological decade ahead. Sheryl Garratt, editor of The Face between 1990 and 1995, may have got started a little earlier than acid house, among the DIY culture of post-punk, but she has no doubts about the entrepreneurial potency of 1988 'n' all that. "So many people became swept up in that world, swept up in the possibilities. People phoning their bosses while on holiday in Ibiza and saying they were never coming back; that kind of thing.

"It was incredibly entrepreneurial," she recalls. "It really felt like the barriers were coming down. All of these people feeling empowered to quit their jobs and make money creating stuff for this little scene that had really excited them and that now was growing really, really fast. Whether it was designing club flyers, selling T-shirts, selling drugs, promoting your own club night, realising that there's a trade in these white labels and starting to sell them out of the back of a van. So many avenues. It just felt so liberating. People would be like, 'I'm going to make a film about that'. And the next minute, they've got a Camcorder and they *are* making a film about it. And then people took it further – lots of my friends overnight quit one job, and suddenly had a little agency business doing something to do with club culture. I had friends in Birmingham who started selling tickets for raves up and down the country, and it really set them up to go and do different things."

The quote from Robert Elms raises this in the context of the new romantics, but deeper into the Iron Lady's reign an interesting question that's often debated, never really resolved, is if all of this acid house get-up-and-go can be considered a reaction against then Prime Minister Margaret Thatcher or more a symptom of Thatcherism. "I think it was both, I really do," Sheryl continues. "It's only looking back now that I see we were all pulling ourselves up by our bootstraps and starting our own businesses. We saw it as totally countercultural, but actually we were doing exactly what she told us to do – except in a way she would never have approved of."

Much as the music and the culture surrounding it drove people towards creative and entrepreneurial endeavours, the socio-political milieu was a major contributor, too. In the UK (and, in various forms, in other countries, as well), there were relatively lenient policies, at least by modern standards, around unemployment benefits (a so-called 'dole-ocracy'). There were accessible housing benefits as well, and a squat culture running in parallel. Cities were significantly less expensive places to live in. Ducking and diving was doable, and talk of a required 'safety net' of privilege and wealth, much less of a thing. All of which meant it was considerably easier for far more young people to sidestep life in the everyday world.

"Now?" Sheryl continues. "That idea that anyone can get into a big city, make some mates, start selling a fanzine in the queue of the Haçienda or wherever, make a bit of money and have a good time, I think it's much harder to do. People have to worry about paying their rent, above all other things. And that leads through to when I look at the music industry today, it just looks more middle-class than it did. That working-class thing of some kids just throwing a band together and doing something interesting – there isn't much opportunity for that anymore."

Carl Loben, editor-in-chief of DJ magazine, also saw the ways into creativity that the music culture, combined with a more accommodating world, provided back then. "There was this strong feeling of, 'How can I contribute? What's my role?' They didn't want it to all stop on a Friday or Saturday night, and I do think it provided an entry point for people and, from there, a way into the big, wide world. It was so DIY. The gatekeeping was relatively limited. You'd have people thinking, 'Well, I haven't studied graphic design for three years, but I've got ideas, and I want to give it a go.' The fact that they hadn't adopted all of the rigidness that can come with a degree often gave them a more leftfield outlook in their creativity.

"You can't ignore that back then you could get away with being on the dole for literally years and scrape by while you tried to develop your place and role in dance music," Carl continues. "Now, unless daddy is a hedge fund manager, I don't see how you can do it without having the full-time day job, and that's not necessarily conducive to finding your creativity."

Recording artist Adamski – who will tell us about his brushes with brands and lawyers in the next chapter – was among a number of UK artists to take the fast track to fame (albeit often fleeting) in that period, flashing from life on the dole to Top Of The Pops in a near instant. "I was at number one and on Margaret Thatcher's Enterprise Allowance Scheme, which was really just a bullshit thing to get the unemployment figures down. I got 40 quid a week and was also still getting my rent paid by the council. It was all kind of serendipitous, and I'm sure that's not nearly so possible these days."

When Ben Kelly thinks back to designing the Haçienda, an opportunity that came to him through the autonomous nature of youth culture, he believes it set him up not so much with the right skills but with the right attitude. "I'd never designed a nightclub before, and the clients had never commissioned a nightclub before. But I then took that thinking through into my own design practice. A lot of people choose to specialise in one area of design, one they are comfortable with. I was like, 'Fuck that, we'll do retail, offices, residential; we'll do it all.' There's a fabulous amount of naivety to that, yet it allows for creative freedom, and that's how it all started for me."

These days, Ben Kelly is a visiting professor in interior design at The Royal College Of Art and a professor in interior design at Kingston University. What advice does he give his students? "My advice to them: be independent. Don't be working for the man. Don't be swallowed up by the corporate machine. But that's so much easier said than done. It's a nightmare world out there," he frowns. "How is it even possible to be independent these days, to be rooted in underground club culture and survive? But that's where originality and creativity and the necessary scope for naivety have to come from."

Ian Anderson from The Designers Republic also found direction through music rather than the routine career ladder. He similarly questions whether the same would be possible today: "There was never a phase of me finding my feet working for other people. My design course was being around music and connecting it with the things that excited me visually. People have more access to tools and digital stuff these days, so that's good. But opportunities to actually experiment in these underground club scenes: I think that's much harder now."

While the success stories relayed here can easily sound like isolated exceptions to the rule, the opportunities created by club culture have also taken on more socio-structural forms, presenting rising tide moments for all. Common People's Tom Armstrong contends that club culture once platformed working-class creativity en masse – not just for a lucky few. "Especially from the '90s onwards, clubs legitimised working-class creativity in a way that hadn't existed before. I think the dial turned. Certainly from my frame of reference, working-class culture had often involved appropriating upper-class styles. But this era marked a turning point – suddenly, high fashion and the upper-classes started emulating what was happening at the football, in clubs and on the streets. I think clubs really did that – they made a lot of that happen. Of course, it didn't create jobs for everybody but it did create visibility."

For The New Statesman in 1988, Cynthia Rose reported on a similar twist of the dial, though one more specifically focused on Black culture and entrepreneurialism. In a piece titled Jazzie B And The New Black Economy, she tells the then-nascent story of Hornsey's Trevor Beresford Romeo, aka Jazzie B. The founder of the north London production outfit, band, label, club and record store, Soul II Soul, he and others on the soul scene such as Trevor Nelson – then at pirate station Kiss FM and running his Madhatter parties – were, as Rose explained, establishing 'a completely alternative entertainment sphere; one which is powered by Black aesthetics.'

She goes on to note the reluctance of Jazzie B and co in relying on the support of established systems or media. 'It's unsurprising Jazzie B should feel ambivalence about the media. Truly interracial and composed of the young and the officially marginal, London's entertainment underground is rarely represented in the media. It supports its own cottage industries – booties *(bootlegs)*, clubs, mixes, pirate radio and boutiques. From fanzines through to semi-slick mags such as Soul Underground or Straight No Chaser, it has started to foster a leisure press of its own. But the single mainstream commentator to comprehend its size and importance has been comic Lenny Henry. His pirate DJ character Delbert Wilkins benefits from primary-source smarts: Henry is the chairman of pirate Kiss FM, which claims an audience of 200,000.'

Back up the M1 and M6 again, from London to Manchester. The UK has produced many influential clubs over the last 40 years, but perhaps none that has communicated itself as strikingly and unmistakably as the Haçienda. Since marketing, communications and the connections clubs have made with the outside world are key tenets of this book, it's no surprise that we find a wealth of material here. One person who was deeply embedded in everything that unfolded at the Haçienda is Mike Pickering. Slurping tea from a mug with PICKERING emblazoned across it, he now lives in Kent, on the English south coast, but his head is very much still in the story of Manchester.

It's all tied up in his own narrative, too. He fanatically bought records from his pre-teen years onwards – "I was always the one who brought along the box of seven-inch singles." He first met Rob Gretton, later to be co-director of Factory Records, aged 16. They were both Man City fans and, at an away game against Nottingham Forest, found themselves hiding from a mob of skinheads. "We were in a bush in someone's garden and it was the beginning of a beautiful friendship, you know. All the way through to when Rob died *(as the result of a heart attack in 1999, aged just 46)*."

In the years soon after, Mike started a fanzine called Modern Drugs with Martin Fry, later of ABC. Reviews of early Joy Division gigs were a staple feature. Then, figuring punk had blown through, he left town to work in restaurants in northern Holland. He would meet up with Joy Division and manager Rob Gretton whenever they headed to Europe. Around the same time, he got in with a bunch of people who'd squatted in an old waterworks in Rotterdam. Mike and a friend cleaned out the pigeon shit from one of the larger rooms, built a stage, moved in a generator and started a club called Rotterdam Must Dance. They persuaded plenty of the Factory roster to come over and play (New Order's third gig was there); also Human League and The Cure. "Rob was visiting one time," explains Mike. "And he said, 'This is fucking great. It's amazing. You've got to come home. I've got an idea.'"

That idea was the Haçienda, where Mike soon found himself booking the bands and DJs. He was also in an outfit called Quando Quango, described as Fela Kuti meets Kraftwerk and best known for the driving electro track Love Tempo, which reached number four on the US Billboard Dance Chart. While Quando Quango (there was also a follow-up project, the more house music style T-Coy, and the fabulous track Cariño) never really made much of a dent on the UK, it was a different story in the clubs of NYC.

"Larry Levan was playing us and so was *(Danceteria resident)* Mark Kamins," says Mike. "And so I found myself, this young scally from Manchester, right in the middle of the Paradise Garage, Danceteria and Fun House. We played live for Larry at about four in the morning once. I'm like, 'Wow, this is absolutely brilliant and there's not even a fucking bar.' We were thinking that this is how we want our club back in Manchester to be. No door policy and definitely no DJs talking on the microphone."

Back at the Haçienda, Mike channelled this experience into something relevant to their city and their culture. He refined the expectations put on the DJs to something closer to what he'd witnessed across the Atlantic and, indeed, he disconnected the microphones. Struggling to find DJs who understood what this underground NYC style of playing was about, a next chapter began. "So I figured I better start DJing myself," he says. "And I guess that's an example of what clubs could do back then: these opportunities that open up for you. Suddenly anyone could do what they wanted – or that's at least how it felt. Punk changed the attitude and then clubs and dance music changed it even more. It had felt such a grey, dark place and then this other world lit up for you – a bit like a dancefloor really. And The Smiths, New Order, The Stone Roses, Happy Mondays, all these bands that are so important in the city's history, they all met at the Haçienda. Everyone hung out at that club. It was a meeting place for creative people. In fact, it *created* creative people.

"Everyone talks about the Haçienda from '88 onwards. But from '82 to '88, it was pivotal in Manchester's cultural history," he continues. "All of that led through to things like the dean of Manchester University saying they'd had the biggest ever intake. Tourism, too. Before that, no one in their right mind wanted to go on holiday to rainy old Manchester. Then it hit a next level when ecstasy arrived. It sometimes feels like an over-told story now, but it remains true. You'd have bankers, doctors, bricklayers, football hooligans, clothes designers, all different walks of life wanting to be part of this thing that let you think about yourself, about who you could be, differently."

Following the Haçienda years, Mike co-launched the hugely successful Deconstruction dance label, founded the equally successful outfit M-People and, in his A&R capacity, signed the even more successful Calvin Harris. Next to writing a book with journalist and one-time pop Svengali Paul Morley, Mike claims to be easing into semi-retirement. He's not exactly inundated with brands that want to work with him, he jokes, though adding, "I might get Saga Holidays." On the few occasions he does DJ, he avoids playing purely for the, as he calls them, "gravers". Meanwhile, the lasting impact of those distant days in Manchester continues to astonish him. "I go back up there for the match or whatever, and there are murals about that time in the Northern Quarter. There are things painted yellow and black. I walk into a bar with my son, and I'm painted on the wall! My son is like, 'Fucking hell…'"

For a while, Mike says, he was concerned that Manchester would get too locked on the rearview mirror perspective, "hooked on nostalgia, too much like how Liverpool is." But he sees progress – be that the very cool White Hotel venue, situated out in Salford's industrial wastelands, the far more mega-scale Warehouse Project, or new club Amber, which promises no phones, local DJs and five-pound door fees.

Asked to pinpoint a primary difference between clubland then and today, he responds, "It's a tough phase. Obviously, that's partly because it's so expensive and just a bit of a fucked up world right now. But the clubbing fraternity needs to take some responsibility too. Maybe this just sounds like an old man speaking, but all the big DJs from my era had a club night. Danny *(Rampling)* at Shoom, me at the Haçienda, Graeme *(Park)* in Nottingham, Frankie *(Knuckles)* at the Warehouse in Chicago, and so on. Everyone had a night. Now, everyone does an hour and a half, and there's a lineup of about six stages. People need to think more about clubbing in the sense that we did: places where you shape your community or tribe. Where you develop your sound, not duplicate everyone else's sound, playing the same fucking records you hear in every club, in every city."

"39 years!" Staying in Manchester, I'm speaking to DJ Paulette, who's reflecting on how long she's been in and around dance music (and one assumes you can add another 10 years or so of loving it as a kid, listening to soul, funk and disco). Published in 2024, her book, Welcome To The Club: The Life And Lessons Of A Black Woman DJ, looks back across those years. It talks about her career and changing times in the music industry. She explains the challenges of cracking through those ceilings she mentioned earlier, and the impact of race, class, gender, sexual orientation and location. "It surprised a lot of people," she laughs. "It showed people who I am. When Gilles *(Peterson)* read the book, he said, 'Wow, I didn't even know you'd been married.'"

Also in Welcome To The Club, she remembers the time she was told, "No club will ever book a Black, female DJ with grey hair." Regardless, she battles those odds week by week. Not long before we speak, she's at Amsterdam Dance Event, firing up a multi-generational crowd. She played back-to-back sessions with The Blessed Madonna at this year's Homobloc party. There are shows on 6 Music, Apple Music and Manchester's music, arts, culture and community station Reform. Track back across those 39 years, and early on, she got to spin tunes at Number 1 Club, one of Manchester's first gay nights. Later, she worked in PR for Mercury Records and A&R for Azuli and Defected. She's played at clubs in countless countries and whole seasons in Ibiza.

All of these dance music moments and experiences have played a part in shaping her, but Paulette cites DJing at the Haçienda's Flesh night as the most instrumental. Running from 1991 to 1996, hosted by promoter Paul Cons, it was a night which updated attitudes to queer clubbing in the UK. Inclusive and carnival-esque, it was important to clubbers – and important to Paulette, too.

"For somebody like me, a young Black, queer woman in the north of England, getting into the music industry felt like a series of shut doors," she says. "No one in London was letting me in. I did get work at a local radio station *(Piccadilly Radio – she sprayed her application with CK's Obsession perfume to get noticed)*. But really, DJing at the Haçienda gave me the true way in. It opened a portal. Suddenly, all of these record labels that didn't want to know me were keen to talk and send records to me."

It was also, Paulette says, about the blend of people you'd cross paths with in the club. A mix of creative minds combined with an egalitarian spirit. "You got to meet people and make connections in clubs then. It wasn't as VIP as it is now, where you don't get influential people mixing with your ordinary, everyday punters. It wasn't so velvet rope in the late '80s, early '90s. Everybody was on the dancefloor together. So you would get *(performance artist, club promoter, fashion designer)* Leigh Bowery on the dancefloor with *(Pet Shop Boys)* Neil Tennant and Chris Lowe and *(fashion designer)* Pam Hogg, and then the people that worked at *(iconic fashion store)* Geese. But then also all of the people from the city council, all raving together on the same dancefloor."

Flesh, she rightly points out, is a club that often gets pushed to the fringes of the Haçienda narrative ("Which is crazy, not least as it actually made the place money, unlike most other things going on there."). Its role in opening portals wasn't confined to the DJs, though. Designers associated with the club, like brothers Trevor and Craig Johnson, played a pivotal role in communicating Flesh's bold reclamation of gay slurs and slogans like Queer As Fuck, which featured across flyers and other materials. The club's famously sharp and spiky flyers also mixed up football and queer culture in unexpected ways. One event was dubbed Flesh FC and carried the strapline: For leftfooters and shirtlifters. Since then, the Johnsons have become mainstays of Manchester's design scene, with a client list that includes Manchester United, Manchester International Airport, Granada Television and Manchester City Council.

This all gets Paulette thinking about Swing, the hairdressers in the Haçienda basement. Complete with Factory Records catalogue number FAC 98, it was another signal of club culture's then potency for joining the dots and fostering opportunity across multiple fields. In an interview with Electronic Sound, chief stylist at Swing, Andrew Berry, explained, "Once we got it up and running, I'd spend my days in the basement cutting hair, then go upstairs and spend my nights DJing in the club."

But clubs now? In the context of the change and flux we've been hearing about? "It's depressing to say, but it does feel harder these days to use these worlds as launchpads. I mean, it was incredibly hard being a female DJ when I started, but it's a different kind of hard today," Paulette reflects. That said, she points out the risks of getting glued to a purely retrospective framing of the problem. While a creatively-minded collective 30 years ago might have centred their activity around the physical setting of a club night, today it's more likely to be a hybrid – a digital platform complemented by occasional events.

"Everything that finishes is always replaced by something else," she reasons. "While nightclub culture as we know it might be struggling, we have to keep our eyes open for how the next generation is going to develop it. When raving started, phones were attached to the wall, and now they're the thing that is filming, recording, connecting. That kind of connectivity is immensely significant. And people are going back underground, too, away from the huge events. They're getting inventive with small spaces and outdoor spaces. Or maybe they're doing a house party and streaming from it, doing the radio from the toilet, or whatever. So they're doing two things there. They are doing a small, intimate thing but putting it online to create a bigger following. So, at some point, in some way, maybe it will explode. Perhaps it will find enough of a following to become a tent at Coachella, or wherever."

All is not broken

As DJ Paulette has just capably described, where there's a will, club culture invariably finds a way. We've heard about the past's great opportunities and the challenges around representation and access that now weigh heavily on what once felt like a less encumbered underground. But while there are resonant lessons to be drawn from those earlier decades, the clock is not turning back. It's also worth remembering that though club culture may have created opportunities then, society's biases and power structures in those long-gone days pushed very hard against social mobility indeed. A rose-tinted perspective, therefore, is ill-advised.

In the spirit of optimism, it's time to hear more from those within club culture and dance music who believe that an abiding energy source prevails – offering a near-unique opportunity for talent (and their ideas) to emerge from the underground. True to its remit, the Night Time Industries Association (NTIA) remains steadfast in its conviction that clubs are a cornerstone of cultural and social change. Its report, Dance Music's Impact On Communities And Culture, explores how various scenes continue to intersect with and shape broader culture.

'At the very forefront of clubbing's avant-garde, interior designers and architects experiment with new VR and AR equipment, light shows push AV limits and musicians innovate sonically, collectively conjuring sensorily spectacular environments. While not every venue exists at this bleeding edge, or has the cultural significance of New York's Mudd Club or Manchester's Haçienda, clubs still play an important role in their city or town's creative scene. As well as being places for creative people to congregate, the clubs themselves operate like participatory theatre productions. Amid the synthetic sounds and under artificial lights, grassroots creativity thrives. Today's club photographers become tomorrow's high fashion photographers, club flyer designers become creative directors, video makers become directors, fanzine writers become culture journalists. For a generation paying off student loans, often required to take unpaid internships, clubs provide de facto creative apprenticeships for those who will go on to shape the next generation of mainstream culture.'

That's the industry's party line, but there's a similar belief in club culture's ability to find new ways in the face of adversity from many of those I interview. Next to being a photographer, curator and responsible for the excellent What We Wore book celebrating the history of British street style, Nina Manandhar is a fashion communications teacher at Central Saint Martins. She believes clubs and the collectives that form around them still offer something unparalleled. "It's harder, for sure, but I think there's still a space for people to put on a night, to build a community, to make money, to create their ecosystem. You can take more agency. You can make some money for yourself. That's empowering, and that's what I think is so important about these cultural spaces. The potential to build something, to create a network and to all rise together."

She cites examples such as east London's PDA parties, creating a safe and motivating space for the queer and non-binary POC community. Also, the No Signal radio platform and accompanying night Recess, examples of club networks elevating Black British talent. "It's about building a collective, really, isn't it? You come together as a communal force. Through it, people are doing styling, making music videos, DJing, doing things in the industry. It's strength in numbers. Not just you against the world but you and all of your like-minded people. It's that collective spirit that enables people to carve out space. And then you can invite people into your space. You have the licence. You are the hosts. You can build contacts in the industry. You can build your clout and your status."

As part of her work with year two students at Central Saint Martins, Nina asks them to design a public-facing event. She remarks that they almost always opt for something set in the night. "It's incredible how many of them choose a club as the type of event – so much so that I think I'm going to have to discourage it in future," she laughs. "But it just shows the power of club spaces. This sense that it's what unites them. People might be working across different mediums, but the club spaces are where they all come together. You network there and there's a kind of collective joy to it all. Also, this sense of, 'How can this be used for me, positively, to build up my career?'

"I think people are still willing to take those risks, even those from disadvantaged backgrounds," Nina adds, referring to the lower stakes involved in these ventures. "It feels different to the risk of, say, deciding you're going to become a fashion designer. That's a very long path to go down. Whereas with starting a club, it's more about seeing what happens. And you can still find spaces, even if you have to look in different places these days."

While acknowledging that opportunities for those from working-class and minoritised backgrounds have diminished in many areas of the creative industries, Ollie Oshodi still sees promise in the resilience and vibrancy of club culture. She also recognises the confidence that a new generation exudes in what they can gain from this culture. "It feels like a generational change thing," she says. "A new generation using all of this after-dark experience they're gaining, their creative projects and side hustles, increasingly confidently. Probably out of necessity, they're maximising it; making a selling point out of it."

The absence of spaces for club nights in gentrified cities, coupled with the heightened risks of operating without a safety net of privilege, all count against creativity flourishing. But other factors push the other way. Whereas once much was left to luck and chance, to the assumption that 'one thing would lead to another', now the systems, resources and means of support are on a whole different level. People and their communities have had to get organised if they are going to make things work – and organised they have got.

Many I speak to reference Funding With Mina, a platform created by London-based DJ, producer and Earth Kicks label founder Mina in the wake of the pandemic. Each month, she highlights funds, grants and opportunities to help people catch a break in the dance music industry. These missives are backed up by workshop sessions designed to demystify the application process. Another go-to resource is The White Pube, known for its extensive library of successful funding applications to learn from. Resident Advisor also contributes with Doors Open Jobs, a not-for-profit platform for electronic music jobs and opportunities. Their mission: 'By expanding access to opportunities and resources, we aim to drive equitable change in the community – breaking down barriers and diversifying the music industry, one initiative at a time.'

Elijah, the UK grime scene polymath, is another big organiser and advocate. Among his endeavours has been a podcast series with Crack Magazine and the BIMM Institute Bristol, dedicated to more imaginative ways to set artists on successful paths. His Yellow Squares format on Instagram and Twitter has him dispatching concise and frequent proclamations primed to keep underground DJs, producers and promoters on track and motivated. These have made their way onto billboards, too. Interviewed about Yellow Squares for the street media company Build Hollywood's website, he said: "I'm trying to be less abstract about the positive change that I want to explore, and actively doing it. Like when people say music brings communities together – how? With this, I can post something and someone will come back straight away. It's not theory."

Black Artist Database is another support system consistently and positively brought up in my interviews. Originally launched in 2020 as Black Bandcamp, it rebranded the following year but maintained its volunteer-led focus on compiling a vast list of Black-owned record labels, DJs, producers and artists. Adding workshops and partnerships to the project, co-founder Niks Delanancy – who also DJs as NIKS – described the initial inspiration to Jaro magazine as the "structural mistreatment of Black folk in the underground electronic industry."

Jamz Supernova is among those keen to praise the efforts of the Black Artist Database. "They've been really instrumental, such a good talking point in the industry," she says. "Questioning things but, importantly, also offering solutions." You might know Jamz (aka Jamila Walters from southeast London) for one of many things. Her DIY Handbook podcast, recounting the stories of how musicians and other creatives have navigated modern world challenges. Her award-winning shows for 1Xtra and BBC 6Music. The diverse sounds (from techno and UK bass to a gamut of international genres) of her Future Bounce club night and label, and her globe-trotting DJ exploits.

Ask her about club culture's role in creativity and the creative industries more broadly, and she draws from a recent trip to Berlin. She played there with Rafiki, a collective of DJs from South and East Africa and the Balkans, who curate an Afro-diasporic mix of sounds, jumping from house and breakbeats to amapiano and gqom. "I could see it all there," says Jamz. "They *(Rafiki)* all work in different aspects of the creative industries and it all sprung out of nightlife. A love of dance music brought them together, but their skills reach out across production, editorial, social media, strategy and all kinds of creativity.

"See, when you go back to the origins of starting a club night, you literally have to learn how to do everything," she continues. "From the aesthetics of the night, the sound, the social media, doing adverts, designing things. Throwing a party is a very hands-on thing to do. Generally, you can't afford a big team, so you do all those roles yourself."

This is all writ large in the earliest days of her own dance music backstory, too, first running some nights called Edit with friends in and around Dalston, east London; also a Kaytranada 'unofficial after party' in Brixton. "One of us was running a company selling unusual laces, so he knew a bit about creating brands. One of the DJs was good with photography. Someone else worked in a bar and knew a bit about managing people and timelines and things. It was all very DIY and so much better for it.

"It teaches you entrepreneurialism. Resilience, too. Okay, all your friends will show up for the first event. But the second and third, they can be the hardest. Get to fourth and fifth, and maybe it's all going somewhere. But in all of this, you are putting yourself on the line in a way you won't be if you're at university or in a regular job."

She agrees that many conventional venues are less willing to take risks these days on fresh faces in club promotion, but that there are always alternative options surfacing (she mentions south London's Carpet Shop – which did indeed used to be a carpet shop – from the Corsica Studios team). She affirms that good ideas coupled with boundless energy continue to find a way through. This means that club culture can still cultivate egalitarian opportunities and that if we can't see them, perhaps it's because we're not looking in the right places.

"I think so. It's there," she continues. "Plenty of the places I play are put on by those who could be described as marginalised. There is still space for it, and of course, it is still important. But I guess it might be harder for people to see. Things tend to end up in their own little ecosystems. For instance, you might not think that Black people are in clubs raving to dance music. But they are – it's just not happening in the clubs that you are going to. Someone like Supa D *(Hackney-based, house to amapiano DJ who made a name for himself on Rinse FM)*, he's selling 2,000 tickets for massive events. Or others might think, 'Oh, I don't see many South Asian people out at clubs.' But there's a massive and growing scene dedicated to a South Asian take on raving."

A plus point to clubbing in a digital age, Jamz feels, is that while we might not always know where to find these facets of club culture that operate outside of the mainstream, they're increasingly finding their way to us. She cites that a number of Boiler Room performances that have attracted significant interest have included a strong aspect of cultural heritage. One she mentions is Panjabi Hit Squad's boisterous debut from Southall. Also, the shows from Lady Shaka – who's of Māori, Tahitian, Cape Verdean, Tokelauan and Samoan descent – flying the flag for the Pasifika community. Meanwhile, Nooriyah's Boiler Room set caught the attention not just through her focus on music from SWANA (the South-West Asian and North African regions) but by her father serenading the crowd at the start. It has since notched up a mighty three million streams.

"It's all very related to identity," Jamz says. "Like, 'I am all of these things, and I'm going to translate them into my DJ set.' These things are starting to really appeal and will more and more be part of the mainstream conversation. And that's an advantage of everything online – being able to see kinds of representation that would otherwise be invisible to you. You look at those clips and you see these other people playing this music, and then you look in the crowd and you see that there are people who are not from the same culture as the DJ and they're really having it. That encourages people to feel they can get involved."

Event promoter and mentor Ahsan-Elahi Shujaat is another who's experienced the upsides of how digital platforms have made the world smaller, illuminating different corners of club culture. Next to Ahad Elley (DJ and music producer), Dhruva Balram (journalist and creative producer) and Provhat Rahman (music producer and founder of the Daytimers art and music collective), he's behind Dialled In, an organisation dedicated to furthering South Asian talent – both on stage and back of stage. He's speaking to me from Nepal, where they are programming events with Boiler Room.

"I'm seeing firsthand the potential to expose more people to aspects of club culture they'd never have encountered before," he says. "The world is getting infinitely smaller thanks to technology and platforms like Boiler Room. You can now see what's happening globally – whether it's something niche, fun, or unexpected – and think, 'Wow, I never knew that.' For example, discovering that Uruguay has a vibrant scene or that Mongolia's club culture is about full-on, amazing techno. You watch it, take it in and then feel inspired to create something that speaks to you. And that's what we're doing here *(he's also headed to Nepal, Bangladesh and Pakistan with Boiler Room).*"

We'll be back with Dialled In later to hear about their work in education and mentoring. Here, Ahsan is telling us about their events and parties ("Though ultimately it all links up – they support each other."). He's among those who believe that club culture still packs the power to launch people to sustainable success in music and the wider creative industries.

"I joke about this with my mates all the time – I think putting on parties is like doing an MBA," he smiles. "Absolutely. There's no worse feeling than losing money, and someone I used to work for once said to me, 'Never trust a promoter who's never lost their own money.' The vast majority of people I know who are doing amazing things in the creative industries started out putting on parties. Some of the most senior people in agency land started out as promoters and now they're running agencies with turnovers of five or six million. It's such a common thread. There's definitely a synergy there."

The nature of that synergy with the creative industries? "I think the whole lifecycle of a marketing campaign can be mapped onto organising an event. I say this to young people I work with all the time. You see all the different facets – there are the creatives who want to be the stars, the DJs, and that's great. Then there are people really into the design side, even if they've never touched Photoshop. There are those drawn to spatial design who end up working on projects like National Theatre productions. And then there are the organisers – the ones who discover, through putting on a party, that they're basically project managers. If you can manage 15 people, run a big event and look after the safety and wellbeing of 3,500 attendees, you can probably handle just about anything. In all of this, it teaches you how to work with people and how to procure a service. Booking a DJ or a live artist – there's a process, a negotiation. It teaches you to lean into your strengths. There's a weird addictiveness to putting it all on the line – and doing things in club culture always feels like that."

Dialled In, seemingly like so many forces for change in modern club culture, has its roots in the lockdown, and the pause for thought that came with it. While there had been the much-touted so-called 'Asian underground' scene in the UK in the 1990s – exemplified by artists like Black Star Liner, Talvin Singh and Nitin Sawhney, and club nights such as Outcaste and Anokha – it had faded away. Reasons given include that the novelty wore off and the media went chasing new trends; also that after 9/11 doors to the mainstream started to close for Asian artists. This meant, for the Dialled In team: "There wasn't really anything in the underground club space to progress. For us later millennial generation and Gen Z people, there wasn't really an immediate precursor to build on. We were starting afresh."

A mere four months after first cooking up the idea of Dialled In, they were running their first festival in Walthamstow, east London. Daytimers and Pxssy Palace hosted stages; Ahadadream, Aisha Mirza, Almass Badat, Aroop Roy, Auntie Flo, Bake, Chippy Nonstop, Freshta and Haseeb Iqbal all played. As did SBTRKT and Skrillex. "We were wondering if anyone would buy a single ticket, but then it sold out," Ahsan recalls. "It was all very raw but it definitely resonated with people. We saw what they were getting from it and that pushed us on as a collective to think about what else we could do."

Since then, there's been further festivals, a classical concert at the Union Chapel, a stage at Printworks and the growing Boiler Room collaboration. Ahsan says there's much more to come. Among their priorities is striking a balance: creating spaces where South Asian creativity can thrive within its own community while also improving representation in mainstream club culture.

"It's great that we can do these events where it's centred on our community first and foremost. That's beautiful for people, and creates a sense of identity and belonging," Ahsan acknowledges. "But we don't want to monopolise those artists. I don't want any of these artists to be forced to only play South Asian focused events – that would feel so disappointing. We'll never stop doing our own stuff, but we definitely want to be able to support and develop people so that they can go off and have success on bigger stages. We almost want it to be like they don't want to play for us because they're too busy, and that it's kind of a problem if they do have to come back to play for us. I want people to go and sell out Drumsheds and places like that. That makes everything better for everyone to be able to do that."

Part of the challenge right now in clubland creating opportunities, Ahsan reasons, is it's the 'middle' that's getting squeezed. "Wherever I go in the world, if you have a niche, something community-based, people are bought into it – they'll come in droves, religiously supporting everything you do. If you're operating at the larger end of the spectrum, backed by a global brand, economies of scale suggest you'll probably be alright. But the more interesting mid-level stuff is suffering," he explains, commenting that Fabric is a rare exception to the rule. "People have less disposable income, and there are fewer places to go out. Even venues like The Warehouse Project need to worry about this. They will eventually need younger promoters – new energy. They'll need the creativity of these people, moving that creativity from smaller rooms to bigger rooms. Without that, we hit a dead end."

Ahsan, like most I speak with, sees an industry that, for all the lip service paid, remains painfully slow to change. If that makes for predictable if depressing reading, what he's witnessing from an emergent generation of clubbers is quite the opposite. "On the one side, Gen Zs have been given the worst hand imaginable, but in a countercultural creative sense, it's fucking sick out there," he enthuses. "If I was younger, I would be going out all the time. There are so many things happening that I wish were available when I was younger, so many good collectives and communities. So I think things have changed. Just not as much up the bigger, mainstream end of the scale as the senior people there may wish to believe; or may wish to give themselves a pat on the back for."

In terms of a collective embodying positive change, Jamz Supernova sings the praises of Pxssy Palace – a name that comes up repeatedly in conversations for this book. Widely regarded as an exemplary model of club culture's progressiveness and reinvention, the collective was formed in 2015 and describes itself as championing 'intentional nightlife, celebrating Black, Indigenous and people of colour who are queer, intersex, trans or non-binary. We provide space to dance, connect and engage, whilst encouraging consent, sexual freedom, pleasure, expression and exploration of our authentic selves.'

Pxssy Palace's impact extends beyond club nights, encompassing a website, podcasts, mini festivals, political activism, fundraising and education programmes. A standout initiative, PP Support, serves as a bridge between partygoers and security or venue staff, prioritising attendees' wellbeing. They also run a taxi fund, supported by audience donations, which helps those unable to afford a safe journey home. White, straight friends of QTBIPOC attendees are welcome but pay higher ticket prices, ensuring entry costs remain accessible for the core community. Through a combination of thoughtfulness and playfulness, Pxssy Palace crafts dancefloor experiences that are genuinely welcoming for all.

"I think we will look back and be like, 'Wow, they really changed the landscape of safer raving,'" says Jamz. "We weren't thinking about this stuff before they came along. I'm not queer, but I wanted to go – though not until I was invited. I like the way they make you question why you want to go and whether you should be taking up space. They do it all in a way that's friendly, fun and considered. And then I went to one, and they had these dancefloor manifestos, or commandments, about things like non-consensual touching. I just hadn't seen anyone doing that in such a bold, powerful, yet accessible way. It was non-preachy. And now, increasingly, we expect all raves to have some kind of perspective on this stuff. Which makes what they were doing revolutionary."

Underground club culture: severely challenged, then, but far short of defeated. Admittedly, the focus here has been on the UK, but these positive tones surely traverse borders; the determination cutting across cultures. Comparing the attributes of different generations (Gen X vs millennials vs Gen Z) tends to be a farcical process. But, even if not dealt such a favourable hand in terms of access to space or the room to manoeuvre without a financial safety net, it's hard to contest that the current wave of dance music trailblazers and scene-shapers have mastered the art of adaptation.

Ahsan from Dialled In describes this as a move towards 'conscious clubbing', a term used by others I speak to as well. "When I was younger, dance music was escapism in its purest, rawest form," he reflects. "But now, I feel there's a more collective understanding of what coming together means. When I first started going out, it wasn't about that. It was just about getting as loose as possible."

Or perhaps, to fine tune the point, it has always been about 'coming together' but that nothing particularly tangible was done with that togetherness before. It was a nice idea and a warm feeling to go dancing with, but it wasn't mobilised in any meaningful way. Whereas an underground community was once something you drifted into, now there is more intentionality – an awareness of its collective power and how it can support and help individuals.

Ultimately, this ladders up to a greater respect for, and understanding of, the role of education in the otherwise make-it-up-as-you-go realm of club culture. We'll cover the burgeoning interest in teaching and learning further in. But for now, it's back to Tom Armstrong from Common People. Perched outside a cafe in Shoreditch – home over the years to many great club nights but also a case in point of a district where opportunities for DIY endeavours are now not so easy to find – he closes things out with some wonderfully expansive views on what makes after-dark creativity a different kind of creativity. Furthermore, why this matters the most to those often marginalised and minoritised.

"There is something spiritual going on," he asserts happily. "I don't mean like fairy magic. I mean on a fucking subatomic molecular level – there's something that happens to humans when we get together in a space to listen to loud music, especially repetitive things. It's like a transcendental experience. And what that does is it takes you to a place that you cannot access in your nine-to-five, day-to-day life. As far as history records go back, music and festivals have been a part of civilisation because it's a form of escapism. And the people who need that escapism most are the people who are marginalised. These experiences have the biggest impact on the people out there who've not been given the best opportunities in life.

"So that, I think, is why club culture has been such a strong vehicle for working-class people," he concludes, speaking in part of his own experiences. "It's an ancient, encoded thing taken to a completely different level through technology and modern clubbing. You walk out of those clubs with ideas you cannot get in an office or a brainstorm. You're a changed person."

and learning in the [illegible] for now, a week to [illegible]. Armstrong from [illegible] memory. Besides, I noted outside a cafe in Shoreditch [illegible] home over the years, not any great delights but also a [illegible] point of a distinct [illegible] opportunities for LGBT encounters [illegible] so easy to find [illegible] somewhat wonderfully [illegible] takes up [illegible] a different kind of [illegible] who [illegible] to those often [illegible] around [illegible].

There [illegible] going on [illegible]

[illegible] something that [illegible] expect [illegible] [illegible] what [illegible] [illegible] [illegible] have [illegible] and the people [illegible] who [illegible] marginalised [illegible]

5. A LOT OF SPLASHING GOING ON

Two things happened at once in the 1990s, and they converged on each other. Youth marketing came of age and dance music grew hugely in reach and appeal

From clumsy moves on the dancefloor to the definitive endeavours of the Red Bull Music Academy

In the '90s

Somewhere in the world, dance music always seems to be having a moment. A time and a place where the constant of the underground finds new dimensions and is bolstered by further allies, producing something more crossover and higher profile. Even accounting for personal bias – it being a moment of this kind that I was close to – dance music in 1990s UK can objectively be considered the biggest, noisiest and brashest of these ascents to the surface. From the charts to media, fashion to drug scares – it really couldn't have got much more on top of the zeitgeist.

Depending on which (well-told) story you run with, it started in London, briefly at a club called The Project, then more robustly at Shoom, and inspired by trips to Ibiza. Or it started in Manchester, at the New York-informed Haçienda. Either way, what started small and tentative in the late 1980s soon crashed into the national psyche as 10,000-strong raves, replete with funfairs and bold – if rarely convincing – claims to the power of the turbo sound on offer. They happened in warehouses and on airfields. Police were given the run-around, the tunes were anthemic, and the pretensions often associated with club culture gave way to a cheery accessibility – something like a secret world but also open to all. Chuck in MDMA, wideboy rave entrepreneurs, football firms and the latest threat to the wellbeing of our youth was good-to-go. Mainstream media proceeded to froth and holler about acid house non-stop for a year.

Eventually, with the law firmly on the offensive, the huge illegal raves started fading out. But far from admitting defeat, dance music dusted itself down and pulled off the unexpected. It completely dominated the 1990s. Oh sure, some boys going by the names Oasis and Blur sold a lot of records and created their own media furore, but out there in everyday UK, it was club culture that ruled the night. It was the last of something and the first of something. The last of the large monolithic youth tribes – rockers, punks and so forth – that had presided over previous decades. And the first indication of a youth culture in which the tribes would splinter and merge and do so repeatedly. People were picking and mixing with increasingly careless abandon. Not so long later, things were turning digital, scarcity of access to music and media was becoming a thing of the past, and a fragmentation that started in the 1990s leads through to the so-called post-tribal youth culture and fluid identities of today.

Throughout this period, the genres multiplied, and specialist dance media, from Mixmag to Kiss, developed an authoritative tone. Superstar DJs, superclubs and super-hubris. It was a decade in which club culture went 'lifestyle' and – to some extent – gained mainstream media respectability. It was also the decade in which youth marketing increasingly drew attention. Agencies specialising in it, often rooted in PR and events capabilities, launched in considerable numbers, connecting brands with the culture of young people in a giddy pursuit of credibility. 'Word of mouth' became a recognised strategy to consider alongside more conventional advertising techniques. By the decade's end, caricatures like Nathan Barley provided painfully sharp parodies of what had become more commonly known as 'yoof' marketing. Safe to say, earnest debates about 'authenticity' were starting to be raised in countless meetings and email exchanges.

Geoff Glendenning headed up UK marketing at Sony PlayStation at that time. They were one of the first brands to embrace this opportunity, including the then bold strategy of positioning themselves as a lifestyle or subculture offer, rather than simply a games console. He reflected on those times in an interview with gamesindustry.biz: "There was this revolution in youth culture at the time. So we positioned PlayStation in the UK to an 18- to 30-year-old market. We made the brand edgy. We made it cool. We didn't pay for any endorsement. We gave hundreds upon hundreds of PlayStations away to very cool people. I didn't say they had to talk about it. There was no social media then. It was truly word of mouth. And that word of mouth was a spark that spread amongst youth tribes and friendship groups. It was very underground.

"I knew that by giving a PlayStation to a top DJ they'd love it," Glendenning continued. "And they're cool amongst their friends, they'd have their friends round, they'd play it, and they'd effectively become an ambassador for it. We created an army of ambassadors. It wasn't a cool brand because the advertising was cool, it was cool because the movers and shakers and influencers of youth culture were out there saying that Sony really knew its stuff. I employed culturally connected people, who worked in music and fashion and taught them marketing. Because you can't teach a corporate marketer youth culture."

Of all the 1990s environments youth marketing aimed to occupy, dance music was the most alluring. There were fiercer, more clandestine corners of club culture that offered resistance, but in superclubs and new festival formats, brands were accommodated with ease.

Carl Loben is editor-in-chief of DJ magazine, globally known for its Top 100 DJs poll, and – since 1991 (more years still if you count its previous incarnation as Jocks) – a survivor of multiple shifts in media and music. "It's gone from just being a magazine to events, mini-documentaries, livestreams that we do from the basement," he explains. "But in all of this, we pride ourselves on quality, and thankfully, that's something clubbers and music fans still seem to respect."

He's been writing about dance music since the early 1990s, as well as DJing, promoting, running a label and releasing the odd record. At the outset of the 1990s, he remembers friction when brands first came knocking, a UK club culture that was pretty resistant to their advances. "I recall people using terms like 'corporate infiltration'. I remember when having your music in adverts was frowned upon – that was one of the ultimate forms of selling out. Of course, eventually, it would be a vital way to earn a living when record sales dropped through the floor. Things like Moby's Play *(famously the first album to have every track licensed to a commercial, movie or TV show)* marked a change there.

"There were some earlier outliers. Like Rizla and Hooch *(the prototype brightly coloured alcopop that found favour in some corners of clubland)*," Carl continues. "But I guess with them it was more like them finding themselves a part of club culture, asking 'What the fuck is going on?' and deciding they'd better embrace it. I saw more signs at first in places like Germany than the UK. I saw brands appearing at Tribal Gathering *(the UK festival decamped to Munich in 1994)* and Mayday *(a huge annual rave event, staged variously in Berlin, Dortmund and Frankfurt)*. But as we got toward the millennium, club culture in the UK was becoming far more mainstream and far easier to co-opt."

DJ Paulette, whose presence in 1990s dance music touched all bases from playing clubs to PRing records, also recalls a shift that saw rave culture go from out-of-bounds to very much the place to be for brands: "At the time of Castlemorton and the Criminal Justice Bill, brands weren't going anywhere near dance music. Repetitive beats and mass gatherings were highly frowned upon. By '96 and '97, things like Tribal Gathering are happening, and brands want in. Alcohol brands, energy drinks and mobile phones – they had technological advances to sell to a young generation."

From her vantage point as editor of The Face, Sheryl Garratt had a clear view of this evolving relationship between youth culture and commerce. Later to write the 1999 book Adventures In Wonderland, a highly regarded account of how the dance music story unfolded in the 1980s and 1990s, her route into journalism started with writing about post-punk and two-tone for fanzines in her hometown of Birmingham, but dance music ruled supreme over the period when she was setting the agenda – with a brilliant grasp for the mood of the young nation – at the most influential lifestyle magazine of the time.

"Those early efforts by brands to get involved, there was definitely a time where people were putting their toe in, finding it a bit hot, pulling it out," she says. "There was a lot of splashing going on. Sometimes what they were doing went well. Sometimes it was really trashy and embarrassing, and everyone would just kind of giggle about it. How I remember it is Ministry Of Sound were particularly bad at taking some money to put up a banner behind the DJ. It just seemed a bit weird – and not at all thought through."

Nevertheless, momentum gathered through the decade, with more brands dipping in a toe. The awkward splashing about, however, also continued. In 1996, in The Face, Stephen Armstrong documented the frequently clumsy comings together of clubs and brands in a piece titled Pretend That We're Cred – How Big Business Hijacked Club Culture. 'The multinational drink and cigarette companies are looking to hitch the nation's youth to their marketing bandwagon, and big clubs are their latest route. The corporate logo is everywhere,' he reported. He was referring to Ballantine's sponsoring the by then omnipresent Cream club's Paris excursions, Sony PlayStation taking a room at Ministry Of Sound and ubiquitous cigarette brand Silk Cut hooking up with northern clubbing institution Renaissance for a tour.

Quoted in the same piece, Mark Ratcliff from the Murmur market research agency issues the kind of caution still put out today: "Chucking money at a big nightclub says nothing, except that you have a lot of money and are trying to be trendy. To impress people, you genuinely have to give something back, not just line some cokehead promoter's back pocket."

Sometimes, the engagements did indeed go beyond chucking money at sponsorship opportunities – though not strictly with much giving back in mind. I stumble upon an academic paper examining how British American Tobacco promoted its Lucky Strike brand through a global partnership with the Ministry Of Sound. This led me to a 1996 internal BAT document that had found its way online. Under the title of Consumer Insight & Innovations Project, it stresses the need for credible on-the-ground research to understand the YAUS target group – that's Young Affluent Urban Smokers.

It also highlights the imperative of catching up with how youth-savvy companies like Nike and Levi's are operating. The proposed approach includes establishing a network of trend scouts to uncover emerging cultural happenings ('Scouts will preferably be hedonists with good skills, yet aware of what's happening in the outside world'). Elsewhere in the report, there's a reference to a 'consumer insights steering group'. Listed as examples (there's no indication these people had been approached) of who would be doing the steering were Ministry Of Sound boss James Palumbo, Irvine Welsh and one Frankie Knuckles. Even by today's standards, the proposed budget for this project was a very solid £2 million.

Despite reservations expressed about the level of craft and nuance that went into these early brand engagements, Sheryl – who since her days at The Face, has been editor of The Observer Magazine and now coaches and advises clients in the creative industries, including high profile names in music, acting and writing – does in hindsight think the big club institutions were getting something right in their ambitions to project an ever more omnipresent image. "I think the superclubs from then were quite an easy target for negativity when you're talking about branding and commercialisation. But in a lot of ways, I thought it was very smart how the Creams and Ministrys and Renaissances turned themselves into brands and, because of that, then attracted brands."

She concedes it was getting expensive to lay on the type of clubbing experiences that people wanted and, with everything from DJ fees to the costs of audio-visual set-ups notching upwards, it was unlikely the money could just come from the door charge to a young, and not particularly affluent, audience. "The cost of the Ministry sound system was incredible. The money did need to come from somewhere. It's easy to point a finger and say those clubs turned it all commercial. But I remember walking into Ministry the week it opened, hearing that sound system and thinking, this is the first time I've heard anything like this since Paradise *(Garage)*. Before that, the sound systems in London, at places like The Wag, were just terrible."

It's a late Friday afternoon in mid-November when I speak to Lohan Presencer, the executive chairman of the Ministry Of Sound Group. He says he may fall asleep any minute, but that seems unlikely as he amicably chats away at 120 bpm. He's been at Ministry for a remarkable 25 years, including 16 years as CEO. He tells me about a book he's written, a warts-and-all account of life at one of the original superclubs. He's been strongly warned against publishing it but lightheartedly contemplates doing so when on his deathbed, leaving the legal fall-out to others. "I'll let the defamed people, as they will claim to be, take it out on my estate."

He's also recalling some of the club's earliest partnerships, including Sony PlayStation having a dedicated room. A brand that truly embraced the decade, this paved the way for them setting up spaces at over 50 clubs in the UK alone. Around the same time, PlayStation also produced a flyer distributed at Glastonbury with the words More Powerful Than God emblazoned across it. The flyer was split into perforated sections, providing roaches for joints. "We were the fucking zeitgeist, absolutely," contends Lohan. "Trevor Beattie *(then creative director at TBWA London, PlayStation's ad agency)* was all over us. He was the God of advertising and loved the idea of mixing gaming with music and fashion. That was a great partnership because we were getting some of that weird 'third place' *(surreal PlayStation advert directed by David Lynch)* cool coming down on us. We had precisely the young people they wanted – not kids but people taking drugs and heading to Ministry Of Sound."

Lohan grew up in a musical family; his father was an opera singer who went on to run a jazz club. His younger brother, Gerard, was a "young jazz prodigy," playing in their father's club at the age of 11 and going on to be part of the acid jazz scene. Now a renowned trumpeter, he's played with Herbie Hancock, Chick Corea, John Dankworth, Norma Winstone and Ronnie Scott. Needing to find a niche of his own, Lohan planned to be a record producer. He went to the University Of Southampton – "I couldn't get on a studio production course, so I did a degree in acoustical and vibration engineering." Of more significance, with early 1990s rave culture igniting, he became the entertainment officer at the student union. Soon, he was promoting parties for 2,000 people. "Electronic music, raves, drugs – I fell for the lot."

All of this led to a job at a music promotions company in London, followed by one as a market analyst at Warner Music. He then got promoted to head of TV and was heavily involved in all marketing campaigns. On the side, he started getting ideas for compilation albums, with some of them – geared to disco and 'summer grooves' – getting a release and doing well.

"And I noticed this thing going on," he says. "These three night-clubs, Cream, Renaissance and Ministry Of Sound, had all released compilations in the back half of '95, and they were selling in significant numbers. And although there'd been compilations before that – Dance Hits This, Dance Zone That, Now That's What I Call Dance Bollocks, and so on – these were different. They were based on a nightclub. Yes, DJs were mixing them, but people were buying this music because of the club's power as a brand."

He was introduced to James Palumbo, Ministry's somewhat notorious founder (now also known as Baron Palumbo of Southwark). They worked on some joint venture releases, before Lohan moved over to the club full-time. They set up the Defected and Relentless labels and, all the while, the compilations kept on coming. Indeed, in Lohan's time at Ministry, an incredible 70 million of them have been sold.

"We were having number ones all over the place, and I was whipping out compilations off the back of that and selling half a million here and 400,000 there. You were getting a nightclub experience in a box, and you had the branding of a nightclub on the box to authenticate it, to endorse it. The majors couldn't do that with dance. Then, we would make these very stylish TV ads and spend a lot of money on them. We would take a genre like UK garage and take people on a journey. We contextualised the experience. And we always considered ourselves aspirational to the mainstream. That was what we did. We weren't just selling a double pack of CDs. We always said we were selling lifestyle products."

More than just music fandom, this sense of lifestyle was precisely the magic dust that attracted brands into the fray. The same notion of creating brands to appeal to brands that Sheryl Garratt raised. Effectively, these advertisers and sponsors had two fronts to operate on: the Tribal Gathering-style festivals and, presenting a different context, the super-clubs. "The 1990s showed something new in youth culture," Lohan believes. "It was a new commercial opportunity, and we were the biggest club going in the greatest city in the world."

As the decade progresses, club culture becomes so ripe for commercial leverage that it's acceptable material to riff off in the most mainstream of advertising. Alix Sharkey picks up on the theme in a 1999 Guardian article subtitled: 'If even big corporates aren't scared to buy into the E generation, has club culture lost its way?' The piece starts by taking aim at the Fabergé fragrance's sponsorship of the launch party for Human Traffic, the movie about clubs and drugs in Cardiff. It then swerves into a full-force assault on marketing's co-option of clubbing. He calls out a spot for Hall's mentholyptus drops, featuring a tube train that turns kaleidoscopic and hallucinatory ('Get a rush with Hall's mentholyptus'). He opines that DJs are in adverts for cars, beers, sneakers and hair products. A 'trippy ad' for the Rover 200 gets the once-over. So does a Prodigy-like one for Lion Bar and a London underground poster for the Berocca vitamin tablet ('You're right, a lot of successful people in the City are on something.').

Speaking of Fabergé (owned by Unilever, the parent company of Ben & Jerry's, Marmite and endless other staples of kitchen and bathroom cupboards), their rave dalliances sailed too close to the wind for more conservative society to cope with. They launched their Fusion fragrance with a campaign that showed imagery similar to wraps of powder and a line (sorry) that proclaimed: 'The only thing to sniff in nightclubs'. A blasting from anti-drugs campaigners duly followed in The Daily Telegraph newspaper.

All aboard

Dance music in the 1990s presented an interesting challenge to the alcohol industry. Drinking had, by and large, been a fixture of nightclubbing since the birth of the discothèque. But the illegal raves of the late 1980s and early 1990s (perhaps taking subconscious cues from the ethos of David Mancuso's Loft) were noted for the dearth of alcohol on sale, with water just about all that clubbers were consuming (in liquid form). All the same, and not to be defeated, this was a new generation and a new culture for drinks companies to endeavour to nudge up close to. As clubbing shifted back into licensed venues, that started to look viable, too.

Writing in The Atlantic in 2015, Chrissie Giles maps the UK's long and generally (over)enthusiastic relationship with alcohol. Come the 1990s, Giles notes, quoting alcohol researchers Fiona Measham and Kevin Brain: 'The drinks industry wasn't going to miss an opportunity like that. It saw a chance "to reposition alcohol as a consumer product which could compete in the psychoactive night-time drugs economies." The industry launched new and stronger drinks, which it targeted at a young and culturally diverse crowd. First were strong bottled lagers, beers, and ciders. Then came alcopops, including Hooch, in the mid-1990s. A few years later, drinks containing stimulants such as caffeine and guarana arrived. It was all part of the industry's desire to recast alcohol from a bloating depressant into a pleasant-tasting, stimulating drink that fitted the youth culture. The dance scene, say Measham and Brain, helped bring about a "revolution in the 1990s alcohol industry."'

Sheryl Garratt reflects back on that period: "I remember quite a sense of panic among the alcohol brands. This huge and growing concern that suddenly everyone was going out all night and drinking water; that different to previous generations young people weren't really drinking alcohol. They were scared. So they started trying to get in on events, clubs and one-off parties. At first, the cooler brands, like Absolut vodka and Sapporo beer, but then the more mainstream brands, too. And then you suddenly start seeing luridly coloured alcopops, and the marketing was kind of like, 'Hey, this isn't really alcohol; it's pop. You can have this at the rave.' Those drinks marketers' minds must've been in overdrive."

One mind potentially in overdrive, trying to make sense of all this in practice, belonged to Richard Taylor. More recently, he's held senior marketing positions at Selfridges, NatWest and in the healthcare sector. From

1996 to 2003, he was at Budweiser, first as a brand manager and consequently as international marketing director. "I was always a party person," he starts. "And I guess the music and marketing combination was always of interest to me. The first activations I can remember – things like Red Stripe at Notting Hill Carnival – they intrigued me. I did marketing at my polytechnic and did my thesis on youth marketing."

In recent times, the Anheuser-Busch-owned Budweiser brand is best known, in Bud Light form, for so-called 'culture war' run-ins. Partnering with transgender influencer Dylan Mulvaney, it evoked angry conservatives and anti-LGBTQ+ activists to call for boycotts – followed by criticism from the LGBTQ+ community for the brand's muddled responses to the boycott demands. Back then, it was launching Bud Ice and, as Richard describes, wanting to position it as "the party beer for the party generation."

Richard says: "You have to think back to what things were like then. It was a pint drinking culture, so any beer in a bottle, followed by the alcopops in bottles, they could shake things up and position themselves as club drinks. If you're in a tightly packed club and dancing, you're more likely to want something in a bottle. So the challenge for us was how to make something of that. And the other good thing for me was that Bud Ice was seen as the younger brother of Bud. It had a lot more freedom. You didn't have to report back to America in the way that you would on Budweiser."

Step one in this process was recycling a US Budweiser advert. Specifically, one with ants carrying a bottle to their ant hill, pouring it in and then the ground vibrating, as if they had their own boombox down there. Richard switched the US track for something that would forge links to UK club culture. Ooh La La by Wall Of Sound-signings Wiseguys had already done the rounds among DJs and more dedicated record buyers, but returning in the Bud Ice advert, it hit number two in the UK charts – "Back when the charts actually mattered."

But taking a big beat track onto the TV and into the Top 10 wasn't truly dropping the brand into dance music, Richard concedes. "We got thinking about what else we could do to cement this position as the dance music beer, the party generation beer. There weren't so many options back then in terms of big events that were focused on dance music. But there was Tribal Gathering."

Tribal Gathering had grown out of earlier megaraves such as Raindance and, as its name qualifies, set out to join the dots between techno, drum 'n' bass, house and more. It became a prominent fixture of 1990s electronic music culture, staging huge, well-organised festivals that garnered as much attention in NME and Melody Maker as the dance music media, and booking most DJs of the decade and countless live acts – of particular note, a rare performance by Kraftwerk in 1997. "I remember reading the write-ups of earlier Tribal Gatherings in mags like The Face and thinking it would be the perfect encapsulation of what we wanted to be, and where we wanted to be," Richard explains. "Ultimately, what we wanted to be supporting, too."

By 'supporting', Richard is referencing the then-nascent, now imperative, drive for brands to not just show up with a truckload of banners and logos. To avoid passivity and piggybacking. The thinking goes that unless you're bringing something of substance to the party, you can easily be switched out in partygoers' minds by the next uninvolved brand to turn up. It's logical stuff, but it's still easier said than done. "The whole thing at the time was you can't just badge," Richard confirms. "You've got to contribute to be credible, contribute to the overall experience. So we decided to create the chill-out lounge, and then we got a bit 'marketing literal'. So, as well as lots of the necessary white bean bags, we had these bizarre sculptures of ants. In hindsight, I'm not sure that was the most sensible thing to do. A few people looked quite confused, some actually very freaked out, by that."

Clearly on a marketing mission by this stage, Richard acknowledged the brand's progress but still wasn't entirely feeling it. "It was okay, but I wasn't that impressed, and I guess I mean both as a marketing person but also as someone in my mid-20s at the time, and what I thought we were bringing to the party. I felt we could do a lot better in terms of contribution to the overall experience. So then we moved to '98."

They switched to supporting Creamfields – then located at Matterley Bowl near Winchester, and soon to morph into Homelands, which Bud Ice would also jump in with. He estimates securing a presence at Creamfields only cost them £15,000, and they locked in beer distribution rights, too. "I'm not sure people understood the commercial value back then. We would earn more money than we spent. It was a win-win, really." Berlin's Love Parade was another destination for Bud Ice. Also sponsoring Ministry Of Sound's show on Kiss FM. But, best of all, in Richard's eyes, there was the Bud Ice bus.

"We figured we wanted to sponsor multiple dance festivals and events. We decided we needed a stage that was ours, for our DJs, and that we could move from one place to the next. We reckoned we needed a bus." They found a 1970s model and called up Cymon Eckel of Boy's Own, XOYO club and Riki Tik bar repute to design it for them. "He was inspired by Evil Knievel and drag racing. Think flames down the side of it."

Richard Fearless, Norman Jay, Jon Carter, Una Bombers, Faze Action – that's to reel off a few of the DJs, all bringing strong credibility with them, who graced the flame-adorned bus. "It became a familiar sight for a lot of young people. People were disappointed if they didn't see us there." The bus later transitioned from Bud Ice to Budweiser branding. Later still, Norman Jay used it as his Good Times stage at carnival, eventually without the branding. "I wonder where that bus is now," Richard muses. "It has some stories to tell."

Much like his bus, Richard would also move from Bud Ice to Budweiser. Music, if less dance-specific, remained important in the marketing mix, including large-scale sponsorship of the V Festivals. A return to clubland came in a series of UK/USA DJ soundclash sessions when Budweiser sought ways to make their American heritage appealing to young British clubbers.

"People talk about how brands can become credible in these moments like they have some magic solution. But the truth is, it's a real challenge, and at the time, lots of promoters and DJs were pretty wary of the idea of working with brands or any commercial deals," Richard remembers. "And it took quite a while for dance music to go legitimate in the eyes of brands. We were all feeling our way, but at least we had a lot of space. Bacardi, Sony PlayStation, Ericsson – I'm sure there were others but not that many."

Ericsson indeed. The mobile phone had long associations with UK rave culture. The brick-like early iterations were synonymous with warehouse event promoters. By the late 1990s, SMS text messaging had a significant popularity surge. Initially designed for telephone engineers to send network status updates to each other, youth culture got hold of this innovation, appreciating its affordability and convenience (and developing a fear of 'picking up the phone' in the process). Suddenly, a whole new means of communication was born. No surprise, then, that mobile brands – some of them now long lost – figured among the investors in club culture.

Ericsson sponsored dance magazine Muzik's awards and, according to the advertising trade title Campaign, used a network of 'lesser known DJs in underground clubs' to promote its new 768 range. In 1999, they took a further step, as per Bud Ice, sponsoring the vast capacity Homelands dance event, replete with nine themed arenas and most DJs under the sun. From our tech-saturated perspective, a quarter of the way through the 21st century, it's interesting to reflect just how novel and powerful the emergence of new devices and digital services, in parallel with electronic dance music, was back then. Campaign explained Ericsson was 'vying to woo the trendy youth audience' and that 'the company would have its own area at the festival which it will fill with new phones designed specifically for young people, and demonstrate how e-mail *(ah the days of hyphenating email)* can be used with the phones.' Ericsson's channel marketing manager added: "Dance music is a perfect link for us because of the technology involved. Our association with the scene has made us a credible brand to the youth market."

Lifting logos

As seen, the more superclubby or festival-approved dance music got the less sense of risk brands felt in taking space and finding opportunity. The easier it was to see the commercial fit between their presence in the night and the aspirational, next gen-oriented focus of their strategies. The bigger the audience they could reach per activation. It all makes for quite a juxtaposition to the start of the 1990s. In the first month of that decade, the twitchy beats and euphoric piano of N-R-G by self-styled keyboard wizard Adamski had ascended out of clubs and warehouses and was charting in the UK and US. It was wrapped in cover art featuring a Lucozade bottle – except with his name replacing the brand's name. T-shirts were printed up, too. It was a nod to the energy drink's newfound role within rave culture as a fixture instead of alcohol and a means to a lift (if another were needed).

It was not, however, a well-received nod. Lucozade owners, SmithKline Beecham (now GlaxoSmithKline), threatened Adamski – who with singer Seal would have an even bigger hit, Killer, just a few months later – with legal action for using the bottle without permission. Eventually, they settled out of court, with a £2,500 donation made by the record label MCA to the Nordoff Robbins music therapy charity.

Wearing a beaten-up straw hat and a Seditionaries-style Vive Le Rock T-shirt rather than anything featuring a sports hydration drink, Adam Tinley (aka Adamski and, at times, Adam Sky) is sitting in his garden on the outskirts of Vienna, recalling events from back then with a mixture of weariness and good humour. "I know it became this rave drink, served at Shoom or wherever, and it augmented ecstasy. But to be honest, it made me think of having the flu – being off school, in bed, sweating and feeling shit, and my mum giving me a glass of it. When they contacted us to complain, I remember thinking, 'God, this isn't fucking fair.' But I didn't mind giving money to that charity."

Indicative of how brand attitudes to club culture were evolving in that period, it wasn't long before Lucozade ran their own adverts, complete with an N-R-G strapline and a distinctly ravey feel. "I was gobsmacked," Adam continues. "After all that legal hassle and coming after us like rottweilers, it would've felt fairer if they'd actually used my track."

Building on earlier observations, Sheryl Garratt notes the state of flux as brands and media wrestled with what to do with the dance music phenomenon in that period. "It felt quite weird and schizophrenic for a while. You'd look at a newspaper and, on the front, they'd be screaming for acid house parties to be stopped. That kids on E were biting the heads off pigeons, that type of thing. And then, 20 pages in, there'd be some kind of guide to clubbing with Pete Tong. Then TopShop would have a little fling with smiley T-shirts, then clear them all out again. People weren't sure if this was something to make money out of or not. It was all very clumsy, really."

Lucozade and N-R-G was by no means the only example of club culture taking the identity of brands and doing what it wanted with them. Not so many years after Adamski's brush with corporate litigation, T-shirts with Kellogg's Special K logo were a common sight on the dancefloor – the association with a breakfast cereal switched for the drug ketamine. There were plenty of MDMA pills with brand logos, too. The Mitsubishi ecstasy tablet became as legendary as any DJ or club night. The emblem of this rather unremarkable car brand that someone in an underground drugs lab in Holland decided to press onto MDMA pills was soon transitioning to T-shirts, record covers and necklaces. Later, Starbucks would be among other brands that adorned pills. By 2001, the Dutch Synthetic Drugs Unit counted 121 different brands being used by ecstasy manufacturers. Come the mid-2010s, there's a story that MasterCard called off a major sponsorship deal in the dance music space at the 11th hour when the existence of small pink MDMA pills embossed with their logo became a topic of media conversation.

Back in the 1990s, branding influences purloined from the outside world wasn't limited to a presence on clothing and pills. Early work from designer Ian 'Swifty' Swift saw him sampling Chanel's logo for club flyers. He would later earn his stripes alongside Neville Brody at The Face, then taking over art direction at jazz-centred Straight No Chaser magazine and designing everything from Foster's Ice 'billboard graffiti' to TV graphics for Peep Show.

On a more widescreen scale, it's over to Club USA in Times Square, Manhattan. This place became a major haunt for the 'club kids' – a late 1980s and early 1990s scene inspired by drag, punk, fetish fashion and performance art. The aesthetic leaned into narcissism, nihilism and heroin chic. You'd also see the club kids at Limelight, Palladium and Tunnel – like Club USA, all spots owned by Canadian 'club king' Peter Gatien. Eric Goode of Area fame designed the interior. Decked out in big screens and mashed-up commercials, Club USA's design took significant cues from its Times Square location. Interview magazine described it as 'an explosion of corporate logos and advertising – there was a mural of Kraft Macaroni & Cheese.' Another club kids destination, Disco 2000 at the Limelight, had a darker take on the role of advertising. Milk cartons in the US then often featured photos of missing children in a bid to raise awareness. Disco's 2000 flyers depicted a milk carton with club kid pictures and the tagline: 'It's 1995. You know where the children are!'

At the other end of the decade, brands again appeared on dancefloor fashion, completely without their say-so. Whereas before it was T-shirts adorned with logos for breakfast cereals and sports drinks, this time, the motifs on display came from a more premium place, with less bootlegging involved (OK, there was some of that, too). They arrived in tandem with a sound called UK garage – essentially vocal, disco-inflected US garage blended with elements of jungle and rave.

Running roughly parallel with the equally well-dressed R&B sound of America that gave us TLC, Destiny's Child and Mary J Blige, UKG followed a pattern of working-class-led youth cultures where dressing up is threaded into the codes of the scene. You can take this back as far as the mods of the 1960s, for instance. To a principle that if you're going to get caked in mud on a building site all day or work behind a counter in a garish polyester uniform, you are determined to dress beyond your means in the evening (the same principle also has it that the posh kids tend to go out looking scruffy by comparison).

While the favoured labels, including Versace, Moschino, D&G and Iceberg, differ markedly from Special K and Lucozade, the logos were just as conspicuous. This wasn't the so-called 'quiet luxury' we hear about today (think TV series Succession). You didn't buy any old Moschino. You purchased the item as liberally smothered in the brand name as possible. Described variously as 'off-key Mosch', 'pattern Mosch' or 'crazy Mosch', the use of colour, typography and images was striking in the extreme. Other symbols of luxury were displayed, too. A senior Moët & Chandon marketer reportedly once headed along to the Sunday night home of UKG, Twice As Nice, to understand why much champagne was being shifted through the place.

Another youth culture theme is at play here: co-opting brands and giving them new meaning and a different aesthetic relevance than intended. It's unlikely the creative and marketing directors at these fashion houses envisaged nights out in Vauxhall or King's Cross as likely settings for their clothes. But then they weren't asked. Speaking to Hypebeast, Andres Branco, founder of the Wavey Garms fashion platform, said of this incongruence: "I could never work out how the very camp Moschino two-piece outfits from the catwalks of Milan were being worn by the most gangster geezer from Hackney."

This logo-laden phenomenon wasn't unique to UKG. Harlem's Dapper Dan had paved the way in the 1980s and early 1990s, pioneering a streetwear-meets-luxury ethos by reprinting monograms of

Gucci, Louis Vuitton, MCM and Fendi on tracksuits, leather jackets and bomber jackets. With gangsters and rappers prominent among his clientele, Dapper often commented that the logos weren't sufficiently conspicuous on the luxury brands' own creations.

In a 1988 feature for US magazine Spin titled Homeboy Fashion, writer Frank Owen investigated the trend: 'But why are homeboys so fascinated by these design logos that were intended for haute bourgeoisie consumption? Dan puts it this way: "We take anything that symbolizes the upper crust and give it that extra street flavor." Rather than simply aping the lifestyles of the rich and famous, homeboys are recoding the trappings of affluence, caricaturing mainstream consumption, re-using, remotivating and retransmitting – the age-old game of youth subcultures. In many ways it's the sartorial equivalent of digital sampling.'

This pattern of cultural appropriation and belated recognition – a reimagining of luxury, rooted in audacity – was therefore simply finding a new expression in the UK garage scene a decade later. Indeed, following a five-year climb from pirate radio to the pop charts, those were heady days for UKG. The sound of crews, including Dreem Team and Pay As U Go Cartel, blasted from London clubs (like Bagley's), holiday resorts (Ayia Napa) and shops. Lots and lots of clothes shops. Nina Manandhar is a photographer, curator and fashion communications teacher at Central Saint Martins. She covered UKG's luxury predilection in What We Wore, her book on British street style. She also heard a lot of UKG through a part-time job back then at one of those clothes stores, Morgan de Toi (not as upmarket as other labels referenced here, but a firm favourite of the scene all the same).

"I think there was an optimism, a positivity that came with New Labour getting into power," she reflects. "People were reacting to that, and in the ways that made sense in their world. I love how all logos being shown off in such a big and loud way questioned the standard rules around taste and what you put on display. It was a code for wealth. How did people afford it? I don't know. There was undoubtedly a beg, steal and borrow attitude to designer labels. I wonder if there was some kind of offline version of Depop that they all tapped into."

So much has changed in the subsequent 25 years, and not just the emergence of socially primed ecommerce platforms. More recently, luxury brands have wised up hugely to younger, more urban audiences, particularly Black youth, whose influence on style has always been as undeniable as often lacking the credit owed. A co-opting of designer labels by street culture has morphed into a deliberate strategy, with brands now actively courting this demographic, designing with them in mind. From 'gangster geezers' in Moschino to a marketing blueprint, fashion houses are finally acknowledging the radical innovation and style born from Black communities.

Facing numerous incoming court actions and police raids, Dapper Dan had a long spell in the shadows after his 1980s heyday. But then later, those same fashion houses that had tried to shut him down came knocking, as they belatedly recognised the influence of Black culture and streetwear on the luxury category. In 2017, Gucci released a jacket they described as a 'homage' to Dapper Dan – a version of one he'd made for Olympic athlete Diane Dixon in 1989. Others saw it as a straight rip-off and by one of the very corporations that had previously shut him down for copyright infringement. Relationships thawed when Gucci brought him on to design a capsule collection. In 2018, the French house launched an appointment-only store, in tribute to his original boutique. It was the first-ever luxury store in Harlem.

RBMA: a different energy

The rapid 1990s escalation of brand interest in club culture naturally had signals and traces that came before. It grew from first forays into music more broadly in the previous decade. Ah, the 1980s. MTV, blockbuster albums, CDs, the beginning of the global audience and the notion of 'the consumer'. If ever a decade knew how to commercialise entertainment, and so much more besides, it was this one.

In a 1987 piece in San Francisco bi-weekly music title BAM (Bay Area Magazine), Dave Zimmer reported on the proliferation of rock music in advertising. He considers the future of these relationships, with an ad exec telling him: "As demographics shift, I can see agencies using more '70s groups, a lot of the Woodstock groups are already in spots. I'm still waiting for some Black Sabbath and Ozzy Osbourne songs to turn up in campaigns."

The ad exec continued: "Music can be an incredible selling tool. And right now, the market most advertisers are going after encompasses the 18–34, 24–40 age groups. These people grew up in the '60s with The Beatles, the whole Motown era. Music was a big part of their lives."

Zimmer also debates whether giving over music to adverts should be deemed an endorsement by the artist. It turns out there was quite the spectrum of ways in which bands responded to these opportunities at the time. On the thoroughly willing side, Crosby, Stills & Nash embraced the chance to have their Teach Your Children in an Apple commercial to the extent of sprucing the song up for the occasion. "Graham *(Nash)* liked the presentation so much he insisted on doing a new vocal and updated the lyrics slightly," their manager explained. "The whole idea of the spot was to show how to prepare your kids for the modern world, which is part of what Teach Your Children is about."

At other times, it wasn't nearly as harmonious a picture. Zimmer raises the case of Nike using The Beatles' Revolution in an advert to launch the Air Max sneaker. The spot, Revolution In Motion, was created by Weiden+Kennedy, the agency that built much of its formidable reputation through its longstanding partnership with Nike, including devising the 'just do it' line. It's stunningly powerful commercial art, shot on Super 8 and mixing playground athletes with John McEnroe, Michael Jordan and others. The Fab Four, however, didn't see it like that. They were stymied by the fact that Michael Jackson owned the rights to their back catalogue by this stage. Nonetheless, they filed a $15 million lawsuit against Capitol/EMI, Nike and Weiden+Kennedy through their Apple Corps business. Nike came back with a full-page ad in the Los Angeles Times, explaining their side of the story – to summarise, they felt they were being used as a pawn in a battle between Apple Corps and EMI. Predictably, the case was settled out of court, with details of the terms kept strictly under wraps.

This backstory of music and brands from before the 1990s, from when the role was almost exclusively to soundtrack whatever message the paying party wanted soundtracked, highlights how much more layered the exchange of value would become a decade on. By then, as we've seen, youth marketing had come of age and brands were seeking more active and authentic involvement. That's when an initiative, still considered by many as the absolute A-grade in brand endorsement of dance music, first emerges. It subsequently motors on for over two decades, connecting, educating, narrating and inspiring a generation of global advocates of underground music. All courtesy of the deep pockets of a slightly nasty-tasting (well, each to their own) energy drink.

So, in Berlin in 1998, a filmed interview started the ball rolling on something big. The interviewee is Jeff Mills, architect of so much of the Detroit techno sound. Bespectacled, wearing a leather jacket, he's as assiduous as ever as he moves through topics like loneliness on the road, the conceptualism underpinning his X-102 releases and how he copes with the damage his ears have suffered. The interviewer is Torsten Schmidt. He's the co-founder of Yadastar, a Cologne-based marketing agency with an obtuse website and a proposition centred around the statement: We Believe In True Encounters.

Set to run for 21 years, Red Bull Music Academy, so often pointed to as a high water mark in credible culture marketing, was underway. The broadcast quality production standards would follow later (the sound is sketchy, the footage wobbly). However, other factors that would become associated with the initiative – the thoughtfulness of

Schmidt's approach to interviewing, the curiosity of the audience and the questions they ask – are present. So much would follow from these humble beginnings. Academy events oriented to learning and the transfer of knowledge, set in locations as varied as Tokyo, New York City, Melbourne, Cape Town and São Paulo. Workshops, club nights, studio spaces, in-depth editorial (including an occasional newspaper called the Daily Note) and a steady stream of radio.

There was a singularly impressive roll call of appearances in the RBMA (as it was commonly called) lecture series: A Guy Called Gerald, Alec Empire, Arabian Prince, Andrew Weatherall, A$AP Rocky, Alexander Robotnick, Amadou & Mariam, Arthur Baker – that's just scratching the surface of those listed under, as you may have noticed, the letter A in this epic roster check. Its boot camp style nurturing of new talent was significant, too. Getting accepted onto one of the programmes was hard, but if you did, so much was possible through the holistic support provided. Hudson Mohawke, Objekt, Nina Kraviz and Flying Lotus are among those who owe a debt of gratitude to the academy's mandate for helping artists climb skywards.

It was, by any measure, a phenomenal undertaking, which everyone I speak to who had some involvement with RBMA attests to. Everything appears to have been planned in meticulous detail and with high intentionality. There was a strong emphasis on getting beyond the obvious, on joining the dots and shining bright lights on those less often recognised for their contributions. Speaking to Pitchfork writer Marc Hogan in 2017, Many Ameri, the other co-founder of Yadastar, said: "When you're looking at the academy itself, the intention is basically fostering creativity. When we leave, there is a new structure that has grown from these people collaborating that would usually not work together. And they continue doing that afterwards."

Against a backdrop where brand engagement in dance music more often concentrated on prominent signage and pushing sample products, this was something else, and the wider media recognised it as such.

'For 20 years, RBMA has served as the gold-standard example of how to use corporate funds to support art on the margins with practically no conditions attached,' wrote The Guardian in 2018. 'Celebrating its 20th anniversary, the Red Bull Music Academy has become a creative meeting space that rivals the IRCAM in Paris or Berklee College in Boston,' noted El Mundo. And the New York Times: 'The company's commitment is strong, and also thoughtful. Its concerts tend to double as history lessons, often spotlighting underappreciated artists and scenes. In the music world, it has been, with exceptions, a rare example of corporate largess deployed with aesthetic care, making for one of the most invigorating musical series in the country.'

Carl Loben from DJ magazine notes the ground shift it created, too: "It hasn't all been plain sailing since then, but from Red Bull Music Academy onwards just throwing, say, 100k at sponsoring something, without investing in it in any other fashion, wasn't good enough. There's more of an understanding that investment should go further than that – investing in young talent, or diversity, for instance."

Reaching one of the Yadastar duo to hear their story was a struggle. Various cryptic responses to emails were received across several months in communication with Torsten. Sample response: 'Hello there, squire! Cheers for the flowers – may I ask to what or whom I'd owe such honours? It seems all a wee bit far away, but yes, would be curious what more you'd be able to tell us about your endeavour? With regards, Torsten.'

But it wasn't hard to find others in the music industry with something to say about RBMA – and what they had to say was almost universally positive. Nicky Siano reminisces fondly about his own lecture slot, recorded in New York City in 2016. You get the sense that he believes it was an important factor in his renaissance, in his own mighty contribution to dance music reaching a wider audience. "Red Bull was the gold standard, really, wasn't it?" he says. Gold standard is an often used term whenever RBMA is discussed. "It was like, wow, this is so well put together. The fireside chats, they were so in-depth. A nice, intelligent audience that wanted to hear what you were saying; the interviewers were so good, so informed."

Björk claims RBMA brought about a U-turn in her thinking around brands and music: "Being a punk, I've always been sceptical of big brands... I've repeatedly gone to amazing gigs Red Bull Music Academy has organised and they really have their heart in the right place. They just seem to be giving so much to that community, especially to electronic music. So I decided to drop my brand-snob thing and embrace it."

King Britt, who ran RBMA workshops, featured in the lecture series and played at their parties and on their radio, is another who does not have much but utter positivity for the initiative. Speaking from San Diego, where the Philadelphia-born dance music veteran is now based, he reflects: "They *(he means Yadastar)* had this beautiful dream of celebrating and archiving the culture, and the music that they loved so much. And it could only really have happened in Europe, especially in Germany, because there was so much more respect for the culture there than here. They created incredible studios – state of the art, next level. And they didn't need their logo everywhere. Not on everything. They just came in, provided funds and built this community around the world that was so dedicated and involved, and it grew into this beautiful, beautiful archive."

King had them to thank for some last-minute funding of his 2014 Moondance celebration of Afrofuturism at MoMA PS1 in New York City. With Shabazz Palaces among the live acts set to feature and Hank Shocklee the panellists, he had a short time to plug a large hole in the budget. "I had two weeks to find the funding and they came good. MoMA wasn't interested at first. They just imagined big energy drink logos everywhere. I think they were astonished when they realised it wasn't like that with RBMA." Not to get too carried away on the commercial Kool Aid, but under-the-radar benevolent acts by RBMA are mentioned by many I speak to. For instance, when pioneering DJ and producer Andrew Weatherall first came up with the idea of his Music's Not Everyone radio show (later to run on NTS), it was Red Bull in London who made their Tooley Street recording studio available to get the first three shows down, with no fee or request to be factored into the marketing or communications of it.

Tom Dodd from William Morris Endeavor (WME) spoke to us earlier about how immersion in club culture fired up his own journey in the music, brand and entertainment industries. Here, he's looking back on his time as head of artist marketing at Red Bull and leading Red Bull Music Studios London. It's a role that had him up close with RBMA, particularly through the Paths Unknown events. These explored under-represented narratives and unexpected partnerships, with Odd Future's Syd, Toddla T, Kesha Lee and Stefflon Don contributing.

"I remember my very first meeting with the team from RBMA, and I've never had a more thorough briefing in my life," Tom smiles. "They really thought about what people would take away from these experiences they created. To a level that no one else was caring to think about it. It was very beautiful really. And it's been hard to replicate the standard, for sure."

Theo Gentilli, co-founder of 'music first creative agency' Warm Street, got one of his early breaks through working on an RBMA tour. He adds to the chorus of people whose exposure to the academy had a career-shaping impact. "The concepts created were driven by the music itself, not consumer insights or marketing data. It focused on what was shaping the music scene at the time. It wasn't about creating a campaign concept and then fitting music into it. All of which I thought was refreshing and powerful. It was about letting the music inspire everything, rather than relying on typical marketing strategies."

"The Red Bull guys, they left so much of it to Yadastar," Tom from WME continues. "They had this very light touch approach but also one about really supporting the scene. Like, interview these people and talk to them about the culture – and maybe put a logo in the background, but it's not essential. Perhaps they'll have a drink of Red Bull while they're interviewed, but probably not, and that doesn't matter, either."

No forcing the product to centre stage. No overbearing agenda. This all sounds so un-brand-like. More incredible still: this peripatetic adventure went on for 21 years. Most brand initiatives in dance music are lucky to last two years. "They kept going when most brands were giving up and tapping out," Tom Dodd continues. "And all giving up for similar reasons: the bosses and owners of the company couldn't see anything tangible enough in how the marketing was impacting the brand."

You can't help but be struck by the difference between RBMA, with its focus on getting the details right and forging lasting and credible community connections, and Red Bull's activities in a different cultural field: football. Get past the vastly more significant sums of money and media noise compared to leftfield music, and you arrive at something not dissimilar in how much the game matters to people and how it offers escapism, a means of expression and a sense of identity.

However, when Red Bull bought SV Austria Salzburg in April 2005, community sensibilities appeared to rank low. The club was renamed FC Red Bull Salzburg. The badge remodelled to resemble Red Bull's logo. The longstanding violet and white kit was switched to red and white. A similar empathy deficit was on show when they purchased fifth-tier German side SSV Markranstädt in 2009, relaunching it as RB Leipzig and propelling it into the Bundesliga. Criticism took various forms but particularly centred on concerns that the new look club was betraying principles in German football – the so-called 50+1 rule that deters big investors and, instead, skews to the significance of fan voting rights. Supporter protests included a severed bull's head getting slung onto the pitch. There are worried looks in Yorkshire, England, now, with Red Bull taking a stake (albeit a minority one) in Leeds United.

Red Bull has also faced scrutiny closer to its music and cultural marketing efforts, particularly following a 2020 corporate event at which a presentation included slides depicting racist stereotypes. The incident, first reported by Business Insider, led to the dismissal of Florian Klaass, the company's global head of music, entertainment and culture marketing, along with other top executives. The same year, the Wall Street Journal reported that US employees had raised concerns about the company's inaction on the Black Lives Matter movement. Also in 2020, the business picked up flak of a less political nature when it cut back on its culture marketing – with music festivals and the Red Bull Presents live music series canned.

For balance, I also researched if there were many (any) dissenting voices in dance music over RBMA. They're largely missing, though Matthew Herbert (also known as Herbert, Doctor Rockit, Radio Boy, Mr Vertigo, Transformer and Wishmountain) did go on record to the New York Times in 2013 to air his reservations: "My overriding impression of any music industry Red Bull tie-in is that the brand is always louder than the art," he said, at odds with others who've described RBMA branding as conspicuous by its absence. "I don't think one would come away from any interaction with them thinking that they were interested in anything else other than selling caffeinated sugary drinks."

A more prominently polarising factor in Red Bull's history is its co-founder and leader, Dietrich 'Didi' Mateschitz. Inspired by the energy-boosting effects of a Thai beverage during his travels, he launched Red Bull in 1984 with Chaleo Yoovidhya. Known for his low-profile yet tightly controlling leadership, Mateschitz rarely spoke publicly but stirred controversy with anti-immigration and pro-Trump remarks when he did, particularly near his passing in 2022 at age 78.

Viewing Red Bull primarily as a marketing powerhouse (production was outsourced), Mateschitz allocated 20% of revenue to promotion, prioritising extreme sports first, then music initiatives, including RBMA. Until 2019, that is. In its final year of operation, RBMA launched Bass Camps, described as four-day residency programmes dedicated to education and celebration, at which up-and-coming artists exchanged ideas with legends and pioneers. These were staged in

Stockholm, Havana and Calgary, with Holly Herndon and veteran R&B singer Swamp Dogg among the typically broad range of contributors. And then, that was it. RMBA was gone.

A statement from Yadastar looked back with pride over their activities in more than 60 countries and on all of the creativity and community energy that sparked from the work. It referenced a mutual parting of ways with Red Bull and concluded with: 'The world is full of great ideas. This was one.' Flying Lotus and Hudson Mohawke were among those tweeting their respects. Media coverage implied disputes over setting new budgets for RBMA and positing the impact of regime change at Red Bull. However, the brand chose not to elaborate on why RBMA was closing now – the lack of reasons given perhaps the only real perceived misstep across the 21 years.

"So much detail and quality and care. And then they close it down so quickly without, I think, really answering the questions about why it was being shut down," remembers Nicky Siano. "The withdrawal could have been handled better." While the reasons for RBMA's canning are shrouded in some mystery, the recurring theme when discussing it with people assumes effectiveness metrics and KPIs – or, more, the lack of them – were a leading culprit. Several commented it was impossible to say if the needle was moving on anything significant to the brand (such as awareness, affinity, or sentiment) as objectives hadn't been set.

Many Ameri spoke about this at the time as if it was no big deal: "Red Bull is not in the world of music to make money off music. We are entering this with no need to make everything work financially – we can focus on presenting things that are interesting and use that freedom." You get the strong sense that, through some entirely unreplicable alchemy of right time and right blend of personalities, next to an unusual corporate structure and strategy, RBMA just *got away with it.* Which is great for the work it produced and the legacy created – but, perhaps, less so in terms of a blueprint for others to follow.

"They invested an incredible amount of money in it, but it was hard to play it back to all of the bosses of Red Bull because they didn't know much about music or the seismic impact it was having on this culture, and that would also ultimately be its demise," believes Dodd. "I couldn't tell you about sales and how it transferred to that, but the impact on dance music, surely that's undeniable," adds Siano.

Undeniable, perhaps, but measurable? Measurability sits at the core of contemporary marketing. Whether a TV spot, a billboard, the sponsorship of a racing team or the funding of a global and multi-tentacled electronic music programme, data is necessary to support the business case. If the right data is being collected is regularly debated – there's an oft-shared line that 'just because something is more measurable doesn't mean it's more effective.' Proceedings get more complex still when what is being measured is cross-channel, cross-market and as liberal in the number of touchpoints involved as RBMA. "That's exactly what they wanted, metrics," Tom from WME believes. "Nowadays, they can calculate metrics differently. They can put a price on the amount of likes, shares and interactions the social media is getting but it wasn't like that then."

Evaluating the socials is, in fact, just one component in campaign measurement. Brands also spend a lot of money with insight and analytics agencies trying to put a value on the return of their investment in advertising, sponsorship and other marketing activities. Reflecting on his days at Bud Ice, Richard Taylor recalls their challenges in pre-social media days. "We were very hot on measuring things in the sense of brand tracking metrics *(consumer survey-based monitoring and measuring of a brand's performance over time)* and we could see the impact of advertising in this. But sponsorship of events and driving buses around the country, this was all very new. Not many people were doing it. It's probably fair to say it was more art than science in how we measured it."

Which is a way of saying they relied more on qualitative than quantitative research to gauge success and to pinpoint improvements. Whereas quantitative research uses data to measure performance – typically issuing surveys pre- and post-activity, or to those who were 'exposed' versus those who weren't – qualitative research concentrates on interviews and observation. It entails listening to what people say and watching them, photographing and filming them to note their actions and behaviours at events or in the build-up to them. Right or wrong, it's not hard to envisage which of the options out of quantitative and qualitative evaluation holds most truck with less creatively-minded purse string holders.

All the evidence suggests RBMA effectively snuck through the system. Powered by the passion of those shaping it, and perhaps aided by some obliviousness at a C-Suite level in Red Bull on how to operate in electronic music, which had them leaving it at arm's length, it motored on for over two decades. And while officially it's gone, in other ways, it isn't. The online content, the feature articles, and the lectures live on as some of the very best of their kind; an incredibly rich archive touching on so many aspects of dance music culture.

Eric van den Bogaard is the creative director of London and Amsterdam-headquartered culture marketing agency Protein. "RBMA has left a bull-shaped hole that's still not been filled since 2019," he says. "And by this I mean something really adding substance, sharing knowledge, creating opportunities for education and for people to meet. That's one of the best things brands can do: bring people together through their resources and facilities." In his Pitchfork interview, Ameri summarises rather perfectly what RBMA did that was different, that mattered, that was truly contributory: "If you just reproduce what the music world out there can do by itself, there is no need for a brand to be involved in culture."

Learning from the Academy

Was measurability, or the lack of it, really behind the shuttering of Red Bull Music Academy? Though initially it looked unlikely I would get to ask anyone at Yadastar about this firsthand, the email exchanges with Torsten

Schmidt eventually became less cryptic. He apologises for how unavailable he'd been, explaining a double whammy of moving house ("too many records and books – it's killing me") and having a master's degree to complete. Finally, we set up a time to talk. He plans this for when he's on one of his dog walks, saying he finds these good occasions for reflection.

He's an amiable guy, and he's fascinating to hear from. The care and consideration he and his Yadastar partner Many Ameri put into RBMA is writ large in his response to every question. We get to speak about a week after the sad and untimely passing of the Glasgow DJ, producer and Numbers club/label co-founder Jackmaster. He was another in the long list of those who contributed to RBMA. Next to interviews and other inputs to the programme, he appeared on a 2014 UK tour alongside Kompakt's Kölsch and fellow Glaswegian Nightwave.

"This has brought back many thoughts," Torsten starts quietly. "It's put me in a lot of contact with people who came through the Academy. And even though it's so long ago now, like a different, pre-pandemic lifetime, the bonds feel so strong." The bond. That's a telling term in how Torsten thinks about what mattered in this vast and doubtless life-consuming endeavour. He talks more about the friendships forged than the deals struck. You only need to look at the myriad lecture sessions he hosted, now to be found on YouTube and Red Bull's digital domains, to see those bonds materialise. There he is, vibing to Pat Metheny tracks with Goldie in Barcelona in 2008. Joking with De La Soul's Prince Paul in Cape Town in 2003 over the first record player owned by the De La Soul producer (it was a Mickey Mouse record player). Listening compassionately to DJ Storm in Berlin in 2018, as she reflects on the loss of her friend and DJ partner Kemistry in a driving accident. Going far, far back in time with disco originator Giorgio Moroder in New York in 2013, including him lamenting on passing the opportunity to score the movie Fame.

Torsten, whose beard is now longer and greyer than in those videos, mentions that his house move has got him thinking about the sheer volume of material RBMA produced. Along with shifting his records and books, he's transporting to his new place the printed transcripts from every interview and copies of every article published. All of the files of videos, audio and images. It takes up a lot of shelf and hard-drive space and serves as a reminder of how far-reaching and, let's be frank, really fucking huge an undertaking it was.

I'm keen to hear from Torsten how it all started. My earliest (and now vague) memory of Red Bull showing interest in dance music was in 1995 when I headed on a press trip to Zurich. The purpose was to interview electro pop eccentrics Yello, and various of the collaborators (such as Carl Craig, Carl Cox and Jam & Spoon) who'd worked on the remix album, Hands On Yello. Red Bull took up a presence at this PR junket, with branding and product samples to facilitate us 'influencers' waxing lyrical about this caffeinated, yellow drink with others. Torsten first recalls it thus: "Initially, it was something your snowboarding mates would bring back from Alpine holidays. It would be great to have a crate of it for your party. We were all still suspicious about the taste," he laughs, "but that's how I remember it starting."

In terms of how it started for Torsten, he was born in the mid-1970s in Thalfang, a village in the Hunsrück region of western Germany. Through his childhood and teens it was, he says, a "hyper-militarised" place to be growing up, dotted with US army installations and everything that came with that. Which included PX (post-exchange) stores where the troops and their families could buy American things. Inevitably, these things found their way into the hands of others. In Torsten's case, it was tapes, records and Jordans that caught his attention. Another local quirk brought about by the US presence was an unusual number of club venues in out of the way places with "insanely good sound systems" – either with service people on the decks or local DJs, who'd purchased vinyl from the visitors. Record stores specialising in imports, and heavy on Chicago and Detroit releases, started to surface, too. And if you tuned in to AFN (Armed Forces Network) radio at the right time of the evening, you'd hear fresh dance tracks there as well.

Combine the American influences with Germany's own commodiously-stocked timeline of electronic music breakthroughs (the nearest big city to his village was Frankfurt, home to Dorian Gray – a club situated in Hall C of Terminal 1 of the airport, and which from 1978 to 2000 played host to disco, then new wave, then EBM, then techno sounds), Torsten was all set to jump into this culture. He started making a name for himself in German dance music, primarily covering the scene as a writer and editor. Starting on fanzines, he would later contribute to the Süddeutsche Zeitung and Die Zeit newspapers and work on the editorial teams at Groove and Spex – a dance magazine and music/pop culture magazine, respectively. He recalls how, from these journalistic beginnings, the Academy adventure started to take shape.

"It was a very slow snowball, which was good in many aspects. I got to know the guy *(Many Ameri)* who became my business partner for 25 years. He had previously worked in an agency *(Berlin PR and events business, Haebmau)* I knew about. Writing never paid much in the 1990s, so you'd have conversations with these types of companies. They could see, even in Germany, the explosion of this youth culture. Events like Love Parade with 10,000 people one year, 50,000 the next, 100,000 the one after and then half a million. They decided they needed to market to these raver individuals, so would contact the few media outlets involved in this world and invite people like me in. You'd then walk into the meeting, and they saw you weren't much older than 20; they were like, 'Oh wow, target audience right here. We need this person as a consultant.'

"I was getting a fair amount of these consultancy things," he continues. "Some of them were OK, most of them were not. So, I was getting reluctant quite quickly. I guess a lot of it didn't sit comfortably with my background in DIY culture and the spirit of the rave movement, the holy gospel of Underground Resistance, and what proper hard work meant. But anyway, I heard via a mutual friend that this guy *(Many)* had been requested to come up with something interesting, so you should check it out. Then we spoke on the phone a bit. And then, about four or five people gathered in Italy for a weekend. We knew that Red Bull saw that all of these people in clubs and recording studios, people keeping late hours, were consuming their drinks, and they were wondering what would be a good way to give back to this culture. The questions we were asking ourselves on that trip to Italy: 'Are these guys actually serious about investing in education based on nocturnal cultures and nightlife?'"

That trip to Italy marked the start of Yadastar and the first threads of what would become the Red Bull Music Academy. Torsten says that as well as himself and Many, the others in attendance were music and subculture journalists. Then, for one night, they were joined by a member of Red Bull Germany's marketing team. "Afterwards he was apparently worried," Torsten explains. "He said to his seniors: 'How on earth are these guys supposed to help us? You can't even see the shoes under their trousers.' I don't know, I guess it was a baggy pants phase."

What was the nature of the deal that Yadastar signed with Red Bull? Or between the Academy and artists? "Everything for years and years and years ran on a handshake basis," he responds. "It was a word of honour thing. If a new country were added to the mix, then maybe an Excel sheet would be drawn up. Other than that, it was about relationships with the people in charge *(at Red Bull)* and persuading them about a project. And if they said go, the rest of the organisation would follow.

"And then, before you knew it, you'd find yourself doing a symphony for 100 car sound systems right in the middle of downtown LA. These people who own the car sound systems are having the time of their life," he smiles, recalling A [For 100 Cars], an RBMA activation with Japanese visual and sound artist Ryoji Ikeda. "Because for once, they're not getting tickets from the cops; they're right out in front of the home of the Los Angeles Philharmonic, or the LA Times, or outside the LAPD HQ or the Broad Museum. They are there – blasting their systems."

As with the brainstorming session in Italy, dance music journalists continued to play a significant role in the development and delivery of RBMA across the years. Among the regulars: London writer and radio presenter Emma Warren (recently fêted for her book Dance Your Way Home); NYC-based author, historian, documentary film producer, DJ and curator Jeff 'Chairman' Mao; and Barcelona-residing American journalist, musician and DJ, Philip Sherburne (he coined the term 'microhouse', no less).

"So many of us involved were coming up as journalists," Torsten nods. "Or maybe to call us journalists isn't quite right, but people who had been instrumental in writing about different scenes, starting fanzines or propelling existing fanzines closer to magazine levels. And all of these contributors, they knew which kinds of artists and producers and DJs would make for engaging interviews.

"It was still a very hidden world," he continues. "Many people were legendary because no one had heard them speak. So to know the people who actually had spoken to person X or Y or Z and could tell you he would be great, or she would be fantastic, was amazing. But the next challenge was that, as incredible as these people were, they did not always feel comfortable in a room in front of lots of people. We needed to confront this: teaching them how to live with that awkwardness. To make sure that we could document these stories properly, all personal vanities had to be put aside."

The Yadastar team were clear and adamant from an early stage that educating and knowledge-sharing, conducted in a style befitting of club culture, was core to RBMA's intentions. They were, in fact, quite resistant to letting parties take up too much attention. "We thought it might take away from the educational experience. But we had people telling us that if we wanted all of this talent to gather, to speak, to contribute, it would make it a whole lot easier if we could provide them with a significant gig that was probably outside of what they would normally do, and probably have higher production values than their usual bookings."

Torsten explains there were other challenges in gathering access to the people and stories that would populate this colossal body of educational material, covering every corner of club culture, electronic music and adjacent genres. Particularly with artists from the past, there was gatekeeping to contend with – those who wanted these stories kept in more rarefied circles. Moreover, there hadn't previously been many attempts to truly surface these narratives or to tell them in less abbreviated and edited form. They had to design their approaches carefully.

"It seems quite weird now, looking at all of this great educational content we brought together and that's out there on the internet for anyone to access, just how many weeks, if not months or years it took, negotiating and persuading people to move away from an old school stance of 'knowledge as power'; and not wanting to relinquish that power.

"A lot of these histories were not recorded. There were hardly any books around about it all. This was one of the main impetus for us to create this project in the beginning. People, pioneering people, had not had the opportunity to talk properly, in their own words. It was just soundbites that supported the main story arcs established by certain media *(one assumes he means primarily the UK dance media)*. We were strongly of the opinion that people are a little smarter than just consuming these media stories, and that if you put lots of different perspectives in front of them, they would make up their own minds and engage in actual dialogue around these facets of history."

RBMA's ascendance coincided with the exponential growth of digital media. This gave them a level of reach that the dance mags of the era couldn't get near. But it also raised the bar around what education meant. More underground and subcultural knowledge was now available across different platforms, forums and so forth, and dance music's next generation was consuming it at pace.

"You remember those moments of entering the specialist record stores, having to work your way into being worthy to be able to purchase a certain copy of whatever record?" he laughs. "You get to 2010, say, and you have these insanely knowledgeable kids involved in the Academy. I remember one band flagellating themselves for only discovering Arthur Russell a year ago. They were aged about 19! I had to tell them, 'You're miles ahead of where I was when I was 19.'"

With more people becoming more knowledgeable, this required RBMA to go further and deeper. "Yes! We had to provide even more context, more detail," he confirms. "And then, with the events, we could go further still. Putting the faces of these creative legends out there, opening up the chance to engage with these incredible humans, these incredible characters. It was a great gift to be involved in it all."

With a few exceptions, most marketers I speak to for this book get to tell me about campaigns, programmes and initiatives that have played out in club culture over a year, maybe two. Torsten and team got to do theirs over 21 years. He feels that longevity was partly achieved by being given the room to develop RBMA at its own, unhurried pace.

"So in between sitting in Italy and going, 'OK, we don't have places where our culture can learn from the best and those who've lived it,' and pulling off bizarre events and a 24-hour radio station, and having this vast archive, and the lectures and articles, and also providing a lot of people with research material for their books and documentaries, there was a long part where I guess we were insanely lucky to test things and experiment without too much attention."

By his estimation, the Academy events in New York City in 2013 and 2014 felt the most significant leaps upwards in prominence – compared to, say, the smaller-scale sessions in locations such as Dublin, Rome, Seattle and Madrid in earlier years. NYC in 2013 boasted lectures from Ryuichi Sakamoto, Egyptian Lover and James Murphy. Brian Eno presented his visual art piece 77 Million Paintings, Sakamoto performed at the Metropolitan Museum Of Art and Giorgio Moroder played his first ever US DJ set at François K's Deep Space night. Elsewhere around town, Skream, Kim Gordon, Masters At Work and Four Tet figured among the 230 artists playing or DJing.

There were drone music and improvisational sessions. There was the United States Of Bass project, platforming regional bass music styles with Afrika Bambaataa representing NYC, Egyptian Lover (Los Angeles), DJ Assault (Detroit), DJ Spinn and DJ Rashad (Chicago), Big Freedia (New Orleans), Scottie B (Baltimore) and DJ Magic Mike (Orlando). The mentorship programme hosted 62 students, chosen from more than 4,000 applicants. With costs covered for flights and accommodation (at the upscale Ace Hotel), they received two weeks of tuition from the music pioneers in attendance. RBMA mirrored German education practices here: two classes of 30, with lecturers given an ex gratia payment of a few hundred dollars. And there was more: a main recording studio, radio booths and smaller 'bedroom' studios for students and RBMA team to use.

Why stop there? The work in 2013 served as a prototype for RBMA morphing into something even more gargantuan, adding 'festival' to its descriptor and debuting back in NYC the next year. "All of a sudden, this thing is so big that it's a month-long festival, and we're highlighting all these great subcultures that were instrumental to the city, and introducing new audiences to parts of their own heritage," Torsten continues. "And The New York Times does 18 big write-ups in one month alone."

There was a lot to write about. RBMA staged a Larry Levan Street Party. It was part of a local initiative to rename King Street, once home to Paradise Garage, as Larry Levan Way. They gathered 20,000 signatures for the petition and livestreamed the whole thing. The Garage's famous membership cards were revisited, with attendees invited to create 2014 versions in custom-built photo booths. Lecture conversations were more extensive than ever. Topping the bill: a rare chance to hear from D'Angelo, with highly respected Black music writer Nelson George moderating. A string of workshops linked up-and-coming local musicians with RBMA luminaries. Red Bull Radio broadcasted live from various festival events as well as from Red Bull Studios. An eight-part video series was launched, celebrating iconic New York City anthems and the drum machines that made them. Among the cast: Arthur Baker, Black Moon's Evil Dee, Peech Boys' Michael de Benedictus, Man Parrish, Suicide's Martin Rev and Johanna Fateman of Le Tigre. Those same drum machines were on show at an exhibition called beat:repeat NYC. William Onyeabor's incredible Nigerian synthesiser music was reinterpreted live by David Byrne and Hot Chip. Leaving no opportunity for creativity unchecked, different illustrations were commissioned for every festival event.

And then the club nights. To pick out a few, an indoor market in Williamsburg was transformed to celebrate dance sounds and styles native to the New York and New Jersey area: housing, voguing, flexing and Jersey club. Dancehall ruler Bobby Konders and house legend Todd Terry played and, ably demonstrating RBMA's attention to detail, a very long article was written to accompany the occasion. Underground favourites Mister Saturday Night took over a regular house for a night. The Lit City Trax label, meanwhile, brought the heaviest bass sounds to a decommissioned strip club.

With so much happening under the RBMA umbrella in a city so brand and advertising-oriented, it's hardly surprising that senior figures from those industries were among the crowds turning up at the events. They were often tapping Torsten or Many on the shoulder, too. "We had all these huge companies saying they want something like the Music Academy. We'd ask: 'Yeah, but do you have three or five years – at least! – to build this up from the ground?' And them: 'No, we report profits each quarter. We need it delivering next month, or at least by Christmas.' And we tell them that we know they will pay us a lot of dollars and our offspring would appreciate it, but it's not going to work. Either you go back to your board and find ways where they give you a long horizon, or it's not worth it from a business standpoint... or any standpoint."

It sounds like the mood music within Red Bull and the processes involved around each RBMA did start to change from the mid-2010s onwards. Torsten is willing to provide some detail, if also a little guarded on getting too far into specifics. "Stakeholder management became the big thing," he acknowledges. "It felt more and more like being in the International Olympic Committee, something huge and complicated like that, having to manage all these different committees, not just person X or Y to persuade."

As RMBA entered its final years, aside from the increasingly complex politics on the Red Bull side, it seems Yadastar already had plans to refresh and update the approach. "It's a long time, 20 years, to run something. For some of us, it already felt the time to take back seats, to keep it fresh in new cities with new people having an influence. And having strong memories of our disgust in our teens for older people going on about Led Zeppelin at length, I think we were always pretty conscious of when to lead the way and when to step aside, stop waffling and leave it to others."

But you weren't planning to call time on it? "No. When it closed, there were several reasons and mainly organisational ones on the client side. The owner was getting old, and with half of the company owned by the family, they were having their version of the Succession drama at the time.

"Quite a lot of this was kept away from us, but probably having the chance to know more about it would have saved losing so much hair later on," he continues. "But still, you could feel that there was a lot of internal jockeying for positions going on. And besides that, the company had grown into a multi-billion dollar company, bringing its own challenges. It would have got harder to persuade more conscious characters in dance music that it was a good idea to liaise with this sort of benefactor."

Meaning as painful as on many levels it doubtless was, the evidence was growing for Torsten, Many and their team that this was an appropriate moment to bring down the curtains – whether the circumstances were within their control or not. "Yes, there were a number of reasons why it was good to make sure it closed down then, and in the right way, in an orderly fashion."

I ask Torsten why the closure announcements in the media were so vague. "What was being said in the public arena felt a totally different beast, and not always very close to what was actually going on. But there were enough reasons why it was wiser to not get involved in that sort of thing. Just to make sure that everyone who worked for us had a decent severance package and knew long enough in advance, so they could start looking for new gigs."

As for performance metrics and KPIs, these seemingly were not the deal-breakers many had assumed. At least not compared to the Roy family-esque Succession wranglings within the Austrian company. "Well, you could tell when all of these data measuring companies got involved," Torsten nods. "That was a whole different level of agency that did not exist when we started. All of a sudden, participants had to do post-event surveys, all of that kind of stuff. So I guess in the final years, yes, there was a lot more measurability. But it often looked good for us. If you just take the earned media market value of something like the New York Times pieces on events in that city, I imagine they easily offset the budget spent. And that's the other thing: our budgets were a lot smaller than people expected them to be. As much as I would love to have lots of money up in the attic to live off for the next five generations, I think that everything being budgeted reasonably was part of the formula for the project's longevity. You might pull off one project with a ridiculously big budget, but it won't work for 10 years or longer."

At the time of wind-down, Torsten hoped RBMA's lasting legacy would be systems, structures and ripples of influence that would drive creativity in electronic music for years to come. He notes unhappily that the pandemic, coming a year after the closure, derailed some of that potential. "Near the end, we were bumping into people we'd been working with for years and thinking, 'Oh, we just hope what we've done is strong enough to sustain them for years to come.' But then we never really got to find out because the pandemic dealt such a major blow to so many independent entities in dance music and club culture. Even RBMA couldn't protect against that."

The systems and structures were impaired. The ripples of influence, meanwhile, proved much less stoppable. Hence, even half a decade after RBMA's shuttering, the exploits of the Academy are never far from the conversation when I'm interviewing people for this book. Torsten acknowledges it's no easy undertaking for others to get to the level of RBMA, but says he's unmoved by what he sees from most brands.

"Something that I've always felt strongly about, and which is rarely discussed in a sufficient manner: why aren't more people prepared to take up the baton? If totally average guys like us can do this, how come others haven't come forward to support youth, the arts and public and civil society? We always put this as a challenge to others to do better, but too often we've seen the cheapskate version with aims to produce very quick results. And I find that very disappointing."

Torsten continues: "I would have expected a lot of people to go, 'OK, here's what we can do. This is how we can do this better, or how we do something similar in sector X, Y or Z.' Because clearly this whole idea of getting people together to share knowledge and ideas, particularly in the physical space, is absolutely what the world needs. Not more budget ending up in unfortunate channels, especially in this political climate. We need to find ways to stop this downward spiral, this race to the bottom. We need to help people find these connecting moments and see how much strength they can develop from working together and from the stories they share."

Like many others I speak with, Torsten places much of the problem here on short-termism. Heads of brand and marketing jumping between companies. Performance-based marketing that prioritises instant results over the merits of more enduring brand growth. Quarterly cycles and pressure from investors and boards. Ever-greater jostling over the allocation of budgets and the rush for data-driven strategies – even if they are not very good strategies.

"I remember getting off so many Zoom calls with major corporations and being absolutely certain that none of the people I was speaking to would even be at this company a year on," he laughs. "How on earth are we supposed to get them to buy into a project and build something that will outlast their stay? A lot of the successful projects involve clients that are underwriting it with their own personal character, with their taste, with their integrity. It's part of what persuaded people to join in. When it's just a whole lot of people switching positions every other minute, it increases this whole notion of the faceless, global corporation.

"I mean, I get it," he continues. "They are living in expensive areas. They're raising kids. And you'd talk to people in these corporations and discover that a third or a half of their annual salary would come from bonuses, and that those bonuses are tied to certain KPIs. Of course, they don't care about project X, Y or Z if it does not affect their KPIs. But I wish we could have more power to discuss how to work these projects into their KPIs. These could be simple things in many ways, but through them, we could be more successful."

It appears that Yadastar is largely dormant at present. Torsten is grinding his way through not one but two MA degrees at Frankfurt's Goethe University. However, returning to the frontline of firing up imaginations through culture doesn't sound entirely out of the question. While brands are still part of the equation, he says he'd set the aperture wider in future. Funds, foundations, philanthropy, public-private partnerships, government, arts organisations, fan-led kickstarters – he believes all these and more deserve consideration. "Absolutely, I'm interested," he confirms. "I'm more than happy engaging with anyone serious about improving something and who can look past the next quarterly report. We need to find ways to stop this downward spiral that I mentioned. People need help with this. They need more help now than they did two decades ago."

We get talking about the RBMA archive. The same one that, in hard copy form, is causing Torsten's shelves to groan. There is so much of it up there online to read, watch and listen to. It's an incredible collection of work and, overall, most of it still seems to be in place. But sometimes, a link leads to a dead page. Some I speak to fear more of the RBMA content will inevitably get lost or removed over time. Case in point: Paramount wiped out over 20 years of MTV news website content at the press of a button. "Eight years of my life are gone without a trace. All because it didn't fit some executives' bottom lines. Infuriating is too small a word," exclaimed one former MTV editor. A number of those I interview for this book say that, somewhere in the world, there should be a definitive archive of dance music and club culture's heritage, and Torsten concurs.

"I make sure there are backup copies of everything. But I must stress no one is trying to sell anything here. However, it is nice to think that if the British Library or the Smithsonian Institution or whoever was interested, this body of work could be made available to them."

A closing question, asking him (somewhat ambitiously) to pinpoint a favourite RBMA lecture, brings some final reflections on everything accomplished. "It's a cliche, but too many to name one! So many that are kind of hidden away in your mind, but then you're watching ARTE *(publicly funded German/French culture channel)* and every other project or music documentary you see on there has touchpoints to what we did. You're like, 'Oh, that was actually not a bad gig!'

"I'm pretty sure almost any of the up-and-coming people we worked with would have made it – whatever made 'it' is – without us," he concludes, back in characteristic modest mode and dog walk almost complete. "But there's something insanely satisfying about how we brought so many people together and how all of the energy created then propelled all of these people and their ideas around the world, touching so many other people. It perhaps doesn't get better than that."

Andy Warhol, Keith Haring and Kenny Scharf – underground art as Absolut advertising

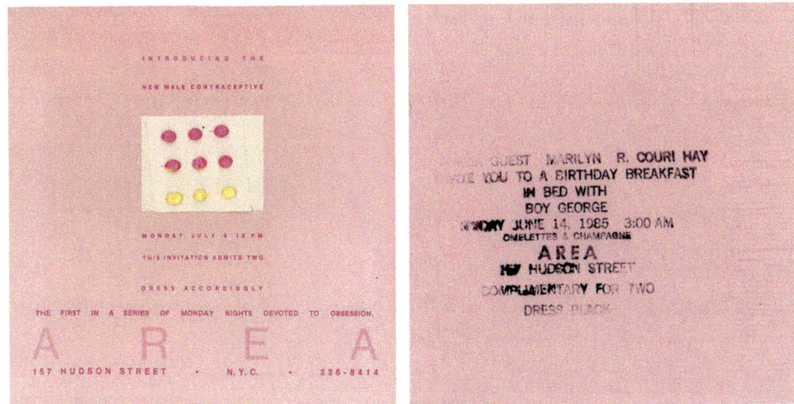

Invite to Area club Obsession night with Boy George guesting

Campaigns from Fiorucci's disco years, including singer and drag queen Divine

FIORUCCI
A B C
B C A
C A B

NEW STATESMAN SOCIETY

US$1.75 air IR £1.47 UK £1 17 June 1988

Black economy

A thriving underground enterprise culture has grown up around music—bootlegged vinyl, pirate radio, warehouse parties. It's a black economy powered by black aesthetics, but its consumers are often white. Sample it inside.

Gibraltar: Duncan Campbell exclusively reveals why the SAS shot to kill

Occupied: on patrol with the Israeli army on the West Bank

The New Statesmen Black Economy cover with Soul II Soul's Jazzie B

Night Fever exhibition at the Vitra Design Museum

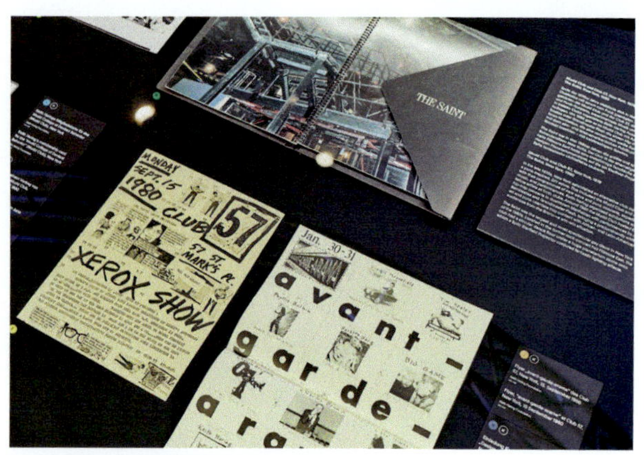
THE SAINT
MONDAY
SEPT. 15
1980
CLUB
57
57 ST.
MARK'S PL.
XEROX SHOW
Jan. 30-31
avant
garde-

Palladium

W
PLEASUR

WipEout: Futurism book marking 30 years of the techno-soundtracked racing game

Ben Kelly and Virgil Abloh collaborating on Off-Set and the Ruin installation

Electronic Beats parties

King Britt and Blacktronika

Sisu DJ courses in Liverpool and London

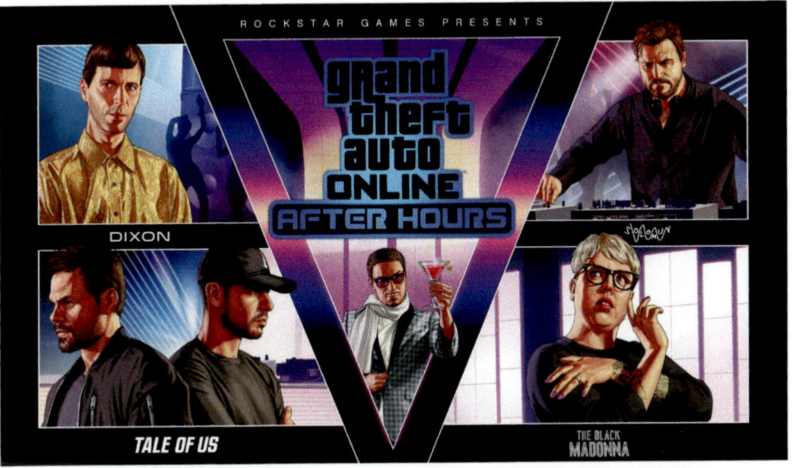

Grand Theft Auto – livestreaming with The Black (now Blessed) Madonna, Tale Of Us, Solomun and Dixon

KFC's Colonel Sanders as DJ

Berghaus take Fabio back to the rave fields

6. THE MODERN TENSION

From the early 2000s to the life of the contemporary culture marketer

This is the frontline – those mastering the implications of brands entering subculture to take space as sponsors and supporters

Navigating the noughties

It would be tremendous to show an ever-upwards tick from Red Bull Music Academy onwards. More nuance, more creativity, more attention to the quality of the relationship between brands and dance music. More of everything that RBMA lit the route for. In truth, it's been a more chequered relationship. Something went right in that case that hasn't necessarily been easy for others to follow. Perhaps RBMA landed at a particular moment in the music marketing evolution where the size of opportunity looked big enough to warrant the spend, yet the metrics were vague enough to have it all approved and signed off as a leap of faith. Or, as several people I spoke to have said (in various words), maybe no one's had as much money to burn as Red Bull at that time.

More auspiciously, perhaps clues to the next big step lie among the smart ideas we'll hear about ahead, from those on all sides of the much-sweated-over value exchange. If not on the same scale, there have been exciting and meaningful campaigns and programmes since RBMA. There has also been greater scrutiny of the role played by brands, particularly since the Black Lives Matter movement and demands for action against systemic inequality and social injustice. The pandemic inevitably derailed many initiatives. Momentum was lost that is now being regained. From the disruption and reprioritisation, new ways to create and collaborate are in consideration.

Back at the start of the 2000s, dance music found itself in a somewhat troubled place. The millennium eve superclub events suffered from poor attendance, and while pockets of the underground of course continued to thrive, more commercial aspects of the scene struggled to maintain the peaks of the 1990s. It wasn't until EDM's explosive rise in the US in the early 2010s that mainstream interest reignited substantially.

However, it was in those difficult early 2000s, in Berlin – where club culture energy resolutely refused to run low – that something interesting called Electronic Beats began to take shape. Something enduring, too. While Red Bull Music Academy may have been the first to lay down a long-term blueprint, this initiative has now outlasted it. In fact, unless anyone knows differently, it holds the title of the longest continuously running brand-meets-dance-music initiative.

The work of Deutsche Telekom, the German telecommunications business best known globally for T-Mobile, Electronic Beats has clear parallels with RBMA. Under the mandate of 'sharing freshly gained knowledge with the community, and forging new connections', there has been a number of component parts over the years. Parties and podcasts. A focus on editorial in print and digital form. A (now defunct)

DVD series called Slices. Telekom Electronic Beats TV on YouTube, featuring everyone and everything from Maceo Plex, FJAAK and Lauren Flax giving the lowdown on their studio set-ups, to revisiting genres such as Belgian new beat, 1980s EBM and 1990s dub techno.

It's never been as global as RBMA, focusing more on Europe, particularly Eastern Europe, recently. Nor has it achieved quite the degree of acclaim. Nonetheless, it's a significant achievement, big on craft and getting the details right. Interestingly, and perhaps unlike RBMA, that's included getting the effectiveness metrics right.

Ralf Lülsdorf is the architect of Electronic Beats at Deutsche Telekom. He's friendly and deeply passionate about music, especially techno and hip-hop, but he also comes across as someone astute in navigating corporate environments. "I'm 57, an old fart. I've been doing this for 25 years, learning how to fight these fights to get the budget each year," he smiles. Numbers do much of the fighting for him. In measuring success, his ammo includes issuing surveys to those exposed to Electronic Beats activity and those not exposed (known as the control group) – to demonstrate that Electronic Beats has moved the needle on how Deutsche Telekom is perceived. He analyses engagement across social media channels and press coverage. Also in his locker, something called implicit testing – a research methodology that, unlike explicit measures reliant on participants consciously expressing their thoughts and feelings, seeks to uncover deeper, often subconscious responses less easily articulated or contradicting more explicit ones.

"People have to respond to the questions very quickly in an implicit test, meaning the response is coming from somewhere deeper," he explains. "It's been brilliant for us. It's meant we can demonstrate how EB is helping with brand objectives. With something like 'creating memorable moments for people', for instance, which has been an important objective – we can measure what is happening implicitly."

Exhibiting much enthusiasm for everything achieved in his role as head of music marketing at Deutsche Telekom (outside of Electronic

Beats, he's masterminded more mainstream partnerships, such as with the Rolling Stones, Robbie Williams, Katy Perry, Pink and Billie Eilish) and in his near 30 years in the company (impressive when marketers typically move on every two or three years), Ralf is someone who, regardless of the mood or level of support in the corporation, has stuck passionately to his agenda. It took a while, he explains, for Electronic Beats to find its true shape. Emerging out of a desire to create a youth marketing strategy, at first Deutsche Telekom's music activity was scattershot – different festivals, different genres, different messaging.

Also worth noting is that Many and Torsten from Yadastar had a hand in early iterations of his music activation work. Similar ideas and ways of operating were coalescing. It was a four-day event that Ralf staged in Cologne to promote Deutsche Telekom's prepaid offering, Xtra, which set a more distinct track towards Electronic Beats. "We had the local Kompakt guys there, of course. Guidance from Chicago. Roger Sanchez, Ian Pooley, DJ Deep – it was like a who's who of international house music."

From there, Ralf – who recalls his early experiences in clubs as featuring a preoccupation with the sound systems and lights ("That was my passion. Not really the girls – more the technology") – saw a strengthening case for electronic music being the brand's focus. "I thought, 'OK, we don't want to be associated with technology from the past. We don't want people thinking about old school desk telephones.' That's a difference to a Jack Daniel's or a Harley Davidson. They're telling stories about the wood of the barrels or physical craftsmanship, and it makes you think of guitars and guitar music. Hip-hop, I love, but the lyrics can be very specific to a market, and I wanted something more international than that. With electronic music, even though obviously Detroit and Chicago are where much of it started, Germany has claims to it as well, and that works for a company called Deutsche Telekom. Lastly, there's something good about the fact that anyone can make this music – the way the tools of production have become so democratised feels a good fit."

Liz Hunter was the launch editor on Electronic Beats. She'd arrived in Berlin as a curious 24-year-old, seeking a break from London and immersion in the creativity and community stemming from the city's famous techno sound, and clubs like Panorama. "Amazing city. Amazing people. This sense, with the wall coming down, of freedom meaning so much more to them," Liz remembers. "A desire to party – and as no one has written any rules yet, we'll write our own."

She could draw on some experience interning at, and then writing for, The Face magazine back in London. But the Electronic Beats gig – secured through club scene friends and acquaintances – was her big break. She explains that the magazine was initially designed for an internal audience only. "It was about convincing internal stakeholders that electronic music wasn't this awful, scary thing that would fuck up their whole business. That it's not just about staying up very late and taking loads of ecstasy." The first edition came out in 2005, five years into the wider Electronic Beats initiative. "I didn't think it would be more than a one-off project," she continues. "So when I was told, 'Guess what? They loved it. They want to do it quarterly and for real people,' I was completely blown away. I felt validated that my gut decision to just move to Berlin at a whim was right."

From there, the issues rolled out. Cover artists included Trentmøller, Theo Parrish, Juan Aitkins, Yello, Róisín Murphy, Miss Kittin and Alter Ego. Initially, the editorial had a lifestyle edge, covering adjacent topics like travel and fashion, but over time it hunkered down to focus on techno and electronica. "I guess this was the very beginning of what we now call content marketing," Liz continues. "There weren't loads of brand magazines, and particularly not about a kind of music that was exploding out of cellars in Berlin, morphing into this global thing, with all of these interconnected strands. There were a few things to sort out with the brand. Like having to use their font, and debates over the design agency to work with – they wanted one in Munich; I said it had to be one in Berlin. But mainly, they were not breathing down our necks at all."

Mirroring so much of what we've heard about RBMA, sweating the details is a big theme when Ralf lifts the lid on Electronic Beats. He talks about how his visuals team (many with a background at Berlin's Love Parade) concentrates on using T-Mobile's familiar magenta brand colour in projects and lighting, decreasing the need for more obvious signage and use of the T logo. And now the visuals are going AI: "You can type in something crazy, like 'horses flying through the sky, shitting magenta bombs', or whatever. And then AI creates videos and moving imagery from that prompt."

Thinking about the Electronic Beats journey, Ralf affords a grin, saying it has all been "a mixture of real, serious strategy and a lot of cool things happening by accident." They marked 20 years of this planning/serendipity mix with a 300-page book available to buy through their website, including contributions from Honey Dijon, Billie Eilish, Bryan Ferry, Ellen Allien, Nina Kraviz, Daniel Wang and Dixon. It's a lavish piece of work. For Ralf, publishing it was also about reinforcing a certain point.

"When we created the 20th anniversary book, of course I wanted to tell the history of Electronic Beats. But it was also to do with the fact that I give lectures for those in the creative and music industries, and often people talk about Red Bull *(Music Academy)*. Always Red Bull, and less often Electronic Beats! This is what hurts me. We've existed for longer now, and I never get tired of telling our story – how we did it and advice for how others can do it."

Ralf, who's as happy discussing David Mancuso and The Loft as his own marketing campaigns, is now readying himself and the team for the 25th birthday of Electronic Beats. There's no trace of a drop in energy. Grand-scale events and content are in development. Doubtless, there will be reflections on changes that have unfolded across that quarter of a century, too. "So much has changed," he nods. "You had superstar DJs back then, but now it's much more DJs as brands. Peggy Gou paid to dress in luxury items and earning incredible fees. Some have gained, for sure. The big DJs who understand the value of being a brand. But it feels like the clubs themselves are currently the losers. The dilemma of creating safe spaces in these very commercial times."

There are other brands-in-dance-music activities we could reference from the early 2000s. Among them, Sony PlayStation (continuing their late 1990s exploits) and Diesel were noisy in grassroots and DIY music around then, albeit less wedded to club culture. But Red Bull Music Academy, which we closed the last chapter with, and Electronic Beats, as we've started this one with, serve as good markers of a modern era of initiatives – those where more innovative formats and more considered design are beginning to show.

Taking cues from them, a plethora of initiatives from a spectrum of brands (OK, alcohol brands more than any other category) have followed. Plenty have been pretty smart, carefully considered and designed to offer something of value to clubbers and to club culture alike. But none have proved as enduring as these two. Or spoken about in the hushed tones with which RBMA, in particular, is still greeted (such is its reputation, quite a few I talk to assume it is still running). Fear of commitment looms large here. Senior marketers jumping between jobs, brands jumping between strategies and budgets jumping between pots (or being removed from all pots). Factors like these make maintaining any sort of north star trajectory hard to muster. In all of the uncertainty, it sure takes people willing to fight for the cause.

Tom Dodd, who earlier shared his RBMA experiences as head of artist marketing at Red Bull and now works at the William Morris Endeavor agency, picks up on this theme. "It's often the brands that have a culture department within their marketing department or a cultural lead within their marketing department. Someone who's prepared to go into meetings and stand up for this stuff in front of the managing director.

"We would often say the first year is when you've got to embed yourself in the culture and do something good and useful for that culture. And then, maybe in the second year, you can push that a little bit further and start to inject the brand. And then, in the third year, you'll start to see the rewards of that. But getting people from the first to the third year is the hardest thing, and you would often see them drop out in year two. It's just really expensive and also it takes time to build trust."

Tom Armstrong from Common People, who we first heard from in chapter four, considers what staying power means in the context of contributing to culture: "I think earning respect is a big thing. You can't just throw money at it. If a brand wants to become part of something rooted in, say, working-class or marginalised creativity, no one should be rolling out the red carpet for them. I mean, if you want to be in music culture, if you just turned up to a record shop and spent a grand on records and bought everything that you thought you should buy, it doesn't mean that you're accepted into that world. You have to keep turning up for years, spending the money and engaging. And then your opinion is respected. Culture is a living thing. It's a collection of humans, and you have to treat it as something with feelings and emotions. Brands, hard as it is for them, have to do that."

Before paranoia sets in, dance music isn't getting singled out here in terms of a quick wins mentality. The pursuit of snappy fixes and immediacy is rampant right across the marketing communications industry and a topic of heavy discussion. In a Marketing Week interview, Sir Martin Sorrell, formerly CEO of the world's largest advertising and PR group, WPP, and now founder of digital advertising, marketing and technology services company S4, noted short-termism as the biggest threat to future growth in the industry: "The average life of a CEO in position is around six to seven years, a CFO is around five to six years, and the people we tend to deal with more – the CMO – is around two to three years."

"I think one way around this short-term flipping and switching is trying to get brands to commit to funds," Tom Dodd from WME continues when asked about ways to combat transient priorities. "More than a campaign. Like a pledge to invest in communities and culture that, in theory, they can't back out of so easily."

More on funds to follow. Meantime, Tom explains that in his day-to-day role at WME, he's predominantly thinking from the artist's perspective. He's trying to understand what makes them tick and therefore the partnerships that could apply. Endorsements, sponsorships, licensing, product collaborations, content creation, tech integrations, events, social media promotions – the angles to work are expanding, and the fit between artist and commercial partner is paramount.

Much like in the world of brands, some artists are comfortable with quick fixes, while others only approve fastidiously planned collaborations. Though there are myriad reasons artists choose to work with brands – or avoid them – and the types of partnerships they're comfortable with, he believes these differences can broadly be divided into two camps. On one side, some commercially-minded artists view brand collaborations as part of their job and a key source of income. They'll promote products, engage with their fanbases, and essentially "play the game" with minimal fuss. "And then there are those who are very idealistic and who think about these things in an utterly different way." That Tom follows this observation by mentioning Aphex Twin comes as no great surprise.

"One that always comes to my mind was doing the deal for Aphex Twin at Red Bull. It was the first brand deal I believe he's done. The reason why he wanted to do it was because his show is very expensive and he didn't want to undermine or lose any intensity in terms of lighting and sound quality and the visual concept. To do that and to make it viable, he needed some support, and he was open to Red Bull because of the work they'd done with RBMA. He was like, 'OK, Red Bull's not a perfect company, but it's made a real difference within music.' That contract that I did with Aphex Twin, I think it maybe had like 300 track changes on it. It was one of the most complex deals I've ever done in my life. It was all thought about *meticulously*. And impressively! Everyone wanted to get the best out of it."

The shows, at London's Printworks in 2019, boasted a custom-built stage set with numerous lasers and 306 LED panels, blasting out visuals from long-term Aphex collaborator, the elusive Weirdcore. "It was challenging but worth it. It was a very beautiful show. I believe you rarely have an artist leave a show when they've done a brand integration and be 100% blown away by the experience, because there's often friction. It's like, 'You got to post, you got to do this, you got to do that.' These are the things you've agreed to in the contract, but the artist isn't really into it. That happens a lot, and that's fine. I think it's just life. But actually, Aphex Twin left that show completely bowled over."

It's a broad church for sure that we're spending time with in *Selling The Night*. The definition of what is 'dance music' is a malleable thing. Perspectives on what the value exchange should be when hooking up with brands, as Tom from WME has already intimated, differ just as broadly. This, though, is contingent on snagging yourself an opportunity in the first place. In realms less abstract electronica and more superclubby, we're back with Ministry Of Sound executive chairman Lohan Presencer. Displaying characteristically brutal honesty, he explains the challenges of working with brands when you're no longer considered the freshest face on the block.

"I still get 300,000 people a year through the club doors, which is pretty much the same as 30 years ago. But you talk to somebody in the marketing department of a cool brand, and they say, 'Oh, Ministry, isn't that for your mom and dad?' Fuck off," he advises. "I'm sure others will argue differently, but we're the most famous club in the history of the universe. Our brand is more recognisable in electronic music than nearly any other electronic music brand anywhere in the world. Pacha, that's the only one that possibly comes close.

"Koko *(the venue formerly called Camden Palace)* has got loads of brand partners and I've got literally no one right now. I'm sort of over it – except obviously I'm not because I'm moaning about it..." He pauses – deep breath – then sets off again. "Brand partnerships were great until they weren't. A great one is where each partner benefits from it in some way; where the collaboration makes total sense. So when things are presented to us, we look at them and decide is this positive or negative? Positive is when it takes you into a category you'd like to be associated with, with an audience that chimes with yours, where there might be some cross-pollination. Negative is when it's just about the money."

He shudders slightly when he recalls a partnership with Nissan and their Juke model from around 15 years ago. They took a room at the club, where a sound system was installed inside one of the cars. "And then they did a Ministry Of Sound edition Juke, which had a *slightly* better sound system and was black, with the Ministry logo on it. None of us thought it was cool. We were like, 'This isn't a fucking Lamborghini. What's the excitement?' But we made 300 grand from the deal, so… yeah…"

Message in a bottle

"My job really is to make sure that the brand stays relevant in culture." Maxime Henain, Absolut's global head of culture, collaborations and partnerships, is explaining his role. We first heard from him in chapter two when revisiting the brand's participation in 1970s New York clubs. He started out with Absolut 15 years ago in a more generalist advertising role. Enthused by the more specialised gig he's transitioned into, he relishes the cerebral grappling over what culture is and where Absolut can figure that comes with it.

"Culture is a big word, but we break it down to four territories where we've always played and still want to play," he explains. "Fashion, art, entertainment and music. My job is to make sure that we work on partnerships with like-minded individuals, brands and communities that can help us bring all of this to life in ways that are exciting and subversive but also entertaining. It has to work for our consumers. In fact, we're consumer-obsessed in how we do this. Even more so than with our normal advertising."

His work includes managing their longstanding partnership with Belgian electronic dance music festival Tomorrowland, which, among other things, manifests as Absolut x Tomorrowland bottles designed to 'spotlight a shared belief that what unites us is stronger than what divides us – and together we can create a better tomorrow.' The job is nothing if not varied. Elsewhere in culture, he can also be found signing off limited-edition tomato vodka pasta sauces made in partnership with Heinz and inspired by supermodel Gigi Hadid's viral social media recipe for spicy vodka pasta.

"We don't see ourselves so much as a vodka or spirits brand," he continues, borderline evangelically. "We're a lifestyle brand. We're art-obsessed. We're music-obsessed. We're fashion-obsessed. We're values-, inclusivity- and diversity-obsessed. It's always been like this, and it will always be so."

Absolut take their cultural backstory seriously. New joiners to the company get given a copy of Michael Roux's My Absolut Life, the book we drew from in chapter two. They have an archivist on the payroll whose job is to document stories, art and imagery, and share all of this during induction sessions. Maxime takes this cultural backstory very seriously, too. "When I joined, the first thing I said was I'm just a custodian of this brand. I'm here for a period of time. Someone will come after me, and someone was there before me. We stand on the shoulders of what our predecessors did, and they've been building the legacy of this brand quite incredibly for 45 years. The job is just to continue that legacy."

As much as maintaining legacy and principles is important, like never before, demonstrating results is now, too. For Roux, in his book, it all sounded so simple what success meant back then: 'My philosophy was that I was not doing things to get something out of somebody. We would do risky things. For instance, we did many things with the gay community. I did it to fight the bigotry. Then, the press would pick it up. My philosophy was, if you're doing good, you'll do well.'

Today, explains Maxime, the KPIs for cultural collaborations vary depending on a project's scale and nature. They range from broad, commercial metrics to more niche, localised ones. Each KPI plays a specific role, whether linking efforts to increased sales or in generating earned media (exposure from journalists, influencers, customers or the public). Some KPIs try to track cultural relevance in more nuanced ways, such as how the brand lands within specific cultural movements in a particular city. While much can be monitored and measured, gauging the true ROI remains, he concedes, an art as much as a science (cue aghast spreadsheet jockeys).

But anyway, he shrugs, sometimes you need to park scrutinising the metrics. Instead, you settle for the ethnographic benefits – getting out there among clubbers and on dancefloors. It's an acceptance that this is messy stuff, and you need to feel it as much as put a number on it. "There is nothing better than seeing what people are doing. I'm not talking about the drinking so much. I'm talking about what they are wearing and what they are listening to. What are they doing when they're not dancing? You're not going around asking questions about 'Who are you, what do you do and what do you read?' It's more about observing, and this is the most valuable data for me. Sometimes, it validates what you think matters to clubbers. Sometimes, it invalidates it. But it's always important to take all of this in and use it in your future work."

He talks about the risks of consumer fatigue. So many drops and collaborations, integrations and activations. When your favourite cereal is collabing with a sneaker brand, you know the game's getting crowded. What once was designed to make people sit up and take notice now threatens to be greeted by a collective *whatever*. "It's important to never stop thinking about different, better ways for us to spread our values around inclusivity, diversity and mixing people from different walks of life," he says. "Doing so with like-minded talent, communities, brands and institutions."

He also feels a growing tension in the music industry. Escalating since the pandemic, the gap between the haves and have-nots is widening. Massive DJs earning lots of money and most other DJs earning very little money. Or expected to play to earn 'exposure' – the equivalent of the unpaid internship – a system hugely favouring those from a healthy socio-economic background. Absolut do need to be at the big events, Maxime concedes: "We're a massive brand. We must be visible." But they also need to keep innovating their methods for supporting more underground environs. "Without that, we lose depth."

These days, Absolut is owned by Pernod Ricard. Once, that was simply a kind of anise-flavoured apéritif. Now, it's a vast empire of 240 brands, no doubt all jostling to make a dent of some kind on culture. There are wines, spirits, non-alcoholic options and ready-to-drinks, including familiar names like Chivas, Malibu, Beefeater and Jameson. Another brand in the portfolio – specifically in the Chivas Brothers group – is the Scotch whisky, Ballantine's. While not able to boast the long-prevailing clubland connections of an Absolut, they've been one of the noisiest entrants to the scene in the years since RBMA was shuttered, and much of that noise has come via True Music.

This is the name they give to their music platform, their means of bridging links with the culture of clubs and the night. Like every instance of brands-in-dance-music, it has some critics (even RBMA had a few of them), but more dominant is the sense that this is an initiative that has evolved positively since launching in 2014, cognisant of a changing world and the need to move far beyond rudimentary brand badging exercises.

Ballantine's partner throughout the lifespan of True Music has been Boiler Room, the dance music broadcasting, events and content business that's grown to epic proportions since it launched, a few years earlier than True Music, in 2010. Sold to ticketing business Dice in 2021, then in early 2025 to Superstruct Entertainment, Boiler Room has certainly been met with criticism. Some of it is rather surface level, such as the general mirth around the set design of DJs filmed surrounded by gawking fans. Other concerns are more deep-rooted, including its policies for paying guest artists and the eyebrows raised over the £800,000 it received from the UK government's culture recovery fund during the pandemic. Nevertheless, there's no denying its colossal impact, beaming a vast list of highly credible DJs to fans worldwide.

Dan Maurice is a global senior brand manager at Ballantine's and, since joining the business in 2017, has been key in setting the course for True Music. He summarises the journey so far: "The brief at the start was that whisky was thought of as stuffy and the audience as old *(the alcohol industry often thinks in terms of finding more 'uptempo' occasions for 'downtempo' drinks, envisaging this as a route to growth)*. There was an ambition to re-energise the brand. To bring in a new audience, and to do that through something people really care about: music.

"Boiler Room was three or four years into its own development, so it felt like a good time to be working with them as a way into youth culture and to changing perceptions of our brand. I think the first two years were very much about testing the waters, finding out what worked, what resonated with the markets, so we could understand what would give us longevity. Basically, we were defining what True Music was.

"Then it became more about how we drive credibility at scale. So arguably a bit closer to a sponsorship badging thing, but with more depth. And getting the artist mix right. People who were quite big or breaking through, but without just resorting to the most obvious big names. So at the time for us, that meant working with a Seth Troxler, or a Nightmares On Wax, or a Maya Jane Coles. Credible artists with interesting stories, but certainly not what you'd label as international superstars.

"All of that felt good in so much as we were building the platform and awareness. But we started to feel it wasn't that ownable," he reflects, showing a refusal to rest on laurels that has served True Music well. "Working with someone like Seth is great, but how many mixes of his have you seen on YouTube already?"

Dan mentions that, unlike many brands in the Pernod Ricard portfolio, Ballantine's sales are less skewed to the US and UK markets. This allowed them to consider their role in dance music differently from that of others. "We shifted our focus to spotlight local talent in Africa, showcasing new music from South Africa, Cameroon, Ghana and Kenya. We didn't necessarily have the budget to take massive headliners to some of these places, so the model was all around celebrating local scenes and talent. We showcased new, exciting genres that audiences outside those regions hadn't been exposed to before and we found it resonated globally.

"Music fans were discovering new genres like amapiano from Johannesburg, so that gave us kudos. It also gave these artists a platform to reach an international audience, which was huge for them. It was the perfect alignment for us: we tapped into a niche and used our brand's scale and reach to introduce new sounds to people."

Afrobeats, Afrotrap, Afro-R&B, amapiano, local takes on house music – these are some of the genres that True Music has lent support to through events (and follow-up content) across South Africa, Cameroon, Kenya and Ghana. Kwesi Arthur, La Même Gang, Amaarae, Oskido, Kat La Kat, DJ Raybel, DJ Maphorisa, Symatics, EA Wave, Taio, Locko, Askia, Dope Saint Jude and DJ Lyle have featured. Familiar names for many engrossed in underground dance music across the continent, but something fresh and fascinating for most elsewhere. Ballantine's were excited by the response, both inside and outside of Africa, and figured this could differentiate them from others operating in dance music.

There's data to back up that case. Views of the hashtag #amapiano were up 166% across global social media in 2023. Stats from Beatport showed that, though techno and house genres were still the most popular, Afro-house had risen from 18th spot in Q1 2022 to ninth in Q3 2023. Editorial coverage also captured the enthusiasm, with everyone from the BBC and New York Times to Mixmag and Refinery29 charting the appeal of amapiano, with its raw basslines, heavy kick drums and a name rooted in the Zulu word for 'the pianos'. Looking ahead, there are predictions of South Africa's three-step sound – think deep house meets amapiano – going global. Also, of growing international interest in artists from Uganda, Rwanda and Tanzania, from Lusophone and Francophone Africa. As their involvement deepened, Ballantine's recognised that celebrating these artists and genres wasn't the total of what they could offer to the communities they were engaging with. Mindful of likely questions about the substantiality of their support (brands claiming 'ownership' of things is a precarious business), Ballantine's turned their focus to more structural ways of furthering electronic music culture in sub-Saharan Africa.

"We knew we were onto something, but then we started thinking more about what these music communities needed to stay healthy and fresh," Dan explains. "It's all well and good showcasing amapiano, but what infrastructure might that scene need – is that something we can play a role in? So, I guess this is where we started to dial up the sense of activating with purpose. How could we develop education programmes or create access to recording studios or improve the sense of clubs offering safe spaces to people?"

The pandemic's transformative impact on culture has become a recurring theme throughout *Selling The Night*. For Ballantine's Dan Maurice, it was a game changer in shifting people's openness to new experiences – sparking curiosity for music from across the globe. He also reflects on how, while many brands were quick to retreat from music when lockdowns began, True Music chose to stay the course, reinforcing their commitment to the scene.

"We did feel a responsibility to support those communities and those scenes, so we kept doing stuff through lockdown. We gave grants to 20 artists in that first year of lockdown, allowing people to continue showcasing their talent and broadcasting online. I think that was when we felt we'd been accepted and people acknowledged we're doing stuff for the right reasons; that we hadn't simply used the communities and the artists for our benefit, and then when it got a bit difficult, just fucked off."

When you look at True Music across Africa and beyond, you're struck by the number of dimensions to it. There have been pop-up studios in places like Delhi and Soweto; partnerships with Defected Records in Croatia. There is the True Music Fund: £100,000 split between 10 recipients yearly. Among those who've benefited: the Africa Rising Music Conference, a female-led event championing the African music industry; Planet Wax, a record store, dubplate cutting studio and bar in New Cross, southeast London; also in London, No Signal, the online radio station centred on the Black diaspora; and Barcelona's queer scene-representing club night, label and platform, MARICXS. As with Red Bull Music Academy, measuring this and understanding what each strand does for Ballantine's brand must be technically challenging.

"We're very open about how we do it," Dan explains. "Every two years, we'll do a full equity study going into four or five markets we've activated in over that time, and doing a pre-read and a post-read *(in campaign evaluations, a pre-read is conducted before a campaign to understand audience perceptions and establish baseline metrics. A post-read takes place after the campaign to measure its impact in changing attitudes toward the brand)*. If you pay enough, you can paint a false picture by inflating the numbers and driving views and impressions on social media. But asking the consumer, that's where you'll get the real answers. We can show how things like brand preferences, likelihood to recommend and so on are changing."

Clearly, it also doesn't hurt that Ballantine sales have grown year-on-year in key markets since the inception of True Music. "We probably can't say it's all down to the music," he laughs. "But while there's that upward momentum, and our True Music work is resonating so well, we're definitely going to take some of the credit."

Dan's own story in music includes studying music production at university. This was a potential career path until something hit him hard: "I love making music, but I also love daylight. I'm not sure spending the next 25 years in a windowless room was for me." Instead, he got an internship at Universal's Mercury label, followed by a permanent role – back when digital was quaintly called 'new media'. "It felt like the Wild West and also probably the most fun time of my career. One minute setting up MySpace and Bebo pages for artists, the next picking up a Camcorder and having all of this backstage access to big names." He also got to work in the distribution side of the business, giving him exposure to white labels, specialist imprints and the early 2000s dance scene. Next came a move to Sony PlayStation ("I had a kid, needed to earn more money"), working on marketing for the Spotify integration into PlayStation and their Champions League and FIFA World Cup activations.

Then, the Ballantine's opportunity. "Do I like music and drink? Yes! So it sounded like the job for me. I felt there could be a chance to do something with depth here." Dan acknowledges that Red Bull Music Academy has influenced both True Music and his own principles for how brands engage in music. Through True Music surveys, he's also aware of RBMA's influence on others. While it may have closed in 2019 (though admittedly, some other Red Bull music activity is still happening), "When you ask people what brands they most associate with music, Red Bull still comes first."

He continues: "You can't overlook that they had a *serious* amount of money to invest, but still, they came across as supporters. They built respect in a way that others have struggled to. I think people understood they weren't taking advantage and were shining a light on important artists and under-represented communities."

He says True Music is finding a similar benefit from its investment in supporting artists and creating content to reflect this support. It engenders a long tail of engagement over time. "Someone like Black Coffee, I think we first worked with him in 2015 on one of our early shows in South Africa. Now he's playing with superstars in Ibiza. But there's our content out there from 10 years ago, and people find it. They realise the support we were giving early on, and there's something very powerful in that."

Also evident is that True Music's success comes from not standing still. The term 'platform' is used frequently and often vaguely in culture marketing, but it's fitting here. It's enabled True Music to be more than a singular initiative, helping it avoid running out of steam by reflecting on strengths and weaknesses, and retooling as a result. When we spoke, and after a couple of months of downtime from activations to take stock, Tom was fresh out of meetings focused on the next decade of True Music.

"We've done a good job with Boiler Room and hitting that younger demographic, but how can we now emulate Red Bull Music Academy a bit more?" is how he puts it. It sounds like this will partly entail whisky moving back into its own, less youthful lane – also acknowledging that dance music isn't just for young people anymore. "We're thinking of different ways to do it. Boiler Room is all about a cutting-edge 18-to-25-year-old audience, but they don't stay with people much after that age. We're considering how we complement that with ways to build longer-term relationships, staying with people as their tastes in music and the culture surrounding that music evolve. That said, it will always be about using our global reach to support artists and communities and to facilitate keeping this culture alive."

Ballantine's isn't the only alcohol brand that has seen value in connecting with more nascent dance communities. Miller's Miller Mix tour with Beatport took them to Almaty in Kazakhstan. In the documentary video accompanying the live show, local DJs and promoters like Nazira, Midclassgypsy and Gato Azul explain how stymied dance music is due to the shortage of venues across Central Asia. We also get to see the Miller Mix parties, local scenesters doing their stuff, a DJ school in action and, just a couple of times, shots of the beer in question. "Miller Mix is putting Kazakhstan on the global map," enthuses Almaty DJ ET.

For others in beer, it's less about the location and more about riding a trend. For instance, phone bans. Anyone interested in club culture has probably seen one of the videos on X, TikTok and similar, mocking the sight of clubbers who are not joyously waving their arms in the air but instead using them to hold their phones aloft. And clubs are taking action. 'No phones on the dancefloor' has increasingly been the response. What started in Berlin's queer party scene and at venues such as Tresor, UFO, Planet, Snax Club and, some while later, Berghain, then arrived at London clubs like FOLD and Fabric. Tellingly, it has now travelled as far as the conspicuous clubbing epicentre, Ibiza. Specifically to nights at Hï Ibiza and the Pikes hotel club ('Keep your phones in your pocket and your mind on the music', they advise via Instagram).

Themes swirling in the phones versus no phones debate include how self-expression and the rights of others to stay out of sight in the subcultures of their choice are being inhibited; the impact of peer pressure (one person gets their phone out, everyone gets their phone out); and, of course, that no one needs to see another vid of a DJ bro mid-drop ever again. "Essentially, you're not present in the moment," psychologist Charlotte Armitage explained in a Time Out article. "So instead of smelling, hearing, sensing what is going on around you, feeling the sound vibrations, you're staring down into a brightly lit phone."

Entering the debate, Heineken. At Amsterdam Dance Event 2024, they 'hacked' Barry Can't Swim's DJ set, deploying infrared light to create an invisible-to-the-eye display, observable only when viewed through the phone's camera. Whenever someone held up their phone to film the DJ, a message would appear on it advising them not to. It would also recommend downloading Heineken's latest app. Called The Boring Mode, it blocks all other apps, notifications and, of course, the smartphone camera for a limited period of time. Barry seemed to cope reasonably with the hacking. "When I heard about the new anti-smartphone concept, it was something that struck a chord with me," he offered up in the press release. "With live music, of course you are more present and immersed if you are giving it your full attention, rather than taking a video on your phone. And without phones, the energy is definitely different – people are more connected on the dancefloor."

Not everything is bottled

Alcohol. So much alcohol. While there are some naysayers around drink's involvement in dance music – specifically, whether it adds or subtracts from the atmosphere and the sense of inclusiveness – in broader terms, you cannot really debate its place as a lubricant of the night. But what about other categories of brands? Who else has headed for the dancefloor? We've touched on telecoms with T-Mobile, and there are plenty more in that sector worldwide who, if not to the degree of Electronic Beats, have put money into dance music.

Ralf at Deutsche Telekom spoke earlier about "creating memorable experiences," a strategic objective that Electronic Beats delivers on. It's going to be interesting to see how telecom brands react to the fast-growing trend we've touched on for banning phones on the dancefloor – essentially the expectation that we trust our own memories rather than those recorded on our mobiles; how self-expression and communal experience should trump the right to document everything going. Time will tell if this challenges the permission that telecom operators have to take space – and create memorable experiences – within club culture. One assumes many marketing minds are considering how to respond to this cultural shift as we speak.

Aside from telecoms, there are cars. In 2015, Volvo's XC90 launch included a significant collaboration with Avicii. "He stretches us a bit outside our comfort zone," Alain Visser, Volvo's senior vice president of sales, marketing and customer service, told Marketing Week. "We like that despite being a world star he's still quite understated. Volvo likes to be that as well. We leave it to the other car manufacturers to be aggressive or arrogant." Aiming for an 'intrepid adventure for music lovers', Land Rover's Defender division plotted up at dance music-focused festival, Lost Village. They had their own stage called Outpost. Brand fit: it was a stage in the site's most rugged, isolated corner. In a similarly rugged-looking setting far away in Ibiza, Sven Vath is beamed out across socials, pictured getting into *his* Defender. Supporting copy, which one feels could have done with some refining before sharing, reveals: 'As a global ambassador for @defender, I see the values of endurance, strength and reliability reflected. Timeless design and superior comfort merge to be ready for any challenge, without compromising style or functionality.'

DJ magazine's Carl Loben has also spotted cars cropping up incongruously: "I went to Sónar *(enduring Barcelona electronic music and associated arts festival)* this year. It was a great event, but it was an eye-opener seeing what looked like a car showroom there *(a partnership with Nissan's 'most rebellious model', the Juke)*. It felt more like what you'd expect to see at Dubai Airport. Imagine that back in the day!"

Inevitably, it doesn't stop with the categories noted so far. There have been chocolates – cue David Guetta helping Cadbury celebrate the 100th anniversary of Milk Tray. Vapes and chewing gum. Soft drinks, cosmetics and hair care products. Rideshare providers and financial institutions. While some connections here between the category and club culture may seem tenuous, they're often justified through a brand positioning statement – how a brand sets itself up versus competitors and communicates its unique value to consumers. Once upon a time, a bank was a place to keep your money, and a drink was a thing to quench your thirst. Thanks to positioning statements, the quest for brands to meet human needs often takes on a more elevated and abstract status now. 'Creating moments of joy and shared experiences'; 'Connecting people with possibilities'; 'Turning ideas into reality'; 'Empowering you to live your best life'. These are all made up but might as well be real and demonstrate how club culture can be made to fit across so many categories.

If automobiles and chocolate boxes take us to incongruent places, fashion, like alcohol, snaps us back to the more familiar aspects of the night. Earlier in our story, we saw how Fiorucci found a home in New York's disco culture. From high street to high-end, fashion has increasingly invested in club and dance music partnerships since the 2000s. A 2023 Vogue Business article highlighted how fashion brands have, in particular, aligned with multifaceted online dance music platforms like Berlin's Colors – founded by ex-advertising industry professionals and dedicated to letting artists showcase their music 'without distraction'. The article also examined partnerships with NTS, the online radio platform that began in Hackney and later expanded to Manchester and Los Angeles, which have flourished in fashion circles.

Fashion is teaming up with something tried and tested here. Dance music's presence across digital platforms has always been significant. Particularly at the more electronica-y end of the spectrum, it was probably online, at scale, before any other genre of music. There have been newsletters, bulletin boards, communities and forums stretching back to the early 1990s, with artists like Coldcut flying the flag for them before most indie bands had got a modem. The pandemic – as ever, the accelerant to end all accelerants of change – ramped things up even further. Livestreams came into play, creating opportunities unlimited by geography.

The benefits of working with dance music platforms of this kind (of course, Boiler Room can be included here, too) become evident when you consider the multiple touchpoints they offer: the reach of online, the energy of events, the power of community. Fashion brands who've teamed up with NTS include Diesel, whose support included backing a 17-hour east London rave with an array of club collectives; also, radio roundtables discussing issues affecting the clubbing sector in the city. Patronage of Colors has come from Burberry ('celebrating local talent and creativity') and, with yet more celebrations, adidas Originals ('celebrating creativity in all its forms – music, art, style and movement'). "Being able to lean into music discovery, talent and culture is something brands can't buy, and that's why collaboration is so necessary," music partnership consultant Tessa Solan reasoned in the Vogue Business article – though they do of course buy those collaborations. "You can't buy support and true, genuine interest. That's where platforms like NTS or Colors have always been consistent and authentic, and brands need that authenticity."

Good sport

In fashion and apparel, sportswear adds a different dimension to the relationship between club culture and style. Namely, sport. A cultural convergence has been steadily unfolding, with a Venn diagram that merges football and basketball, in particular, with music, clubs and fashion. DJs and rappers alike take to the stage and streets in football shirts. There's a recognition that the power of fandom lives in both spheres. Boiler Room teamed up with Umbro, enlisting DJs like EZ and Jyoty and youth culture photographer Ewen Spencer to document the collaboration. Behind it all: 'celebrating the unifying power of both the football pitch and the dancefloor, acknowledging the intersection between club culture and the beautiful game.'

This trend is part of the same redefinition of style – how it presents itself, where it draws its energy from – that has seen Paris Saint-Germain FC collaborate with Jordan (a brand deeply rooted in the NBA and previously nowhere near European soccer leagues), even opening a store on 5th Avenue in NYC. It's in the work of designer and creative director Ted Philipakos, who has transformed the shirts of relatively lowly clubs like Venezia FC and Athens Kallithea FC into luxury athleisure items. It's the New York Knicks hiring Kith founder Ronnie Fieg as creative director. Not typically known for progressiveness, Major League Baseball is getting involved too: the New York Yankees joining forces (well, they are part-owned by the same investment group) with AC Milan for a co-branded lifestyle collection. Milan deserves another mention, with Jordan choosing to open its first concept store there instead of a city more traditionally associated with basketball.

The trend goes deeper – and becomes more structural – with initiatives like Stormzy's adidas-backed Merky FC. A football club, recording studio and sports gaming hub in Croydon, south London, Merky FC aims to 'nurture the voices of tomorrow' and provide a 'safe space for all to express themselves'.

These cultural collisions make particular sense in the case of hip-hop and its offspring, like grime. The sentiment of lifting people and creativity from the streets is both powerful and provocative. But not new. For over 40 years, sportswear has been in close company with music and the culture that surrounds it. It's an association that turned sportswear into streetwear and, by common account, it all started in 1973, when Puma released the Clyde, a signature sneaker for New York Knicks point guard Walt 'Clyde' Frazier.

Known for his style both on and off the court, Frazier's collaboration with Puma resulted in a shoe that became iconic not just in basketball but also in streetwear. He was one dapper guy, a purveyor of the so-called pimp look (think wide-lapeled suits, fedora hats and mink coats), which preceded sportswear on the streets and in the clubs. At the same time, outdoor courts in places like the Bronx, Brooklyn and Harlem were switching the tone of basketball, and ultimately the NBA, to something with more swagger and improvisation. Something more deeply connected to Black culture, too. Clive Campbell, the Jamaican-born, NYC-bred DJ who, also in 1973, was busy prototyping the hip-hop sound on Sedgwick Avenue in the Bronx, would use the tag 'Clyde As Kool' in his graffiti days. This was down to Frazier being his favourite player. Eventually, he'd streamline that to Kool Herc (the Herc is Hercules abbreviated, and due to his six-foot-five-inch height), and hip-hop folklore was underway.

In an interview with Versus, Jason 'Scully' Kavuma from London's No Signal – known for radio, events and amplifying Black voices; and, as mentioned earlier, recipients of funding from Ballantine's – points to similar parallels between music and football as there is with basketball. "I think both music and football are associated with the working classes. With football, all you need is a ball and therefore anyone can play it. And when it comes to music, all you need is a decent voice and an understanding of flow and rhythm. I think the access point for both is more obtainable because of this. Anyone can 'get in', but the thing about both of them is: the better you are, the further you go. It feels like a place where there's true meritocracy. If you're really good at football, you're going to succeed. If you're really good at music, you're going to sell records. Obviously, there's outside factors that can change this, but that is the simplest way of putting it. I think that is why they're so synonymous."

It's no surprise that the NBA and football are getting most of the love here, but this trend stretches further, reaching places with a less self-evident cultural fit. Swiss sportswear brand On, for example, marked the 2024 US Open with 'an electrifyingly unique fusion of sport and rave culture' at their Brooklyn Clubhouse Nights. The events featured a tennis match commentated on by the hosts of the hip podcast How Long Gone (self-styled, and only half in jest, as targeting America's 'bi-coastal elite'). Later, the court 'transformed into a pulsating dancefloor', with DJ sets from Yaeji, Memphy, Oscar Nñ and Young Teesh, plus a specially curated selection of cocktails. In the words of the press release, it was 'a one-of-a-kind celebration of the intersection between sports, music and entertainment.'

"Football is the biggest and most global sport. It has the most money and the widest, most diverse fanbase. So, it feels like it's at the bleeding edge. But tennis, rugby, cricket, golf, running – there's an appetite across numerous sports for some of this." We're hearing from Corey Pellatt, CEO and founder of the same Versus we quoted Jason 'Scully' Kavuma from. Corey is no slouch at insight on all sports, but football is his heartland – hence *Versus* is positioned as a media platform and fan community championing 'the future of football and its rising influence on new music and culture.' It was conceived with the same multi-set Venn diagram of cultural intersections mentioned earlier. As their comms blurb explains: "A new generation of players and fans have changed the rules, and the beautiful game is now more important than ever. Contemporary football is hyper-connected and culturally fluid – interacting with fashion, gaming, music, and activism."

Speaking from Versus HQ in Brixton, south London, Corey explains a journey that began at 16 when he started a student magazine. He was spinning all plates, from selling the ad space to local businesses to designing it and interviewing people like Tinie Tempah and Rizzle Kicks. This led to a role on the UK launch of Complex, the American platform dedicated to Black culture and style, founded by Marc Eckō of Eckō Unltd fashion brand fame. Complex is also known for ComplexCon, an annual event that blends immersive experiences, panel discussions, much streetwear and live music performances from artists like Skrillex, Travis Scott and Playboi Carti.

As Complex sports editor, Corey saw a course of direction for football that mirrored the NBA's cultural rise in the US. Moments like Liverpool players Mario Balotelli, Daniel Sturridge and Raheem Sterling going viral for blasting out Drake in the dressing room, or Stormzy performing Shut Up during Anthony Joshua's ring walk for his 2015 fight against Dillian Whyte, crystallised this vision. Being of an entrepreneurial bent, these experiences also encouraged him to leave Complex and start Versus.

Explaining what needed disrupting in conventional football media, he says: "When you look at Talksport, Sky Sports and so on, and how they've historically covered players getting involved in music, attending fashion weeks, launching their own fashion lines or even dancing when they score a goal – it's all been cynical. There's no respect for self-expression, diversity or the aspiration for a non-toxic football culture. That felt so far removed from what we were seeing: the Paul Pogba and Stormzy transfer announcement when Pogba joined Man United *(an adidas-led viral video that spawned a wave of remixes)*, Hector Bellerin being far more expressive than anything we'd seen from footballers before, or Umbro collaborating with Off-White and Virgil Abloh. Something was clearly shifting in football's influence on culture and society. And when I say culture, I mean music and style. When I say society, I mean anti-racism, gender equality, sustainability and mental health."

This isn't solely about club music in the narrow sense of house and techno – but it is about Black music and electronic music more broadly. Corey highlights projects like OM Records, launched by Olympique de Marseille to build connections between the club and grassroots music in the city. He mentions the Man United x adidas shows on NTS, blending Manchester's musical heritage with sets from old-school icons like 808 State and newer voices such as Tarzsa and Kisa. Versus itself has driven initiatives like the Blue Creator Fund with Chelsea FC and the Chelsea Foundation, empowering a new generation of creators across disciplines, from music to poetry. Then there's the New Balance-backed Basement Cup, featuring mixed-gender teams from the worlds of fashion and influence, paired with DJ sets by Tiffany Calver, Just Jane, Raaandy & Rickinzi and Karetorical. Corey also points to AC Milan's introduction of NBA-style front-row seats at the San Siro Stadium – where stars like Jay-Z have shown up (AC Milan's backers include LeBron James and Drake in their consortium).

"In football right now, it's quite like that NBA journey through the '70s and '80s," Corey continues. "What Walt Frazier was doing back then is sort of what someone like Jules Koundé *(the Barcelona defender who's ruffled feathers by being seen in skirts and boots with 'slight heels')* is doing now. If you look at how Allen Iverson embraced music in the noughties, that's what Paul Pogba did years later."

All of this blending and borrowing is not without obstacles, however. Change comes slowly in some circles. Football clubs are typically risk averse, sensitive to anything that may offend more traditional fans ("Put it this way, clubs don't yet have culture teams"). And among younger audiences, there is still a need to ensure the right sensibilities aren't lost in pursuing innovation. "When we poll our audience," Corey says. "They do want more style and music in the game – but they also tend to be anti the Americanisation of European football. Things like the introduction of tunnel fits *(as in the carefully styled pregame outfits that basketball players wear while walking through the arena tunnel to the locker room)*."

It's a complicated space to operate in. Fans, players, agents, managers, clubs, investors – there are many cohorts to introduce these cultural forces to. "But now it's started – parties, raves, all these things adjacent to football, we're sure to see more of it," Corey signs off. "There'll be friction, I bet, but you've got to be excited by the idea of that."

The culture marketers

What kind of people work in these roles at the intersection of music and marketing? What motivates them, and what are the commonalities between them? All those I meet – and we've told several of their backstories already – clearly love music. It's no act. Whether it's the first time they heard hip-hop, a teenage trip to Ibiza, fumbling around on a home studio set-up or starting a local club night, they can all speak of core memories forged from that love of music. In earlier times, you figure many of them would have worked for record labels rather than on the marketing communications side. But then the music business, in its more conventional form, hasn't exactly shimmered with positivity over the last 20 years – even if it does seem to have found some new sparkle (and profitability) of late.

Autonomy is coveted by them, too. Blurring the nine-to-five with what happens outside of work hours is seen more as a plus than a problem. They do, however, almost all mention occasions of feeling conflicted: is it really possible to square a love of music with the requests of brands? Are they supporting subculture or merely extracting something from it? And in the end, who gains more from the collaboration – the underground or the corporations?

But next to this conflictedness, there's a strong sense from the majority I speak to that brands ultimately *are* part of the youth culture matrix, something they've felt since they were growing up. Adverts, products and media next to scenes and sounds – counterculture and consumerism rubbing together, often without much rationalisation of whether it made sense. A 'necessary evil' is sometimes used to describe brands getting close to culture – a deep-pocketed means to an end. But for many, there's more to it than that. There's a sense that brands aren't just a presence in the culture; they can be participants, collaborators and, maybe occasionally, even creators. After all, they grew up equally obsessed with sneaker behemoths like Nike and adidas, and the cultural clout they packed, as with independent record labels or club nights. Perhaps it's about who's appropriating from whom in this relationship – the mutual exchange (or tension) between culture and consumerism.

With so many mentions of the culture word figuring above, it's no surprise that the creative industries, ever keen to refine and reconfigure, have eked out a tentative new field of work – a new role – in this liminal space. We've heard the term a few times already: culture marketing. Though light on formal definition or criteria, it currently makes up for that with plenty of energy and the spirit of venturing into the unknown. Perhaps eventually it will become more narrowly codified. For now, we can think of it as a profession focused on embedding brands in culture to boost their resonance with specific consumer groups. It's also a bit of a Swiss Army Knife career – part strategist, creative, PR, trend expert and more.

While it's hard to pinpoint exactly when the nomenclature 'culture marketer' (or variations of it) first emerged, there's no doubt it has proliferated over the last decade. A decade, likely by no coincidence, in which the term 'culture' (wars, etc) has peppered debate and rhetoric. Client-side (as industry parlance puts it), these roles unsurprisingly first appeared in fashion, sportswear and alcohol companies – brands already leveraging entertainment partnerships and tracking early adopter trends. But you also started to see specialists in other categories, such as FMCGs (fast-moving consumer goods; the large corporations producing everything from sandwich spreads to shampoo), where the culture in question would more likely centre on family or home life; or banking institutions, where it might involve thinking holistically about wealth and life journeys beyond the buttoned-up world of interest rates and risk assessments.

Agency-side, larger, more conventional creative and media shops began to augment their teams with culture experts, sometimes creating entire departments. Alongside this, countless more niche agencies (many predating the interest shown by bigger agencies) offered their own spin on connecting brands with culture. Different techniques for identifying opportunities and implementing projects that – when all went to plan – positioned their clients among the things in life that matter to people. Phrases like 'culture-first strategy' and 'moving at the speed of culture' started to populate pitch decks, and the industry nodded along knowingly. And while culture marketing isn't solely about music, it's clear why it has become a popular route for many brands – given music's deep emotional connection with audiences.

You can expect to encounter this type of role in various settings, then. So far in *Selling The Night*, we've predominantly seen culture marketers seated in global corporations, but Kazim Rashid shows another option. Originally from Manchester, now ensconced in Berlin, he's chief creative officer of the dance music content, community and ticketing platform Resident Advisor and its 23:59 agency. Described as an 'incubator for ideas, creativity and culture', 23.59 is in place to work with brands – and designed to diversify the parent company's business model, making it less reliant on ticket revenue. It's a popular course of action in specialist media circles.

Before Resident Advisor, Kazim was in similar roles at Mixcloud (running their Loud creative agency) and at Virtue, Vice's brand solutions wing. Earlier still, fresh out of university, he ran his own record label and website. There was DJing, obviously, and making videos for friends running fashion labels. "My first step into branded content." Not long after, he started working for Warp Records, eventually becoming their head of marketing. He's consulted for i-D and Business

Of Fashion. All the while, he's managed a roster of artists, including veteran producer Nightmares On Wax. Quite the hybrid career, one that has given him insight into how people respond to brands entering music subculture from different perspectives.

"In my early days, it was interesting seeing the divide," he says from Resident Advisor's suitably industrial offices in Mitte. "You'd be in the room with one bunch of people and they'd totally get how brands and dance music could work together – even that there was a necessity for them to work together. Then you'd be in another room, say with some more traditional independent record label people, and they'd still see it as selling out, a dirty game. People just didn't get it. They couldn't work out how to do it. It wasn't sync ***(aka synchronisation, licensing music for use with films, TV, advertisements and video games)***, and often they even struggled with that. It was something unknown; they couldn't see how what they did could lead to these collaborative moments.

"It all felt very new at the time," he continues. "Trying to balance the commercial needs, the brand needs, with creativity and doing something worthwhile and that deserved to see the light of day. Nothing felt very optional for me in this, though. Older artists may have built enough of a solid audience that they don't think they are reliant on brands. But for anyone who's not five good albums deep, the requirement for revenue streams to be outside the traditional record business is enormous."

For those like Kazim, this was less a new skill to reluctantly learn and more a given. It was how they assumed things would need to be in an underground music world fiercely rocked by everything from algorithms and streaming to the demise of venues. "All the way through, my work has been treading the line between commerce and external money from brands and delivering integrity-driven creative outputs." And does he have a code, an operating system, for how he strikes a balance between the two? "For me, an important one is making sure that the things we take money for are the type of things we'd like to do anyway. Using other people's money to do what we want to do, if you like. Another is making sure that this external money is used to enhance the cultural space. And primarily in the work I do, that means making sure the artists feel the benefit, too."

One example Kazim raises of when it was a brand, rather than a record label, that backed an early stage artist is Gaika, the south London rapper, singer and producer who's picked up descriptions like 'gothic dancehall and industrial electronics'. His 2018 debut album, Basic Volume, came out on Warp. But before that label was willing to jump in, Carhartt WIP effectively provided the early seeding.

"The labels were cautious. It felt too risky. No one wanted to sign him; we just couldn't get the funding. He was getting attention, there was excitement but we were running on fumes – just me and him, doing absolutely everything, making all the videos, making all the content, paying for it all ourselves. Then Carhartt gave us 25 grand, and it was life-changing. It bought us a year and meant we could go on tour. He smashed it, and then suddenly, labels were offering deals. Without that startup capital from the brand, I don't think we'd have got to the point of doing the record deal, or at least got things in a strong enough place to get a good deal. I think that's an important lesson. We're in an age where the more traditional areas of the music industry – as in the labels – are so cautious and risk-averse."

Commissions for 23.59 have included Breaking Through, a WeTransfer initiative showcasing new artists, and Lift LDN, a Nike platform launched to promote the Air Max 720, blending big names like Peggy Gou with rising talents such as DJs Danielle, Fauzia and Imogen. They accompanied the launch of Rockstar Games' Grand Theft Auto V update by hosting the first-ever in-game livestream, where The Black (now Blessed) Madonna, Tale Of Us and Solomun wore 'fully mapped suits to record their actual movements' during their sets in the Los Santos nightclub. For Absolut, 23.59 created Alternate Cuts, a content initiative celebrating independent party promoters. Kazim describes the source of the work as 80% responding to RFPs (request for proposals), 10% driven by end-of-financial-year budgets that need to be hurriedly spent (a godsend for many agencies) and 10% from Resident Advisor developing an idea and taking it out to raise capital for it.

Does he think there's anything specific to how dance music responds to brand opportunities compared to other genres? "I think underground dance music, perhaps inevitably, has more of a chip on its shoulder about how to work with brands than hip-hop or pop. What's cool, what's not? What feels like it has integrity, and what doesn't? It still feels that anything to do with brands is perceived to be on the wrong side in that discussion.

"If you ask me, it's easier to get money out of a brand than a record label, which says a lot about the industry at large," he shrugs. "And what they want is different. They *(brands)* might want their logo on your poster or for you to wear their shoes. What they don't want is 50-to-80% of your rights for the next 25 years."

Kazim adds that, while he's certain brands can be positive partners for new artists, making sure the partnership is in a good place is not something you can ever sleep on. "I would say that's a never-ending task. Constant work. The expectations of artists and brands are usually misaligned at the outset – and that's reasonable to expect. Handling that relationship requires a huge amount of sensitivity."

We've spoken with culture marketers in brands and at agencies, but plenty are freelance. Originally from London but now based in Marseille after an on-a-whim pandemic move, Ollie Oshodi is a brand and culture consultant and another whose passion for music is unmistakable. She wanted to be a music journalist from as early as she can remember. Her first club experience was Whirl-Y-Gig – an outlier institution brimming with global beats, hippy vibes and a grand finale where a giant silk parachute would be lifted over the crowd.

She moved through genres, from house to drum 'n' bass, UK garage to grime. At university, she wrote essays on the difference between

London and Manchester club culture. There were internships at record labels, followed by a series of marketing roles focusing on music and subculture. These included positions at the Frukt agency, as UK managing director of Fader magazine and its Cornerstone agency and, since 2020, as an independent consultant on projects for brands like Airbnb, Spotify, Google, YouTube and adidas.

She notes that a couple of stand-out projects have been for Converse and Smirnoff. The former was the Rubber Tracks initiative, partnering with studios in Tottenham and east London to allow artists to record without fees – while allowing them to retain full rights to their music. "The glory days of brand culture marketing, where you didn't need many metrics," she smiles. The latter, Equalising Music, a campaign that centred on amplifying the voices of the LGBTQ+ community in club culture – highlighting their pioneering role and working to create more opportunities for the future.

"For me, that was a good example of thinking carefully about the challenge and not making assumptions," she elaborates about Equalising Music. "Rather than just charging in there and assuming you know what's right for that community, it started from a perspective of wanting to learn. We set up roundtables, bringing in different people from the community *(among the more high-profile contributors: Honey Dijon, French ballroom scene icon Kiddy Smile and British transgender model and dancer Lucy Fizz)*. Co-creating the approach and listening. It's important to think and operate like that."

One of the challenges, Ollie believes, is that brand money still tends to support iterations of dance music that stick to the accepted lineage of acid house, rave culture, European techno and so forth. Despite some progress, there's still a long way to go until more of this money reaches, for instance, dance scenes rooted in Black or Asian communities. "It feels like there's quite a narrow view on it all and a constant nostalgia for rave culture. I find it interesting that, when I was 17, I'd be looking back at early rave culture, thinking, 'Oh, my God, this is amazing.' All these years later, there are other waves of young people who have the same nostalgia for a period they didn't experience. I get the appeal. It's powerful. But I think there's a gap for something else. Brands need to get braver."

Of course, attempts at bravery aren't helped much by instances such as the Daily Mail howling at adidas for its support of drill artists. A 2019 article, researched with all the carelessness and scant regard for facts we've come to expect from that paper, accused them of having 'blood on their hands'. But it's not always the fault of rabid newspapers. There's a lack of understanding about other scenes on the brand side – about what does or doesn't 'align' with their 'values' – uncertainty caused by a lack of diversity within marketing teams.

We get talking about how to encourage brands to focus on utility, the resources and support they can provide behind the scenes, rather than expecting to be the life and soul of the party. But also that there's a flip to this – the need for DJs, artists, promoters and managers to get smarter in how they work with brands, understand the industry codes and behaviours, and be more willing to collaborate. "When you consider how important a revenue stream this is for artists these days – potentially their main route to earning a living – they need to think more like co-creators with agencies and brands. Not view it like they are there to be pulled about by them, to just put up with it in return for some quick money. You need to work out how to get on with people."

Indeed, for all of the emphasis on tight strategies, bold objectives and commercial synergies, so often in my conversations with culture marketers, what seems most important is a healthy grasp of a pretty timeless thing: people skills. Suspicion and expectations of the worst mark the starting point of many attempted brand-meets-subculture unions. Time-honoured frictions between artists and commercial people surface. It's easy enough to understand why. But, say the culture marketers I chat with, it tends to be counterproductive for DJs, artists and promoters. It puts them on the weak side in negotiations.

It cuts both ways, of course. Stereotypical conduct plays out on the brand side, too, and our culture marketers often find ourselves right in the middle of wrangles. From curating the CTM festival to promoting and DJing at the Leisure System nights at Berghain, Michail Stangl is a man with deep connections to Berlin club culture. He's operated as a lead programmer and curator for Boiler Room and advised brands such as Google, Converse, Apple, Audi, Native Instruments and Budweiser. Contributing to a Resident Advisor podcast on branding in dance music in 2018, though one assumes not speaking specifically of the clients he works with, Michail cut to the chase when describing the dynamics of how deals tend to be struck and how projects are designed.

"Unfortunately, the process is traditionally structured that the clueless brand manager gives that budget to a very clueless advertising agency that then gives it to an even more clueless sub-agency, and they then find the person on the ground, and then when it trickles up back to the brand, a distorted monster of the original idea arrives, and this is why we get a lot of really awful event concepts. So, the job of a lot of the players who understand the process is basically expectation management. But also setting boundaries. Of course, those who've paid for things should get what they've been promised, but also to protect those who don't know how to protect themselves. Which is quite often artists... protect them not to get sucked into something they might not understand, because it's a very complex process."

At no time does Theo Gentilli describe brand managers as 'clueless', but he is keen to help them become even more clued up. He's the co-founder of Warm Street, another agency operating in the culture marketing space – though, unlike 23.59, not one affixed to a media platform. They describe themselves as a 'music-first creative agency bringing big moves to small screens'. Something they've been focusing on recently is offering brand-side marketers ways to immerse themselves in music culture. Or, as they put it, 'to step beyond their desk'.

Calling this programme Beyond, they've brought together a diverse group, from the head of entertainment at Nike and the head of social at Adobe to social media managers from various brands. Mixing levels of seniority is an important consideration, with those more senior often eager to learn (or maybe unlearn old ways) from those with less experience. The programme includes trips – sometimes by hired bus – to festivals and clubs, networking events and thought leadership roundtables. It's all part of how he sees the role of an agency like Warm Street evolving.

"When we started, most agents, managers and record labels didn't understand how brands work. Now they understand them well enough not to need an agency to help navigate it all so much," he explains over lunch in a London pub, painting a somewhat different picture than Stangl's more damning one. "They're more confident working on these partnerships directly and don't always feel they need a translator or a facilitator." Theo is a little nervous about what this (along with other topics we'll get on to) means for the future of culture marketing. But, someone who thinks deeply about how his chosen trade is evolving, he prefers to concentrate on the positives here: a sense that they can play a more elevated advisory role in times ahead and less that of just the doers and fixers.

"Before, it was more just like, 'What's cool? Who can you get us involved with?' Now, it's sharing a deeper understanding and being experts in lots of different techniques and methods. So one thing we're doing is mapping the touchpoints of how consumers can be reached via music. If you have a graph where the Y axis is grassroots to mainstream, and an X axis that's tried-and-tested to be more innovative, then you can start to plot the different methods onto it. So festival sponsorship will often be tried-and-tested and mainstream, but we can start to show brands how they might evolve through different stages. Or invest more in some areas but try smaller, innovative ideas in other areas. Basically taking clients on a journey that's more strategically sophisticated."

Theo's been in and around club culture since he was 18. At university in Bristol, he ran a ticketing business. "It was a loosely run operation, with all transactions done in cash, which gave it a bit of a feel of being in The Wire," he jokes. A summer spent in Berlin shaped his thinking further. "The scene blew me away. The city felt like it was at a tipping point, experiencing a major shift. The clubs were vibrant and fun. And unlike the UK, where day parties weren't part of the culture, Berlin was full of them."

Back in Bristol, he put on a daytime party in a basketball court. "That marked the beginning of my journey into promoting. I was deeply involved in that scene for about four to five years." He was part of the crew that organised the highly regarded Just Jack nights and was responsible for taking the likes of Theo Parrish, Underground Resistance and Gerd Janson to the South West. Eventually, the late nights started to take their toll, and he looked for other ways, further back from the frontline of party promoting, to be involved in a world which excited him culturally and entrepreneurially. An opportunity to work on a Red Bull Music Academy tour then materialised.

"They needed help navigating the music scenes in each location and I really rate it that they came to us, that they recognised the importance of understanding local nuance," he explains. "You can't just assume that a London-based team can effectively manage the dynamics of a scene in another city, especially in places where the ecosystem is fragile and has its own ways of thinking." A highlight of his work with RBMA, he beams, was bringing over US jazz-funk pioneer Lonnie Liston Smith and setting up a roundtable discussion between him and Gilles Peterson. He was sold at this point on moving into the culture marketing field and, alongside friend and fellow Bristol scene collaborator Robin Shaw, launched Warm Street in 2015.

The business now hosts a team of creatives, strategists, producers and marketers. Projects that Theo calls out include working with Berghaus on Press FWD, where the focus was on celebrating rave culture and its overlap with the great outdoors. Among the outputs: "We took Fabio to do a photo shoot at the first outdoor rave site he ever played with Grooverider. You're building a real sense of story into the fashion shoot. Putting these fascinating people from a scene into product campaigns is exciting."

Another project he flags saw Warm Street bringing together Ray-Ban with HomeBass, the father-and-son-led touring rave that sprang to life, guerilla-style, during the pandemic. Blasting forth from a white van, it carries with it the spontaneity of earlier times. "There were challenges, and it was a struggle at first. There was a lot that people needed to learn and get their heads around. But the results were way above and beyond what we'd have achieved with a partnership with Mixmag or whoever. People 100% cared. They were excited by it. They'd been following these guys for ages, so getting to see them doing their first brand partnership felt like witnessing the next stage of the story and seeing them have this success."

A few weeks later, and on their return from dates in Sydney and Melbourne, I'm speaking to the HomeBass duo, Si and Jackson Long, along with their manager, Thor Sutherland. Theirs is an all too rare success story from outside of conventional clubbing, with those who've rolled up to join them in their van making for an impressive list – DJ Zinc, Fatboy Slim, the Ragga Twins and Eats Everything included. The 'door' fee at a HomeBass rave: generally nothing at all. The genres covered: all points from house and techno to jungle, dubstep and UK garage. Confirmation of where each party will be: invariably dispatched last minute. Surfing the margins between legal and illegal raving, having played everywhere from quarries and forests to the heart of Shoreditch, they're buoyant with enthusiasm for where to take the HomeBass story next. They're pretty happy with how – *eventually* – their Ray-Ban partnership turned out, too.

"I guess it started because we liked some of their new designs – these very 1990s, sort of rave-y styles," begins Si Long, the father in the pairing. He can call on a clubbing history himself that stretches back to the

1990s – running Birmingham's much-loved Wobble house night. "And then, obviously, the money side of things. When we do our pop-ups, we give everything for nothing and need to get some money in from somewhere. And then the exposure for HomeBass, just being involved with such a cool, iconic brand."

Thor adds: "I think it positions us in more of a commercial lane, rather than as the guys that throw illegal raves and nothing else. That's definitely powerful. On the flip side, there were a few struggles. I think sometimes, when you're working with these big corporate companies, they don't quite understand how the event works. Sometimes, you know, there's compromise.

"We got there, and the events were great," Thor continues, expanding on their meetings with Ray-Ban. "But there were some challenging days in the build-up. We weren't quite able to align what our brand is with what Ray-Ban's is. We didn't want to, I guess, 'give in' and lose our core values. Doing that, just because we're getting some money, would come back to haunt us."

The factors that needed ironing out had less to do with what kind of presence Ray-Ban could take up at the events and more, well, quite a few other things. Thor explains: "It was, what's the lineup, where will the parties be, what's the stage going to look like? Is it going to look a bit too corporate, a bit too polished? What's the experience for the fan? Will they turn up and get strip searched on the way in and made to feel like they're going into a maximum-security prison? That's what's most important, really. The journey of the raver and how much fun they have at the event. That's what's special about the underground scene. If that's removed, that goes against everything we stand for."

They explain that partnerships such as this – and understanding how to navigate them – go a long way to shaping plans for where HomeBass heads next. There is no rulebook, they say, to how you balance out the integrity of the underground with collaborations that provide necessary funding and exposure, so they will need to learn as they go.

"It's the finest of lines," Thor continues. "Go too far, and you are corporate. A sell-out. But it's worth exploring this as much as we can so we can keep offering this underground alternative to a sometimes boring club scene. Like, we've just been to Australia and thrown a load of unlicensed raves, and it's been paid for by Monster *(energy drink)* – which really is something when you think about it. Them having the trust to invest in something like us! That, for me, is a big win for the underground."

Back with Theo from Warm Street, we talk further about what it's like dealing with different producers, artists and DJs – the gamut of sensibilities and differing perspectives on what constitutes reasonable compromise. As much as it's easy to assume this is all about hard-nosed deal-making, the stuff of entertainment industry legend, the reality is shaped more by the ability to listen and to deduce fears and motivations.

"It can form in one of a few ways," he says. "One is you have the much more artistic side of the industry. They will always be a lot more difficult to work with, and you've got to think about what the right concept is for them. You then have the really principled side of the industry. Those who are actually going to read a brand's social impact report and metrics and, in part, use that to decide if they want to partner with them or not. And this is a question that comes up more and more. People are checking the leadership to see if it is diverse. They're wondering if there's anything that will impact them in a partnership that they would rather stay clear of.

"And then there's a lot of artists for whom things have happened very quickly. A track has gone viral; they've got a record deal. They might not have performed out yet, but already they're commanding the attention of brands. The challenge is they don't know what to expect or where to draw the line. They might not really have thought through their principles yet, so it can all get a little random."

Turning to the other side of this equation, the brand people, Theo says that as much as they'd like to design activations that connect in better ways with underground culture, they are often up against conservative forces. A robust case of 'you won't get fired for hiring IBM' – the adage implying that choosing IBM was considered a safe, risk-free decision in the corporate world – often plays a significant role in their decisions. It's hard for them to take risks with their brands – or their jobs.

"It's tempting for brands to work with a Live Nation. You get access to a portfolio. You get scale. They will do all the reporting, and you're paying a premium for the overall service. But what you get from it can be very limited – like three social posts per festival. And it all tends to be a bit 'plug-in', cut and paste. Your brand could be switched for any other brand. With a Live Nation, yes, you'll get an awareness metric, but I'm not sure you get deep engagement and we need to challenge brands more on this, on what they invest in. The average brand-side person will say, 'Well, I would if I could.' But that's a good challenge. We've got to help them with this."

At times in our conversation, Theo exhibits an even bigger dose of conflictedness that most who work in culture marketing suffer from – as in, is it really possible to bring brands, art and community into the same room. He raises concerns over becoming a type of gatekeeper: "Once upon a time, the gatekeeper would have been the magazine editor – now, conceivably, it's the culture marketing person, creating opportunities for the ones they chose to create them for." He also worries over how little climate change is part of the conversation in his work: "It's the biggest emergency we have on this planet, but I still don't think many artists or DJs know how to talk about it or try to influence change."

With all of this in mind, he laughs it would be easy to walk away at times and find a field of work with less of the "modern tension" of underground alongside overground. But no, there's a flipside to focus on. To professionalise further. To create strategies and solutions that enable brand money to get through to those who will benefit the most from it. "I fundamentally wish there wasn't such a need for culture to rely on brands, but while we work at alternatives, it just is the case. And it means we need to work hard to help them *(brand-side marketers)* get alternative forms of investment and engagement signed off," he says.

"I've always found it frustrating how many advertising campaigns do so little for culture. If we can create even a small shift and divert just 0.5% of that spending into the right areas of music, that can have a huge impact on creating a healthy ecosystem. So our philosophy has always been that to do better work in music, culture and community, we need to translate our efforts into a commercial context. In doing this, we can unlock more budget for ourselves and, more importantly, the communities we work with. That's something to really get our heads around."

Representing

Most people we're speaking to here are looking out for the interests of a brand, a media platform, events or artists. Elsewhere in the sprawling modern dance music matrix, there are those more focused on representing the industry in its totality. Speaking from his native Edinburgh, Finlay Johnson is in this cohort. He's the chief operating officer at the Association For Electronic Music (AFEM). Founded in 2013, in the decade since this not-for-profit has come to represent 270 company members in 29 countries. It describes itself as 'an independent, democratically run global trade association created to connect and represent the common interests of those companies and individuals whose business is electronic music.'

What started out prioritising issues like keeping festivals afloat, mitigating piracy, improving health and wellbeing in the industry and addressing inaccurate royalty statements from performing rights organisations has, remarks Finlay, grown in scale and professionalism, allowing it to contribute to a wide range of topics confidently. As we speak, for instance, there's the issue of the DJ revenue-sharing platform Aslice closing. Techno fixture Richie Hawtin has been airing his disappointment across social media about how few of the great and good of DJing supported the donation-based proposition, which worked by voluntarily sharing set playlists and contributing part of performance fees to the artists whose music had been played. "The closing of Aslice is a huge disappointment," lamented Hawtin. "Perhaps the biggest disappointment that I've felt in our community, our scene, since I've been part of it." Meetings and conversations then ensue to discuss AFEM's position on the issue, what role it should play, and how it can best support its members.

Looking at the initiatives, campaigns and resources now offered by AFEM illustrates how complex and layered what was once a far simpler and largely underground space has become. Also how, as a more significant industry, it's held up to greater scrutiny. So next to ongoing work around improving royalty distribution and health and wellbeing, there's guidance on carbon neutrality and monetising DJ mixes. There's a confidential helpline for victims of sexual harassment, anti-racism workstreams and a diversity charter. They've formed an emerging technologies working group, grappling with all things web3. They offer resources on everything from approved DJ download sites to how to obtain a visa to tour in the United States.

Finlay's background was in live events and at William Morris Endeavor. He started in the mailroom, then assisted in tour management for Björk, Lady Gaga, Taylor Swift and Fatboy Slim. He became part of the team working for Black Coffee, Peggy Gou, Benji B and Virgil Abloh, as well as managing house and tech-house heavyweights Mark Knight and Michael Woods. Across all of this, he remarks that he got to understand: "Approaches to different fan bases, the positioning of artists, how the industry *really* works."

As befits someone in this role and with his background, Finlay comes equipped with many opinions on many topics. We start talking about how conversations between brands and artists or brands and event promoters typically take shape. "When they *(brand-side people)* come to the artist or the club promoter or the record label, they say, 'We care about the culture. We want to preserve it. Want to be a part of it.' When they go to the CEO, looking to get the budget signed off, they say, 'This is a youth market that is very hard to define and get into. If we invest in this way, we align ourselves with an audience that does not consume TV. They're not buying magazines or newspapers. They are wary of mass commercial advertising. You will not reach this audience unless you embed yourselves in their culture.'"

In parallel with this perhaps inevitable brand-side need to be fluent in two languages, he also sees artist-side changes in how the conversation unfolds. "I think when artists now choose a management agency, one of the conversations is, 'What are my options with brand deals? What does that landscape look like?' You look at an agency like *(Los Angeles-headquartered sports, music and entertainment giant)* Wasserman, and they're hiring brand agents – people who don't spend their days talking to promoters but instead talking to Gucci and Chanel and Ray-Ban, and figuring out what kind of artists they want and what their budgets are.

"And when these agencies bring on artists, they'll sit down with them and ask questions like what social causes they care about; what were the last five charities they donated to; would they ever do an advert? These questions are asked at the outset so you can then put them in front of the right brands at the right moment. There's a lot more preparatory work that goes on these days. They then know how to behave, how to talk to these brands and what the brands will expect in advance."

Of course, all of this schooling, advising and optimising circles us back to a theme already touched on previously: DJs/artists not just working with brands but *becoming* brands. Hey presto, we're also back to Peggy Gou. "She's working with Ray-Ban now, co-designing, and I think these merchandise lines have become incredibly important for artists like her," Finlay continues. "For many artists, these brand collaborations become a form of career longevity – like a pension plan. Even after they stop DJing, they can live off fashion consulting and other ventures. We're seeing more DJs think about their legacy and invest in areas that generate income beyond their DJ fees.

"A slightly different type of example," he adds. "Adam Beyer's Drumcode *(a label that's become a radio station, a festival, an extensive merchandise line – and that's no doubt about to become something else, too)* has grown into an entity that doesn't rely on him being there for it to succeed. DJs are increasingly putting their money and time into projects that can sustain them long after they've stepped out of the booth."

Reintroducing someone else we've heard plenty about already, Finlay got to see firsthand what happens when different spheres collide when Virgil Abloh played at London's Fabric venue. "We booked him to play alongside Benji B, which was significant because Fabric had never done a celebrity booking before. Fans were holding up their phones with messages like, 'Will you sign my shoes?' They were literally trying to pass sneakers through the booth for him to sign. It was surreal. Fabric is a place for dancing, and suddenly it felt like a mix of an authentic musical experience, because it was that, but with a strong fashion focus. It was clear that people didn't see Virgil as just a DJ or just a fashion designer – more like a multidisciplinary brand. I think we'll see more figures who can seamlessly shift between these worlds."

We move on to identifying patterns and common themes in how brands engage with dance music today. With the days of simply hanging up banners behind us, I suggest that these approaches often fall into three overarching categories – though brands frequently blend elements of each. The first centres on creating content: documenting events, artists, collectives and scenes. The second is experiential, focusing on IRL immersion and interaction through which to reflect the brand and, at times, incorporates product sampling. The third revolves around providing utility and resources, offering funding, education and tools to support clubs and the communities they serve.

"That seems fair," he nods. "I think the era of having your logo on things is fading. It's about being much more embedded now and yeah, it's either more content-led – things like interviews and films with DJs and artists. Or it's about interesting production. Things like Beavertown having a stage that looked like an art installation at Secret Garden Party. It's not just about plastering up the logo. But if the stage looks ridiculously creative and you've integrated the Beavertown colours and the Beavertown skull, the brand's iconography is built into the party – and that becomes very Instagrammable. Or, yes, funding. But I'll be interested to see where that all goes. You're keeping club spaces alive, but how are you measuring the return on that investment? What are the conversations internally and do you even have any metrics?"

On metrics, Finlay raises an interesting point about how the trend for banning phone cameras in clubs might skewer some of the most favoured of them. "You'd imagine for 90% of brands, big among the ROI metrics will be how many unique clicks or views they've had. That seems flawed now and will only get more flawed. Phones are getting banned from more and more clubs." He cites Damien Lazarus' night at Hï Ibiza as one of them. Lazarus, he of Crosstown Rebels, Day Zero and Get Lost, explained his decision in an Instagram post: 'From open to close, we take pride in creating a totally unique environment, centred around the mystical temple, it's a proper session where we lose our inhibitions and can enjoy a sense of freedom as we enforce our groundbreaking 'No Phones' policy inside the room.' Finlay continues: "Hï Ibiza, in my mind, is one of the most commercial club spaces in the world. That even they have a no-phones policy shows where this is going. What will your metrics be now?"

Outside of the three categories I mooted, Finlay astutely raises a bunch of other ways to cut and slice what's happening in this space. One he thinks about distinguishes between those he describes as 'native' to the scene and those not. "Compared to a Beatport or a SoundCloud, say, those that are not should pay a higher price to be involved because they're not intrinsically providing anything of value to the sector. They're not an existing provider of a service to dance communities."

He also senses a potential divergence in the paths of luxury and premium fashion on the one side and more general consumer goods on the other. "I think we'll see a split in how brands approach sponsorship. Consumer goods will likely focus on events and event series. Brands are aware of the risks of putting everything with one artist – they could tweet something controversial today and see their career end tomorrow. To mitigate this, they take a broader approach. Like Ballantine's, which could have sponsored Black Coffee directly but instead chose to back a wider South African activation with Boiler Room. It's a strategy that spreads the risk and allows them to work with multiple artists under one umbrella.

"Then high-end fashion will target individual artists, being more selective in their partnerships. They'll choose just a few key figures, and instead of simply writing a cheque, they'll offer a stake in the organisation. Like the Jordan model *(it's estimated that Michael Jordan's partnership with Nike – going far beyond the routine endorsement model – has made him a billionaire and then some)*, where there's more involvement, commitment and shared success."

Most roads in *Selling The Night* lead to some kind of reference to Red Bull Music Academy, and that's the case again, speaking to Finlay. What's particularly compelling for him is the role it played in documenting club culture. It set out to respect the less-told narratives, bringing in the right voices and looking beneath the surface level stories.

"One of the biggest challenges for dance music perhaps isn't a lack of funding. There's VC money coming in at all angles. The real issue is how to capture and preserve what's already happened," he feels. "Like, we've recently seen a resurgence of eras like electroclash, with themed parties and a renewed interest. But much of that culture wasn't properly documented. I think there's a huge, unexplored opportunity for a brand to invest in and own a lasting piece of culture. How long will someone like Peggy Gou remain popular, or how long will Boiler

Room stay relevant? But if you have one of the few interviews with an artist like MF Doom, who will undoubtedly *(and has)* become a cultural icon within certain circles, that content holds value forever."

We're also returning to topics we previously explored in the context of museums and exhibitions: bringing permanence to what is typically ephemeral. "If a brand were to propagate an archive, it would be far more meaningful than sponsoring festivals like Creamfields," Finlay continues, warming to this theme. "What if there was something like a British Library but dedicated to the genre? A permanent space that housed every record ever made. That's a fascinating idea and one that would make celebrating these artists easier while they're still with us. They deserve recognition while they're alive and well, more than just a crowdfunding campaign for medical bills when they fall ill without a pension *(he's referring to situations such as Balearic pioneer Alfredo, who needed help with hospital costs after suffering a stroke and has since passed away)*. For me, creating a not-for-profit resource to archive and protect these cultural moments is the most impactful thing a brand could do if they're serious about cultural preservation."

Brand sounds

This chapter has concentrated mainly on the type of brand incursions into dance music that – whether dubbed activations, programmes, campaigns, projects or something else in this vein – generally blend one or some of the following: events, content and PR (and then broad swathes of social media activity to follow). But there are other ways in which brands and dance music get close to each other and through which value – including money – change hands. Jingles, sync deals for movies and commercials, audio logos and product sounds – this is just some of the terminology and component parts of what's steadily getting wrapped together under the umbrella title of sonic branding.

One definition I come across describes sonic branding as a holistic approach to a brand's use of music and sound across all relevant touchpoints. Break it down, and it's about advocating for brands to give as much consideration to what they sound like as to what they look like. It highlights music's ability to evoke emotions and forge memories – I once worked on a project for Spotify where we demonstrated that people could recall the music from holidays a decade ago more vividly than the visuals of the destination – and, ultimately, its role in enhancing brand recognition.

Jingles are, of course, almost as old as the radio itself, catchy/irritating melodies associated with promoting breakfast cereal, household cleaning products and the like. In terms of a modern age for sonic branding and when that may have started, consensus suggests it came when a then beleaguered McDonald's (its stock price at a seven-year low) aimed for its first unified global campaign, something that would help them connect with people in every culture.

Out of this came the missive I'm Lovin' It. First surfacing as a track featuring Justin Timberlake, Pharrell Williams and Chad Hugo, it then returned in a McDonald's advert (also featuring Timberlake). And it's never, ever gone away since. Different iterations have been produced, but the song remains the same. It's proven globally relevant and eminently flexible. It is as mainstream as can be but also unifiable with skatewear collaborations with Palace or when artist Kerwin Frost conjured up adult-intended happy meals with limited edition collectables. 'Fast forward 20 years and the I'm Lovin' It sonic is still delighting listeners and conjuring up visions of delicious comfort food,' trumpets Radiocentre, who have some skin in the game as the representative body of commercial radio in the UK.

Thinking wider than jingles, about how music and sound can be leveraged in different and less familiar ways, a notable player in sonic branding is MassiveMusic. Founded in Amsterdam in 2000, they now have 10 global offices. Their staff are called Massivians ('even our chief financial officer was a drummer', they remark on their website). They have steadily added to their services as the definition of sonic branding has flexed, and the available channels to work across have expanded and fragmented. For instance, they now highlight that they're an official TikTok sound partner – creating 'fresh-out-of-the-studio tracks for brands, instead of licensing existing ones' – with an emphasis on music that inspires community participation. They work on 'audio identities' for clients. User experience sounds – think notifications, alerts and button-click noises. Custom compositions to drop across multiple channels. Access to rights-safe music catalogues. Global compliance, music strategy, research and evaluation. There's a lot to it. 'Sounding shitty never looks pretty', they tell us in their sales material.

Roscoe Williamson is their global creative strategy and innovation director. He played a key role in launching their London office and, in keeping with the vast majority who feature in *Selling The Night*, fondly recalls his own rites of passage in music. In his case, the new school break scene of the early 2000s, producing, promoting and DJing alongside the likes of Plump DJs and Stanton Warriors ("That was my passion. Then I started fusing that with an interest in the advertising world").

The day job has him developing strategies for the Premier League, Colgate-Palmolive, eBay, Gymshark, The Wikipedia Foundation and the aforementioned TikTok. Factors in this include considering the relevant audience and markets (aka countries), mapping the competitive set, and understanding the nuances of brand objectives. From there, he likes to declutter the topic by thinking on two fronts: they're either creating owned assets for the brand – such as its own music or sonic logos – or curating for the brand, shaping its place within the broader music sphere. The former, he says, plays to marketing goals where achieving distinction and consistency are dominant; the latter, to tapping into trends and scoring cultural relevance in fast-paced fields like sport, fashion, food, movies, media and, of course, music itself.

"When I started here, 11 years ago, I was pounding the pavements, eulogising about sonic branding," he remembers. "But there's been a huge sea change since then. We've had research to evidence how underused, but how effective, audio is in branding. The arrival of smart speakers has made a difference, too, in how people think about the role of sound. And, of course, music plays a major role in social media. It's all so different."

And what about dance music? How does that figure within sonic branding? Given it typically avoids many of the conventional structures found in rock and pop genres, it creates different opportunities. The emphasis on repetition and building atmosphere, as well as the cognitive shortcuts to thinking of modernity and innovation (key for many companies), gives dance music its own space in sonic branding. "It's got details and layers," he agrees. "All of this is very important when designing with brands in mind."

Then there's the fact, laughs Roscoe, that it's the type of music that most people at agencies like MassiveMusic are listening to, dancing to. "We're all living in cities like New York or London or Berlin, and it's the music we interact with. It's almost a blessing and a curse. It's got to the point that it's become a bit of a joke thing to say we can't allow any Jon Hopkins or Bonobo in a brand playlist. It's everywhere! Any dance music that's organic-sounding and slightly orchestrally infused is considered the perfect blend for a lot of brands. But even when you ban those types of artists, other composers working on brand projects copy the same styles… and so it goes on."

Getting brands to move on from the obvious appeal of the cinematic feel that comes with a Jon Hopkins or the accessible downtempo global sounds of a Bonobo is a fascinating challenge, he says. He mentions a microchip client, ASML, that was more fixated on change and disruption than fitting in and for whom MassiveMusic looked to mirror the complex processes of their work by 'deconstructing pitch into polyrhythmic components.' In other words, something more challenging than standard-issue chilled beats. He believes clients are slowly coming to understand that drifting further and further into "sonic homogenisation" will be the opposite of using sound to stand out and be memorable. The future might well be somewhat more jagged and jarring. "I'm seeing people wanting to push the envelope further. Things that are more abstract and less obviously melodic. Closer to sound design and more atonal."

MassiveMusic and parent company Songtradr's The Music Of Sportswear report, presented as a thought leadership piece in 2024, examined the role of music in the US sportswear category. The report underscored the prominence of electronic music in sonic branding. Assembling insights from 'music psychologists, music experts, and data scientists' and leaning on their proprietary MusicIQ scoring system, it found electronic music the most commonly used genre, with hip-hop trailing by about a quarter and alternative music further behind at roughly a third less. They also investigated moods: 'energetic' wins out, followed by 'dreamy' and 'calm'. A detailed analysis of eight major sportswear brands notes that Nike uses music in 92% of its content. The report (designed to generate business, after all) was also an opportunity to showcase MassiveMusic's capabilities, spotlighting an innovation for the Swoosh brand back in 2008: a custom mashup of French electronic duo Justice's Genesis and heavy metal tracks that earned all important viral status.

Sometimes, the role of dance music and electronic music is far less elaborate – less about bespoke creations or highbrow objectives like soundtracking an entire brand experience. Instead, more prosaically, it is licensing music for synchronisation in adverts. As mentioned, the atmospheric qualities and lack of a traditional verse-chorus-verse structure make dance music – and adjacent genres – particularly well-suited for this purpose. While this practice has been around for decades, it reached new heights with the release of Moby's Play in 1999. Initially a commercial flop, the album – a restrained mix of field recordings and lazy beats – seemed poised to mark the twilight of Moby's career. However, it eventually struck a note by being the first album to have every track licensed to a film or an advert.

Rolling Rock, Volkswagen, Nordstrom, American Express, France Telecom, Bosch, Bailey's Irish Cream, Thorntons and Maxwell House were just some of the recipients of sounds from Play. With this level of exposure, the album became big – *really* big – a coffee table staple of its time. Facing criticism for his prolific licensing, Moby defended himself by saying he was paving a path many others would inevitably follow. And he wasn't wrong. What happened with Play was less a one-off anomaly and more a first-of-its-kind blueprint for the industry.

Vice described it as the advent of a new kind of advertising music ' that specifies a geographically formless, airbrushed but distinctly urban world.' Speaking to American Songwriter, Moby was quick to point out there were limits to the deals he'd make – none with tobacco or fast-food companies, for instance – but otherwise seemed comfortable enough with his part in this omni-metropolitan airbrushing. "In the early '80s, I played in a hardcore punk band, and the term 'sellout' was tossed around quite a lot. There were some really hardcore anarchist punks who believed that if you charged money for a show, you were a sellout. And there were people who believed that if you made a seven-inch record, you were a sellout. Basically, every musician who is involved in the commercial exploitation of music is ostensibly a sellout. I eventually realised how absurd that was."

Blacktronika's King Britt sees net gains in dance music gracing adverts beyond just the cash earned by the individual. "Electronic music in adverts – the perfect combination! I was watching TV, and this DJ-oriented Courvoisier advert came on, and, oh my God, I see Moodymann's on there. The fit is great. I mean, I don't drink but Courvoisier is big in the African American community and Kenny *(Dixon, aka Moodymann)* has it on his rider. It's a perfect marriage. Insane! It shows a community being lifted, too."

He also recalls an advert for the Ford Focus from 2000, which ended with the strapline Detroit Techno, and bounced to the sound of No UFOs by Model 500 (aka Juan Atkins). "We're in the factory, the robot is at work, the rivets are going in," Britt recalls joyously. "To tie in culturally all these things: Detroit, the automotive industry, Ford and techno. That was important. It brought eyes to Detroit, and I honestly think it contributed to things like the Detroit Electronic Music Festival *(starting the same year the Ford spot launched and a forerunner to the city's Movement event each Memorial Day)* getting the go-ahead. People used it as a springboard, rebuilding how the city was perceived, and starting to think of it as a vibrant, rather than decaying, place."

One of the most eye (and ear)-catching of transfers from underground to overground came in 2019, in the shape of IKEA's first-ever UK TV Christmas ad. On it, household objects start spitting bars, lamenting the state of the place, with this channelled through a dis-track by grime artist D Double E.

Speaking at a Nicer Tuesdays industry event, the executive creative director behind the work, Hermeti Balarin from the agency, Mother, explained some of the process: "The client and the copywriter were both massive grime fans… We told him *(D Double E)* to make it how he'd make it for his album, and that's the secret to why it's loved. I was also told it would have to be at 140 beats-per-minute, because that's how grime goes." Writing in The Guardian, Jeffrey Boakye, author of Hold Tight: Black Masculinity, Millennials, And The Meaning Of Grime, praised: 'D Double E has done the thing that we must truly celebrate – he's eclipsed the machine and brought grime to the masses. And that might just be the biggest gift of all.'

Some brands try to weave an intricate connection between themselves and the music. Stone Island Sound, for instance, has the Italian label describing 'sound as a form of research' – a nod to Stone Island's approach to creating clothing, which begins with experiments on fabrics and how they hold dyes. Their press blurb fails to elaborate on what nature the 'research' takes here exactly; instead, it concentrates on the news of upcoming playlists from Hackney-based producer and rapper John Glacier and Brooklyn singer, DJ and producer Yaeji.

It's interesting to note the randomness of which gems are brought back into service for advertising purposes. Some way from the world of luxury apparel, creative agency Leith's 2024 work for the Luton Airport Express train service ("One of London's best-kept secrets") features a fictional rap collective, So Rapid Crew, covering a version of So Solid Crew's 21 Seconds. Titled 32 Minutes, the track bears lines such as: 'With plenty of seats for yo'/space for yo' bags to stow.' And not forgetting: 'Now we've 31 minutes to go/from only a tenner or so/spend the rest on a travel pillow.'

Nerves and flux

I come away from these interviews – primarily conducted with those on the frontline of trying to make a success of brands taking space in dance music – with a sense of an industry in flux. There's a nervousness about what the future will bring. I hear a strong appetite to keep learning, to keep improving on – even reframing – the value exchange. But doubts and discomfort, too. Is it *really* possible to add value? Are brands willing to go further still, or will a retreat now follow? If tensions are an inevitability of culture marketing – of bringing together very different energies and emotional operating systems – it seems there's something in the constitution of club culture and dance music that is producing particular sensitivities.

It should be said that I'm writing this in a period that has been spectacularly tough for the marketing communications industry en masse. While global economies have remained relatively strong, many categories have become spooked. What started in the tech industry, with lay-offs and, as Meta CEO Mark Zuckerberg put it – while ditching staff and improving profitability – the 'year of efficiency', permeated out to redundancies across media, apparel and consumer goods categories, eventually hitting marketing communications agencies themselves. With the undetermined threat (or opportunity) created by generative AI lingering heavily in the air as well, it's been a phase of company reorgs, delayed projects, scarcity of briefs and slashed budgets. Small wonder the mood music has occasional melancholic moments in the conversations I have.

"If you're focused on a big market, if there's a downturn, the culture marketing can be first to go," says Dan Maurice from Pernod Ricard. "In alcohol, it's back to thinking off-trade *(industry talk for drinking at home, and therefore point-of-sale and in-store promotions)*. Back to discounts. Back to the basics."

"When the going gets tough, culture gets cut. We need to do more as an industry to show the commercial value of proper commitment," comments Theo Gentilli from Warm Street. "Sometimes I question what within this might be a bubble that will burst, with brands moving on to something else." Then he smiles, recalling why he landed up doing this work in the first place: "But this is what I do. Maybe after all of this *(he means the commercially challenging year)*, it will be time for a reset, and we should be excited, not scared, by that. We can keep improving our methods and how we can meaningfully contribute to music communities. Sustainable ideas, accountability, tangible action – I'm here for all of that."

Further rays of sunshine come in an autumn 2024 research report from Soundcloud. 'Electronic Music Fans Are The Most Engaged Worldwide', it declares. 'Electronic music fans are leaned-in, engaged listeners. Electronic music fans are superfans, over-indexing for all music activities. Compared to fans of other genres, electronic music fans are: 52% more likely to comment; 104% more likely to share; 85% more likely to repost.' If brands want to speak to engaged people – and by God, they do; engaged people are deemed far more receptive to advertising and promotional messages – this means they will want to work with electronic music fans and may more readily move in their direction. The power dynamic, therefore, looks positively balanced for dance music. Be gone with having to compromise… right?

Lutz Leichsenring represents Berlin's Clubcommission, an organisation set up to care for the interests of nightlife in that city. More detail on his painstaking work in the next chapter, but he closes out this one with observations on how there's never really escaping compromise. Those people skills our culture marketers have told us about will never go out of style. "Not all cities have supportive governments to work with like here. Sometimes, brands can be your only option if you are looking for support. But whether it's brands or government money – it's always a compromise, *immediately* a compromise. You have to steer the conversation in the right direction. You keep your thinking fixed on the community. You have to find the people in the organisation or business who support you and who understand the community. That's the person you want to work with. It's still a compromise, but it can be a *nicer* compromise."

7. BRINGING A GUN TO TURN DOWN A RADIO

A notion called the creative industries has grown and grown, and club culture has been swallowed up in it

Alongside this, gentrification and a multi-pronged fight to keep clubs alive

Creativity as industry

In 1997, Tony Blair and New Labour were serenaded into power (after 18 years without it) by Things Can Only Get Better, the crossover dance smash by D:Ream. Despite the uncomfortable sight of politicians Peter Mandelson and John Prescott dancing together to that tune, a generation felt its moment had arrived. Complete with attestations from Blair and co of the good to come from globalisation and modernisation, it was a landslide victory. It marked a fresh start, awash with a youthful feel and progressive energy not unlike 1990s dance music itself. "I remember clearly, there was this wonderful sea change, and the nation had this feeling that there was a need for change," Peter Cunnah from D:Ream said more recently in a Guardian interview, then noting that Iraqi war controversies now have him regretting the association. "Everyone was really behind it and giving Labour the benefit of the doubt. But after the war, I became politically homeless."

Long before the conflict in Iraq tainted New Labour's legacy, the generational optimism they ushered in came with something called Cool Britannia in tow. First used in 1967 as the title of a song by the Bonzo Dog Doo-Dah Band, this time around, Cool Britannia was the wrap-around headline banner for a hotchpotch of music, fashion, media, art, cinema and more. It was a new kind of British pride and an acceptable patriotism. It was Britpop, the Spice Girls and Trainspotting. Alexander McQueen and Stella McCartney. Damien Hirst, Tracey Emin and the so-called YBAs (Young British Artists). It was the music videos and advertisements of directors like Jonathan Glazer (such as Surfer for Guinness, soundtracked by Leftfield's Phat Planet).

It was the remodelling of football (England and Premier League) and nights out in Camden boozers. It was the members-only Groucho Club and different nights out in Notting Hill (also, painfully, it was the movie Notting Hill). Cream and Chemicals Brothers were in there, too; all things big and comparatively accessible in dance music were thrown into the Cool Britannia mix. The British flag was back on show again, and a high (or low?) came when soon-to-be-married couple Oasis' Liam Gallagher and actress Patsy Kensit appeared in bed on the front cover of US magazine Vanity Fair. 'London Swings Again!' the headline proclaimed. Emphasising this point, the bed was adorned with a Union Jack duvet and cushions.

This outbreak of triumphalism would prove to be short-lived and without direction. By the early 2000s, the notion of Cool Britannia was rapidly fading out of sight. Music and broader cultural tastes were changing (not least hip-hop and streetwear were becoming globally omnipresent). Economic disparities undermined any sense this was something for all (rather than a product of a fast-gentrifying London).

And, truth be told, no one could pin down exactly what was the shared substance across all facets of Cool Britannia anyway (other than perhaps a zippy energy and some good cheer – even when majoring on heroin addiction in the case of Irvine Welsh's tales from Edinburgh). Later still, some would even accuse it, perhaps fancifully, of displaying early traces of what would steer the country to Brexit tub-thumping.

But if Cool Britannia was mostly a flimsy marketing construct, a temporary gain for New Labour and the nation's branding, beneath it sat developments with bolder and more structural ambitions in mind. The new government's recently formed Department For Culture, Media And Sport (DCMS) produced the 1998 Creative Industries Mapping Document. This assessed the impact – particularly economic – of 13 very loosely connected fields of activity: advertising, architecture, the arts and antiques market, crafts, design, designer fashion, film, interactive leisure software (aka video games), music, performing arts, publishing, software, television and radio. According to the report, the common ground was 'their origin in individual creativity, skill and talent' and 'a potential for wealth creation through the generation of intellectual property'.

A Creative Industries Task Force brought together ministers and civil servants with entrepreneurs from those aforementioned fields, working on tax relief schemes, export campaigns and skills development to further the cause. While those starting out in these fields – as freelancers, interns, first jobbers and the sporadically employed – may not have understood the minutiae of what was happening behind the scenes, nonetheless, the advent of something called the creative industries sounded compelling and worth being part of. It felt like an approving nod towards DIY artistic and entrepreneurial endeavours – including those in club culture. Validation that these counted for something and could take you to more established areas of creativity – complete with more reliable remuneration – such as in advertising and TV, if that was your bag.

Writing for The Guardian in 1999, investigating how dance music culture was intersecting with other spheres of creativity and corporate activity, Alix Sharkey saw this mixing and merging on show at the then very hot advertising agency HHCL – probably best known for work with Tango, including the 1991 Orange Man commercial, with Gil Scott-Heron's gravelly voice-over. Covering new tech and starkly different attitudes to work/life balance than we tend to see today, Sharkey spoke with Jon Leach, head of strategy at the agency.

'According to Leach, advertising's shift towards club culture has been driven by changes in technology and working practices. Leading me through HHCL's open-plan, 'hot-desk' offices – where desks and computers are not allotted, but open to whoever needs them at the time – he takes me to a studio at the far end of the building, where a couple of twentysomething creatives are toying with Cubase music software, writing their own drum 'n' bass tracks on Apple Macs for rough edits of film proposals – which have been shot on DV cameras, downloaded straight into the computer and edited on Avid software.

'"Basically, they use the same editing and music software as most jungle producers and directors of dance videos. A lot of these guys download their work, take it home on their laptops and continue to work there," says Leach. "You find that they're actually designing with club-type music playing at the same time through their CD-drive, so the gap between their working environment and their leisure environment is not so great. And a lot of people doing this kind of work are single men and women in their 20s, who go out a lot. They work long hours and go out straight from the studio, or go home and crank up the Apple to play computer games. There's a lot of interweaving of work, leisure and culture. The distinctions have almost disappeared. Basically, we buy them the kit and let them do what they want, as long as they continually provide us with new ideas. We get to know about new trends in club culture at almost the same time as the punters."'

Creativity as class

Adding further dimensions to the notion of the creative industries, the American urbanist Richard Florida released an influential book called The Rise Of The Creative Class in 2002. Compared to the DCMS interpretation, he broadened the scope in this 'class' to include professionals in fields such as technology, science, education and business, effectively aligning with something closer to the idea of the knowledge economy. More telling to *Selling The Night*, he spoke of 'cool cities', the clustering potential of places with strong queer and bohemian/hipster communities; their significance for the economy and the role therein of art galleries, music venues, independent cafes and vibrant nightlife. The creative class perspective has since been criticised on several levels, not least as elitist. By the time I interview him for a project in 2022, Florida's written The New Urban Crisis, an attempt to find solutions amid the darker forces at play in cities – economic segregation, the housing crises and that most catch-all of terms, gentrification. "I saw that we needed to develop a new narrative, which isn't just about creative and innovative growth, but about inclusion being a part of prosperity."

Many interviewed for this book express a strong sense of conflict with the creative industries, with being part of the so-called creative class, and the factors churned up by each. Particularly in the UK, they bemoan how far down the agenda the creative industries slipped in the years that the Tories were in power. The sense that all of this extraordinary subcultural creativity, produced not only in London but Bristol, Birmingham, Belfast, Manchester, Leeds, Sheffield, Glasgow and beyond, is perceived as insignificant, low of brow and low of value. It's unfathomable to them that it isn't held in greater esteem.

"The mainstream remains heavily indebted to working-class culture. Just look at grime, which has dominated British music for the past decade – yet we've failed to celebrate it. We've lost something." This is Tom Armstrong from Common People, the non-profit set on addressing the diminishing opportunities in the creative industries for those from working-class and low-income backgrounds. We first met him in chapter four, where he shared his own story of how immersion in club culture opened a path to working in the wider world of creativity. Outside of grime, we're reflecting on 15 years of Tory rule (they were voted out days before we meet) and their weakening of 'brand Britain' through utter miscomprehension of what was in front of them. "Britain is this ex-colonial power that probably shouldn't have had such a positive representation on a global scale, considering what it's done in the last few 100 years. But everybody was looking to Britain as a miracle of soft power – until *they* came along. And that soft power that they've wasted, that was all accumulated from the everyday creativity of working-class people."

Alongside frustration with those in power dismissing innovative ideas from grassroots and non-hierarchical sources, there is also unease about the economic motives driving the creative industries. The focus on commercialisation overshadowing genuine creativity. Limited tolerance for more niche or experimental work. The gig economy exacerbating fragile employment conditions. Generative AI stoking uncertainty and further threatening opportunities for human creators.

Adding to all-things neoliberal, there's that hot potato of our age, gentrification, too. Often for those in the creative industries, it triggers dismay at feeling both a cause of it *and* a victim of it. Concern for the displacement which follows what initially can feel like well-intended regeneration. A creeping, incremental transformation which the creative industries/class undoubtedly has a hand in. Early stage gentrification – that often thrilling mix of old and new – invariably leading to something more culturally flattened, closed off to broader society. Moreover, in all of this, while the Instagram and TikTok-approved aesthetic of polished concrete-floored coffee shops may prosper, the place for club venues, in many cities, is squeezed to the margins.

Clubs can function both as instruments of gentrification and casualties of it – signals of the early stages of urban change, then later booted out of neighbourhoods as the next stage of change presides. A 2016 Resident Advisor feature by Max Pearl laid bare a particularly pronounced example of club culture's role in gentrification in New York City. It reported the scene from a warehouse party called The Bronx Is Burning in Mott Haven, a high poverty neighbourhood. The name referred to the 1970s period when vast blocks of the borough were razed to the ground by landlords burning down their own buildings to collect insurance money. DJs at the event included Brooklyn breakbeat techno trailblazer Frankie Bones and none other than year zero hip-hop pioneer Kool Herc. The writer describes the decor as poverty-themed ('cars riddled with bullet holes and garbage can fires').

More unsettling still, the piece reveals that the event was bankrolled by a real estate investment firm: '"We're developing about 2,000 apartments along the waterfront in the South Bronx," said Keith Rubenstein, head of Somerset Partners, the real estate investment firm that funded the event. He spoke to a reporter from Women's Wear Daily while models mingled around him. "Tonight is an amazing opportunity to introduce a whole new world to the South Bronx, and celebrate its heritage."'

It's an extreme example of how gentrification leverages culture, for sure, but the general principles it worked to are not uncommon. In Rebel Cities, anthropologist David Harvey's 2012 interrogation of where urban living meets socioeconomic change and resistance, he reports: 'The commodification of culture and the arts is now firmly entrenched in the spectacle of urban redevelopment.' Or, as Richard Florida put it in The Rise Of The Creative Class: 'What the creative class is looking for are communities and places that offer high-quality experiences, an openness to diversity of all kinds and, above all else, the opportunity to validate their identities as creative people.' Nights out with burning bins and fantasy poverty seemingly included.

Where's the club?

To enable club culture to remain, as Common People's Tom Armstrong puts it, a test bed for ideas from the streets and those under-represented and marginalised, you need two things. One, as we cover throughout this book, you need representation from those communities in the clubs. The other is that you've got to have the actual clubs, the venues in which to do the testing. Clubs always come and go, and the number of them you find in a city will inevitably vary across passages of time. But the trajectory at present is tracking in an ominous direction. Media outlets routinely report on the latest club venues to bite the dust. Dig into the statistics, and we hit on figures as shocking and dispiriting as those around representation in the creative industries (see chapter four). About three-quarters of UK nightclubs have closed since 2005. Continue on that path, and according to the Night Time Industries Association (NTIA), there won't be any left at all by not-so-far-away 2030.

The NTIA accused the UK government in 2023 of "intentionally" closing down nightclubs and venues across the country, stating that, unlike other countries in Europe, the sector was viewed as "a burden on policing and local government." Pointing to rising outgoings on almost all fronts for those running clubs and requesting that VAT is reduced for the sector, Michael Kill, CEO of NTIA, said: "The closure of nightclubs transcends mere economic repercussions; it represents a cultural crisis endangering the vibrancy and diversity of our nightlife. Nightclubs serve as vital hubs of social interaction, artistic expression and community cohesion, making their preservation imperative."

Predictably, the threats to night culture and its economy cannot be put down to one thing. Next to rising costs, there's the lasting impact of the pandemic – including a switching off from IRL experiences that some have found hard to switch back on. A preference for fewer, bigger nights out, with this particularly impacting midweek clubs (work-from-home habits can't help much here, either). NTIA's

2024 Electronic Beats, Economic Treats report, in partnership with the Audience Strategies research agency, estimated the total spend on nightclubbing in the UK (taking in everything from transport and pre-drinks to entry fees and outlay in the club) to have shrunk from £1,699 million in 2022 to £1,457 million in 2023. So much for the heavily touted Roaring Twenties to follow in the wake of the pandemic shutdown.

In the same report, Carly Heath, the night-time economy advisor for Bristol, issues a rallying cry for what club culture offers a country beyond the fiscal benefits. "Electronic music fans are active participants in the creation of underground culture. The connection between DJs and the dancefloor is reciprocal. I feel there is magic created in the call-and-response moments wrapped around a perfectly placed rewind. For me, dance spaces are all about the people – without the ravers, there'd be no rave. Dance spaces deserve celebration for their significant contribution to British culture, yet the financial support and public funding for our culture is woefully inadequate. I'm hopeful that future generations will recognise club culture as a British cultural institution. The government should better support the scenes of today to create the legendary artists of the future. The unending fight for our right to party is a battle cry for our night-time economy."

With less talk of rewinds, Ministry Of Sound Group executive chairman Lohan Presencer views this from a somewhat more hard-nosed commercial perspective ("It comes with the job"). He explains the brutal and relentless battle of keeping a club going in London. "Every single day is war. Fighting with my landlord, fighting with the council, fighting with local property developers. I am literally in one of these fights all the time. There's always someone trying to sell the land from under us, build flats next to us, complain about noise. Then this fucking government *(he means the new Labour one – he doesn't sound keen)* has just taken away all of our rates relief. Do you want to get into my club? It costs the same on the door as it did 30 years ago, right? But my staff costs and my DJ costs and my beer costs and my electricity costs are not the same as they were 30 years ago."

The secret to Ministry's success, where others have fallen by the wayside? "It's only because we're big, bad and ugly. We sue people, and we make lots of noise in the press. Every other fucker gets shut down. James *(Palumbo, Ministry of Sound founder)* was from the world of high finance. And James understood litigation from a young age. And James taught me litigation early on, and how to use the law and political lobbying. Most young club venue owners are lost here. Their creative entrepreneur sensibilities are crushed by the might of others."

He comments that, while he's not the biggest fan of Amy Lamé, London's first night czar – appointed in 2016 by London mayor Sadiq Khan, she stepped down from the role in late 2024 – she was offered little support and no budget. He also mentions that one of the Ministry's masterstrokes has been securing a 'deed of easement', protecting the venue from the threat of noise complaints. It's one of very few to have been issued in London. "How else could we survive?" he continues. "Does London want to have a night-time economy? Does it want to have clubs? Or does it just want fucking flats? We need all of the protection we can get."

As much as it would be convenient to claim clubland is only suffering because of malevolent forces conspiring against it, it would be remiss to skirt over changing trends in entertainment and socialising. More typically writing about clubs, gigs and the hedonism that goes with them, Fader reported in 2024 on the burgeoning enthusiasm for bingo among young audiences. They're 'increasingly partial to live entertainment over boring nightclubs', the story remarks. There is some cause for optimism for those into dance music, however, with news in the same article that 'bingo raves' are now a thing in cities such as New York, Chicago, Los Angeles and Philadelphia. One specialist promoter, Bingo Loco, promises a frantic-sounding combination of 'dance-offs, rave rounds, lip sync battles, throwback anthems, confetti showers,

CO2 cannons, conga lines and prizes ranging from international holidays, cars, air fryers, lawnmowers and so much more.'

But before we go thinking that novelties such as bingo nights have taken over and that these are now the go-to 'IRL experiences', the truth is people are going out less often. And when they are, there's a tendency for going to bigger events (less frequently) over smaller ones (more frequently). It's an occasional night in the converted IKEA building that houses Drumsheds in Tottenham Hale, not a weekly commitment to a sweaty basement in Soho or Shoreditch. There has also been a shift to people preferring to engage in social activities earlier in the evening rather than late at night. The cost of living, safety concerns and less drinking are all impacting here. Perhaps impacting most of all, the sheer convenience of our devices and all that can be streamed from home. Dance music as a community is now as likely to be evidenced through what forms around independent online radio platforms as offline, in the real world.

Speaking to Red Bull Music Academy's The Daily Note, a free daily newspaper distributed in New York back during the 2013 Red Bull Music Academy, DJ Prince Language (promoter of nights including NegroClash and Stoned Soul, and producer for the likes of DFA and Editions Disco) articulated the course of change: "The internet has had the greatest, and arguably most detrimental, effect on New York. Pre-internet, it can be reasonably stated that most dance music was primarily heard in dance clubs, by people dancing in a specific, communal context. People went to clubs to hear music that could only be heard there. Actual physical spaces like clubs simply don't matter as much – this has diminished the power of both the spaces and the music played within them. Clubs may not be the centre of dance music anymore."

In shifting from in-person dance music to an online iteration, a contribution is being made to the so-called 'loneliness epidemic', and one that disproportionately affects young people. American political scientist Robert D Putnam, in his heavily-discussed 2000 book Bowling

Alone, detailed the decline of social capital in the United States since 1950. He argued that spending less time with others eroded two forms of social capital: bonding capital and bridging capital. The former arises among similar people, the latter among those who are different. Putnam linked these two forms, showing how they reinforce one another. Supported by data, he argued that the decline in bonding capital had triggered a corresponding drop in bridging capital. This, in turn, contributed to the worsening polarisation, friction and mistrust between communities that have become hallmarks of the modern world.

Revisiting the work in a New York Times interview in 2024, he spoke of a nation that is now even "more divided, more lonely and less confident about the way forward." He adds: "I think we're in a really important turning point in American history. What I wrote in Bowling Alone is even more relevant now. Because what we've seen over the last 25 years is a deepening and intensifying of that trend. We've become more socially isolated, and we can see it in every facet of our lives."

Clubs themselves can reasonably be seen as spaces where bonding and bridging capital coexist, with personal connections forming alongside broader, cross-cultural exchanges. NTIA are keen to stress that the benefits of dance music are not just economic. Their 2024 survey of the genre's 'engagement, culture and connections' concentrates on the community cohesion it provides, and the inclusivity and mental health benefits that come in tow. Dance and electronic music events improved the emotional and mental health of 80% of their survey participants; and 75% felt a sense of belonging at them, and strong social bonds. As one of their club-going research participants put it: "My entire friendship circle has come from meeting friends on the dancefloor."

Kazim Rashid from Resident Advisor's 23:59 agency, who we heard from extensively in the last chapter, is also in no doubt about why protecting club culture has a purpose more significant than simply making space for hedonistic behaviour. "I don't think it's just about keeping clubs open for the sake of keeping clubs open. It's about preserving integral social spaces for people who need them. These social spaces are hugely important to young people. I think they should be preserved with the utmost integrity. You shouldn't need to be a fan of clubbing yourself to understand that these environments are very important for people, for social progression and cohesion, for dialogue and health. If you make no effort to preserve clubs, isn't that much the same as not preserving community centres or libraries? For me, it's the same attitude as that. It's that the powers that be don't see the value in social spaces that are largely for working-class, inner-city people."

Some good news strikes in the UK in the week I'm writing this chapter. The government announces a new policy instructing that every ticket sold at an arena or stadium show should include a financial contribution to support grassroots venues, promoters and artists. Quite how this will be implemented remains uncertain at this point. "The ball is firmly in the court of the music industry to quickly and voluntarily establish the mechanisms for delivering the grassroots ticketing contribution… get this done or expect a statutory levy," said the Music Venue Trust, a charitable organisation formed to combat the closure of venues. Nonetheless, it has high hopes, describing it as: 'The single most significant shift in over 50 years of British music. Together, we have actually changed things for the better – and together, we can do even more. There is light at the end of the tunnel for grassroots music venues.'

Berlin resistance

Among the terms most readily splattered across *Selling The Night*, gentrification is sure to be right up there with 'authenticity'. This catch-all descriptor for the process by which developers transform neighbourhoods from low to high value lurks in most conversations about the shuttering of clubs. Williamsburg, Shoreditch, Kreuzberg – debates have raged long and hard around the impact of change in these and many other hot districts. The stages are familiar: artists and outsider communities move into an affordable area that's experienced decline; politically liberal-progressive professionals follow; those with significant wealth come next; and the original residents – plus most artists and outsiders – are displaced. And across these stages, the role of nightlife often transitions from the very reason people are flooding to the district to something considered a noisy, dangerous, undesirable irritant.

The 2012 book The Gentrification Of Nightlife And The Right To The City by York University's Laam Hae looked at how this process played out in Manhattan's East Village as far back as the 1980s. 'The gentrification of the East Village explicitly hinged on the aesthetics and ambience that the neighborhood's countercultural and bohemian artists had created [during] the 1960s and 1970s. The media's attention to this [movement] gradually changed the popular picture of the neighborhood from low and marginal to central and interesting.' Later, Hae notes, the trajectory was for those same countercultural and bohemian artists to be squeezed out; valuable and cherishable in transition but without lasting usefulness.

Across the Atlantic from the East Village, as experts on night culture go, Berlin's Lutz Leichsenring is probably unparalleled in how it intersects with government and commerce, creativity and environmental factors. He started out promoting hip-hop and street artists, then collaborated on an early German dance music website, along with running clubs and restaurants. In 2009, he became the spokesperson and executive board member for Berlin's Clubcommission, a body set up to represent the interests of nightlife in platform debates and discussions, including at sessions of the Federal Parliament. As Clubcommission put it: 'We function as an intermediary between our members, the media, public authorities, institutions and businesses and promote the members' interests as well as the general cognition of the scene. Furthermore, we represent the scene in commissions, political occasions and abroad.' They also – and more evocatively – proclaim: 'Who is there to speak out for a scene that consists of committed individualists? Who represents the interests of a subculture that defines itself by being separate from the world of business? And who organizes an industry that actually stands for planned irrationality?'

The Clubcommission first took shape in 2001 in the wake of several threats to the city's vaunted night culture. These included intensifying club raids and town planning decisions that suggested a perilous future for venues like Tresor, Bar25, Klub der Republik and the Knaack-Klub. If Clubcommission started in protest mode, since then, it's widened its remit to include lobbying, developing legal frameworks, defusing conflicts between clubs and local residents and providing start-up assistance and advice for the next generation of event promoters. In turn, it's offered the direction and inspiration for countless other organisations and night mayor-style positions to spring up in cities worldwide.

While the application was submitted by Rave The Planet, the electronic music-supporting non-profit started by DJ and Love Parade founder Dr Motte, Clubcommission also had a hand in Berlin's techno scene joining the country's UNESCO list of intangible cultural heritage. It's a status usually granted to more traditional activities (Slovakian bagpipe culture was a recent addition). "Congratulations to all the cultural creators who have shaped and contributed to Berlin's techno culture," Dr Motte said on social media. "This is a major milestone for the entire culture, and our joy is beyond words."

Lutz combines his role at Clubcommission with work he conducts under the VibeLab banner, a consultancy he established in 2018 in partnership with Amsterdam's former night mayor, Mirik Milan. VibeLab describes itself as 'a research, consultancy and advocacy agency dedicated to supporting creatives and preserving nighttime culture.' One of their first projects was the Global Nighttime Recovery Plan, a set of reports providing guidance on how nightlife should bounce back post-pandemic. Their Creative Footprint work, developed in partnership with professors from Harvard, deployed mixed-method research techniques to examine the cultural value of club culture in Berlin, New York, Tokyo, Stockholm, Montreal and Sydney. They've produced reports for initiatives in cities ranging from Malmo to Nashville and, indeed, Berlin – the most recent came in the wake of the city's Watergate club announcing its closure after 22 years, with its owners lamenting that the night economy still hasn't recovered after the pandemic. They've collaborated with IKEA, advising on how to engage with creative communities hunkered down in tech and VC bro-blitzed San Francisco. Another project, NightSchool, offers EU-wide peer-learning sessions for new starters in the nightlife industry, emphasising minimising the environmental impact of after-dark cultural activities.

Making sure their work doesn't get too lost in theory and abstraction, they commit to running at least one party every year. Case in point: Sexy Mess, an event staged with New York's House Of Yes at Amsterdam Dance Event, championing inclusivity, performance and, of course, good music.

"It's interesting to see what different cities are doing," Lutz starts when asked about the broad view of developments and best practice his work affords him. "Nashville, for instance, is marketing itself very well as a music city but probably needs to do more to actually support new music. Sydney is a good example, because they lost so much of their nightlife through bad policy-making, and now they're investing back into it. But when it comes to successfully aligning with politics and administration, I think Berlin is ahead of other cities."

As ahead as the city may be in this respect, it's undoubtedly faced many gentrification challenges in the years since the 1989 fall of the Berlin Wall. A quarter of a million new residents arrived in Berlin in the high growth years between 2012 and 2017, many exhibiting the traits of what we'd now call the 'digital nomad' set. By 2018, a telling moment came with investor Warren Buffett's real estate arm upping the ante on the 'financialisation' of the housing market by entering into a deal to sell high-end apartments in the city. But Berlin knows better than most cities how to fight back. In 2021, locals voted overwhelmingly in support of a referendum that called for drafting a new law to socialise nearly a quarter of a million apartments, pushing back against powerful real estate investors and their control over rent prices. Berlin's penchant for firebrand activism surfaced more recently through bouts of vandalism of Amazon Tower in the Friedrichshain quarter. The company's plans to make a floor in the building available free of charge to non-profit organisations were met with claims of social washing.

The story of Berlin's clubs and techno is deeply entangled with gentrification. It plays a paradoxical role, both driving and resisting the polishing up of the city that, in 2003, Mayor Klaus Wowereit famously described as "poor but sexy". It's a story that's attracted legions of tourists and new residents, along with the relentless investment that follows. DJ Laurine, originally from Italy, is one example. She came for the weekend and, as she told El País, never left. Now, she co-runs the Slow Life label and plays at iconic venues like Berghain. "I realised that everything I needed to be happy was here." But clubs have also actively resisted gentrification. Many have championed local communities, fighting to preserve spaces and leading campaigns to protect venues from being redeveloped into luxury apartments or commercial spaces. These clubs have become hubs for activism – sometimes through formal events, but more often organically, where those wanting to push back tend to gather.

This push back seeps through into the wider creative industries of the city. Writing in 2024 for It's Nice That, a platform targeting the global creative community, Milly Burroughs reported on a drive against the homogenous design aesthetic that comes with having lots of fintech businesses rolling into Berlin. Independence and analogue techniques were instead finding favour. 'While much of the design world appears increasingly dependent and interwoven with big tech and AI, Berlin's subversive voices are rallying against these digital advances in typically defiant style. The city's young designers are more likely to be found attempting to replicate grungy, analogue design techniques in digital mediums to promote their community radio show or artist-owned creative space than finding use for Midjourney or Runway, and imperfect street and lo-fi rave aesthetics have returned to the zeitgeist.'

Lutz's work often has him mingling with those who have little interest in which way the underground and those on the fringes are shifting. Key to his mission in many cases is showing the worth of club culture to those who don't care a jot for house music or DJs, for the craft of tune selection or the nuances of the mix. These are people who need a bigger picture rationale for its role within urban planning and what's increasingly termed as placemaking – developing strategies for cities that emphasise community engagement and the social aspects of space.

VibeLab's Berlin Nighttime Strategy programme, for instance, is commissioned by the distinctly dry-sounding Senate Department For Economics, Energy And Public Enterprises. Focus areas of the work include the promotion of sustainable tourism, protection from noise conflicts, social anchoring of the night-time economy and the foundation of a forum to support this. To his mind, this meticulous focus on the factors underpinning the creation of cultural capital supports Berlin in the competition it's in against other cities around the world – the pressure to secure both residents and visitors, driving economic growth, preventing decline and boosting global reputation.

"These so-called soft factors are vital if you want to attract people to live and work in your city. Especially for this young generation that is now starting their careers, being part of something is more important than consuming something. They see a city not just as an infrastructure but as something where you can participate, contribute and share values, and club and music culture is an essential aspect of this. When so many cities are losing their identity and all looking the same. When there's this sense that you drink coffee in the same kind of places in every corner of the world; that all shopping malls look the same. When there's all of this, club culture adds back individuality."

This brings us back to Richard Florida's creative class premise – though with Lutz airing the same reservations that the American urbanist's argument generally receives. "I think what Florida missed in his analysis to start with, though he has become wiser on since, is that you need to make sure you don't become a victim of your own success," Lutz continues. "And you learn how to steer against certain negative trends, such as potentially harmful forces within real estate. When you look at Berlin, it was never a very beautiful city. It was always the culture that made it interesting and attractive. If you're losing that and letting gentrification take away the cultural individuality of a place, you're just an ugly city, and then why should people come? You're losing your appeal."

Niklas Effenberger, a research associate at the Fraunhofer Institute For Industrial Engineering IAO and a collaborator with VibeLab, raises points on the nighttime.org knowledge exchange platform around how cities in after-dark mode are rarely granted the same level of consideration as in the day. 'I spend most of my working time on projects on sustainable city development. When I bring up the topic of the urban night in this professional context, I often encounter similar reactions: either a grin or a confused look. A reaction that seems to ask, 'This is a fun topic, but what exactly is the connection to what we're doing here?' ...These reactions suggest a perception that the night is maybe a topic more for leisure, relaxation or socialising and distinct from 'serious' urban issues.'

Professionalising these topics is, Lutz believes, essential in elevating the conversation around club culture. Given the sheer volume of media coverage prophesising the death of nightlife in the last few years and the copious pessimistic data points (some of which we shared earlier in this chapter) backing up that coverage, it's interesting and refreshing to hear him highlight reasons why club culture, with a stronger voice, may gain advantage from more macro-level societal shifts.

"I see some mega-trends that are likely to be beneficial to night culture," he confidently asserts. "One we've been thinking about is climate change. There are things that we've always assumed we'd do in the day that are starting to happen more at night. All kinds of things. Construction work is happening more at night in some cities. Festivals and other events are starting later in the day, because it's too hot earlier. All of this means there will be more people out at night, so more attention will need to be paid to how to manage the night, as there will also be people trying to sleep. I think this better management of the night will be advantageous for club culture and where it fits it.

"We all know that more people are working from home and shopping from home. We can all see the empty office spaces and retail spaces," he continues, shortly to hop to plan VibeLab's guest appearance at the upcoming World Urban Forum in Cairo. "If real estate owners want to breathe life back into cities, they need to consider the role that culture can play in drawing people in. We have to be at the table when these decisions are made about how inner cities are reshaped. And I think this all means there's a good chance that club culture will be moving back into inner-city spaces – reclaiming what we've been pushed out of in recent times."

Laws and listening in NYC

The more you explore the world of those campaigning, lobbying and planning solutions for keeping nightlife buoyant, the more you learn that Lutz Leichsenring is likely to have offered them guidance. Ariel Palitz is one of them. In 2018, she was appointed the founding director of New York City's Office Of Nightlife, part of the Mayor's Office Of Media And Entertainment. It's a role that she held for five years, and one she had, in a sense, been preparing for most of her life. "I'm a native New Yorker, born and raised," remarks Ariel, a proclaimed 'Jewish-Rasta-Buddhist', soon after we meet. "I always joke that you go from spin-the-bottle to bottle service here."

She started hanging out in nightspots early in her teens, all set for the 1990s 'club kids' era that burst loudly and brashly into Manhattan's nightlife – a whirl of heavy makeup, elaborate hairstyles and bold accessories, blending punk with rave and a flair for self-aggrandisement. When still at school, she was helping founding club kid Michael Tronn – notable for his sprayed and shellacked 'unicorn horn' hairstyle – running the guestlist for his themed nights at Club Mars – the hyper-cool, multi-floor spot that, among other claims to fame, was where Moby started his DJ career. After college, there was fundraising for the Lower Eastside Girls Club ("I've always wanted to serve the community") and jobs in PR, at record labels and in and around bars and clubs. In 2004, she took over an East Village venue that was about to go under, renaming it the Sutra Lounge and running it until 2014. Big nights there included a regular Tuesday hip-hop jam featuring the likes of Kid Capri, Tony Touch, Kool Herc and DJ Premier.

Quite early on, though, the place became famous for something else: the New York Post ran a piece ranking Sutra Lounge as the 'noisiest bar' in Manhattan, with the most complaints to the city's 311 number. 311 is a hotline designed to report non-emergency issues, make complaints and request municipal services. "What a badge of honour," she laughs. "I lived above the club and woke up to lots of news vans and reporters wanting to hear about all of the noise I was creating." She found out that the overwhelming majority of those calls had been made by one "chronic complainer" – someone with a track record of hitting 311 whether in earshot of noise or not. It was a turning point in Ariel's life. "I wound up being activated and politicised at that moment to not only defend myself but the industry as a whole. Because I had been a witness to how this really beautiful culture had been vilified and criminalised and underappreciated and over-enforced."

More in spite of how the city functions than because of it, nurtured by community rather than administrative structure, it's sometimes a wonder how NYC ever attained such legendary nightlife status. Challenges are manifold and longstanding. Put bluntly, the city that never sleeps hasn't wanted you to dance much. There was the 1926 New York City Cabaret Law, which was finally repealed in 2017. As well as demanding that musicians apply for a New York City Cabaret Card (Chet Baker, Charlie Parker, Thelonious Monk and Billie Holiday were among those who fell foul of it), it prohibited dancing in all venues selling food and drink unless they had obtained a cabaret licence.

Such a licence was expensive and hard to obtain, with the law often accused of targeting those in marginalised communities. The targeting was notoriously unambiguous in the actions which preceded the pivotal Stonewall riots of 1969, the constant persecution and police raids of gay bars. There's the strangulating influence of the city's zoning laws to contend with as well, an attempt to drive orderly development that's forever criticised for its inflexibility and inequity, furthering the forces of gentrification in the process.

As far back as the prohibition era, menaces have often come in the form of overzealous and occasionally tyrannical statesmen. Ranking high among the more recent characters in this camp: Rudy Giuliani. Better known of late as one of Donald Trump's sidekicks, he took office as mayor in 1994, bringing with him an obsession with the 'broken window' theory. This decrees that relatively slight misdemeanours automatically lead to more serious crimes being committed. It was a perspective that manifested as his Quality Of Life campaign, a clampdown on minor offences and, by extension, activity in and around the city's club scene. It's often cited as the leading cause of death of NYC nightlife energy in the 1990s and the end of the club kids era (though Tunnel club promoter Michael Alig's arrest and subsequent guilty charge for the murder and dismemberment of fellow club kid and Limelight doorman Angel Melendez, after a fight over drugs in 1996, doubtless didn't help either).

Ariel Palitz's brush with notoriety over noise complaints had her delving deeper and deeper into understanding the red tape and the flawed dynamics of the city's relationship with its nighttime self. She joined her local community board and was a founding member of the New York City Hospitality Alliance. "There was so much that was wrong," she remarks. "You can go back as far as the probationary era, and the night economy and nightlife had never truly been officially recognised as an asset, rather than a liability."

The 2016 Resident Advisor article quoted from earlier, The Bronx Is Burning, concluded that New York City should mirror European cities in appointing someone to act as an ambassador, helping the nightlife industry and the city to understand each other. Two years later, that's what Ariel became. In September 2017, Mayor Bill de Blasio signed legislation to establish the first ever Office Of Nightlife. "I read the job description, it was basically my biography, and I applied," Ariel recalls. "I believe hundreds and hundreds of other people applied. Eight interviews, a 1,500-word memo, 30 letters of recommendation and ultimately an interview with the mayor, and I got appointed."

At this point, the hard work started. While there were learnings and best practices from other cities to consider, NYC had a set of puzzles of its own to solve. "I was completely making it up," Ariel happily admits. "I mean, I had people like Sound Diplomacy *(a consultancy on the creative industries' impact on community development and economic growth)*, Marik *(Milan from VibeLab, Amsterdam's former night mayor)* and Lutz to turn to, and they were so important. But really, this is a Herculean industry in a Herculean city with endless problems and challenges. So I did a lot of meditating and trying to stay positive. But you know, you can do anything when you've run a nightclub. Nothing to do with working with the government is as intimidating as that."

Early stages included surrounding herself with people who could help her understand the language of government and a 'listening tour' across the five boroughs, bringing together venue owners, workers, performers, elected officials and, crucially, the residents too. "We filled out huge halls, and everybody thought I was absolutely insane. Everybody thought it would be uncivilised. War! But I knew it could work. I intentionally chose beautiful places – synagogues, places of worship – and made playlists, creating the right vibe. I requested that people listen as much as they talk."

She took what she heard and designed ways to, as she puts it, foster "empathy in the city." She wanted everyone to listen to what it's like to be running a club and have someone who cannot hear any noise weaponise the 311 complaint system. She also wanted venue owners to learn what it can be like for those neighbours living nearby and the reduction it can bring to their quality of life. Five years down the road, Ariel looked back on the notes she took in the early days and deduced she had achieved everything she set out to do.

She's rightly proud of introducing a number of tangible and positive changes to the city – some underway in her period with the Office Of Nightlife, some not taking effect until more recently. She instigated disbanding the city's MARCH (Multi-Agency Response to Community Hotspots) approach to dealing with nightlife issues. Initially established by Rudy Giuliani, it was the driving force behind many raids on clubs and acknowledged by the current mayor, Eric Adams, to have been "abusive and intrusive" in form. Instead, there is now CURE (Coordinating a United Resolution with Establishments) – a 'solution-oriented' programme under which 'enforcement will be a last resort'.

She also brought in – we're big on acronyms here – MEND (Mediating Establishment and Neighborhood Disputes), a free mediation and conflict resolution service with a remit including quality of life issues between residents and businesses. With it came a reduction in the power held in making anonymous complaints, and a greater emphasis on sifting legitimate grievances from the less legitimate. This, in turn, reduced the overuse of stretched police resources, as they were duty-bound to attend whenever a complaint was made. "It's like, you're bringing a gun to a knife fight. Or not even a knife fight," she sighs. "You're bringing a gun to tell somebody to turn down a radio." She set up the Narcan

Behind Every Bar campaign to bring life-saving opioid overdose prevention training, tools and resources to the nightlife community (Narcan is a medication used to rapidly reverse opioid overdoses).

Ariel ended her tenure in the Office Of Nightlife in 2023 (she passed the baton to Jeffrey Garcia – among other things, founder of the Latino Cannabis Association). Since then, she has consulted in similar fields, finding solutions to global after-dark and hospitality challenges. She has also recommended launching a permanent New York City nightlife museum, which she hopes will one day become a reality (a temporary exhibition is planned for 2025). Such a museum, she says, would emphasise the importance of preserving club culture for reasons that go beyond the purely commercial.

"For many of those in the queer community, for instance, it is their chosen family. It is their safe place. It is where they can express themselves and also be compensated. And we noticed what happens when you take this away during the pandemic. For some people, it felt like their safety net was gone. It was like the oxygen had been taken away from them. We set up online therapy to fill the gap. I think the pandemic validated that nightlife is a necessity, not a luxury. And for many reasons – culturally and economically; for self-preservation, self-care and survival. People really need people."

Another influence in changing the course of nightlife in NYC is Greg Miller. He's the founder of Legalize Dance, which pushed hard for and contributed to the success of relaxing the zoning laws and repealing the Cabaret Law. His weapons seemingly a mix of mighty legal firepower and karmic good vibes. He's also behind Dance Parade, a non-profit celebrating diversity by 'presenting as many forms of dance as possible.' Particularly striking in the mission statement on Dance Parade's website is the following: 'Our root is social justice. Our rhythm is unity. In the 1800s, ballroom dancing was deemed devil's work. In the 1920s, New York City enacted the Cabaret Law to stem interracial dancing in Harlem jazz clubs. Nazi Germany banned 'anarchistic' swing dancing in the

1930s. Even today, although the Cabaret Law was repealed, racist era zoning laws still prohibit dancing in 80% of New York City. We stand for all dancers, including you.'

The inaugural parade was staged in 2007, with over 2,300 dancers from 75 organisations winding down Manhattan's Broadway and Fifth Avenue. Among the participants: DJs Danny Tenaglia and Kool Herc, and b-boy originators the Legendary Twins. Dance Parade thrives to this day, with over 10,000 now taking part.

Taking inspiration from the transformative role of dancing in our lives – whether to banging house, Armenian folk, or Brazilian zouk – Greg draws on his experiences at festivals like Burning Man and with the '5Rhythms' meditation movement, first devised in the 1970s. "It's about getting out of your mind and into your body," he tells me breezily, a man seemingly unfazed by NYC's maelstrom of pressures.

"The Black and Latino communities, the LGBTQ community – they thrive in nightclub situations and these laws have all been set against them," he continues. "That, for me, can be considered structural racism. For 91 years, the Cabaret Law was suppressing culture. We should never have a law against dancing and wonderfully, Mayor de Blasio came to think that and say that."

The red tape of America seemingly has no bounds, however. The challenge now, Greg continues, is that, even with changes to zoning and the end of the Cabaret Law, it's New York State's Liquor Authority, aided by the community boards, that decides which venues can host dancing. "No community board should force bars and restaurants to post 'No Dancing Allowed' signs. Local communities and small businesses, particularly those centred on the marginalised, should be allowed to flourish. The problem is the state is a lot harder to sue than the city. But still," he smiles, thinking ahead to the fight with the New York State's Liquor Authority. "We have some lawyers on our side who are totally fucking amazing."

8. CHALLENGE IT ALL

Should club culture even aspire to be part of the creative industries?

How can dance music work differently with brands – or not at all. Resistance is surfacing and from many angles

Marketing or funding?

October 2024 and it's the time of the year for Amsterdam Dance Event – or ADE, as it's more commonly known. This near 20-year-old conference, festival and all-around celebration of four-to-the-floor sonics – also commonly known by its bright yellow flags and banners – does a concerted job of ensuring that brand logos do not swamp proceedings. Nonetheless, there are partners out in force. Porsche cars are driving industry people about town. Heineken fridges are glowing in the dark. G-Star is handing out the official ADE rucksacks. KLM is flying in the DJs and Dyson is all set to launch its OnTrac headphones, complete with the heartfelt belief that: 'Dyson has been at the forefront of technological innovation, initially focusing on powerful motors for vacuum cleaners. Recognising that these motors generated significant noise, Dyson invested heavily in research to minimise it, mastering the control of sound waves, frequencies and attenuations.'

Amid this whirlwind of all-bases-covered activity is the presence of the German digestif brand, Jägermeister. Next to its signature green bottle and – in association with another business that has figured heavily so far, Red Bull, the Jägerbomb – it has long been associated with partying. The bomb is a concoction the brand is trying very hard to leave behind, but it has other traditions in the after-dark world to build on. Much of the early work in positioning this drink, conventionally associated with more sedate occasions, within the noise of the night is attributed to Sidney Frank. Eventually to become a billionaire businessman and philanthropist, he can also lay some claim to the success of Grey Goose vodka. In the 1980s, when he was the importer of Jägermeister to the US, he promoted the drink heavily in party settings. First among students, including in the form of jello shots, before hitting a broader aspirational audience. New York magazine enthused back then that he was a 'promotional genius' and had made a 'liqueur with an unpronounceable name, drunk by older, blue-collar Germans as an after-dinner digestive aid, synonymous with 'party'.'

When I research near-vintage Jägermeister PR material, it seems that once upon a time the parties in question had a strong heavy metal flavour to them. Associations were made with bands such as Metallica, Mötley Crüe, Pantera and Slayer. More recently, it's all been about dance music. And under the title of Save The Night, it's been about something that many conversations in *Selling The Night* have gravitated towards: funds and funding. By which we mean dedicated financial resources established to support creative, cultural and community-driven projects. That's funds from brands in this context, encompassing a growing line of thinking that, if your brand is benefiting from something in culture, the value exchange with that 'thing' should be more enshrined than what can sensibly be left in the hands of the fickle marketing department.

It's a commitment, then, to partnering in ways which, in part or in full, moves the remit out of that marketing department. It puts it somewhere where the metrics can be less short-term, where initiatives aren't so prone to biting the dust when one CMO replaces another. The exchange of value could be summarised as follows: for the subculture, it's support with fewer strings attached and a more enduring purpose; for the brand, presenting yourself as a more genuine cultural ally, perhaps even settling overdue debts for past leverage.

Tom Dodd from WME puts it this way: "These businesses are multi-billion dollar operations, making money out of the culture of music, often Black music or music from gay communities. They have a duty to invest back into the culture without shouting about the fact they're doing this being the number one point in the objectives. Yeah, it can be addressing the same communities or subcultures that the marketing department is addressing, but it's about behaving in a different way."

At ADE, along with a showcase of some of the previous recipients, Save The Night leads on a talk from grime figure and industry thought leader Elijah, with him advising how to successfully apply for the fund. The origin story of the fund, meanwhile, takes us back to the pandemic period, when it was initially considered more of a short-term rescue plan to help clubs and collectives that were struggling to stay above water. It offered financial support but also, in those times of isolation, online drop-ins and master classes through which to cultivate dialogue and connections.

The Jägermeister team then started to assess what an enduring version of Save The Night could do, specifically in addressing challenges such as gentrification, sustainability, safety and inequality. Kea Kleihauer joined the brand as a senior manager in global culture and experiential marketing around the time these plans were unfolding. Speaking from her home in Berlin, she says: "As we looked at the impact of our pandemic-era work, we recognised an opportunity to turn this support into something foundational, rooted in our brand values. So unlike many partnerships that end up feeling temporary, we committed to a long-term relationship with nightlife, one that benefits the community."

Today, the centrepiece of Save The Night is a yearly call-out for club culture-oriented ideas and innovations, with investments of up to £100,000 made to successful applicants. Judges have included the creative director of Fabric, Jorge Nieto, Jamz Supernova, Elijah, Jaguar and Jayda G. Jägermeister proudly claim to have supported over 1,650 meisters (that's the name they give to movers and shakers in the network) and 1,225 projects (though certainly not all to the tune of £100,000) in more than 60 countries. The submissions they invest in are diverse: it could be funding for an app that seeks to improve safety and security at night, or a mentoring scheme creating opportunities for young bartending talent from under-represented communities.

The two big winners last year, Kea continues, were: "One was from Northern Ireland – a documentary and research project *(called Free The Night)* to highlight how nightlife has struggled in the past 30 years since the end of the Troubles. In a country that's been torn apart, they emphasise the need for club spaces and nightlife culture to make connections in a divided society. The second project *(Studio Can-V)* was in Nairobi, Kenya. It's about establishing recording studios for local artists. Access to recording equipment and facilities, allowing them to develop their art. It's bridging a gap for artists who might otherwise struggle to find suitable environments for their work. And the studios are designed to be transportable, as many artists travel long distances to reach the city centre. By making these studios mobile, we're supporting a wider range of creatives."

When asked about guardrails or principles they apply when deciding what to invest in, Kea responds: "We have a clear checklist that each project needs to meet. On one side, we have globally run projects, managed by my colleagues and me, such as a fund where creatives can apply with their ideas and receive up to 100k in funding. Then we have local markets – our 150 markets. Each can apply for budget support.

For example, a market like Indonesia might propose a project to help a marginalised community, outlining details on how they'll spend the funds, the community impact and the long-term goals. We then have specific questions for these local applications, like which communities they're supporting, the project's long-term objective and a breakdown of budget usage. We're very conscious about avoiding ethics-washing, so we want to ensure the funds go beyond just a social media campaign. We also require them *(the local market office)* to co-invest, so there's always a share of both global and local budget. If we just cover the costs, it's easy for local teams to be less committed. Shared investment helps ensure they follow through with execution and quality.

"It's been a journey, though," she admits. "Early on, we'd see proposals saying, 'Oh, we have this big brand event with a DJ who happens to be LGBTQIA – can we get funding?' That's not what this initiative is for. We're not just paying for talent to make a token statement."

So part of Kea and team's work is mediating these conversations with the local markets, navigating cultural differences. "Yeah, exactly. Sometimes we're called the Woke Girls, because we're the ones talking about how we can make nightlife safer! Talking about LGBTQIA representation; doing the *fancy cultural stuff*," she laughs. "There can be friction in this process but it's also a valuable learning dynamic. We have open discussions to explain that our values – such as being allies to these communities – are non-negotiable. We won't deviate from them because it's core to who we are and who we support."

I remark that this all sounds very complex and involving for a brand to commit to. Embedding this work in a place in the business which protects it from the fluctuating status of quarterly budgets must be vital. "Oh yes, I think we're definitely lucky," she nods. "We give the artists and meisters lots of trust and then we as a team are given trust by the business. They see the importance of this work and the need for freedom for cultural marketing to be done well. It's easy for a brand to think, 'Let's just do another promotion or campaign and hope it boosts sales.' But this is different. And even though the industry is struggling right now, they understand the importance of keeping this going. It's reassuring to know our projects aren't in jeopardy. Cutting back would be costly in terms of losing the reputation we've built over the past six or seven years."

Save The Night, Kea explains, is viewed as a core pillar within the business – and one around which other club culture initiatives can orbit. One of these is Night Embassy, described as a community-driven platform with a remit to provide support for a next generation of creative talent. Asked about the relationship between Save The Night and Night Embassy, Kea says: "With Save The Night, we try to set the foundation and make sure that there can be a future of nightlife. Then with Night Embassy, it's about defining that future. What will it look and sound like? How does it come to life? That's the distinction for me."

Eric van den Bogaard is the creative director at London and Amsterdam-headquartered culture marketing agency, Protein. He's worked on Night Embassy since it started in 2019. He had a key role in the design of Save The Night, too; and through running his own agency prior to joining Protein, can point to a 12-year working relationship with Jägermeister. "I know them well," he smiles, talking from his home in Amsterdam. "What I always give them credit for is that they genuinely dare to take risks in working with creative communities, trusting them and what they want to do. They aren't briefed to death. It's much more symbiotic than that. Of course, at first there can be scepticism among the communities and artists we work with. But it's actually funny to see when we take them to Wolfenbüttel where Jägermeister is made, and you can observe them defrost in a matter of hours. Obviously the product helps a bit with that, but it's genuinely like being immersed in the brand and feeling, 'Wait, actually, I can relax. I can trust these guys.'"

Eric, who's résumé prior to agency life includes spells as a music journalist and a DJ, talks in more detail about how Night Embassy works: "It's been five years now, 10 markets, and the basic premise of what we do is we land in a culturally interesting place. We identify emerging communities that we think are interesting, relevant, urgent at that moment in time. We distil and understand the essence of this local culture, and then we find community leaders to help us identify talent who we then work with to put together a nightlife programme. So this year, for instance, we're doing Paris and Warsaw. But we've been to Tokyo, São Paulo, Johannesburg, Nairobi – so many places over the years.

"One of my favourite examples is this ballroom event we did on the edge of the Alexandra township in Jo'burg," he continues." You literally couldn't walk 20 or 30 metres outside the venue because it's one of the most dangerous places in the city. Yet within that space, you have this whole queer community in a sort of weird venue where God knows what happens normally. And these audiences actually mixed. It worked, and it was a beautiful occasion. You could see the encounter between these two groups that never meet. For me, that's where the magic really happens in what we do. We've also brought the queer community into Shibuya, Tokyo. It really was the first time for them to be on full display. In Nairobi, it was the same thing – having someone voguing on stage at a brand event, which is unheard of there.

"And there's just so much more we can do," Eric adds. "We land in different cities and find that everyone is struggling with similar challenges and questions. When we bring them together, they can learn from each other. One of my dreams is to build a global, open-source platform where everyone can contribute and collaborate. It hasn't fully come to fruition yet, but I'm confident it's the kind of thing I can work on with Jägermeister. We've been cultivating this global community for a while now, after all."

The symbiotic relationship between the Save The Night fund and initiatives like Night Embassy is an important consideration, too, says Kea: "Artists often come back after a project saying, 'Hey, this was fantastic, and I'd love to do more together.' That's also where we can step in with Save The Night, to continue the momentum, ensuring that once something like Night Embassy wraps up, we're there to support any new projects they want to realise. It's about keeping the relationship genuine. It makes me proud: if one of our partners approaches us with a project and asks for financial support, I'd say we're able to help about eight out of 10 times because we keep a budget set aside for this."

While Save The Night and its various offshoots benefit from a positioning within the business as a fund, rather than campaign (albeit the distinction here is probably open to interpretation), the need to report back to the C-suite and to evaluate remains. I'm curious how refined their approach to this is. Work in progress looks to be the most fitting description.

"In the beginning, we jumped in without much formal planning, focusing more on getting things done on the ground than on creating an elaborate strategy," Kea says. "Now, with the importance of CSR *(corporate social responsibility)* to our company identity, Save The Night has become a core pillar. Every employee at our company should know what Save The Night stands for. But no, our reporting hasn't been particularly sophisticated so far. Each project we support is so unique that it comes with its own set of KPIs. Sometimes we're tracking attendance at an event; other times, it's a straightforward donation we're providing with less measurable outcomes.

"Because of this, we launched a comprehensive impact reporting system to gauge our brand's impact on communities," she continues. "And by the end of this year, we'll be able to share for the first time clear data on our impact. It's a system that involves a backbone of various smaller metrics – things like visitor numbers, people reached, and donations made – which then feed into a more complex calculation to assess our overall influence.

"One of the most important things for us – and especially for me – is to avoid any hint of ethics-washing. I'm very conscious of not making claims that we can't substantiate. We have to be very careful and ensure we have evidence to support anything we claim. Otherwise, people could quickly accuse brands like ours of saying we're making an impact without any real proof of what we've achieved."

If the number of times it's mentioned in our conversation is anything to go by, ethics-washing – essentially a derivation of greenwashing, and a term often associated with big tech corporations and their self-regulatory shortcomings – seems to be a hotter topic at Jägermeister than most places. Speaking as an outsider to the business, Eric adds: "Honestly, I think you're too cautious about it. Especially with Save The Night. It emerged so organically and during such a unique time. It took a while before the brand felt ready to communicate about it externally, and in hindsight, I think we could have started a year earlier. Of course, it's generally better to be a little late than too early with these things. But this points to a modesty within the brand that, while admirable, shouldn't be allowed to hold things back. At the end of the day, this is also a PR exercise. It should be mutually beneficial. And sometimes, I do feel like the brand could afford to be a bit more bold in sharing its achievements."

One way they're trying for greater boldness is through thought leadership. Their The State Of Nightlife report, produced in partnership with Protein, researches and presents a range of themes. It covers the move away from 'big box clubs' and back to DIY creativity. The push towards partying with purpose ("The new generation inject politics into partying," comments the Bogotá artist and activist, LoMaasBello, in the report). The quest for different spaces – chill-out zones and meditation spots, not just bars and dancefloors. They also look at the complexities of letting brands in and building trust. Within this, the need for brands to listen, rather than assume they understand all perspectives. Similarly, the need for those within subculture to learn more about how brands work, and the realities of red tape and process. From there, equipped with knowledge, for all parties to have honest conversations; not just to hope for the best.

Asked to consider the duty of care taken by corporations in this exchange, South Africa's Theresho Selesho, described as a cultural entrepreneur, comments in the report: "Brands play a big role in culture because they're one of the biggest investors in cultural projects. They have the responsibility of helping shape a scene because of their financial contribution. They are the ones who are booking or curating or investing in a certain direction. Brands become kingmakers. Some brands know what a big responsibility that is, some don't."

Eric from Protein highlights that progress rather than perfection is the operative term in how they live up to this responsibility. "It's not about claiming we have everything 100% right. That would backfire and no one would believe us. But we can show we're not afraid to be part of these conversations." Findings from the report also help guide the upcoming path of the Night Embassy work and what to invest in, he adds. Effectiveness metrics, meanwhile, look the other way, reporting on the route taken. As with measuring the success of Save The Night, work in progress is the status here.

"We've been evolving from a strictly events-based programme to more of a global platform," Eric continues. "In the beginning, we had simpler metrics focused around these events – things like attendance, PR reach and the number of creatives supported, which were relatively straightforward to measure. Now, though, we're pulling in more data points and it all goes into one *massive* spreadsheet. We're essentially at the same stage as Save The Night, where we're getting more serious about defining everything. The weak spot in programmes like this is when the finance team starts asking about the actual ROI. Since we're mainly focused on brand building rather than directly driving sales, having as much data as possible and metrics we can use to back up what we believe in, helps us protect our projects and budgets."

In the communications industry, brand building is often set up as the opposite of performance marketing – though in truth, it doesn't have to be an either/or. Whereas performance marketing focuses on optimising campaigns in real time and driving direct consumer actions, such as sign-ups and sales, brand building concentrates on nurturing positive, memorable perceptions that convert into long-term loyalty. Big on storytelling and cultural relevance, most consider brand building the more exciting and creative of the two. All good – but also the harder to quantify in terms of investment value.

"If Jägermeister talks about how nightlife is an essential part of its own culture, then obviously we also need to show how we invest in that culture," Kea reasons. "But you need a foundation within the company that understands this is about long-term brand building over short-term selling. There's always that tension – the temptation to do a promotion that gives a quicker return. But the belief here is strong – we fight that temptation! And we're transparent about our motives, too. Without a thriving nightlife, there would be no natural place for Jägermeister. Bars and clubs are central to our identity, and if they disappear, it diminishes who we are as a brand."

Eric emphasises the importance of continuous learning to their strategy – and indeed, that there is still a lot to learn. It's easy to think of dance music and electronic music as a mature industry now. Depending on where you mark the starting point, it's been around about as long as hip-hop has. Yet, while hip-hop's rise to global prominence follows the archetypal hockey-stick growth curve – steady beginnings followed by exponential success – dance music's ascent has been more episodic, decentralised and marked by sudden bursts of momentum and periods of unpredictability.

"Yeah, dance music is still maturing, especially in the mainstream space. It's hard to pin down even exactly what it is anymore, but brands have jumped on board because they recognise it as a key cultural touchpoint – similar to how hip-hop was viewed about 15 years ago. There's a certain excitement around it, yet this rapid evolution brings challenges. You can't just capitalise on the popularity of dance music without understanding its nuances and the communities behind it. And anyone who thinks they have learnt everything they need to learn is crazy. That's when you get people churning out work that's 'sustainability, inclusivity, blah-blah-blah.' Just a dreadful amalgamation of so-called woke-y themes."

Jägermeister are not the only brand to add the terms funds and funding to the lexicon of how they position themselves within club culture. Ballantine's True Music, as we heard earlier in *Selling The Night*, also includes a fund element: '10 recipients awarded a division of the £100,000 fund to help elevate their essential work as they strive for equality in music on a global scale.' Gilles Peterson's Worldwide FM partnership with whisky brand Monkey Shoulder switches the language from fund to grant, with £10,000 up for grabs for grassroots music communities. Their press release highlighted the role of independent venues, radio stations, record stores, collectives and club nights in shaping the UK's musical landscape and energised communities. "We have no idea where this is going to take us but can't wait to see and hear it," said Gilles at the time of launch. In a rather over-scripted explanation, Monkey Shoulder's global brand manager, added: "Monkey Shoulder believes things are better when they are mixed. That applies to our whisky as it also does to music scenes that foster creativity, diversity and new thinking."

Theo Gentilli from the 'music-first creative agency' Warm Street is complimentary about Jägermeister's work but, reflecting on the rise of funds and grants more broadly, he airs some misgivings. "Traditional product placement and sponsorship always felt a bit dirty. Then it became about creating content around the culture. After that, the creator world exploded, followed by the rise of the social media ecosystem. Eventually, it shifted to funds – and I think Black Lives Matter was a key moment that flipped people's thinking. But the sad reality is that most of these funds end up deprioritised or outright cancelled. Very little is standing the test of time."

Brands surreptitiously switching off their good deeds isn't the only issue, Theo continues. Sometimes it's about the thought that goes into initiatives in the first place. "It tends to be quite formulaic. The work that gets signed off has fallen into a bit of a cycle. It's another fund – you're putting forward a sum of money, which is good in some ways, but you're helping one person with a project instead of properly investing in smart partnerships that could offer lasting value to people. I think the tone is often a bit off, too. Many talk about being purposeful, but it often comes across as saviourism – like they're coming to the rescue of communities. It's still very much about giving people fish rather than teaching them to fish. In a better world, we wouldn't even need brands to step in because the political environment would be more supportive of the arts and the communities involved. The teaching to fish would happen there."

Finlay Johnson, chief operating officer at the Association For Electronic Music, also questions the level of consideration that goes into creating this type of initiative. Specifically, the amount of listening that goes on. "Has anyone actually asked those marginalised communities if they want the brand's involvement, and if they do, what would they spend the money on? Because a lot of the club communities that are in these spaces are fiercely independent, and they wear that they are not about to be bought by anyone as a badge of pride.

"He.She.They are an interesting example," Finlay says of the house and techno record label, fashion label and inclusive party collective we've referenced elsewhere in *Selling The Night*. "They're really passionate about developing ways to provide training to door staff beyond what they get with an SIA *(Security Industry Authority)* licence, specifically around engaging with transgender people at the door. But you've got to think so carefully about which brand will genuinely be sensitive to this. What real depth is there to a so-called fund they might offer?"

He.She.They co-founder Sophia Kearney also addressed the dilemmas of bringing brands into clubs that are safe spaces for the transgender community when I spoke to her for Ballantine's Resetting The Dancefloor report in 2020. "It should be about a brand giving money and enabling a community to do something. And not with 10 different restrictions. Or having to give speeches about the brand. Or demanding high profiles, like, 'We want a trans DJ with a million views'. That's unlikely – trans people are marginalised!"

Kazim Rashid, chief creative officer of both Resident Advisor and their 23:59 agency, highlights a similar challenge: the tension between a brand's desire to support those who need it most and the pressure to reach a large audience. "I'm finding brands are enthusiastic about funding initiatives that bring in marginalised communities or focus on emerging markets. The friction comes in striking a balance between this and the expectations around reach and scale of the activation. But it's important to keep this in mind – especially for more experimental artists; and even more so if they come from working-class backgrounds, racial minorities or are otherwise outside of mainstream communities. These are the people who are finding it hardest to secure funding and also the ones who need it the most."

This is where collectives like Pxssy Palace stand firm. Noted for organising nights that 'make space for women and femmes of colour to party free from discrimination', they have mastered how to protect their space while engaging with brands, says Tom Dodd from WME. He believes they're a prime example of an outfit that maintains a strong sense of 'who's in control' in their dealings with brands. "They're saying, 'This is ours. If you want, you can help pay for it, but you're not going to be all over it. And you're not going to have a say about what we do or how we dress or what we look like.' It's protecting a safe space for the LGBTQ+ community. You can't take that from them. If you want to be involved, you can help, but that's it."

Over in Colombia, LGBTQIA+ scene pioneer Ynfynyt Scroll talks about how brand funds or grants could be used to strengthen a scene in the country by bringing in bigger artists to play alongside local talent. "I've tried to book people from other places. That would be positive for us. But US and European artists usually do not go down on their fee to be here. Maybe in the future brands can think of their sponsorship as more like grants – making things possible that literally wouldn't be otherwise."

Regardless of the pros and cons we're hearing, some would argue that the funds we've been discussing – those from brands – are barely funds at all. Instead, they're marketing campaigns in a different wrapper. But funds, of course, come in many forms. In the more conventional sense, there are philanthropic funds, government funds, arts and culture funds, and crowd-sourced funds. These days, though, it's the institutional investors – venture capital firms, private equity and hedge funds – that are probably most top-of-mind when people think of funding.

Here, they play by very different rules. Given underlying objectives, funds from brands can more readily invest in culture – supporting communities, for instance. In contrast, funds from institutional investors are generally focused on investing in businesses rather than culture. A decade ago, the notion that they would find much in dance music to interest them would've seemed far-fetched. Yet, these investors are now very much a part of the ecosystem.

It's a busy space. A growing number of institutional investors are translating this interest into equity positions in dance music's biggest names. Dubai's luxury-focused Five Holdings acquired the Pacha Group (including the Pacha club chain) for $363 million in 2023. The private equity-backed Superstruct Entertainment, with Cream founder James Barton at the helm, has taken stakes in a number of dance festivals, events and platforms, including Boiler Room and Sónar. Plus8 Equity, an offshoot of Plus8 Records, with DJ/producer John Acquaviva among the managing partners, bills itself as an investor in 'early stage opportunities at the intersection of entertainment and technology.'

Speaking to Resident Advisor in 2023, Srishti Das from music analytics firm MIDiA Research explained that, whereas once investors were content to put their money into one vertical (such as a label, or management company), they increasingly want to get behind opportunities that enable them access to music fans across a range of touchpoints.

"They want a distribution system that's interlinked with social media, ticketing or other technology services such as livestreaming, AI or VR." They also want to get behind what's described as culture-driven opportunities. "When you attend a festival or a club, it's a whole experience of entering the world of that space and exploring that space's relationship with design, the neighbourhood, food, fashion and non-music activities like tattoos or wellness – it's a whole cultural experience," Das continued. "There is a clear demand for identity-driven culture, which is why you're seeing genres like Afrobeats, neoperreo and amapiano going global. Investors want a slice of that."

While there is debate about how effectively brand funds can reach those on the fringes or marginalised in dance music, institutional investing shows little indication of focusing on anything other than scale and the pursuit of premiumisation. "We're seeing a split in dance music culture – two separate communities with opposing views," says Finlay Johnson from AFEM. "On one side, you have people making music and going to raves because they love it, and on the other, the professionalised Ibiza-Mykonos-Dubai scene driven by venture capital. This divide raises important questions for groups like AFEM, which originally supported under-represented artists, but now face the challenge of staying relevant in a scene where electronic music is mainstream.

"Venture capital investments are widening this gap," he continues, referencing dance music's 'squeezed middle', a recurring theme in my conversations. "The middle ground is disappearing, leaving artists either as hobbyists with side jobs or as part of multinational operations. Bringing this back to brands, they'll need to decide how to engage with this evolving landscape – whether to counter the VCs by supporting grassroots, authentic dance culture, or to focus solely on luxury night markets like Ibiza, where the audience is more about partying than dance music itself."

Though not strictly addressing a squeezed middle, Jägermeister, interestingly, is a brand straddling both sides here. As well as Save The

Night and Night Embassy, they have a venture capital arm called Best Nights VC. Launched in 2018, it describes itself as an impact investor and, contrary to the venture capital norm, also as community-motivated. From their Berlin base, Best Nights VC makes investments of between $300,000 and $1 million in each funding round. Among their mission statements: 'shaping the future of nightlife by funding it' and 'investing with the aim of bringing people together in real life'.

"We fight against a stigma," Best Nights VC managing director Lorrain de Silva told the Global Corporate Venturing website in 2023. "For many cultural entrepreneurs, venture capitalists are evil. We have two horns on our head because we are capitalists, and the cultural side doesn't fit with that. But they are building great businesses that are scalable, that are generating millions in revenue and are profitable, yet they need capital to grow." Later in the piece he continues: "Jägermeister has a high reputation, and we want to leverage that. We're looking for content platforms, marketplaces for events, dating apps: we want to be a part of everything connected to nightlife as long as it's close to culture and people."

Andrea Rosen is an innovation ecosystem strategist at Best Nights VC. Decoded, that means she spearheads the portfolio management. So while she is involved in the investments and deal flow processes, hers is more the holistic view of what's happening in each of the portfolio companies. She looks at ways to support them and, importantly, ways to connect them with opportunities within the Jägermeister business. Moving from Israel to Berlin for "the tech and the techno," she was first enticed to Best Nights VC because "it just sounded such a different kind of opportunity. They were looking for people with very hybrid experience, and it all sounded so right for me."

"One of the things I love most about working here is that the social impact goes hand in hand with the financial concerns," she adds, doubling down on the balance between purpose and profit. "We're focused on diversifying our portfolio rather than just chasing unicorns *(investment talk for a privately held startup valued at over $1 billion)*. We look for companies that we really do believe in, of course, and that can sustain themselves. But also for ones that have an emotional connection to the community, and some of the ones we've backed are doing this incredibly well."

Previously, she'd held advisory roles related to vertical farming and the future of cities. She's also worked for audio-tech innovator Native Instruments, specifically on their Traktor DJ software. And if anyone questions her integrity as a venture capitalist in club culture, her nearly two-decade DJ career shoots down the doubters. Playing and producing as Androosh, she started in her native Tel Aviv, moved on to Berlin clubs like OXI, and toured extensively across Europe and Africa. In late 2023, she released her debut EP, Proof Of Existence, a big, rolling deep house sound, in collaboration with Hett for the Nervous label.

I ask her what the reasoning was behind Jägermeister launching Best Nights VC. "I think it makes complete sense," she responds. "It started by paying attention to trends in other corporate venture capital units, especially those in food and beverage, where it's clear many support their own supply chains – whether that's through other alcohol brands or complementary products. But we approached it from a different perspective. Jägermeister has always invested in culture, whether through grant funding or other activities. We focused on how we could invest in the consumer value chain, rather than the supply chain – and specifically in tech startups that enhance nightlife and create measurable impact and community value.

"For us, nightlife is a strategic asset," she continues. "Our whole thesis revolves around the idea that nightlife is essential for making cities competitive and attractive to top talent and innovators *(we're back to Richard Florida's Creative Class)*. We aim to foster cultural impact by supporting spaces and experiences that leverage the online-to-offline connection. Anything that brings people together and empowers community building is what we're invested in."

Communities, community building and impact are recurring themes here. But when they come from venture capitalists, we can be excused for thinking they sound opaque. I ask Andrea to clarify what impact they're aiming for. "Nightlife is a broad topic for us," she acknowledges. "But when we talk about its impact, we focus on social impact. How can we address the loneliness epidemic? How can we tackle the challenges brought on by the pandemic? And, most importantly, how can we bring people together again in real life?"

To guide the investments they make, they've come up with a bespoke metric for measuring impact: ranking the number of physical interactions – hence 'best nights' – that a startup can provide. Best Nights VC claim their investments led to 22 million best nights for clubbers and music fans in 2023.

"This aligns perfectly with Jägermeister's mentality," Andrea continues. "It's about creating social impact – helping people live their best nights and making that possible for as many as we can. The formula we use varies depending on the company and product, but we develop a tailored equation for each. We take into account things like how many people the product brings together, how many events they host, and what their product contributes to the market. From there, we're able to quantify the impact they're having. So yes, our startups enabled 21.9 million best nights in 2023. That's the kind of metric we look at. Now, we're expanding our focus to consider other forms of social impact. For instance, we're starting to look at each company's role in fostering diversity, their responsibility in ensuring safety metrics, and how they address accessibility. It's work in progress but it's going well."

It's a fascinating space for a drinks brand to land itself in. And one that starts to make greater sense when looking at what sits inside the holdings portfolio. The Best Nights VC website details 13 startups 'bridging the gap between tech and culture'. Included among them, Togather, an event planning marketplace; Un-Hurd, a data-driven marketing agency supporting independent artists; Soundboks, creating portable speakers to 'enable Gen Z to party anywhere, anytime'; and Woov, an app that allows grassroots festival organisers to build sitemaps, timetables and onsite transaction functionality.

Andrea talks about some of the other companies in the portfolio that particularly stand out for her. "We've made investments across the US, UK and Europe. But, most recently, our first one in Africa. In Kenya, which is close to my heart because I lived there during the pandemic and saw firsthand how vibrant the music and arts scene is. The company is called HustleSasa. It was founded by this very entrepreneurial Chinese-American guy who owns one of Nairobi's coolest nightclubs and has been in Kenya for 12 years. His co-founder is African, giving them a unique blend of perspectives. They've built a marketplace for creators and event organisers to host events, sell merch and more.

"What's brilliant about it is how it tackles the fragmented infrastructure in East Africa, particularly around payments," she continues. "They're solving issues like cross-border payment difficulties, scams and underdeveloped systems. They're essentially like a fintech for the nightlife scene, making things safer and more seamless for creators and organisers; also reducing risks for foreign companies wanting to do stuff in Africa – and that's important. The deal has just closed and should be announced in the next couple of weeks."

Andrea also explains more about 222, based in Los Angeles. "They're a deep-tech machine learning platform that matches people for blind social experiences. It's perfect for Gen Z, who want to meet new people in real life but also in a cool, innovative way. The idea is small groups – maybe five or six like-minded people – are paired up, and you don't know where you're going until just before. Over the night, you might visit two or three places together. It's very fresh, very smart and ideal for tech-savvy young people who want something different from a night out."

Another example from the portfolio she wants to mention is Lex, a New York City-based LGBTQ+ social app that goes beyond dating, also focusing on fostering friendships and communities. This business is further along its journey. When I spoke to Andrea, it had recently been acquired by 9count, a mobile app conglomerate founded by Alex Hofmann, the former CEO of Musical.ly – the app that later evolved into TikTok. "It provides a safe and inclusive way for people in the queer community to connect around shared interests, no matter where they are. In certain parts of Africa, for instance, where it can be especially challenging to be openly queer, Lex offers a way for both locals and travellers to identify safe spaces, meet like-minded people, or, you know, even just find someone to go skateboarding with. They've built one of the most cohesive queer apps for finding friends."

It's hard to argue with the palpable enthusiasm for innovation, entrepreneurialism and solving needs on show here. But, to circle back to some of the comments Best Nights VC managing director Lorrain de Silva made in the interview we quoted from earlier, raising the notion of venture capitalism in clubbing circles often still results in one of two responses: suspicion or confusion.

"Yeah, of course, in being part of nightlife, part of an underground scene, we can talk about sticking it to the man, sticking it to the capitalist agenda," Andrea reasons. "But at the same time, nothing survives without some entrepreneurial spirit. And I'm not going to lie, there is definitely a gap in the market in how to train these more artistic entrepreneurs on ways to build better businesses. I think grant funding is great as a starter for some things, but you do need to think longer term as well. How is this venture going to sustain itself? How's it going to continue to make money? Sure, it doesn't need to be a unicorn, but at the same time, it still has to be able to get to some kind of scale.

"This is why I keep saying there's a significant education and financial literacy gap in the markets we operate in," she adds. "I really believe the entire nightlife economy and industry would be stronger if we could address these gaps. For instance, there's a shortage of solid clubs, labels and festival businesses that could grow with the right investment. We wouldn't invest in all of those – we have a lane to stay in – but there are things that absolutely need tackling here."

Andrea sees improving financial literacy in the nightlife industry as part of Best Nights VC's remit. By addressing this gap, after all, they can source higher-quality startups for their portfolio. "In a place like Berlin, what we notice is that there are creative industry events and VC/startup events, but these rarely intersect. So we try to do that, making things educational and inspirational. We have a commitment to investing in non-traditional founders, but we do need them to be willing to learn about our side of things and this is a way to make that happen. So we organise panel discussions on topics like art, music, social gaming, or Web3, where contributors from diverse backgrounds and without much in common – artists, entrepreneurs and others – come at it from completely different angles. Ultimately, we're building up that literacy."

Investment literacy, startup portfolios, non-traditional founders. It's not lost on Andrea how different all of this is as subject matter compared to older codes of language in dance music – think DIY, making-it-up-as-you-go-along, living for the day (or night). Across the last 10 years in particular, she feels that this dimension of dance music has been advancing at a giddying pace. "I remember going to events like Sónar+D *(the Barcelona festival's tech and creative industries programme)* and seeing maybe a handful of music tech investors – generalists dabbling in the space. Now, it feels like everyone is calling themselves a music tech investor. And we're even seeing the rise of funds focused on culture and arts – that's not something we'd have really seen before. So, yes, there's definitely more activity in the space, but just because it's trendy doesn't mean it's all doing what it says it's doing."

Beware of investors touting caring, sharing phrases but with little to back them up, in other words. Deeper digging is advised. "Take the term community, for example – it's thrown around so casually now," Andrea laughs. "When someone tells me their work is all about community, my first question is, 'Okay, but how are you measuring that?' If you can't measure it, it's just lip service. I've had founders tell me they're focused on building community, and then it turns out their idea of it is just adding in to what they do a few in-person events here and there. That's not community – that's just bro culture repackaged, my friend."

Drink up

It won't have escaped anyone's attention that alcohol, and alcohol brands, are never far away from a mention in this book. Of course, this should hardly be a surprise. Despite some opposing views – and we'll get to those soon – drinking, dancing, music and the night have long been part of the same hedonistic bundle. Add to this the alcohol industry's enthusiasm for associating its products with 'uptempo occasions' (therefore the opposite of the downtempo ones, which are considered indicative of an older consumer), and we find ourselves awash with booze – in both liquid and brand endorsement form.

It's been a partnership with its rocky years, however. As we've seen earlier in this book, the 1990s and the explosive growth of club culture brought a complicated relationship between dance music and alcohol in many countries. The rise of rave – and predilection for MDMA pills and bottled water – posed a real threat to the alcohol industry. But the giants of the drinks industry weren't going down without a fight. They saw an opportunity to reinvent themselves. In the UK, visits to pubs dropped by 11% between 1987 and 1992. The clientele was ageing, and the 'spit and sawdust' surroundings hadn't moved on in decades. But when authorities began cracking down on illegal parties in warehouses, dance music was pushed back into more traditional licensed club venues. Alcohol brands had the perfect opportunity to give themselves a makeover and reclaim their presence.

In 1997, writer Jim Carey described the brewing industry's attempt to 'recapture the youth drugs market' as a 'recreational drugs war'. That same year, journalist and author Matthew Collin, in his book Altered State: The Story Of Ecstasy Culture And Acid House, quoted Fraser

Thompson, then strategic development director at the Whitbread Group: "Young people seem less prepared to sip beer for hours; culturally, they prefer short, sharp fixes. Five years ago, there were fewer alternatives for getting a buzz or getting high. The challenge for the industry is to make alcohol part of that choice." In his 2009 book The Politics Of Alcohol, James Nicholls observed of that period, 'For the first time, the alcohol industry began to market drunkenness as a primary aim of drinking as they sought to compete with other psychoactive youth markets.'

The Portman Group, a trade body formed in 1996, introduced its Code Of Practice On The Naming, Packaging And Promotion Of Alcoholic Drinks in part to challenge this new marketing push. Its success was partial, at best. The reinvention of alcohol was well and truly underway. Alongside luridly coloured alcopops, imported bottled beers and energy drink-infused beverages, came mixology and so-called 'experiential drinking', ready-to-drinks (RTDs) like canned cocktails, new flavours and innovative packaging – all supported by heavy duty club and festival branding and sponsorship. A marriage was made in music-meets-marketing heaven.

The exact size of the alcohol industry's current investment in dance music is difficult to ascertain. However, looking at their investment in music overall, data from sponsorship consultancy ESP-IEG, just pre-pandemic, estimated the spend at around $1.54 billion on sponsoring music venues, festivals and tours across all genres in the US alone. While the global lockdown and the gradual return to socialising likely shifted more of that budget online, much of it went into digital music platforms – indicating that the industry was in no hurry to exit the opportunities music offers.

Adjusting to the cultural and societal shifts brought on by the 2020 pandemic hasn't been the only hurdle for the alcohol industry. A topic du jour in recent times has been the drinking habits of Gen Z, those born from the mid-to-late 1990s through to the early 2010s. The data on this is hotly contested within the industry (especially regarding factors like regional differences and how lasting the trend is set to be), but there are numerous reports indicating a decrease in consumption. A 2023 Gallup poll in the US found that 62% of adults under 35 said they drink alcohol, down from 72% two decades ago. Mintel research in the UK in 2024 claimed that a third of people aged 18-24 do not drink at all. It also found that two-thirds of consumers in that age group are concerned about the emotional impact of alcohol, with a similar number expressing an interest in learning more about mindful drinking.

The term 'sober curious' has entered popular argot, too. It was coined by author Ruby Warrington in her 2019 book of the same name. "Being sober curious means, literally, to choose to question, or get curious about, every impulse, invitation, and expectation to drink, versus mindlessly going along with the dominant drinking culture," she explained. "Not necessarily full-blown abstinence, then, but considering more closely when, and when not, to drink – and the effect that consuming alcohol has."

All of which, naturally, has an impact on the economic realities of clubs and live music. Mark Davyd, CEO of the UK music venue advocacy group Music Venue Trust, commented in 2023: "If everyone became teetotallers tomorrow, you would create a £79 million hole in the ecosystem that delivers live music up and down the country. If everyone stopped drinking, lots more venues would close. Funding throughout the music ecosystem will have to change. The music industry is behind the curve on this, and so is the government."

Similar conversations play out elsewhere. Writer Daniel G Wilson discussed this for the New Feeling website – described as a 'multi-stakeholder co-operative of Canadian music journalists and community members enthusiastically covering the sounds and stories of music across the country/occupied Indigenous lands that constitute Canada'. He considered the obstacles in the way of creating spaces for music in which the alcohol industry pulls fewer strings:

'Creating alternative spaces, not even necessarily to decentre alcohol but simply to offer performance venues outside of a bar or club, comes with its own set of challenges. There are often myriad permits and licenses even just to throw an event, and one wrong piece of paperwork, or omitting paperwork altogether, invites the attention of bylaw officers or municipal police. Such spaces often exist in residential areas, either in houses or lofts, which invariably leads to noise complaints and friction between neighbours, when the underlying desire is simply to have a space to gather and be social and not have to do so in a black box with a bar attached. Starting a DIY space with these priorities in mind shouldn't be so difficult, but the fees, fines, surveillance, violence and potential evictions that come attached make the notion riskier than it ought to be.'

I certainly don't encounter a wholesale dislike for the alcohol industry among those I interview. But there is a greater sense of scrutiny now of the impact that drinking has on nights out, on communities and culture. And, therefore, on what it means to work with, and take money from, the businesses that sell it. Manchester's DJ Paulette thinks about this in relation to Jägermeister's support of Reform Radio, the community station she works with. It's a well-designed brand initiative, one that includes providing paid opportunities for struggling creatives. There's nothing superficial in how it's been put together. But still, she does have to square the good it brings with the fact that it is also engineered to drive alcohol sales.

"They support a lot of the stuff that Reform does, and they do it well," she acknowledges. "But my problem is, I don't drink, I don't smoke, I don't take drugs. So if there's an alcohol sponsor on something, I have to feel very clear about my connection with it and how it's not authentic for me. It's difficult. I'm a difficult customer! But it would be foolish to think some of the listeners aren't also running this debate through in their heads."

When King Britt thinks about how his attitude to working with alcohol brands has changed over decades as a DJ, producer, label founder, club promoter and now educator, he gets to a similar story. In short, that money is there but get hooked on it at the peril of what you really want to accomplish.

"Back in the day, if I'm organising a night, Gilles Peterson is a friend but that doesn't mean it's not going to cost a lot of money to fly him over here to DJ," he says. "You can try to fund that through what you earn on the door, but that's tough. So then you have alcohol sponsors. There's lots of them, and they're willing to fund these things. But then as you get older, you start to think, maybe I don't want to promote alcohol – that's not so healthy. So you look around at who else is out there, and I guess the next stop is fashion brands – adidas, Nike and whatever. Those can work out great, so long as the brand coincides with the aesthetic of the sound. But it all boils down to authenticity, and it's the finest of lines. Because when you take someone's money, they feel as though they should have a say in everything."

King's view on the acceptability – or the lack of it – of letting alcohol brands through the door has hardened further since dedicating himself to Blacktronika (more on this endeavour later), with its focus on educating the next generation. More money is, of course, useful. But when you're shaping something with an enduring purpose, you have to hold your nerve at times. He's not alone here, nor speaking solely for an older generation of club culture voices. In a 2019 Guardian piece examining how 'club-cultural innovation is under threat', Resident Advisor's Will Lynch weighed up the reciprocal value of Smirnoff's Equalising Music initiative – which aimed to address various imbalances in representation within dance music, including (and launching on International Women's Day) a pledge to double the number of women-identifying headliners. This initiative included an industry pledge and the release of a documentary film. Even so, Lynch questioned: 'What does it mean to team up with a vodka brand? It's not the most socially wholesome idea.'

It's a topic also raised by Dr Luis Manuel Garcia-Mispireta, the associate professor at the University Of Birmingham who we heard from earlier; and who researches electronic dance music scenes and their impact on sexuality, tourism and the creative industries. He asserts that even brands with longstanding club connections, such as Absolut's with the queer community, are not beyond accountability. "On one level, you can't question it: Absolut established a good and long relationship with a community that consumes their product," he says. "But then there are conversations I witness where people are saying, 'Well, look, the presence of alcohol in our parties has not always been good.' And actually, for some collectives, there's a push towards alcohol-free events, or at least events where alcohol isn't omnipresent in your face. The past 15 years have been full of opportunities for profit. But let's not forget, also for reputational damage from poor choices."

Back to London's Pxssy Palace – who came up earlier in this chapter and will feature later, too. This arts platform is rooted in 'intentional nightlife', celebrating Black, Indigenous and people of colour who are women, queer, intersex, trans, or non-binary. Their focus on intentionality extends to their approach to alcohol. Speaking to Vice in 2023, Nadine Artois – aka Nadine Noor Ahmad, the Pakistani queer, trans, working-class co-founder of Pxssy Palace – explained how it was a driver behind trying different party formats, including shifting some events to daylight hours. "For one, it's harder to get home at night. It's more expensive," Artois said. "But the main reason is people don't want to get totally legless. They want to savour the next day… What does drinking and hangovers give you? Anxiety. And the world is much more anxiety-inducing than it used to be."

Patrick Topping, boss of Trick Records, known for his sets at DC10 and DJ Magazine's 'Best Of British' DJ of the Year in 2022, staged his Sober October Rave in 2024. With no alcohol on sale at the event, which took place at World HQ in his hometown of Newcastle, he said in the build-up: "I started playing sober in 2017, and it changed my relationship with music and partying, improving my mental and physical health so much. I'm not saying I'm fully against alcohol – every other event I play at sells it. I just want to offer an alternative, where people can come and not feel the pressure to drink but still enjoy that communal experience of raving together."

DJ, producer and Earth Kicks label founder Mina is best known for her digital platform advising artists on how to submit funding applications. She's another who has experimented with alcohol-free events. Speaking at the time about 2023's Club Soft at London's Colour Factory, she said: "I don't have any judgement towards those who drink – plus there are many ways to get lit outside of alcohol – but alcohol-centred spaces are the default in club music, and alcohol just doesn't work for a lot of people, so I wanted to create an alternative space. Club Soft is for anyone who loves electronic music but struggles with late nights or drinking culture."

Ahsan-Elahi Shujaat is one of the co-founders of Dialled In, the party-promoting, education and mentoring collective dedicated to furthering South Asian talent. He was on hand in chapter four to discuss how empowering running club nights and after-dark creativity can be for people. Here, much like King Britt, he explains that as hard as it can be to turn down money from alcohol brands, it's crucial to choose partnerships wisely and avoid anything that undermines your cause.

"I'm as aware as anyone that brands are a large part of the current ecosystem. And we've found partnerships that work – for instance, with Dishoom *(Mumbai-inspired restaurant group)*. It's a nice fit – our audience loves going there, and what we do with them feels natural," he says. "But from the beginning, we made a decision not to work with alcohol brands. That probably ruled out 80% of potential partnerships, which was a big call to make. But it wouldn't work for our audience – not just from a cultural or faith perspective. Some of us might drink, others might not. But because we're a community-centred project first, I wouldn't feel comfortable ramming whatever alcohol brand it is down an 18-year-old's throat. We feel too much of a collective responsibility to our audience to do that."

Of course, as we've seen, the alcohol industry has a successful track record of adapting to club and youth culture drinking patterns. Whereas alcopops and stylishly bottled beers were their fightback weapons against rave, this time around it's probably the rapidly advancing no/low alcohol ranges. A Fast Company piece in January 2025 laid out predictions for the year ahead: 'Many N/A *(no alcohol)* brands are also moving away from their health-centered positioning to make a play for the partying set. They're rebranding away from the simple health option, and into party beverages with just as much nightlife appeal as the hard stuff – as suited for bars and raves for the 365 party girl as a picnic sipper for the morning workout class community.'

Whether visible in the virtuous form of a mocktail or not, alcohol-free club culture is nothing new, and we can trace threads of this back through dance music's history. In multiple countries, alcohol rarely figured at early acid house, techno, rave and hardcore parties. Further back, it was also absent from the loft parties staged by David Mancuso and others in downtown Manhattan. Whether through necessity or design, these storied settings were often soft drinks-only. What's changed, perhaps, is a greater level of activism in how these choices are being made – more cognisance of what alcohol brings to, and takes from, self-expression in the night. "This thoughtfulness is growing," nods Dr Luis Manuel Garcia-Mispireta. "It's not the easy route but sometimes the need to step away from taking the money just becomes too important to overlook. It can turn into the only route."

Deindustrialisation

Themes of protest and dissent – of rejecting the supposedly equitable value exchange offered when brands, and the creative industries as a whole, interact with dance music – are not confined to this chapter. It's a live and active debate, one that everyone I spoke to for this book was eager to contribute to. Across the chapters, we've explored the formation of the creative industries and how different fields were drawn together to form a tangible – and profitable – whole. We've discussed the opportunities available, or absent, for those from marginalised backgrounds within these industries, and the role of club culture in nurturing this talent. We've examined whether brand sponsorship and engagement in club culture are truly giving back as much as they take.

However, all of this is largely predicated on the assumption that, if set on the right path – if representation and access can be improved (okay, yes, quite a lot to fix there) – the creative industries are ultimately and undeniably a net positive. The surface trends might be out of sync, but the fundamentals seem sound. After all, what's not to like about something that combines cultural enrichment, economic growth, innovation, intersecting fields of creativity, less hierarchical career opportunities and the grand-scale realisation of very cool ideas? That certainly feels like what I bought into when the term 'creative industries' first came into earshot. It has always felt like an intoxicating mix of possibilities – something that legitimises all those hours spent deep in subculture, implying they weren't wasted time or destined to lead to dead ends.

But not everyone subscribes to this perspective. For some, it is exactly the *wrong* way to think about creativity and culture – and dance music therein. From this counter view, lumping everything under the nebulous banner of the creative industries isn't about strength in numbers. Rather, it's a parlous route to commodification; to passions being coldly monetised, to prioritising sellable trends, to the unequal distribution of wealth and resources, to creativity as a means to an end, and to the erosion of any subculture that cannot pay its way. With generative AI systems trained on artists' work without consent or compensation threatening to accelerate this commodification – further reducing creativity to mere economic output – a decoupling from the creative industries logic arguably feels more prescient than ever.

A book published in 2024, Culture Is Not An Industry, doubled down hard on these themes. The work of Justin O'Connor, a professor of cultural economy at the University Of South Australia, it argues for a reframing of government policy to position culture as a public good and a human right. O'Connor traces the origins of the 'cultural industries' – as they were originally called – which were designed to legitimise the economic value of cultural production in historically undervalued fields like music, film and art. Over time, however, the concept was co-opted by neoliberal policies, aligning cultural production with entrepreneurialism and market competition. By the 1990s, as we've already seen, the creative industries were all boxed up and good to go, ready for deployment by the likes of New Labour.

For all the fanfare the creative industries have received, O'Connor questions the success of this sectoral convergence, arguing that the contribution to GDP is often overstated. He also notes that economic gains within the creative industries tend to accrue to a small number of large corporations, rather than being evenly distributed among independent creators or local communities. Additionally, he points to the tendency for outputs from the creative industries to be monocultural, with their merits often reduced to metrics such as impact on urban regeneration, tourism, job creation, or plain old units sold.

Instead, he calls for new cultural policies, focusing on inclusion and representation, rejecting top-down approaches and embracing community-led initiatives. In doing so, he positions culture alongside healthcare and education as a public right, rather than a luxury or commodity. Interviewed for the trade website MediaCat in 2024, Justin O'Connor was asked to expand on the concept of the creative industries as a rebranding of what had previously been the cultural industries. "There was a common word meaning cultural industries, they would say 'arts and cultural industries'," he responded. "They decided to rebrand it in the late '90s, mainly so it connected with the whole dotcom digital thing. But in doing so, it expanded the concepts of cultural industries way into what's not creative, basically. So it made it a very difficult concept, but it also displaced the idea of culture, which is at the heart of it. It undermined the cultural aspect of culture. And at the same time, it became increasingly about, 'Oh, it's an industry, it's an economic sector. We've got to grow it.' Whereas that's not the point of what culture is. It's culture for culture, not for economic growth."

Later in the interview, he brings up the topic of hugely powerful corporations that, for all their creative industries pizzazz, are by no means squeaky clean: "We now know that six of the 10 largest corporations on the planet are cultural organisations. They distribute and often produce culture; including Netflix, Meta, Amazon… they're massively powerful, and the creative industries' agenda has nothing to say about that."

As robust a case as O'Connor serves up, he's still drowned out significantly by those who beg to differ. In other circles, the argument continues to be put forward for the creative industries all-in package, in which the work of the largest corporations and smallest collectives are crammed together. In a blog post, Talking Heads' David Byrne applauds the creative industries' positive effect on the economy and on job creation, proclaiming: 'Investment in the arts doesn't cost us money – it makes us money!' Others, from Damien Hirst to Stormzy, have similarly shown backing or been wheeled out to boost creative industries PR drives.

In the UK, advertising trade title Campaign reported on the creative industries' strong presence at the Labour Party Conference in September 2024. They seemed to like what they heard from the newly elected government, who – possibly trying to evoke Blairite sensibilities – pointed to the potential for growth on the near horizon. Opening the inaugural Cultural And Creative Industries Pavilion at the Liverpool conference – three days of panels and fireside discussions with 40 creative partners – the minister of state for creative industries, arts and tourism, Sir Chris Bryant MP, said: "There is nothing better for the UK as part of our soft power, our enjoyment of life, and our understanding of what it is to be a human being than a vibrant, lively arts and creative industries for everybody." Creative UK, the not-for-profit organisation supporting the creative industries, made the case for public investment – with economic modelling to demonstrate that £100 million injected into the sector could generate one billion more for the economy.

"Well, I have lots of question marks over club culture's part in the creative industries," says Dr Luis Manuel Garcia-Mispireta, the author and associate professor in ethnomusicology and popular music studies whom we've heard from across various chapters. We didn't get to speak about Culture Is Not An Industry directly (it was published shortly after we met), but he's certainly an erudite and enthusiastic source of similar themes and sentiment. His work in academia involves researching electronic music scenes, with a focus on intersections between everything from identity to mobility. Though based these days in the UK midlands, much of the focus of these explorations has been in Berlin, particularly through intensive ethnography within subcultures from 2008 onwards.

"I have had mixed experiences – sometimes enjoying, if not privileged access, at least easier access through presenting as queer. But also big disadvantages as a Latino kid in that town," he remarks about Berlin, before talking about the city's role in electronic music. "I describe Berlin as the Nashville of techno. It's an industry hub, with the same sort of patterns of people who want to launch a career, moving there, trying it on, not always succeeding, sometimes moving out after failing to adjust to the subcultural shock of how the place and its scenes actually function."

Whereas many I interview for this book eulogise the case for underground dance music as their springboard to jobs, starting businesses and a way into the broader creative industries, Luis emphasises a different personal narrative. One that casts the role of dance music more as support network than a cheat code for entrepreneurialism. "I've been a raver far longer than I've been a scholar of any sort," he says. "Since 1995. That was my first party. I was 15, 16, and I started off raving in

Canada, in between Toronto and Detroit. From the first, I was exposed to drum 'n' bass and jungle from the UK. From the latter, techno's second wave via Detroit; things like Plus8 parties.

"So I'm a Canadian citizen, but also Latin American – both Peruvian and Colombian. I was growing up as a queer kid at a time of extremely high stigmatisation of queer folks. At a time when raves were one of the places where you could go and escape some of that, at least," he continues. "As a kid, I experienced bullying. I was somebody who was readable as queer very early on; like there was no way for me to hide that from bullies. And going to raves was the beginning of me becoming an extrovert again – like I had been before puberty. As raves, there wasn't that kind of suffocating cage that came with the school peer group. There was a comfort and safety in just dissolving into a crowd of strangers who don't know who you are, who don't have a whole battery of weaponry to aim at you. It taught me how to socialise again. How to trust having interactions, and to be optimistic about them, rather than defensive and wary."

These are themes he built upon in his book, the wonderfully titled Together, Somehow: Music, Affect, And Intimacy On The Dancefloor. Published in 2023, it explores the kind of sharing and connecting that happens between strangers on dancefloors – what he calls stranger-intimacy. "The book is me talking to lots of people, asking them questions like, 'Do you behave differently towards strangers at techno parties, compared to in everyday life? How is it different? Are you more or less open to being in tactile contact with strangers? What do you think about that? What openness do you have towards intimacy, both physical and emotional, in a rave or club setting versus your everyday life?' I went from there." This led him to consider how stranger-intimacy might help people feel more connected to society at large. However, he also addresses if the sense of warmth and togetherness created by clubbing can sometimes obscure deeper exclusions and injustices. And he stresses the importance of distinguishing between the positive, consensual intimacy that occurs in these settings and the unwelcome and abusive forms that can also arise on crowded dancefloors.

Luis shares with me a copy of Bottoms Up, the research-project-meets-fanzine he collaborated on with others from Berlin-based queer nightlife collectives. Defiant, inquisitive and disruptive, it serves as evidence of club culture as an anti-commercial sanctuary, a counter-narrative to deferentially taking a place within the broader creative industries. One of the questions asked in Bottoms Up is, 'What's it like to throw parties and build community at the same time?' Themes throughout its DIY, punk aesthetic-informed pages include: accessibility to both space and funding; sustainability within the scene and in the context of climate justice; healing, particularly in the wake of the pandemic, both through experiences and community; dealing with misrepresentation and stigmatisation, especially in relation to journalists, researchers and data privacy; archiving, and finding ways to document projects without relying on conventional social media; and addressing conviviality and intersectionality, with a focus on recognising and eradicating oppression, including anti-Blackness within communities. This section concludes with the question: 'Are we really together or just... together?'

All of which takes us into headspaces quite different from that of most interviewed for *Selling The Night.* It's a focus on resistance over compromise, with community looking inward for solutions and progress, rather than relying on commercial partners. Self-sustainability – though with a plan to back it up. The power of creativity is central here, but it's less about bridging gaps with other industries and more about pursuing different objectives. "Absolutely," he nods. "The kind of creativity I find most valuable is in queer collectives working as promoters. Many of them aren't focused on making a ton of money, but on community building. They throw parties to create welcoming and safe spaces for these communities. In doing so, they reset the story and remind us of histories before the mainstreaming of rave culture, before bro-step and white frat boys.

"Where I'm seeing the creativity is in things like community care, right? This shift towards, 'What we do is not just throw parties, per se, but we throw events where care and support are stitched into the design.' The rise in seeing nightlife as a community service, if that's the right word. We lost a lot of our people to suicide during the pandemic, precisely because these meeting spaces became unavailable. It became very clear, very quickly, that many of us are dependent on these nightlife spaces to help support our just remaining in the world, in being able to bear all the other things that happened to those who are queer, and those who are POC and queer, and trans folks. This increasing sense of being embattled, under threat, stigmatised and villainised and demonised and so on. The creativity I'm thinking about and which I think matters the most is being used for purposes of healing."

Creativity for healing. Community for healing. This is very much dance music and club culture contextualised to meet similar needs as in post-Stonewall NYC, where queer communities used nightlife as a refuge and space for solidarity in the wake of social and political struggles. In many ways, this tradition of clubs as healing spaces has continued in countless other times and places since – creating environments where individuals could find freedom, expression and connection. Not an easy place for brand sponsorship to occupy space in, right? "It's important to challenge it all," he smiles. "And that includes where brands fit in club culture. For me, this all stepped up from the 2010s. It felt like a move to cash in on EDM, as it was by then called, in the same way that there was for disco in the '70s. But this time, it wasn't just record labels and mainstream promoters driving it – brands were, too."

Luis has also contributed to Berlin club culture as a co-founder of Room 4 Resistance, the queer collective dedicated to a 'divergent club counterculture' and to 'examining the political dimensions of the dancefloor, creating intentional spaces, and advocating for adventurous under-represented artists.' From his experience organising these events, it's only really the companies who are already bringing utility to and actively supporting the scene that can credibly come on board. "Native Instruments, SoundCloud – people like that. I get the sense that there are more actual ravers and clubbers on staff, and therefore a better understanding of what is appropriate to ask for." In general, he explains, the agreements forged for sponsorship and support tend to be more light-touch, more socially and subculturally appropriate.

While turning down ill-fitting commercial partnerships can doubtless offer a sense of satisfaction, it also brings the challenge of finding alternatives. If promoters and collectives want to avoid calling on brands to address their monetary needs, one answer could be public funding, in its many forms. Luis remarks on the impressive scale of funding for more niche arts initiatives in Germany. In 2024, in Berlin alone, culture funding reached €947 million – up €13 million from the previous year, with the target for 2025 set at €1 billion. Commenting on social media, Ruth Hogarth, a researcher at Queen Mary University Of London, highlighted a stark contrast, noting that Berlin's budget is more than double that of the entire UK: 'The city of Berlin's culture budget (population seven million) for 2024 has been set at €947 million. The whole of England's culture budget (population 57 million) for 2024 is £458.5 million. I know there's lottery and local authority funding on top, but it doesn't add up to anything like the per capita spend.'

Public funding is most certainly available in Berlin, then (and the Bottoms Up fanzines talks about improving grant-writing support as a priority for the scene), but Luis also comments on how politicised aspects of receiving state support have become. "If you're a collective that has any members who've ever said anything publicly to do with Palestinian solidarity, it's very possible that you'll be blacklisted." Indeed, in early 2024 the city's Senate Department For Culture And Social Cohesion informed cultural associations of the importance of complying with the International Holocaust Remembrance Alliance definition of antisemitism. Others, however, believe the definition conflates anti-Zionism with antisemitism, undermining rightful freedom of expression – and this debate is expected to continue.

Despite these challenges, Luis believes there is much for other cities to learn from how Berlin supports creativity, suggesting that such public backing creates an important decoupling from the profit-driven imperative of the creative industries. "The argument from within electronic music for ages has been that this is culture," he continues. "What we're doing is an important contribution to human culture more widely – not just a beauty parade for brands – and we should be respected and supported at least in a way that's comparable to how much resource we put into keeping opera houses open. These major cultural spaces would absolutely fall apart if they were expected to survive purely on profit. If they were required to be commercially profitable in the way that nightclubs are.

"So, ycs, that's the argument righr there," he continues, as energetically as at all points in our conversation. "Just because we've come up from a marginal space where we've had to make profit margins to survive, that doesn't mean we don't deserve support. I think that's been a really interesting shift, and one that Germany's been leading on. It's part of a larger direction of travel – where it's not just about collaborating with the private sector, but also the public sector. It's a reframing of electronic music: still subcultural, yes, but no less deserving of support than elite, high culture – especially when both are so economically fragile."

Carl Loben, editor-in-chief at DJ magazine, concurs that other places and public bodies should be taking notes. "We lack that enlightened view of the electronic music scene that places like Amsterdam and Berlin in particular have. And we saw it in the pandemic, how readily the German government and the Berlin authorities invested in the creative community, which included electronic music. In the UK, it seems like all of the money goes to opera. Nothing really seems to go to the electronic music community and that should change. You just need to look at the revenue generated by the dance scene. Surely you'd want to try to nurture it if you're in a position of power."

Comparative data is not easy to locate, but what is is that, of the Art Council England's £445 million assigned for its 2023-26 Investment Programme, a whopping 80% per cent is going to organisations involved in classical music. Redressing misbalances such as this is part of a broader need to shake up perceptions, Carl continues. "In a city like Barcelona, they'll let you have a rave in a museum courtyard. These things can happen in civic buildings and they're not considered dirty or obnoxious. Can you imagine that in the UK?! With the gentrification of so many cities continuing, we'll need to get more imaginative – new spaces, new forms of investment."

Over in New York City, Ariel Palitz, founding director of the city's Office Of Nightlife, has had plenty of experience trying to elevate nightlife's standing. Progress, she feels, is slowly being made. "I've fought hard to have nightlife culture recognised as eligible for cultural funding. It's classist that it hasn't been. It's often dismissed as too lowbrow. But I do believe we're heading in the right direction. The pandemic highlighted just how vital these spaces are for people."

She proudly recalls a symbolic moment at New York City's Lincoln Center – home to prestigious institutions like the New York Philharmonic, the Metropolitan Opera and the New York City Ballet. In 2022, the Center installed a 10-foot-wide, 1,300-pound disco ball to mark the opening of The Oasis, described as the city's largest dancefloor. The space hosted everything from Eddie Palmieri's Salsa Orchestra to Silent Disco sessions. "The first night, I cried. They invited me to speak to the crowd and open it up. It's a perfect example of these two worlds coming together – the above-ground and the underground – in a place that's an icon of culture."

Despite the obvious appeal of dodging the clutches of corporations, switching from brand funding to public funding does exchange one set of complexities for another. In the case of public funding, a key issue is often who the money goes to and who's considered most deserving (which, admittedly, is also relevant on the brand side). We've already seen it raises questions about who deserves funding more: traditional institutions like opera, or underground music. But, when you look more closely at the funding that does make it through to club culture, where the money is being used productively, rather than as a disjointed, ad-hoc life support system is also called into debate.

Finlay Johnson from AFEM weighs in on this point: "I have quite strong views on this matter, and I don't think my views are particularly popular. The most sustainable and reliable source of funding is from the punters. If you can't sell enough tickets to make your event work, maybe the event is too big. Maybe your audience reach isn't strong enough. Should you need this external support to exist, or should you aim to do something smaller and more modest? Perhaps the issue lies with your model, not the funding.

"On top of that, every year, so many organisers have this nervous wait, needing to find out if they'll get the funding," he adds. "Whereas if they're not relying on that funding, they can plan everything better, further in advance, and be much more responsive to the changing needs of the community."

He also raises a topic that comes up in many other discussions: funding application processes are often arcane and bewilderingly hot messes of paperwork. They certainly don't suit everyone. "It can feel like a race for a limited pool each year, and it's not equitable in many ways. If you're really good at writing funding applications, you'll get funding more often than not. If you're not, and perhaps if you're dyslexic or struggle with time management, but you're doing great work in the community, then you probably won't get the funding. And arguably, your time should be spent on that work in creativity and community, rather than on funding applications, which are not simple processes."

Even if the processes aren't necessarily more simple, in a 2017 Pitchfork story, the generally superior nature of Scandinavian arts funding was highlighted. Space disco mainstay Lindstrøm explained: "Whether we have a right or left government, there seems to be consistency in the cultural politics. Norway is one of the best countries in the world to live in, and arts funding is an important part of the social democracy." He also noted that he only grasped the intricacies of funding when he could afford to hire a team to assist with applications. Reinforcing Finlay from AFEM's view about the deficit in long-term planning caused by relying on funds, Lindstrøm acknowledged that there's no certainty over what will be received each year, which means he focuses this spending only on current projects, rather than those he'd like to pursue in the future.

If the onerous stipulations and convoluted demands of arts body funding are a barrier for many, another path is community funding. Often in fact coupled with arts funding, in this realm it can be a combination of kickstarters and crowd contributions, private donations, micro-grants, fund-raising events and membership programmes. In southeast London, the Sister Midnight not-for-profit co-operative has been navigating this space since 2012. Their manifesto is to launch a 'music venue that is owned and democratically controlled by the community; a space that champions local creative talent, and prioritises people above profit.'

Led by DJs, producers and educators Lenny Watson, Sophie Farrell and Lottie Pendlebury, after a series of dead ends and unsuccessful efforts to secure a location, Sister Midnight signed a lease on a former working men's club in the heart of Catford town centre in 2023. Promising a venue that would cater for everything from activist group meetings and soup kitchens to club nights, the next stage was to engage the community. A 2024 story in The Standard reported they had 1,000 members on board and had raised over £350,000 through community investment. Included in this, as top-ups, were industry contributions dispatched with little fanfare – and well-received for it. The Beggars Group, parent to labels such as Rough Trade and XL, gave £10,000.

"We could never have done this if we hadn't set ourselves up as a co-operative," commented Lenny Watson. She also explained that Sister Midnight's course of action first germinated when a record store she was working at was being turned into a cheese and wine shop. "I just thought, 'Fuck that. That sounds like the last thing we need more of. We need music venues.'"

Resistance is plentiful

Freedom for all. Dance your worries away. A nocturnal utopia. We are all equal. We are one… For anyone who's ever embraced the dance music party line, these sentiments will be familiar, likely even hard-coded into their psyche. It's what has been preached to us. It's what we've seen in the visual language of club culture. It's what we've heard bellowed in countless house and disco anthems. All brought together, a form of ideological indoctrination has taken place, and most have willingly imbibed the message. Until, that is, there was a dramatic swing towards change. Over the last half decade, this maxim of equality and togetherness has started to be stress-tested in numerous ways. Dance music has gone through many of the same shocks, traumas and wake-up calls as society at large.

So much that once went unchecked is now under scrutiny. In many ways, dance music has been pulled into the culture wars, with even the idea of freedom up for debate. Neoliberalism has co-opted that term, transforming it from a fundamental human right – something enshrined in international conventions and celebrated for generations through media, heroes and countless songs – into a symbol of selfishness. The negative side of unchecked individual liberty looms large. Talking about freedom now often signals a lack of empathy, a pursuit of self-interest at the expense of others. Dance music's own take on freedom doesn't look so rosy anymore either.

Consequently, ugly squabbles within the dance music scene have erupted across social media. There have been attempts at cancelling figures both justified and unjustified. Radio Slave, Joey Negro and The Black Madonna were among those who either chose or were forced to revise their names. Ghost productions, bias in myriad forms, exclusionary lineup compositions, cultural appropriation, pay-to-play schemes – these issues and more have raged across the socials. Separating what has substance from the noise can be exhausting. However, amid the unsteady sense of friction and backlash, many important issues have been brought to the surface.

Post-Harvey Weinstein, MeToo reached the dance music industry, with repercussions finally hitting abusers. Two features I wrote in the 1990s came up in this drive for justice in the early 2020s: one with techno founder Derrick May, who faced multiple sexual assault allegations (though he has yet to be charged), and the other with Colombian-American DJ, producer and later revealed rapist, Erick Morillo – who took his own life before he could face justice. Many other DJs, producers, managers and label bosses have faced claims and accusations. An industry-wide culture that allowed such behaviour to go unchecked, and where abuse was often normalised or even dismissed, is undergoing significant demands for change.

This momentum crystallised into action, such as When The Music Ends, the film from activist and techno DJ Rebekah. Inspired by real stories of abuse in clubland, it highlighted the lasting impact on survivors and showed ways to take action against unwanted sexual behaviour. Rebekah, who had been raped at 17 by someone purportedly there to teach her to mix, launched the #ForTheMusic campaign, calling out harassment and assault in the music industry, and urging followers to sign an open letter on change.org. The Association For Electronic Music took notice, releasing a code of conduct in 2021, with other pledges and charters following. Rebekah also acted as an ambassador for Safer Dance, a UK initiative set up to train venue staff on how to tackle sexual violence and abuse.

The pandemic brought issues to light such as so-called plague raves – with DJs like Nina Kraviz, Michael Bibi, Tale Of Us and Amelie Lens playing at events where social distancing measures were scarce in the extreme. Sharp questions were also raised over the arts support grant scheme funding offered in the pandemic. Funding to the tune of £800,00 in the case of both Resident Advisor and Boiler Room. One thing tends to lead to another, and soon Boiler Room was also facing accusations of not paying DJs for their performances. They responded stating they'd always paid artists for branded or ticketed events and, as of mid-2020, would also compensate them for 'non-commercial' shows.

Of course, the hardest slam against the status quo came after the May 2020 murder of George Floyd by a white police officer in Minneapolis. The Black Lives Matter movement forced a necessary reckoning through so many aspects of society, culture and capitalism, and dance music wasn't exempt from this scrutiny. Writer, musician, curator and theorist DeForrest Brown Jr led the Make Techno Black Again campaign in New York City. He addressed themes such as Drexciya's notion of a Black Atlantic, "an underwater utopia populated by unborn children of pregnant African women thrown overboard during the Transatlantic slave trade." Writing on his Join The Future website, journalist and author Matt Anniss discussed a conversation with fellow journalist and author Emma Warren. 'She has gone on the record a number of times to say that we have a duty as white writers/commentators on Black music culture to seriously examine whether we are the right person to tell a story. When the story is about Black British communities and cultural movements, would it not be better to have someone with lived experience, from within those scenes and communities, tell the story?'

These debates expanded into a broader call for redress in the representation of marginalised communities in dance music. They also drew attention to the lack of recognition for the invention and creativity from these communities that propelled dance music to its global powerhouse status. When I spoke to Honey Dijon in 2020 about the origin stories that need to be retold, to highlight the people and communities too often sidelined, she responded: "I scream at the top of my lungs about it. I constantly talk about it in interviews. It's there in the way that I DJ, the imagery I put out, what I share on social media. Activism isn't just marching in the streets. Activism is how you live your life.

"What gives me purpose as an artist is continuing a cultural conversation that otherwise would be lost within a generation," she went on. "Who's talking about the Black lesbian contribution to dance music, or the Black trans contribution? I try to shine a light on all of the hidden corners. Frankie *(Knuckles)* and Ron *(Hardy)* got famous, but they're just the ones who made it through."

While progress has been made in club culture, with a high degree of inevitably, not all of that early-2020s energy has been maintained. Pledges that were signed have fallen by the wayside. Campaigns have lost their funding. Loud industry voices have grown quieter. It's a parallel story to what we've seen in other fields. In 2024, US marketing trade title AdWeek questioned why so many brands had started to edge away from the diversity, equity and inclusion promises they made when the BLM movement was at its noisiest.

"The fact that they are now publicly saying, 'We don't need *(DEI)*,' is tantamount to an admission that *(companies)* didn't really mean it, that they don't have values," Ellen Pozner, who teaches management at Santa Clara University's Leavey School Of Business, said in the piece. "It makes us feel like nobody's serious about anything." Marc H Morial, president and CEO of civil-rights organisation the National Urban League, commented on the conservative pressure groups at work here: "The extremist backlash to corporate diversity, equity and inclusion policies is a blatant effort to keep the gates of opportunity locked. Diverse organisations are profitable, thriving, resilient organisations, and we will not allow a small but powerful and influential group of extremists to drag our country down to protect their own narrow interests."

LGBTQ+ news outlet The Advocate got further into specifics in 2024. It reeled off a list of some of the companies that – even prior to the ominous consequences of Trump's return to power – had 'caved to the far right and stopped DEI programs'; among them Ford Motor Co,

Harley-Davidson, Brown-Forman (the maker of Jack Daniel's whiskey), Toyota Motor Corp and Molson Coors. The perceived rise and fall of 'woke' was having sad repercussions.

Closer to home, there was also a sense that, by 2023, dance music was starting to de-prioritise these conversations, and that the impetus to ask awkward questions wasn't quite as pressing as it was. "Has the industry been waking up? It's kind of got one eye open, but the other one is slowly closing again," says DJ Paulette. "No one is sounding quite as enthusiastic as they were in 2020. Are people really making good on the promises they dished out? Around supporting women's initiatives, around helping Black music festivals to launch? Nope, not happening. They're still supporting the same old things in the same old ways, and they're not really pushing to include those currently excluded."

This lack of commitment, Paulette believes, extends to where brands are investing money and resources. "What we see is, the stuff that men do – say around launching a new app to support something in music – versus the stuff that women do, men's stuff gets through quicker. Men's stuff gets supported quicker. Women are way down in the hierarchy and the pecking order. If whatever support they give to someone like Gilles *(Peterson)* they could also give to people like Pxssy Palace. But they don't. It never happens.

"The problem? We live in a patriarchal society. It is just part of the systemic misogyny and sexism that is built into society, full stop. And the only way to get around that is for people to actually start looking outside of what they know; employing people and giving money to people that don't just look like them."

DJ, broadcaster and founder of the Future Bounce club night and label, Jamz Supernova (aka Jamila Walters), whom we met earlier in the book, is in firm agreement here. She's positive about the change she's witnessing from those on the dancefloor. Less so from those with power. "The music industry put out a lot of pledges for people to sign in 2020 – all about promising change. Where are a lot of those pledges now? If we struggle, it's not for a lack of talent – DJs, artists or even promoters. If we keep sliding back, it's often more about who has the money and the decisions they make. It's about those higher up."

Ahsan-Elahi Shujaat from Dialled In, the collective dedicated to furthering South Asian talent – both on-stage and behind the scenes – adds further perspective here: "It feels like we go forwards a bit, then backwards a bit. I mean, I think by the very nature of us existing, it's obviously getting better. But it would be better still – *much better* – if we didn't need to exist. There's still a lot more that needs to be done and, for all of the talk, it's not really happening. For example, when you see lineups drop from some of the bigger organisations, you can often guess eight out of the first 10 names on the bill before they're even announced, if you know the brand. It's predictable. I get it – it's a competitive time and people need to sell tickets. The issue is, these same organisations have put out big statements saying they're committed to change, yet there's no one holding them accountable. There's no unionised presence or structure saying, 'You committed to this, so why didn't you follow through?' No one seems to be holding anyone accountable."

On the theme of representation in lineups, Ahsan goes on to highlight just how deeply they think about it at Dialled In. While much of what he discusses is specific to their focus on South Asian talent, it also underscores the broader lack of proper, beyond tokenistic, attention given to representation elsewhere. The contrast is striking – while some are grappling with the complexities, others are either merely glancing at or avoiding the topic altogether.

"It's a tough one for us," he smiles, aware of the understatement. "We're essentially trying to speak for an entire region, a whole continent. India has 1.5 billion people alone. Consider everyone else and you're looking at around 2.5 billion people from different religions, creeds, ethnicities, caste systems, genders and languages. That's in the back of our minds with every lineup we put together. So it's not just about gender parity or queer representation – it's broader than that.

We can't just focus on artists who are primarily ethnically Indian or Pakistani, even though they are the majority subgroups within the UK. That's important, but what's also great is the emergence of smaller events catering very specifically to communities like the Malay Indian community or Tamil-speaking communities from South India and Sri Lanka. I'm not suggesting every promoter needs to think like this, but they do need to think about these things more than they are."

Cape Town rapper, producer and drag artist Dope Saint Jude was interviewed for the 2021 True Music Resetting The Dancefloor report. They raised frustrations that the brunt of work was still largely sitting with those suffering the injustices: "There's so much to be done. Black artists often have to carry on their shoulders the struggle of their whole community. You can't just be a carefree artist. The responsibility is often placed on the oppressed group but I think it's the privileged people who have to do the work and the reflecting. It's not our job to be educating people all the time." Dope Saint Jude went on to talk about the dangers of box-ticking diversity in how lineups for events were being assembled: "This can all result in tokenism, as opposed to actually thinking about the music. The artist might be selected simply due to their identity and there's a lack of authenticity."

In the same report, Honey Dijon, as is her way, got to the nub of the issue. Which is that, really, no one is asking for anything more than what should be expected as normal in the supposedly open-minded realms of club culture. "All of these things we're fighting for – diverse lineups, diverse dancefloors. This is simply us wanting our humanity and our creativity to be considered as worthy as other people's. That's an expectation no one should be able to stand in the way of."

So some things changed in the wake of MeToo, BLM and the pandemic, but many didn't – not permanently, not fundamentally. Despite the upheaval and calls for reform, the dominant forces within the dance music industry only grew larger. The juggernaut powered on regardless. The term 'business techno' – coined just before the pandemic by Berlin producer Shifted in a snarky Twitter exchange about a Resident Advisor review of an Anja Schneider's EP – gained traction in the years that followed. It was described as everything from 'techno for people who don't like techno' to 'big room techno' to 'maximum profit techno', with plenty of references to capitalism.

Also on Twitter, anti-authoritarian 'Baron Of Techno' Dave Clarke went in for the kill: 'It is the appropriation of techno and pretending to be cutting edge (when anything but), putting social media and presence first, being run by old EDM management styles and have marketing coming first in your businesses with integrity being last, if at all.' Firing off a follow-up tweet, he snarled: 'It is appearing on social media with a new keyboard, saying big things are on the way, but have no idea how to use it, and you pay a ghost producer in Mars bars and a promise to do a warm-up set somewhere for 400 pounds but they have to pay their own travel and hotel.' Soon after, the collective behind Poland's Up To Date festival put out a Monopoly-style board game called Business Techno. The objective of the game: instigate a dance music empire and trade techno properties. The *real* objective of the game: 'To open dialogue about the state of the industry today.'

Any conversation about business techno often leads to one about Boiler Room. The behemoth broadcaster and club promoter has come to symbolise much of the current age in dance music, capturing the tensions between the new era and the old – what it means to be a DJ, to play music for people, and the media, commerce and celebrity that surround that act. When I speak to King Britt, he recalls appearing on the platform in its early days, alongside Run Dem Crew's Charlie Dark and Dego from 4hero. "We put on something pretty special," he smiles.

Asked how Boiler Room's contribution to dance music nets out, Britt has mixed feelings. "In one way, it's been good for dance music – it's brought it into living rooms," he says. "It's good for artists too. They get so many gigs off the back of appearing on it. But Boiler Room don't like to pay *(though they claim to have changed their policies on this now)*, even with big drinks companies supporting it. I guess it's good for the audience who get to go along. It's a spectacle, at least. But it's not so good for the culture of dance music. No one is dancing. Everyone has their phone in the air. If it's something like a live show, okay, cool, you want to document it. But if it's a DJ, just dance!"

Mobiles. So often, they're held up (literally) as symbols of dance music's moral and communal decline – of losing touch with what clubbing is supposed to be, a problem bigger than the act of using a phone itself. As a result, banning phones now starts to feel like an act of resistance. The proliferation of filming and photographing the moment runs alongside what's become known as 'doing it for the 'Gram.' Simon Marlin, aka The Shapeshifters, had something to say about this on social media, specifically in the context of pop-up DJ appearances in intentionally random locations: 'Instead of DJing in a coffee shop, bakery, convenience store etc for socials and content and making yourself look quirky and hip to your many followers, how about you just support a local small nightclub/venue struggling every week to keep their head above water?'

The phones, it is safe to assume, were out in force and raised aloft at the Squid Game rave happening at London's Drumsheds, the month after I'm writing this in late 2024. The night's organiser is Netflix, celebrating the arrival of the second season of the global smash Squid Game. The event promises Korean food, 'plenty of Squid Game fun' and Peggy Gou. 'Ravers. Let's Goouuu!' screams Netflix across its socials, claiming it as the biggest free party of the year. Others on social media remarked, somewhat brusquely, that big, free parties used to mean something else in dance music – something rooted in counterculture and activism rather than consumerism. Someone going by VossLR on Reddit conspiratorially mused: 'It isn't really free, though, is it? They want something from us.'

Much like Boiler Room, the scale-driven spectacle of venues like Drumsheds is also routinely included in debates about modern clubbing. Whether entry is free or, more often, priced high, the trend for fewer, larger venues consolidating power is a frequent concern throughout this book. Theo from the Warm Street agency puts it this way: "I don't think it's good to have 15,000 tickets held with one venue every weekend. It doesn't help the ecosystem. Consumers seem to be having fun, and artists enjoy playing there. But now people are paying £50 to go out once a month, whereas they might have paid £15 to visit Corsica Studios twice a month. As great as the experience can be at these huge parties, that's the worry from a structural perspective."

The general scaling up and pumping up of all things dance music has led, in the slipstream of business techno, to other descriptive terms. There is the 'festivilisation of dance music' (this differs from the museumification, academisation and intellectualisation of dance music – also discussed elsewhere in this book; such giddy times for '-tions'). Clearly enough, it denotes the shift away from basements, bars and small club settings to much larger, and potentially more profitable, environments. A 2024 analysis of the top 50 European festivals by music industry platform ROSTR and IQ magazine found that rock and indie acts in headline slots dropped from 43% the previous year to 30% – a 30% year-on-year decline. Hip-hop doubled year-on-year to 14%. Metal, R&B, country and K-Pop showed modest growth. Pop remained flat. Dance/EDM climbed to 26%, with the accompanying editorial predicting that the genre would clear rock and indie in the following year.

The data also revealed that Fred Again headlined the most across the 50 festivals tracked, performing seven times. Of the approximately 5,000 artists appearing at these festivals, 69% were men – actually up 5% from the previous year. Just 22% were women, and less than 1% were non-binary. The report also noted that five of the 10 most balanced lineups were in the Nordics.

Oftentimes, even things that start off from a good place come under criticism as they grow – and even get 'festivalised'. Manchester's Homobloc, the brainchild of DJ Luke Una and an extension of the Homoelectric club nights, has gone from strength to strength over the past half-decade. Blending DJs, drag queen parades, performance artists and protest, it's now considered more a festival than a club, partnering with the high-profile party production outfit Warehouse Project to put on events at an impressive scale. Despite the quality of the spectacle, criticism has emerged that money is being moved out of the queer community and into the hands of the mainstream. Additionally, the Warehouse Project is majority-owned by Live Nation, a group in which Saudi Arabia's Public Investment Fund is a passive shareholder. Saudi Arabia, of course, being a country where same-sex relationships remain punishable by death.

Homobloc's creative director Sophie Bee responded to the criticism in a 2024 Guardian article, saying: "I've got a personal statement – and this isn't the official Homobloc statement: doesn't our community deserve a global stage? We've fought so hard to be seen, and I'm passionate about that." Later in the interview, Bee said: "My DIY and activist background and nature is that we can only change things from within. We've had internal discussions, and have met as a community. We're still talking about it and kind of figuring it out."

Surveyed in total, what we're hearing here makes for a multifaceted and expansive frontline of conflict – one where, inevitably, money and community are at odds. It speaks of an electronic music and events industry that, by many measures, is bigger than ever, yet a club *culture* that feels increasingly fragile. But as we've seen, the pockets of resistance are as plentiful as the bones of contention. The very human power of joining forces as a means to survive – forming collectives – comes through clearly, playing out in everything from setting up venues and online radio stations to firing up support groups and activist gatherings. Whether this recalcitrance can actually change the course of the mainstream dance music industry, or is more about breaking away from it, remains to be seen. Some I speak to see a polarised picture ahead (oh-so-familiar in the 21st century), with little to connect the two camps.

Whatever divisions may lie ahead, the resistance most likely to impact the core industry in the short-term is clear enough. Challenging the ethics of brand sponsorship is something many I speak to now see as non-negotiable – an issue that those running parties and managing artists can no longer afford to ignore. We've touched on this in the context of alcohol brands, but this goes beyond shifting attitudes to health. It's about the growing demand for accountability that brands are expected to meet. And with social media offering far more effective channels for exposing failures, these demands are becoming impossible to sidestep.

"It's all got to be clean. *Very clean*," says DJ Paulette, remarking on the growing scrutiny of sponsors. "We've seen problems with Barclays in recent years and problems with Booking.com, where people are actually asking for sponsors to be removed because they're not clean." In the case of Booking.com, their sponsorship of Manchester's Pride event in 2024 sparked allegations that the business was profiting from the conflict in Palestine. Drag artist Bimini pulled out of performing, telling the Manchester Evening News: "Booking.com lists vacation homes in disputed territories and has been blacklisted by the United Nations Human Rights Council as a company that has human rights violations concerns. As an artist and activist, I stand for justice and accountability." DJ Paulette continues: "Israel and Gaza, Ukraine, climate change – that's just the surface of a very long list. People in music are asking in a much more intensive way than ever before, 'What does working with this sponsor say about our events, our community, our creativity?'"

AFEM's Finlay Johnson references Shein, the Chinese fast fashion giant, and its sponsorship of Creamfields as a particularly striking example. 'You asked, we listened – Shein returns to Rockstar Energy presents Creamfields this summer!' exclaimed the event's communications, before elaborating on the partnership: 'Presenting the iconic Runway Stage, join Shein to make 2024 your most stylish festival season yet.' "I have to wonder what the conversations were between Creamfields and

Shein, and is the money worth the reputational damage?" says Finlay. "It's fast fashion that doesn't have a good reputation. Also, they've had really bad publicity around child labour in China. Does the Creamfields audience care about child labour, or do they just want to get off their face? Once, you might have assumed they wouldn't care, but I don't think that's the case anymore. There's perhaps a generation gap and an ethics gap – promoters and bookers in their 40s, the audience in their 20s."

Applying pressure to sponsorship decisions is what happens on the surface, where dance music operates at scale. But politics and activism intersect with club culture in more structural ways, too. Here, the emphasis shifts towards fortifying community – and often, it wants nothing to do with brands at all. This manifests most readily on the free party scene, a varied and evolving space within dance music that's anti-capitalist at its core (the clue is in 'free'). Money is raised from within the community – not from brands or formal public and arts funding. It's also as long-standing and central to the dance music narrative as the money-making exploits of Studio 54, Ibiza, superclubs and festivals.

There's a through-line that stretches back to rigs like DIY Sound System, Tonka's house music-infused sessions and Spiral Tribe's high-profile, tabloid-admonished activities. It loops in 1985's Battle Of The Beanfield, when Wiltshire Police clashed with the Peace Convoy, and reaches way back to 1960s countercultural gatherings. It's also highly global, though perhaps with its most consistent presence in the UK. Many of the rigs that roll out across Europe, landing to host large-scale parties in the Netherlands, France, Italy, Czech Republic and beyond, have their origins in Britain.

There's a brilliant knack for reinvention here as creativity collides with defiance and a different attitude to throwing a rave. Look away for a short while, and free partying evolves into something new. Released in 2023, Mark Angelo Harrison's documentary Free Party: A Folk History traced that backstory and made the case for the scene's ongoing relevance today – standing in opposition to an expensive, monocultural club scene designed by and for those with money and power. "The contributions of new-age travellers in shaping modern dance music have definitely been overlooked," said Harrison.

Finlay from AFEM sees the free party scene in strong form and also notes its present-day pertinence: "There are a lot of discussions in trade circles about the pressure on grassroots music venues, but despite that, illegal raves are still thriving. People are finding ways to participate in dance culture, even outside of traditional venues. These are parties that have no desire for a sponsor, no desire for any sort of brand to be anywhere near them. Even if they were offered it, they would not want it, because it's about something that's illegal, free and for the community."

Exploring the free party scene in 2024 for DJ magazine, writer Dave Jenkins said: 'Unlike many aspects of mainstream electronic music, no one gets into rig ownership for bragging rights or empty 'superstar' clout. Certainly not with the £10,000 fine *(fixed penalty notices introduced by the government)* that's been in place since the summer of 2020 during the pandemic.'

One of the people he interviews for the piece, going by the name Kelvin 373, sits in the middle of three generations of free party activism. He was 'born on the road', his mum part of the 1990s scene. Now his daughter is involved too; part of the WickeDnBad crew, joining the dots between fast-paced techno and drum 'n' bass. Musing on the motivations behind these parties, Kelvin 373 explained to DJ magazine: "That's the ethos of a free party, the fact there are no rules and you can do what you want. That will never change. It doesn't matter what generation comes along and takes responsibility for it, as long as they're into it for the same reasons."

While generations within the free party scene share a common ethos, cultural divides often exist between this and other forms of clubbing. Speaking anonymously to, of all things, the Swindon Advertiser, one free party organiser drew a clear distinction between their crowd and the 'conventional' clubber: "A lot of people that attend regulated club events aren't the same as us. Free party attendees find that there's a lot more alcohol at clubs and people just trying to pull girls or pull men. It feels like an aggressive culture, unlike ours which is a lot more relaxed." Yet, these divides aren't always so rigid – many free party organisers also run occasional legal nights or record labels and other dance music businesses, showing how the lines between the underground and mainstream sometimes blur.

One outfit who seem unlikely to be doing that in a hurry, however, is London's Redtek. They pull off the particularly ambitious feat of running free parties in the metropolis rather than the countryside, doing so with an unapologetically caustic political edge. 'London's socialist sound system. Where the party is always right. Against capital in the capital', is how they describe themselves on their Instagram page. In one of their posts, they issue a call to arms for new collaborators: 'It's time to take the next step. Redtek is a machine as efficient as its components, a unit as strong as its members. It needs photographers, videographers, artists and designers, musicians, producers, carpenters, researchers, writers, spies – whatever you think you can offer, offer it now.'

Such are the challenges of using conventional venues that the adoption of alternative spaces is not confined to the more overtly political free party sphere. Outdoor events, of course, have featured heavily across the decades – particularly in the UK, with the well-documented days of orbital raves and M25 convoys. But outdoor partying, often paired with daytime events, seems to have found a fresh energy. This shift can likely be tied to the 'gorpcore' outdoor wear trend – where outdoor living is now positioned as a new luxury – and the growing interest among Gen Z in rambling, birdwatching and other nature-based activities. Where the operative word in the orbital rave era was simply 'outdoors', today it's more often 'nature'. It's no longer just about the practicality of big green spaces; it's about a deeper connection to something beyond the urban and the commercial.

On his Join The Future website, Matt Anniss wrote on the subject: 'The roots of dance music may lie in urban spaces and marginalised communities, but when experienced in rural locations – with or without psychedelic assistance – it takes on a whole new meaning, at least for those who grew up and live in urbanised locations… For city-dwellers in thrall to dance music culture, jaunts to the countryside to dance all night are a relative novelty. To us, the countryside is somewhere we go for walks, camping holidays, weekends away at posh hotels and Sunday afternoon trips to pubs in picture-postcard villages whose residents often cling on to a very traditional (and romantic) notion of the British rural idyll.'

"I think it's an important development," says Warm Street's Theo Gentilli, explaining that projects set outdoors are a hot topic at his agency. "We know that spending too much time in urban environments can make us unhappy. So how do we combat that? By spending time outdoors, including when we're listening to and dancing to music. For me, the bigger message is about sustainability – not asking people to consume less, but encouraging them to appreciate nature. I think that's a better message to land. I think there's something here that artists can get behind – the connection between music and nature, and maybe we'll finally then see more of them having a point of view on the environment. It's the biggest emergency we have on this planet and I don't see very many of them wanting to engage with this."

Sometimes, being outdoors doesn't mean being in fields. By the autumn of 2024, DJ AG (aka Ashley Gordon) is picking up serious plaudits for his decision to livestream from the streets of London. What started on social channels by this point is garnering coverage on mainstream TV news, in 'before we go…' stories. With Skepta, JME and Lethal Bizzle among those showing support for his portable spin on pirate radio, AG views it all as a reaction against the scarcity of venues and places for underground creativity to thrive. He's out three to five times a week, inviting everyone from the famous to absolute beginners to broadcast with him. With 470,000 followers and 2.5 million likes (and counting) on TikTok, he's clearly striking a chord with people.

Speaking to the Capital Xtra hip-hop station, AG responded to a question about how selective he was in who he lets stream with him: "I didn't leave my job to do this to be dictated to. We're never going to gate-keep. When I'm outside, I feel the energy, the pain, the passion… It's all about community, and it needs to stay all about community." By the end of 2024, Time Out has enthroned him Londoner Of The Year.

The guys from the white van rave outfit, HomeBass, whom we checked in with earlier in the book, are as at home in the fields as they are in urban settings like car parks and wasteland scrub. They're adept at popping up quickly, their vehicle arriving ready-packed with decks, sound system, lighting, and branding that nods to the almost identically named DIY emporium. Particularly heartwarming for HomeBass is how many big-name DJs – including DJ Zinc, Fatboy Slim, and Eats Everything – are ready and willing to join their free sessions without requesting a fee.

"I guess once, this type of thing was up against the superclubs *(meaning the likes of Cream and Ministry Of Sound)*," says Si Long, who started out DJing at a West Indian social club in Birmingham, playing ska and reggae at wedding receptions. "Now, it's more like Drumsheds or Printworks. I quite like those places, in a way, but they don't generate the same atmosphere. We play house, we play techno, we play garage, we play dub – not many people do that in those venues, either. The last pop-up we did in Shoreditch – the atmosphere was like electricity, like nothing I've ever experienced in a normal venue. It could light a bulb. It was magical, seeing these kids sprinting towards the van as we started playing. I mean, it's stressful as fuck, too, because you have no idea when the police are turning up or what's going to happen. But that's all part of it."

And how do they deal with the police, if they do show up? "It's a good relationship, especially in London," Si says, his confidence rooted in experience. "They know us now. They're like, 'Oh, here we go again…' They know my first name before I even introduce myself. But it's not in their interest to create tension when a crowd is building. They don't want to cause trouble. We make it clear we'll be done in a few hours, that we'll tidy up and make sure everyone is safe. If anyone falls ill, looking after them becomes our total priority."

While this is about resistance against many of the things that are considered normal in club culture today – the dominance of vast venues, the obsession with VIP and the monocultural tone of production – HomeBass want to push their cause further than some of the more hardline free party rigs. They aim to have operations up and running in the US and Australia before long. There's a soundclash format they want to roll out soon – "crews coming along and challenging us." A label, too. "It's going to be all about bringing through the underground scene," enthuses their manager, Thor. "Artists who normally wouldn't get a look-in; signing amazing dance records and helping them develop – not just signing stuff that's hot on TikTok. Finding this talent and helping them break through from the underground. Break through from the van."

Even when the DJ gets to play under a roof more solid than that of a white van, robust challenges to accepted clubland norms persist. Stormzy's House Party venture in Soho, London, is an elaborate synthesis of the in-home bash – spanning seven floors with actors, performers and interactive experiences; "the only place in London where bedroom DJs-turned-headliners will once again become bedroom DJs". It is nonetheless emblematic of a broader trend where houses have become settings for raves. Michael Kill, CEO of the Night Time Industries Association, blogged about the phenomenon: 'DJs spinning from kitchen counters, GoPro cameras capturing every angle and a curated mix of guests creating an intimate yet electrifying atmosphere. While this reinvention of the house party resonates with a social media-savvy generation, it also raises questions about its broader implications for the night-time economy.'

Back in venues that don't double as abodes, some are invoking an earlier era of arts spaces and communes, including the 'pluriclub' approach of the Italian clubs referenced in chapter three, such as Turin's Piper, which integrated disco, fashion shows and poetry readings. Amsterdam's now sadly closed De School – shuttered due to financial instability and, uncomfortably, claims of harassment by door staff – attracted considerable attention for being a nightclub that was so much more than a nightclub. A concert venue, restaurant, café, gallery space, football tournaments, artist residency, gym, garden – it could flex between them all.

De School may have closed (though, at the time of writing, they are reportedly looking for a new home – one hopes with new door staff), but others are following a similar path. Public Records in Brooklyn combines a music venue, bar, restaurant, record shop, workshop space and outdoor garden. In the neighbouring borough of Queens, there's Nowadays, with Anthony Naples and Avalon Emerson among the residents. The focus here is on community-driven nightlife, offering impressive outdoor spaces (by NYC standards), a strong emphasis on clubbing safety and, during the pandemic, an auxiliary role supporting people and businesses.

New twists on the listening bar theme are emerging, too. Also clubs launching on promises of affordable door fees, no dedicated VIP rooms and venues available for community initiatives during the daytime. Kink and sex-positive party organisers Joyride, meanwhile, stage an alternative Christmas market called Slayride: "Our parties are cultural spaces – cheeky markets, performances, tattoos, make-up and tunes." And rising from De School's ashes, Tilla Tec – a new venture on the same site – includes a queer tattoo parlour, a queer gym and a coffee roasting company as part of its vast complex.

Jamz Supernova is seeing new visions for clubbing environments firsthand on her travels. With BBC London research revealing that there are now more 24-hour gyms than clubs in the capital, she hopes some of this progressive thinking will eventually make its way to her home city. "There's always light at the end of the tunnel," she affirms. "We've always had to adapt to different circumstances across 40-plus years of raving. One thing that's interesting is how we use space differently. What's a club at night can be other things, too – maybe a workspace or a restaurant. Multipurpose spaces with a really strong link to community."

Reflecting on recent gigs, she continues: "You're raving in somewhere like Berlin and you're in an empty swimming pool, an old theatre or some ex-Cold War building. There are lots of ways to get more imaginative with space. I played this place on the outskirts of Milan. It was this amazing, sprawling multipurpose environment – it was a skatepark, a library, a refugee community and then a courtyard where the DJs played."

University Of Birmingham's Dr Luis Manuel thinks along similar lines: "A space that offers clubbing, but maybe also has a gym, a workshop or a restaurant. Broader cultural programming, like concerts, art galleries, installations, that kind of a thing. It puts club culture into a broader context of independent cultural production." And many I speak to who represent collectives and other community-driven initiatives place a similar focus on clubs as places to learn, not just party. Nadine Artois, co-founder of Pxssy Palace, has previously said: "There's no reason why the dancefloor can't be an educational space… It's not just a club night; it's a form of resistance."

In his approach to placemaking and urban planning at night, Lutz Leichsenring from VibeLab and Berlin's Clubcommission also factors in more refined thinking for how club space is used. The benefits, he says, are not just felt by club-goers, either. "Club culture has a duty to be the progressive part of society. It should be pushing to the next level of being inclusive and being forward thinking. I would say you can learn a lot from venues that do things differently like this, and hopefully can create safer spaces in the process. This therefore makes whole neighbourhoods safer. It's really about creating safer cities, not by policing, but by having better communication, by learning from communities and sharing experiences. The more mainstream it is, inevitably, the more it's about making money. The more it's about serving certain niches and special communities, the more it's driven by a philosophy of supporting others."

If, as we've established, protest and politics have always figured alongside hedonism in dance music – with touch points from the Stonewall riots to Underground Resistance's abrasive stand against the industry – then the chaotic and disturbing events of the last half-decade have brought about a renewed vigour. It's also evident that the political discourse doesn't just play out in free party settings. Shortly before the impact of BLM and the pandemic, Grime4Corbyn – the unexpected coalescing of youth support by Stormzy, JME, Logan Sama, Akala and others for prime ministerial candidate Jeremy Corbyn – was the beginning of something new here. Something with less of the tropes of old school socialism, student protest or so-called 'crusties'.

Tom Armstrong from Common People, the non-profit organisation addressing the diminishing opportunities for those from working-class and low-income backgrounds in the creative industries, believes that the politicisation of dance music – or the 'politics of dancing', as it's invariably headlined – has moved beyond the more traditional agitprop groups. "One of the positives in recent years, something that's accelerated since Covid, is that club culture, which was once indirectly political, is now overtly so," he says. "Yes, there's been things like Spiral Tribe and the Criminal Justice Bill, but those were quite narrow and rooted in an anarchist mindset. Now, there are sound systems on protest marches, and so much happening in the Global South, where dance music and parties are being used as direct resistance to oppressive regimes."

One example of resistance in the Global South came in Nicaragua in 2021, when female and non-binary DJ/producer NAOBA (Tamara Montenegro) set up music production workshops for female and non-binary artists. Addressing issues such as gender-based violence, LGBTQ+ discrimination and anti-abortion laws in the country, NAOBA used music as a platform for political and social change. "Music offers me a voice to empower women and non-binary artists," they told Mixmag. "There is hatred and violence towards LGBTQ and trans women, too, so it's a political act for me to make this contribution with my creativity."

Other mergers of dance music and protest around the world include Lebanon, where raves were staged, particularly in 2019 and 2020, in abandoned spaces near demonstrations against government corruption and increased taxation. In Tbilisi, following police raids on queer venues, protesters marched behind booming sound systems, chanting: "We dance together, we fight together."

This politicisation of dance music is also evident in the US, where to no surprise Donald Trump entered the dialogue. Techno DJ Dave Clarke called time on performing in the country, citing the "misogynist, narcissist, racist president in office." Another techno DJ, Berlin's Len Faki, posted a photo of himself giving a thumbs down outside Trump Towers. 'Keep politics out of dance music', some retorted, to which Faki responded all guns blazing: "Techno has always been political. And actually, this is one of the reasons I became part of the scene in the first place. I don't want any haters, homophobes, sexists or racists… neither on my page nor on our dancefloors. You cannot play 'unity' on the dancefloor but betray everything this culture stands for."

Of course, the invasion of Ukraine and the Israeli-Palestinian conflict have both proven powerful catalysts for protest and resistance. There have been many reports of how rave culture has refused to switch off in Kyiv and other cities, even in the face of war. Particularly noteworthy, the Repair Together collective organised 'clean-up raves', fixing damaged homes in recently liberated towns while DJs played. The collective explained: "We came up with an idea, that in order to repair Ukraine after the war, we need volunteering to become the lifestyle of our generation. To make it real, volunteering must be not only physical work but also joyful, social and attractive to people. Since we loved parties so much in the past we decided to combine it. During the second or third clean-up rave, a lot of internationals joined virtually. It felt like there was a demand for such initiatives by young people across Europe. Our mission then grew, from not only repairing Ukraine and uniting local people, but to uniting people globally."

Responses to the Israeli-Palestinian conflict – powerfully linked to dance music through the October 2023 Nova music festival massacre – have played out in all sorts of ways. Sama' Abdulhadi, the Palestinian DJ who's spoken out vociferously against Zionism, was enraged by the US presidential candidate Kamala Harris' unauthorised placement of an image of her DJing at the Movement festival in a campaign ad. "The use of this footage implies that I endorse Vice President Harris' presidential candidacy, which is totally and utterly false," she said of this piggybacking on her Instagram page. "It is deeply offensive to my social, moral and political beliefs and is misleading political advertising…" In New York, the Palestine Forever collective led a DJs Against Apartheid campaign. It included a statement signed by more than 500 DJs, including Logic1000, Nene H, AceMo, Aurora Halal and DJ Haram, and reads: "We, the undersigned nightlife community members, stand in firm solidarity with those resisting occupation and fighting for their right to self-determination. We commit to using our platforms, no matter how big or small, to challenge at every turn the massive misinformation campaigns waged by those who have a vested interest in the destruction of the Palestinian land and people without fear of repercussions."

Forward/Scratch describes itself as a volunteer-run resistance online music publication. With DJs Against Apartheid among their collaborators and proceeds from subscriptions supporting efforts for victims of colonial violence, it sets out to document music and nightlife as tools of political defiance. The focus is currently on Palestinian liberation, but the ultimate remit is global injustice more widely. "We focus on the role of music and nightlife as tools of resistance in the struggle for Palestinian liberation," they explain. "We also feature broader analysis of the ways in which colonialism employs culture to impose violence and confine our political imagination – and how these attitudes manifest at all levels to reinforce the violent institutions we seek to destroy."

A slight step back from the most pressing causes of the moment, Ed Gillett's brilliant 2023 book, Party Lines: Dance Music And The Making Of Modern Britain, dug deep into the moments and spaces where dance music and politics have intertwined over the longer term. It also challenges the standard rave backstory (1988, Ibiza and so forth). The book traces a path from the Windrush generation and shebeen parties to queer spaces and the 1992 Castlemorton Common party, illustrating how activism has surfaced along this journey. Interviewed by Dazed's James Greig shortly after the release of Party Lines, Gillett remarked: "There's something inherently political about a group of people taking control of a space without necessarily having the approval of mainstream society. That could be a marginalised community finding a space of solace and peace for a night; it could mean mobilising 30,000 people to go and seize a piece of common land."

However, he also cautioned against believing that all acts of rebellion and non-conforming behaviour in dance music are genuinely infused with true political intent. "Dance music is desirable, it's alluring, it has a cultural cachet, and I think it's been very easy for successive generations to mistake that for genuine community. So, there's a risk of dance music becoming tokenistic in its politics. You get quite a lot of shallow, superficial feel-good semi-political activity, and there isn't always the space to have deeper conversations."

Dance music's desirability and cultural cachet once gave brands something cool to just hang out with at the party. The shallow superficiality that Gillett references was perfectly fine. No big questions asked. Now, everyone is asking questions. As dance music experiences a social and political awakening, brands are vying to show they can keep in step.

That they can empathise with community needs rather than simply turn up to celebrate the big occasion. Whether brands – constructed entities, corporations in shiny wrappers – can do empathy remains another matter.

"You also get lots of brands interested in leveraging dance culture's sense of outsider cool, which then spills over into how the music is politicised," Gillett continued, getting to the nub of what is so fragile and susceptible to ill-fit here. "So while I think Blackness, queerness, transness and femininity can all be incredibly powerful within a dance music space, those identities can quickly become co-opted and commodified. The cultural capital embedded in dance music makes it a rich target for capitalism, which in turn absorbs that radical energy into itself and quietly deradicalises it."

Teaching defiance

If politics makes for a hotly debated bedfellow of dance music, education is another. Learning and studying seem like polar opposites to in-the-moment hedonism, the spontaneity, free-willed expression and physicality of clubbing. Dance music is about what you *feel*. Not what you've revised or the knowledge acquired (though, to be fair, a legion of trainspotters and record collectors has always run counter to that). Regardless, the shift towards education is real and evident. It may be a generational change, perhaps a reaction to the fractious world we now inhabit – a response to injustices and a growing need to get organised, rather than leave things to chance. The urge to teach people *something* about dance music has emerged as a recurring theme among those I speak to for this book. Intentional or less so, it represents a form of resistance rooted in the clarity that learning brings.

In the industry, the imperative surfaced early and in a structured form with the Red Bull Music Academy. Now it's flowing through the work of countless collectives. It's present in Honey Dijon's bold declarations and it threads across most of the conversations I have – paired with terms such as community and conscious clubbing. What most needs teaching varies depending on who you're speaking with. Often, it revolves around backstories, especially those of pioneers who are Black, female, queer or from communities whose contributions to club culture have been pushed to the margins. It can also focus on how to operate in these pressured times, where just being part of a crew with ideas and energy may no longer be enough to propel you forward. Therefore, how to organise and strategise, how to mitigate against the fact that opportunities and ways in are now less forthcoming. Sometimes, it's down to the fundamentals: how to mix, produce, raise funds, throw a party, release a record or mobilise a scene online. Throughout, talk of mentoring others and dismantling previously tolerated gatekeeping drives conversations as much as big tunes or favourite nights out.

"It's such an interesting topic, how this sits alongside actual clubbing and actually feeling the music. In the classroom we can talk about the sociopolitical context of the music but, really, it's also all about the body. So I tell my students to also get out there and dance. It's something visceral. It's all about freedom. It's about a balance." We're back with King Britt, here ruminating on how learning sits alongside partying. An irrepressible character, energised and fiercely optimistic, we've heard from him across *Selling The Night*, where he's discussed the Red Bull Music Academy, the Area club, dance music in advertising and brands in dance music. He's more than qualified to speak on each of these themes. Now, he's also qualified to teach students about them. As Professor King Britt, he's the creator of the Blacktronika: Afrofuturism In Electronic Music course at the University Of California, San Diego (UCSD), in his adopted home on the US West Coast.

Drawing on science, science fiction, fantasy, history and the African diasporic experience, Afrofuturism is a discursive movement and – though its roots stretch back much earlier – a term first coined by cultural critic Mark Dery in his Black To The Future essay in the early 1990s. It's Sun Ra and author Octavia Butler, Flying Lotus, Jean-Michel Basquiat and photographer Renée Cox. Described as 'forward thinking as well as backward thinking', it chimes with King's objectives for Blacktronika: "To reclaim the narrative around the origins and foundations of electronic dance music, and therefore where it will go next."

King's own backstory is as eventful as that of many of the pioneers who grace the Blacktronika lessons. Before starting "professor life" in 2018, he'd been firmly embedded in independent music, ever since quitting his first job as a 12-inch record buyer for Tower Records in his native Philadelphia in 1991. He had DJ residencies at a couple of the top spots in town, Silk City and Revival. He put out his first track on Strictly Rhythm in 1990, called Tribal Confusion by E-Culture, which cemented his relationship with fellow Philly dance music lodestar Josh Wink. It was a bond that began with them playing together in clubs, including a night called Vagabond, a highly visual experience which moved between various venues. In addition to touring with the likes of Digable Planets and Sade, he started the Ovum Recordings label with Wink. Aside from their own releases, luminaries such as Boo Williams, DJ Pierre, DJ Sneak and Ian Pooley graced the imprint. In 1998, he released the 500,000-selling neo-soul album When The Funk Hits The Fan under the moniker Sylk130.

Into the 2000s, alongside more releases of his own and producer credits with others, Britt spread his creative wings. He hosted radio shows for NTS and, in 2007, was awarded a Pew Fellowship in the arts for his composition work. In 2014, he co-curated an evening of music for the Institute Of Contemporary Art in Philadelphia, running parallel to an exhibition about another Philadelphia great – and fellow Afrofuturist – Sun Ra. That same year, he organised Moondance, a celebration of Afrofuturism at MoMA PS1 in New York City. Red Bull Music Academy helped fund Moondance, and over the years, King featured as a lecturer at RBMA's global sessions. The power of educating others about dance music began to crystallise in his mind, and his route to becoming a teaching professor was underway.

King first headed cross-coast from Philadelphia to teach electronic music production, arriving at the University Of California's computer music department in 2018. It was an exciting new string to his bow: working closely with young people as they searched for their own sound. But he noticed something was missing – something more foundational in nature. It wasn't just about how to make the music, but about understanding the roots beneath contemporary music and putting it all into some kind of context.

"That felt like the bigger work, the more important work," he explains. He also posits that many in academia do not consider these genres sufficiently 'intellectual' to be studied. "This rich and now quite long history of dance music was being left to chance, shared in a scattered and skewed way. It deserved better, and I wanted an opportunity to address that." By which he means the story could largely be found across blogs and articles, sometimes at events and exhibitions, or in random podcasts – more accessible to some than others. Often unevenly told, too, with the appropriate emphasis missing. "Over the years, you know, there was this intentional motivation to erase the Black and Brown history of a lot of this music," continues King, who grew up in a household that shook to avant-garde jazz (courtesy of his mum) and heavy funk (his dad). "Black dance music, you could say, had been gentrified."

Conversations with UCSD's music department ensued, and King was given the greenlight to design a course that, at its core, presented a Black pedagogical perspective on dance music, rooted in lived reality. In addition to RBMA ("They cared, they didn't cut corners"), King points to the 2010s work of Lynée Denise as a source of inspiration, with the queer interdisciplinary artist having developed a 'DJ scholarship' methodology in Los Angeles. Processing what he was learning from these endeavours, he set about laying out a 10-week lecture course for undergrads. "So that these young people, who were loving the newer electronic music that was coming through, would know the history, the lineages and the socio-political context of what they were listening to."

Even the course name of Blacktronika was about following threads through the Black cultural experience. The title – spelt Blacktronica at the time – was first used by Charlie Dark (also known for his music productions as Attica Blues and for founding the urban run and mental health collective, Run Dem Crew) for his multidisciplinary events at London's ICA. King was among the ICA collaborators, and when Charlie Dark moved on to new projects, he asked if he could adopt the title. "Adopted with love; passing the torch," smiles King. "We switched the C for Charlie to K for King *(as in going from Blacktronica to Blacktronika)* to mark the moment."

Blacktronika, the course, charts a methodical route through the eras and genres of dance music. It launched during the pandemic, which meant King had to learn how to deliver it remotely, with Zoom in mind. One of the key aspects of Blacktronika, drawing on learnings from RBMA, is the interview format, where he speaks with an artist or music expert who can truly open up about each phase of the story. The first Blacktronika guest was the now-deceased Village Voice writer (as well as musician and producer), Greg Tate. Since then, Marshall Allen from Sun Ra Arkestra, Common, Jeff Mills, Kathy Sledge, Herbie Hancock, Honey Dijon, Nile Rodgers, Santigold, Flying Lotus, Hank Shocklee, Questlove, Carl Craig, Dexter Wansel, Roni Size and Goldie have all shared their wisdom and counsel with the students.

Sometimes, the format switches to roundtables, with King joined by journalists such as Ash Lauryn and DeForrest Brown Jr – who've been instrumental in ushering in a more defiant reclamation of the Black community's pioneering place in electronic music. At other times, patient and considered explanations of the differences between genres that may, at first listen, sound similar are presented to the young students (for example, deep house compared to early US garage). For many of them, the tracks are completely unfamiliar, though the samples from them often less so. Occasionally, a certain Virgil Abloh would join the students – anonymously, that is. No status-seeking involved, just an interest in how Blacktronika was unfolding.

One aspect of Blacktronika is a series called No Manual. This refers to how technology in underground circles has often been used without formal guidance, leading to tangential innovations, and even the creation of new genres. The role of the cassette tape in early hip-hop editing methods is explored, as is the Roland TR-909, designed for programming but used by some for live rhythmic improvisation in clubs. Also under the microscope, dub reggae icon King Tubby transforming the mixing desk from something restricted to the recording process into an instrument in its own right.

The sum total across all these facets of Blacktronika forms a truly edifying body of work. What's striking about it is the warmth and conviviality with which it is delivered – a balance between not underplaying the significance of the narratives and ensuring accessibility. There's a palpable joy from everyone involved in the good that comes from opening closed gates and letting others in.

"Any moment is the right moment to bring the truth to the forefront. But this moment, in particular, is critical. For a lot of reasons," King replies when asked to reflect on the timing of Blacktronika, amid the cultural and societal fractures in the world. He sees this as especially relevant in the case of the house music story. "Being an educator now gives me a unique perspective. When I started the class, there were 25 students. Now there are over 500. And a lot of that growth is thanks to Beyoncé and Drake – two global superstars diving into house music. Suddenly, these young Black and Brown kids, who didn't know anything about house music – or thought it was exclusively white – are buzzing. They are actually *talking about house music*. The interest has been insane; so many people now want to understand the genre."

What the future holds for house music after its most recent brush with celebrity – and whether it stays overground – remains to be seen.

Also, which other scene, movement or genre might next rise to the surface. Regardless, King feels optimistic about the outlook for Blacktronika – for what it does and how it can impart the truth. "It might not always come across this way, but Blacktronika is a very political class. And really, education has always been part of what's important. Clubs like Body & Soul *(the NYC house music institution)* – that's also education; just late at night. So we're changing the platform – just making the education more tangible. I feel super blessed to be able to do it."

There's so much more he wants to do with Blacktronika, expanding both its scope and the perspective it offers. We discuss the Vitra Design Museum's Night Fever exhibition on clubland design, and he's enthusiastic about the possibility of collaborating with them to add a module to Blacktronika. One suspects there are *many* modules he'd like to add – different formats for storytelling and direction. His plans to take Blacktronika on the road, in various forms, are also progressing.

Indeed, while he had little choice but to consider Blacktronika as an online-only undertaking when it launched mid-pandemic, taking it offline and out of the classroom is particularly high on the agenda for King. This process began, as he puts it, "still in the UCSD bubble," organising club nights on campus. "It was kind of about fun, kind of about stopping it from feeling too much like theory alone," he explains. "It meant the students could come and meet each other. And, yeah! We'd have 500-plus wanting to be part of that. They were getting out of class and into their bodies. They were hearing the music they were studying on a proper sound system."

Since then, he's started venturing outside of the USCD bubble with Blacktronika. He took it to the Geffen Contemporary at Los Angeles' Museum Of Contemporary Art. There's been a monthly film and music series off-campus in San Diego. Festivals with nonprofit organisers Big Ears in the US and Sons d'hiver in France. He's also struck up a strong bond with the inventive, learning-oriented Public Records club in Brooklyn. Steering us back to the topic of brands in dance music, while King can't necessarily control which of them have a presence at events they appear at, he's making a conscious decision to keep corporations and their marketing departments away from direct involvement in Blacktronika. "Oh, my God, I've had all of these brands come to me. 'We want Blacktronika!' they say. I'm like, 'Nope, you can't have Blacktronika!' The reason is there's a major educational component to this. Also, I want to keep it grassroots and a brand would taint that. I honestly can't think of a brand that wouldn't."

King's stance on brand involvement where dance music meets learning is shared by some, not by others. There's a diverse range of providers stepping in to meet the growing demand here. Formal institutions, specialist workshops, festivals, platforms and grassroots initiatives all figure. Some teach technical skills and music business essentials in traditional classroom lectures. In other settings, education is blended with entertainment in the form of panel conversations or, as per RBMA and Blacktronika, illuminating interviews with pioneers and industry movers. It can get hands-on as boot camps, mentoring and shadowing. Then others expand access with online tutorials, global insights, tools and resources.

We've already heard Pxssy Palace describe their club as an "educational space" – a way to "spread our ideals into the wider society." Their next step is securing their own work and learning studio, something they were actively fundraising for at the time of writing. US festival organiser and arts community Afropunk have long embraced an educational focus, offering workshops exploring Black creativity across past, present and future forms. Sónar is another festival notable for its educational initiatives, from collaborative sessions with Ableton, Roland and Native Instruments to partnerships with MIT Media Lab and drop-in lectures on topics such as machine learning in music and sustainable festival practices. Brixton-based Reprezent Radio, instrumental in the careers of Stormzy, Jamz Supernova and Munya Chawawa, is among many stations making a mark in this space. They've hosted free workshop sessions covering radio presenting, production, video content, recording live performances and managing social media channels, with food and travel costs subsidised – thanks in part to support from Converse. Coming along with ambition was important, they stressed. Prior experience, less so.

When Jamz Supernova – who's been involved with multiple programmes and initiatives geared to learning – thinks about education in dance music, it's very much in the context of knowledge as power. A form of soft power, at that. It's a way to reach people who might otherwise put up barriers. "Things are changing and improving in music," she feels. "I mean, I think it would be hard to get away with an all-male, white lineup at a festival these days. But there is absolutely a need to keep the pressure on, to stop things sliding back. That progress comes from education, not from shouting at people or getting angry. It's more about showing them: 'You will have a better night if it's a more diverse night.' We need people to learn more about scenes and different communities, to understand the fantastic things they bring to the mix and why it's important we all have a stage. When done right, learning brings people closer together – you find common ground and appreciate differences."

While Jamz emphasises education as a tool for improving dance music in real-time, Dr Lulu Le Vay is seeking valuable lessons from the past. We last checked in with her when she shared thoughts on disco's legacy. Educating about dance music – particularly its history and the elements most at risk of being obscured by time (and bias) – is integral to what she teaches. She's a strong advocate for King Britt's Blacktronika work, often directing her students at places like the BIMM Music Institute to explore it. Similar to King Britt's concerns, she worries that while there's a new generation eager to make electronic music, they risk losing touch with its foundational roots.

"I work with students who are learning to produce or be singer-songwriters and almost all of them know nothing about these backstories," she says. "My fear is it will all be forgotten unless more people start educating or at least telling the stories. That would be a travesty for those pioneers; they've never received much money, in most cases, so they definitely deserve recognition. And it also won't help the future path of the music, in terms of creating things that have depth."

The dance music backstory has in fact been committed to print on an increasing scale in recent years, with a seemingly never-ending series of weighty books being published. Lulu's issue with this, though, is that much of it adds to the so-called over-intellectualisation of dance music. It's not that accessible, and it tends to come from a narrow perspective.

"You've got the trainspotters, you've got the scholarly articles, you've got your Tim Lawrences (*academic, music historian, author of expansive disco explorations Love Saves The Day and Life And Death On The New York Dance Floor*). Yes, he's brilliant, but he's not telling the story in a way that will reach a wider audience, and as much as he really does care about the things he writes about, he is telling it from the perspective of the privilege which comes with being a heterosexual white male. That can be considered problematic by some. We need to come up with ways to reach different people, the broader community."

Reaching people and community doesn't just mean those old enough for higher education, either. Published in 2024, Elvin Discovers Chicago Footwork is a children's book that aims to strengthen literacy through both words and illustrations inspired by the footwork genre. A Chicago juke music strand that emerged in the early 1990s, footwork is raw, fast-paced, sub-bassy and chaotically strewn with repetitive vocal samples – about as far away from a conventional learning tool as you can imagine. With an accompanying soundtrack by Chicago producer DJ T-Rell, it is community-designed education in excelsis, grounded in relatability.

Relatability is also high among the priorities for Melissa Kains. She never set out to become an educator, but her own encounters with closed doors switched her on to the possibilities. These days, she's the brains behind Sisu, a community and platform to 'educate, inspire and showcase aspiring women and non-binary DJs, producers and behind the scenes roles.' In line with most collectives in dance music, Sisu pushes its cause on multiple fronts: a DJ roster, events, radio, workshops and talks – no doubt with more ideas to follow. Back when she was 17, the Sisu story all started from a personal frustration: she wanted to learn how to DJ, but no one was willing to show her how.

"I so, *so* wanted to DJ," she smiles. "I'd get to play one tune at a party – that was it. No one was teaching me how to mix. I couldn't afford the equipment. The boys were in charge. They were like, 'No, you can't mix, you need to get off and let me take over.' I sometimes thought I was the only girl who was interested in these things – but then I started to think, 'I'm sure there are lots more but they just need the confidence to stand up and say so.'"

The setting for these all-too-brief forays on the decks were bars and basements in Southport and Liverpool, where Melissa grew up. Dance music always appealed to her, and soon she decided she preferred raving to more dressed-up clubbing ("throwing on my trainers rather than high heels"), frequenting the Circus club and, along the M62, Manchester's Warehouse Project. Next to wanting to DJ, she became curious about how to start a club night and the factors involved. Again, she noted just what an "utter boy's club" it all was.

This curiosity and accompanying frustration started to convert into action when Melissa moved to London, taking a position as an apprentice in community arts management at the Southbank Centre. Among the centre's many arts and community initiatives, they were looking for more input from younger people and asked if Melissa would like to design an education course. "I said I'd love to and that I wanted to create a space where women can learn how to DJ," she says. "Basically so they could take the headphones off the boys and show what brilliant things they can do."

She designed a six-week course called Scratch Collective – "Because we were teaching women from scratch – though we quickly changed that, as everyone assumed we were a hip-hop collective" – that went live in 2017. "They had the best equipment. They were giving me the space for free, and they were going to promote it for free. It was an amazing opportunity for me. There was only room for 10 people on the first course, but it sold out in a flash. I immediately had no doubts there was a need and demand for things like this."

Melissa created follow-up courses – spin-offs of the original, too, including a DJ course specifically aimed at South Asian women. While she was grateful for the start the Southbank Centre provided, she saw a greater potential operating independently. "They let me take the course with me," she continues. "By then, I was so invested in it. Obsessed with it. That's when I started Sisu, and the collective feel became vital to it. This sense that we were all learning together, and that you could make a mistake without feeling anxious about it. It was a space where men weren't dominant or leading the conversation."

Taking cues from Saffron, the highly regarded mentoring programme for women and non-binary artists and DJs in the UK's South West, Melissa decided early in the switch to independence that Sisu should operate as a non-profit. "I thought doing it as a business would turn making money into the priority, which would take away from concentrating on the ideals of the collective. And that felt wrong; not why I chose to do this in the first place." Three pillars to bring the Sisu agenda to life were established: events, a DJ roster and, underpinning it all, education. A launch party, naturally, was thrown, too.

"We had this really diverse crew of people along for it, and a really diverse mix of genres getting played," she recalls. "And then the wider industry started taking more notice. They knew they had to diversify their lineups and that we could help with this. Next we started doing call-outs to get others to join the collective, so we could begin to manage artists as well. Now, we've got 65 women and non-binary DJs and producers on the roster. Everywhere from Berlin to Hong Kong. And diversity in the UK, too. Creating opportunities for women DJs in the north, so they don't always feel they have to move to London to find them."

Melissa sends me a follow-up email after our conversation with a list of people from Sisu she'd love to see namechecked. It's far too long a list to include but demonstrates the collectivism here – in other words, the title 'collective' used meaningfully rather than out of convenience. Volunteers who maintain Sisu's forward motion range from accountants and researchers to photographers and event organisers. Then there are the many DJs, such as Vera Borek (aka ona:v), Chiara Capellini (Little Hats), Rosalind Davey (Bitxi), Soraya and Lauren Reid, who also doubles as Sisu's development manager for communities and creative learning.

Importantly, the principles that Sisu's DJ roster adheres to are markedly different than those of the average DJ agency, where ways of working are generally hand-me-down versions of control and ownership that have been a constant in the music industry. "It's all non-exclusive. People can work with other agencies if they like. It's a friendly stepping stone, really, and all of the money goes back into Sisu, so we can build this holistic approach to helping women and non-binary artists, and diversifying the industry at the same time."

There's something of a virtuous circle at work here. The returns from DJ roster bookings fund the educational work – and the educational work nurtures new talent for the roster. At Sisu workshops, whether large-scale occasions such as commemorating International Women's Day at the Barbican, or plotting up at Cafe 1001 in Brick Lane (with the workshopping transitioning into partying later on), typically participants are guided through everything from preparing music files to beat-matching and mixing techniques on Pioneer CDJs. Everything is laid on for them, though they're welcome to bring along a USB of tracks to use, too.

"We get to do incredible things now as a collective like play at Hideout *(the annual dance music festival in Croatia)*. And I didn't realise there were other collectives out there in the world trying to do similar things and that I'd get to talk and collaborate with them all. That's all great, but staying true to the benefits of education is really the core still of Sisu. It's where we began and it's where the greatest need is," Melissa continues. "I see what we're doing as one part of a bigger, live conversation in dance music: panel talks, people like Mixmag sharing important things on Instagram; courses and training. I'm not sure people like me or Sisu would have been listened to once upon a time but now when we share thoughts on, say, lineups and how to diversify and how to avoid tokenism, people sit up and listen. We've got a roster of DJs, a collective, backing up what we're saying. And then topics like harassment. Huge DJs are continuing to get called out for this, and I don't see that stopping now. There are too many people who just will not accept old behaviours coming back."

Next to money coming in via DJ bookings, Melissa and the Sisu collective have explored numerous other avenues for funding. Brands, inevitably, have figured here, though with mixed results to date. "I don't get my hopes up too high when they approach us," she explains. "There's something about the way we work, grassroots in style, and how they work, often very brutal in style, that doesn't blend. It generally feels very rushed and you can put a lot of work in and suddenly they go quiet on you, or just say that they've had a change of plan. In theory there's a beautiful opportunity there, and we could definitely do with their money. But making it actually work isn't so easy."

She says there have been incoming enquiries from brands they've declined for reasons of ill-fit ("Vape brands – when they approach us, it has to be a big 'no'"). The better fits tend to be with DJ and producer tech providers ("The Abletons of this world"). She's also aware that, as impactful as Sisu's work is, it might not pack the big numbers in terms of footfall, eyeballs and exposure that brands expect. "It's a shame. We might not help them reach 300,000 people or whatever, like a festival can. But what we're doing can genuinely change people's lives, and then snowball to change lots of other people's lives. It has a lasting impact beyond that night out – which feels like it should be something worth them backing."

With brands proving tricky customers, Sisu are well-versed in navigating the particulars of funding applications. Melissa points to resources we've referenced elsewhere in this book, such as Funding With Mina and The White Pube ("Um, strangest name ever, but the examples they share of successful funding applications are gold dust"). Funding successes for Sisu include through Youth Music, the National Lottery and Arts Council England-backed charity. Support from them enabled Sisu to bring on paid roles for an events manager and an artist manager. These hires not only bolstered their operations but also reflect Sisu's ambition to influence more than just who's visible on stage. "It's not just about DJs and producers," Melissa reasons. "It's about the sound engineers in the venue. It can even be about who picks you up to drive you to the venue. All these angles are important. As a woman or non-binary person, you are entering what is a very male space and that can really make people feel nervous."

While learning how to raise funds from external sources is important, such is the power of the collective that much of the Sisu magic comes from within. The skills, perspectives and wisdom that sit among their number are a daily motivator, Melissa remarks. But as the collective has grown more global in nature, ensuring the communication channels are fit for purpose has become a priority. "We have online meetings, Discord chats, WhatsApp groups. But really, it all comes to life in person at the events. It's invaluable. Some of the collective have become best friends. They rent houses together. That's where you get the feeling of belonging and being with people you can trust."

A specific example of harnessing the skills within the collective came when Melissa realised that developing clear metrics of success would help the Sisu cause – both by improving their ability to access funding and by holding themselves to account. While there were plenty of costly agencies and consultants who could've helped them with that, Melissa knew the collective already held the answers.

"One of our DJs is a data scientist – next level," enthuses Melissa, who also mentions that Sisu expansion plans – including programming more festival stages, organising retreats and launching a record label – will all tap into the power of the collective. "They wrote a survey for us so we can start measuring our impact. Things like: How many gigs have you played? Have you performed abroad? Have you made new friends and felt part of a community? Have you developed your professional network? Have you released music? Have you done any interviews or radio? Has your confidence grown? That's an important one. In the last survey, 95% of people said yes, their confidence had grown. When I think back to me as a teenager in Liverpool and the confidence I didn't have, that's what makes this all worthwhile for me."

Dialled In is another collective that combines partying and teaching, astutely joining the dots between the two. Earlier, co-founder Ahsan-Elahi Shujaat spoke about their club nights and festival programming. But as important – and fun – as collaborations with Boiler Room and stages at Printworks are, facilitating educational opportunities remains paramount in their plan to advance representation for South Asian people in music.

"We partnered with Boiler Room to produce their first events in Nepal, Bangladesh and Sri Lanka – and now we're heading back to Pakistan for the second time. It's been an incredibly exciting run," he enthuses on a video call from Nepal. "We're showcasing what's actually happening in those places to a global audience. We also have projects lined up in Bradford, as the City Of Culture 2025. Bradford has one of the largest South Asian populations in the UK – around 49%. But break it all down and education, that's at the core of all of this – it's the essential part. I hate the expression, really, but every project we've done has an element of CSR to it.

"We run workshops everywhere we go, to engage with the end user, which is our ticket buyer," he continues. "We're trying to figure out what barriers there are to getting involved from an artistic sense. We're doing this alongside the practical things, like trying to work with South Asian carpenters and builders to make our set props and do our design stuff, the physical parts of festivals."

Dialled In's lockdown beginnings ("It gave us time to think") were born from, as Ahsan puts it: "A collective feeling in the South Asian music, arts and culture space of a lack of representation. In two ways really. Representation within the underground music space, and then within UK culture more broadly, as the largest diaspora group." Vogue India described their impact in a 2022 piece on ascendant South Asian musicians, models and creatives: 'Toppling the very structures that had so far alienated them from mainstream clubs, inclusive collectives like Dialled In are building robust communities on the back of a unique culture of sound.'

On that theme of alienation, Ahsan believes the circumstances tend to differ across minority groups. Once identified, you design your approach accordingly. "I think there are various prongs to this," he says. "From the wider mainstream perspective, perhaps we're not seen as marketable or scalable in the same way other minority groups are. But I also think there's a lack of pathways for people from our community to get into those roles – or maybe they just don't know those roles exist."

By roles here – and echoing what we've heard from others – the emphasis is as much on adding to those behind the scenes as on stage. Dance music has engineered its own corridors of power – there is much to dismantle. "In a way, the artistic talent has always been there," Ahsan continues. "This work is about creating the managers, bookers, heads of marketing and agents. The quote-unquote South Asian world has its own ecosystem and roles within it, but in terms of the wider music industry, no. I've been working on parties most of my life, and I can probably count 10 *(South Asian)* people who have any semblance of power. Of course, there are people like Ajay *(Jayaram, head of music at the huge Broadwick Group, which integrates live music events, venue development and brand partnerships)*, but he's among very few people of South Asian ethnic heritage who are where he is. I can think of three South Asian agents based in the UK. Manager wise, maybe four or five. We get approached by artists all the time, asking us if we know of managers they can work with from our community. And generally the answer is no, we don't."

By the time this book is published, Ahsan and co-founders Ahad Elley, Dhruva Balram and Provhat Rahman will have pushed the button on the next phase of their teaching plans. Dialled Industry, a CIC (Community Interest Company), will be in operation, a move to further systematise how they share knowledge and foster confidence. Dialled Industry will focus on three main strategies. Ahsan explains that one, aimed at opening up pathways into the wider creative industries (he can call on experience himself in agency roles for It's Nice That and Vice's Virtue wing), will be introduced later. The other two, which will be rolled out first, he talks about in more detail.

"There'll be a 12-week career development mentorship program, where someone who's wanting to get involved in a back of house role will be paired with a South Asian industry professional to help them develop. And then after that, they'll get a paid placement within somewhere highly credible like a UTA *(United Talent Agency)*, Broadwick or Resident Advisor, places we have strong links with. Then we'll essentially help them to develop that career goal for another six months afterwards.

"And the other is a live music programme. We're always trying to find new live artists to book, but they're just not coming through, because live is expensive for people. Access to DJing can be as simple as having a controller and an internet connection – you can pretty much start from there. But to be in a band, it comes with costs, and I also don't think South Asian live artists are taken seriously. You have your Nabihah Iqbals and Joy Crookes, and they've done incredibly well. But they also talk about how hard it has been to be accepted as South Asian women in the scenes they are in. So, we're running residencies where we give three bands or live artists access to studio time. Afterwards, they'll perform at some of our shows, with one of them also joining us for our South By Southwest showcase. Of course, it would be great to find an amazing breakthrough artist – but even if not, we start to normalise the idea of South Asians in the studio."

Over in Germany – and similarly removed from the constraints of the formal educational institution – we find a different take on what it means to bolster community. The decidedly cosmic-sounding Academy Of Subcultural Understanding is the latest project from the Tresor Foundation. Born from the legendary techno club that did so much to forge links between Detroit and Berlin, the foundation was started by Dimitri Hegemann – also founder of the club. He's spoken in the past about how he's declined offers from big entertainment groups, seeking to buy the Tresor brand and turn it into a global offering. For him, he says that the path ahead was instead to "continue to dedicate my lifetime to subculture."

The Tresor Foundation's manifesto talks about a commitment to 'preserving and developing endangered or as yet undiscovered cultural spaces, making them available to local people and facilitating and successfully shaping (sub)cultural work by imparting knowledge and experience.' The Academy Of Subcultural Understanding's version of this lofty mission focuses on guidance for young people who aspire to create subcultural spaces in their own towns and cities – not just in the big and fashionable ones.

As Kea Kleihauer from Jägermeister, who has collaborated with the academy, explains: "They teach people from the more rural parts of Germany how to run a club, how to run a collective. But then they also want them to go back to their town afterwards, because in Germany we have the issue that, same as in London, people go to the main city to do their fancy stuff. But these other places completely die out. We've been in discussion with them on how to best support their work, such as maybe to give a lecture on 'Just how do you work with brands? How can you get brand funding?'"

At the time of writing, the next programme – now closed for applications – is scheduled to run from January to May 2025. It promises training in club management, research at the intersections of urbanism, community-building and subcultures, and knowledge-exchange practices that bring young people together with local experts to learn from each other 'in the shared goal of creating sustainable subcultural spaces.'

Speaking to WIP, a magazine funded by Carhartt, Dimitri Hegemann drew parallels between his new work and Fischbüro, an alternative gallery, community and education space he set up in an old shoe shop in Berlin in 1986. "You can't study nightlife at university," he says, before describing his role as: "Finding spaces for young people to explore their creativity. Places for people who can't sleep at night, whose best ideas come after 3.30am. Without these kinds of playgrounds, they leave small towns for bigger cities. I try to be the intersection between them and the authorities, creating communicative rooms for all sorts of creatives, like Cabaret Voltaires. In these spaces, not only do new mindsets emerge but also little micro-economies, which increase the viability of each community."

He is then quizzed on whether smaller cities and semi-rural locations have enough people to sustain such spaces: "I believe there are always enough people for a small, cozy location. Everywhere. My aims are to encourage and coach these people so that they stay where they are but make their surroundings more colorful. I don't think it's healthy when the young intelligentsia move to bigger cities. And today, with the internet, you can be connected from everywhere. The British author Charles Landry says that today, the competition among cities is how to make creative people stay *(much like the Creative Class thinking of Richard Florida touched on earlier in this book).* Creative people not only expect a nice apartment, schools, restaurants, galleries, clubs, live venues or theaters, they also expect people like themselves. They want to meet their people. All of this can bloom in cities with a curated nightlife. I deeply believe that."

Regardless of how conventional or unconventional the educational format or the channels and mediums used, the recurring theme in all of the learning (about learning) in this chapter is that it's by the community and for the community. While there are top-down elements in some places, the focus is more on participation, peer-to-peer, doing and experiencing.

Educational theorist Étienne Wenger first coined the term 'communities of practice' in 1991. He has since described this as: 'A group of people who share a concern or a passion for something they do, and learn how to do it better as they interact regularly. This definition reflects the fundamentally social nature of human learning. It is very broad. It applies to a street gang, whose members learn how to survive in a hostile world, as well as a group of engineers who learn how to design better devices or a group of civil servants who seek to improve service to citizens. In all cases, the key elements are: the domain – members are brought together by a learning need they share; the community – their collective learning becomes a bond among them over time; the practice – their interactions produce resources that affect their practice.'

These communities of practice speak to a broader ideal: that meaningful learning and cultural progress are born from shared purpose and collaboration, rather than imposed hierarchies. Similar thinking also informs deschooling and decentralised learning models, as well as efforts to decolonise education. Beyond particular mechanisms and practices, there is a larger context of societal and cultural development: an affirmation of the belief that creative ecosystems – no matter how small or remote – can thrive when people are empowered to contribute, connect and learn together.

Predictably, the corporate business world, always hungry for something new to add to its endless teeth-gnashing over what constitutes modern-day leadership, has taken a shine to the communities of practice concept. It surfaces in editorial in Forbes and Harvard Business Review. It's credited with how machine learning and artificial intelligence innovations have gained traction across otherwise segregated departments in sprawling corporations like Microsoft. But when communities of practice aren't assembling to cook up ominous AI futures, it's easy to see the conceptual relevance to dance music. In Red Bull Music Academy's vast back catalogue of stories and learnings, in digital forums, in community spaces, in collaborative experimentation, in record stores, and on dancefloors – in all of these settings and more, hope for the future ('hope' and 'future' not often appearing in the same sentence these days) is found.

Across all fronts from learning how to mix, to open a venue, sustain a scene, or lift up pioneer stories that are in danger of being forgotten, this is incendiary, catalytic knowledge. And knowledge, as we so often hear, is at the root of power. Whether a next generation of dance music's multifarious communities is gladly working with brands or vigorously eschewing that route, they will need it. Whether club culture is fully engaged in the creative industries, or more looking inside its own subculture for support and sustainability, it will need it, too. The work we're hearing about here strongly ups the likelihood that a next generation will be doing just that – operating from a position of knowledge/power.

Always sharp at combining the theory with the visceral, soulful and practical, we close out with King Britt. He smiles as he thinks back to his own teenage years. To the times spent pause-editing with cassette tapes, chopping up hip-hop and funk grooves; and, later, experimenting with an entry level sampler that he went halves on with his father. "These kids I teach have been making music since they're about 12. To a high, *high* level. They are so on it that it blows my mind. I'm just trying to give them the history, the backstory. But I'm excited where they can take it next. They are very open to new ideas, and they have a greater window on the heritage of this music than ever before. That's an exciting combination."

Shortly to head back to class, he ends with a characteristic shot of optimism: "Now is the time for the truth. And to build communities around the truth, so that these communities can pass on the truth to the next generation. That, absolutely, is how it must be from here."

EPILOGUE

At the outset of writing this book, I speculated that 'authenticity' would be up there among the phrases to feature most often. I wasn't disappointed. This most culture marketing-primed of terms is bandied about liberally, applied to everything from why brands chase it, to how elusive finding it actually is. Moreover, often, that we've lost sight of what it even means anyway.

At the other end of writing this book, it turns out that 'collective' and 'community' are phrases that have figured just as frequently. The way these terms are sometimes used today in society and media – loosely, indiscriminately – can make them seem as hollow and stripped of substance as the 'authenticity' word. But not so in many corners of club culture. There, they have taken on new energy and greater substance. Community has always been central to dance music, and collectives have long acted on their behalf. However, there is now a deeper awareness of the power and potential they hold. A realisation that exercising it is an imperative, too. What was once simply about the conviviality of being with like-minded folk is now infused with purpose – structures and strategies that support both people and creativity. In an increasingly gentrified, financially-driven world, they have become mechanisms for survival and – at their best – for transformation.

And brands? Perhaps in the future they'll choose the relatively easy route offered by the parallel version of club culture – huge venues, entertainment at its most commoditised and consumerised – where their presence is rarely contentious. However, given the rampant quest for, yes, authenticity, one suspects that won't ever be enough and the culture marketers will be putting in the hard yards. Brands will need to grasp empathic new ways of working if they're to broker win-win agreements with increasingly determined collectives and communities. They'll have to get braver as much in what they'll forgo as what they bring to the party. And if collectives and communities wish to reject brand money, they will similarly need to get sharper in fashioning alternative funding models – not just scurrying after short-term fixes (and the long-winded application processes that go with them).

There were two main directions of inquiry in this book: brands entering club culture as sponsors and supporters, and the democratising capacity for people and ideas emerging from it. Of the latter, despite the spectacular commercial and societal upheaval of our time, the perspective that after-dark creativity is something special and that can't be cultivated in agencies, studios or innovation labs remains steadfast for me. It surely will continue to influence fields as diverse as travel, advertising, fashion and design. Making certain that true originators receive credit and compensation, though still a point of friction, now at least seems more widely acknowledged as a necessity.

Fifty years have passed since disco first made its mark on wider culture. Thirty-five since the 1990s convergence of youth marketing and dance music. Twenty-five since the Red Bull Music Academy laid down an estimable blueprint, and just over half a decade since someone dressed as a fast-food chicken overlord at a brash dance music festival. Selling the night has always been curious and fluid, heavily contested and charged with unpredictability. As long as dancefloors remain significant to people, it's safe to assume they'll continue to hold a lot of meaning for brands, culture and the creative industries, too. The night is far from over.

IMAGE CREDITS

Every effort has been made to trace copyright holders and obtain necessary permissions for the material included in this work. If you believe you hold rights to any content and have not been properly credited, please contact Velocity Press and we will make any necessary corrections in future editions. All credits, unless otherwise stated, are licensed under fair use terms.

p. 1 (top): © The Absolut Company
p. 1 (bottom): © Area
p. 2: © Fiorucci
p. 3: © Fiorucci
p. 4: © The New Statesman
pp. 5–8: © Vitra Design Museum/Mark Niedermann
p. 9: © WipEout: Futurism/Duncan Harris/Thames & Hudson
p. 10: © Ben Kelly Design/Hanna Garcia Fleer
p. 11: © Ben Kelly Design/Jack Hems
p. 12 (top): © Telekom Electronic Beats/Ivan Kassa
p. 12 (bottom): © Telekom Electronic Beats/Nils Leon Brauer
p. 13: © Blacktronika/King Britt
p. 14: © Sisu/Rob Jones
p. 15 (top): © Rockstar Games
p. 15 (bottom): © Yum! Brands
p. 16: © Pentland Brands/Berghaus/Yushy (Aiyush Pachnanda)

BIBLIOGRAPHY

Baron, Naomi S. *Always On: Language In An Online And Mobile World*, Oxford University Press, 2010

Berger, Jonah. *Contagious: Why Things Catch On*, Simon & Schuster, 2013

Brewster, Bill and Broughton, Frank. *Last Night A DJ Saved My Life: The History Of The Disc Jockey (Deep Cuts)*, White Rabbit, 2022

Cameron, Douglas and Holt, Douglas. *Cultural Strategy: Using Innovative Ideologies To Build Breakthrough Brands*, OUP Oxford, 2010

Charles, King and Jones, Kent. *Elvin Discovers Chicago Footwork*, Independently published, 2024

Chayka, Kyle. *Filterworld: How Algorithms Make Everything The Same*, Heligo Books, 2024

Collin, Matthew. *Altered State: The Story Of Ecstasy Culture And Acid House*, Serpent's Tail, 2010

DJ Paulette, *Welcome To The Club: The Life And Lessons Of A Black Woman DJ*, Manchester University Press, 2024

Echols, Alice. *Hot Stuff: Disco And The Remaking Of American Culture*, W. W. Norton & Company, 2011

Electronic Beats, Electronic Beats, 2021

Fataar, Leila. *Culture-Led Brands: Drive Growth, Build Resilience And Cultivate Resonance*, Kogan Page, 2025

Florida, Richard. *The Rise Of The Creative Class*, Basic Books, 2019

Garcia-Mispireta, Luis Manuel. *Together, Somehow: Music, Affect And Intimacy On The Dancefloor*, Duke University Press Books, 2023

Garratt, Sheryl. *Adventures In Wonderland: Acid House, Rave And The UK Club Explosion*, TCL Publishing, 2020

Gillett, Ed. *Party Lines: Dance Music And The Making Of Modern Britain*, Picador, 2023

Gladwell, Malcolm. *The Tipping Point: How Little Things Can Make A Big Difference*, Abacus, 2002

Goode, Eric and Goode, Jennifer. *Area: 1983–1987*, Abrams, 2013

Hae, Laam. *The Gentrification Of Nightlife And The Right To The City: Regulating Spaces Of Social Dancing In New York*, Routledge, 2012 fine

Haq, Nav. *Rave: Rave And Its Influence On Art And Culture*, Black Dog Press, 2018

Harden-Guest, Anthony. *The Last Party: Studio 54, Disco And The Culture Of The Night*, Open Road Media, 2009

Harris, Duncan. *WipEout Futurism: The Graphic Archives*, Read Only Memory, 2024

Harvey, David. *Rebel Cities: From The Right To The City To The Urban Revolution*, Verso, 2012

Hebdige, Dick. *Subculture: The Meaning Of Style, Routledge*, 2012

Jones, Dylan. *Sweet Dreams: From Club Culture To Style Culture, The Story Of The New Romantics*, Faber & Faber, 2020

Kaftandjiev, Christo. *Absolut Semiotics*, Self-published, 2020

Klein, Naomi. *No Logo: Taking Aim At The Brand Bullies*, Picador, 2000

Lawrence, Tim. *Life And Death On The New York Dance Floor, 1980–1983*, Duke University Press Books, 2016 and *Love Saves The Day: A History Of American Dance Music Culture, 1970–1979*, Duke University Press Books, 2004

Levinson, Jay Conrad. *Guerilla Marketing: Easy And Inexpensive Strategies For Making Big Profits From Your Small Business*, Harper Business, 2007

Malone, Jacqui. *Steppin' On The Blues: The Visible Rhythms Of African American Dance (Folklore And Society)*, University Of Illinois Press, 1996

Manandhar, Nina. *What We Wore: A People's History Of British Style*, Prestel, 2014

Maupin, Armistead. *Tales Of The City*, Books 1–10, Black Swan, 2000–2025

McCracken, Grant. *Chief Culture Officer: How To Create A Living, Breathing Corporation*, Basic Books, 2009

Neville, Richard. *Hippie Hippie Shake*, Duckworth & Co, 2009

Nicholls, James. *The Politics Of Alcohol*, Manchester University Press, 2009

O'Connor, Justin. *Culture Is Not An Industry: Reclaiming Art And Culture For Common Good*, Manchester University Press, 2024

Putnam, Robert D. *Bowling Alone: The Collapse And Revival Of American Community*, Simon & Schuster Ltd, 2000

Rapp, Tobias. *Lost And Sound: Berlin, Techno And The Easyjet Sound*, Innervisions, 2010

Rose, Cynthia. *Design After Dark: The Story Of Dancefloor Style*, Thames & Hudson, 1991

Roux, Michel. *My Absolut Life*, The Absolut Company, 2024

Siano, Nicky and Lipsett, Suzanne. *No Time To Wait: A Complete Guide To Treating, Managing And Living With HIV Infection*, Bantam, 1993

Vitra Design Museum. *Night Fever: Designing Club Culture: 1960–Today*, Vitra Design Museum, 2018

Warren, Emma. *Dance Your Way Home: A Journey Through The Dancefloor*, Faber & Faber, 2023

Warrington, Ruby. *Sober Curious: The Blissful Sleep, Greater Focus, Limitless Presence And Deep Connection Awaiting Us All On The Other Side Of Alcohol*, HarperOne, 2018

ACKNOWLEDGEMENTS

Utmost thanks to the many contributors – credited throughout – who generously gave their time to be interviewed for *Selling The Night*. The perspectives I heard were varied, from a substantial range of vantage points, but always fascinating, well-considered and incredibly heartfelt. I learnt something from every conversation.

Similarly, I'm indebted to the numerous writers, artists and industry insiders who I've quoted from other sources in this book – again, all credited throughout. A lot of ground had been covered before I got near this topic – much erudition and reasoned thinking for me to stand on the shoulders of.

Thank you also to family, friends and kindred spirits; all those who shared ideas and angles with me – and/or listened to my out-loud reflections (and occasional fretting).

Much gratitude to Colin Steven for having me on board at the excellent Velocity Press. If you don't already own a shelf-load of their books, please consider buying some. The role for independent ventures in music, culture and creativity could not be more vital in our commodified and play-it-safe world, where trying to do your own thing, in your own way, is harder than ever.

On the publishing side, thanks also to Paris Ferguson (editing), Paul Baillie-Lane (typesetting) and Hayden Russell (design).

And deep appreciation going out to the main character here: dance music, clubs and all the joy that comes with them. Brands will come and go. Creative industries will bend and flex. But whatever iteration of this after-dark subculture works for you, it's always worth believing in. At least it has been for me – for four decades and counting.

THANK YOU

Namechecking those who pre-ordered *Selling The Night* early and direct from Velocity Press. Your support is hugely appreciated.

Robert Abbott, Diamond Abdulrahim, Lodina Agyeman, Julian Alexander, Kelvin Amos, Roshannah Bagley, Sebastian Bayer, Lee Benecke, Beth Bentley, Maciej Biedziński, Mathew Booth, Eric Borgo, Julie Brethous, Guglielmo Bottin, James Buchanan, Tom Cartmale, Aaron Cole, Lucien Coy, Nick Dawe, Simon Dawson, Warren Dell, Nicklas Eklöf, Rhys Ellis, Tom Ellis-Jones, Theo Erasmus, Jarred Faust, Sarah Feeney, Tom Forrest, Peter Foster, William Frank, Andy George, Iestyn George, Nathalie Gibbs, Tim Patrick Gibney, Fred Gifford, Dane Gorrel, Lea Grissmer, Sue Gurner, Josephine Hatch, Edwin Hodges, Will Hogan, Fabian Huismans, Phong Huynh, Deniss Jacenko, Seth Jacobson, Mark Jefford, Torkel Jelvinger, Rebecca Jolly, Aaron Jones, Lora B Kato, Max Keane, Caitlin Keeley, Si Kemp, Toni Kent, Matthew Kershaw, Peter Kormanyos, Sy Kraft, Serena Kutchinsky, Ann-Marie Ledgister, Philippe Llewellyn, Katy Louis, Stef Macbeth, Mark Macdonald, Mark Maddox, Elly Barham Marsh, Gabriel Mathews, John Matthews, Sara McAlpine, Zoe McQuillin, Bram Merkx, Rudi Minto de Wijs, Carlotta Monzani, Jaymie Morales, Andrea Ng, Gabriel Noble, Luke O'Connor, Kalinda Panholzer, Alexandra Pasquinelli, David Passey, Michael Pesce, Sam Peskin, Andrew Powell, Arun Ramanathan, Clemence Rebourg, Marcus Reed, Sophie Rees, Steph Richards,

Jennifer Robinson, Mark Rosenberg, Sophie Rouse, Marco Rovagnati, Anjali Prashar Savoie, Jakob Franz Schmid, Richard Seabrooke, Miles Shackleton, Peri Siolis (aka GLOWKiD), Julia Smaldone, Luo Su, Phil Teer, Antonello Teora, Michele Tessadri, Anthony Topham, Eva Ventura, Dylan Viner, Sebastian Weber, Paul White, Taylor Wiegert, Edward Williams, Jon Wilkins, Craig Wood, Kyle Wright, Sally Young

INDEX

ALSO ON VELOCITY PRESS

THE SECRET DJ PRESENTS: TALES FROM THE BOOTH

The Secret DJ's first two books lifted the lid on what really happens behind the decks in the sometimes hilarious, sometimes harrowing world of the superstar DJ. Now they've reached out to dozens of DJs from around the world - and from every scene and genre – for their own true stories of the DJ life. Tales From the Booth raises the BPM, rounding up an all-star cast of Secret DJs to tell their anonymous stories of what it's really like to rock dancefloors for a living. From strange encounters on tour to side-splitting debauchery and afterparty excess to the seamy and even dangerous side of the industry, this is your access-all-areas backstage pass. You'll never look at a DJ quite the same again.

THE LABEL MACHINE

Nick Sadler

So, you want to start a record label? The Label Machine is the ultimate guide to starting, running and growing your independent record label. You will learn all about the music industry business and how to navigate the tricky dos and don'ts. You will finally understand and take control of your music copyright and get to grips with the legalities involved. You will build your label effortlessly, learning how to professionally market your music and artists – allowing you to reach thousands of fans.

TRIP CITY

Trevor Miller

In the summer of 1989, when *Trip City* was first released with a soundtrack by A Guy Called Gerald, there had been no other British novel like it. This was the down and dirty side of London nightclubs, dance music and the kind of hallucinogenic drug sub-culture that hadn't really been explored since Tom Wolfe's The Electric Kool-Aid Acid Test. Maybe this is why Trip City is still known as "the acid house novel" and an underground literary landmark.

But for 2021, *Trip City* is back in this all-new incendiary incarnation – including a new introduction by author Trevor Miller, a foreword by Carl Loben (*DJ Magazine* editor) and a vinyl reissue of the A Guy Called Gerald soundtrack.

LONG RELATIONSHIPS: MY INCREDIBLE JOURNEY FROM UNKNOWN DJ TO SMALL-TIME DJ

Harold Heath

Written by former DJ/producer Harold Heath, Long Relationships is a biographical account of a DJ career defined by a deep love of music and a shallow amount of success. From the days of vinyl, when DJs were often also glass-collectors, to the era of megastar stadium EDM, it's a journey of 30 odd years on a low-level, economy-class rollercoaster through the ups and downs of an ever-changing music industry.

FLYER & COVER ART
Junior Tomlin

Showcasing the mastermind behind some of the most iconic rave flyers and record covers of the late eighties and early nineties, *Flyer & Cover Art* is a comprehensive insight into Junior Tomlin's incredible back catalogue.

30 years since he designed his first flyer this book documents his work across 160 pages, with commentary and draft sketches provided by Junior himself. The book is 25cm square, printed on premium 130gsm full colour paper. It is the first time his work has been documented and presented in such a comprehensive, cohesive fashion.

BEDROOM BEATS & B-SIDES: INSTRUMENTAL HIP HOP & ELECTRONIC MUSIC AT THE TURN OF THE CENTURY
Laurent Fintoni

Bedroom Beats & B-sides is the first comprehensive history of the instrumental hip-hop and electronic scenes and a truly global look at a thirty-year period of modern music culture based on a decade of research and travel across Europe, North America, and Japan.

Combining social, cultural, and musical history with extensive research and over 100 interviews, the book tells the B-side stories of hip-hop and electronic music from the 1990s to the 2010s and explores the evolution of modern beat culture from local scenes to a global community via the diverse groups of fringe idealists who made it happen and the external forces that shaped their efforts.